Race and Racism in Modern Philosophy

Race and Racism in Modern Philosophy

EDITED BY ANDREW VALLS

CORNELL UNIVERSITY PRESS   Ithaca and London

For information, address Cornell University Press, Sage House,
512 East State Street, Ithaca, New York 14850.
First published 2005 by Cornell University Press
First printing, Cornell Paperbacks, 2005

Printed in the United States of America

Library of Congress Cataloging-in-Publication Data

Race and racism in modern philosophy / edited by Andrew Valls.
p.   cm.
Includes bibliographical references and index.
ISBN-13: 978-0-8014-4033-5   (cloth : alk. paper)
ISBN-10: 0-8014-4033-5   (cloth : alk. paper)
ISBN-13: 978-0-8014-7274-9   (pbk. : alk. paper)
ISBN-10: 0-8014-7274-1   (pbk. : alk. paper)
1. Race—Philosophy.   2. Race relations—Philosophy.   3. Racism.
4. Philosophy, Modern.   I. Valls, Andrew, 1966–
HT1523.R2517   2005
305.8′001—dc22   2005012277

Cornell University Press strives to use environmentally responsible suppliers
and materials to the fullest extent possible in the publishing of its books.
Such materials include vegetable-based, low-VOC inks and acid-free papers that
are recycled, totally chlorine-free, or partly composed of nonwood fibers.
For further information, visit our website at www.cornellpress.cornell.edu.

Cloth printing   10 9 8 7 6 5 4 3 2 1
Paperback printing   10 9 8 7 6 5 4 3 2 1

CONTENTS

Introduction   1

    Andrew Valls

1. Descartes's Silences on Slavery and Race   16

    Timothy J. Reiss

2. Race in Hobbes   43

    Barbara Hall

3. Metaphysics at the Barricades: Spinoza and Race   57

    Debra Nails

4. Imagining an Inundation of Australians; or,

    Leibniz on the Principles of Grace and Race   73

    Peter Fenves

5. The Contradictions of Racism:

    Locke, Slavery, and the *Two Treatises*   89

    Robert Bernasconi and Anika Maaza Mann

6. Berkeley and the Westward Course of Empire:

    On Racism and Ethnocentrism   108

    William Uzgalis

7. "A Lousy Empirical Scientist":

    Reconsidering Hume's Racism   127

    Andrew Valls

8. Rousseau, Natural Man, and Race   150

    Bernard R. Boxill

9. Kant's *Untermenschen*   169

    Charles W. Mills

10. Race and Law in Hegel's Philosophy of Religion   194

    Michael H. Hoffheimer

11. John Stuart Mill and "The Negro Question": Race,
    Colonialism, and the Ladder of Civilization   217
    Anthony Bogues

12. Marx, Race, and the Political Problem of Identity   235
    Richard T. Peterson

13. Nietzsche's Racial Profiling   255
    James Winchester

About the Contributors   277

Index   281

III

Race and Racism in Modern Philosophy

|||

Introduction

ANDREW VALLS

Is modern philosophy racist? Does it matter that Locke defended slavery and helped run companies involved in the slave trade? That Berkeley owned slaves? That Hume thought blacks inferior to whites? That Kant agreed with Hume, and developed elaborate theories on the various races of humans? Are these facts merely incidental, calling for no thorough reexamination of the views of these figures? Or do the facts reveal something deeper about their philosophies, and about modern philosophy itself?

Scholars have been puzzling over these questions for some time now, and no consensus has been reached. For some, modern philosophy, or at least some of the major schools of thought within it—rationalism, empiricism, liberalism, social contract theory—is deeply racist. On this view, the appearance of race neutrality in these theories is belied by a deeper reading, and this calls for a major revision of our understanding of modern philosophy. For others, the racism expressed by some major modern philosophers has no significant implications for, say, their epistemology or their ethics. Rather, on this latter position, any racism expressed by modern philosophers can simply be detached from their philosophical views, and no reinterpretation of these views is required.

It should come as no surprise that some modern philosophers have something to answer for when it comes to race, since the period of modern philosophy—roughly the seventeenth through the nineteenth centuries—was also the time during which ideas about race became fully developed in the West. Most scholars agree that race and racism (as opposed to xenophobia or ethnocentrism) are distinctly modern ideas, and it is no accident that these ideas developed at the time of

This volume has been several years in the making and has benefited from input from several editors. In the early stages of its development, the project benefited greatly from advice by Gayatri Patnaik, then of Routledge Press. At Cornell University Press, I wish to thank Catherine Rice, Sheri Englund, Susan Barnett, Teresa Jesionowski, Roger Haydon and, for her excellent copyediting, Susan Tarcov.

For helpful comments on this introduction, I thank Bernard Boxill, Charles Mills, Sharyn Clough, Jonathan Kaplan, William Uzgalis, and Sheri Englund.

the "discovery" of the "New World," the development of colonialism, the African slave trade, and the racialized institution of slavery. Many explanations have been advanced for why racial ideas developed when and where they did: when Europeans were encountering seemingly very different peoples, race provided a way to understand and explain these differences;[1] this period was also when modern science was developing, which encouraged the construction of rigid categories to understand empirical phenomena;[2] racial categories, starting out as scientific tools, became an all too convenient rationalization for the exploitation of non-Europeans and their lands and resources;[3] and, perhaps ironically, the universalist thrust of modern moral and political philosophy required a way to exclude Others who would otherwise be entitled to equal concern and respect.[4] Whatever the explanation—and no doubt all of these factors played a role—the fact is that modern ideas about race and modern philosophical doctrines developed together in a context shaped by conquest, colonialism, and slavery.

This volume charts the relation between modern philosophy and race by closely examining their connections in the thought of thirteen major modern philosophers. Each chapter is an original essay that focuses on the role of race and racially implicated ideas in a modern philosopher's thought. As such, the volume takes stock of, and contributes to, current debates on race and modern philosophy. It does so at a level that, it is hoped, is accessible to newcomers to these debates while being of interest to those familiar with them.

| | |

One way to begin an exploration of the intersection of race and modern philosophy is by looking at the relation between racist ideas on the one hand and empiricism and rationalism on the other, to see which philosophical approach is more compatible with racist doctrines. Harry Bracken,[5] Richard Popkin,[6] and Noam Chomsky[7] have argued that rationalism is inhospitable to racism, but that empiricism lends itself to racist doctrines. Bracken argues that Locke's anti-essentialism has the implication that there is no essence that unites all human beings, making it possible to treat skin color or any other feature as a defining characteristic—a view that lends itself to racist doctrines. A Cartesian epistemology, on the other hand, makes it difficult or impossible to advance racist doctrines, according to Bracken. At the very least Cartesianism provides "a modest conceptual brake to the articulation of racial degradation and slavery."[8] Focusing on Hume rather than Locke, Popkin argues that "his view about non-whites cannot be dismissed as a fleeting observation. It is intimately related to his thought, and to one of the problems of eighteenth-century thought—the justification of European superiority over the rest of mankind."[9] Noam Chomsky has concurred in this general view of empiricism as supporting racism. Chomsky has suggested that "the [empiricist] concept of the 'empty organism,' plastic and unstructured, apart from being false, also serves naturally as the support for the most reactionary social doctrines."[10] Empiricism is a dangerous doctrine, according to Chomsky, because in denying the existence of innate mental structures or a substantial human nature, it undermines an important ground for claims of human freedom and dignity.

Others, however, have disputed these claims—among them John Searle and Kay Squadrito. Searle finds this line of reasoning "quite unacceptable." First, he questions whether any of the major modern philosophers can be connected to racism, asserting that "[n]either the great rationalists—Descartes, Leibniz, and Spinoza—nor the great empiricists—Locke, Berkeley, [and] Hume [—] were engaged in facilitating a racist ideology."[11] Searle's second point is that if there were such a connection, empiricism lends itself to racist doctrines less easily than rationalism. "If anything, it is a shorter step from the Cartesian theory of the mind to the theory of racial inferiority than from the Humean, because once you believe that there are innate human mental structures, it is only a short step to argue that the innate mental structures differ from one race to another."[12] Squadrito offers a more developed argument against the Bracken/Popkin/Chomsky position.[13] Squadrito argues that historically it is empiricism that has been the more progressive force. Doctrines of innateness, she points out, have often been used to enshrine a particular conception of human nature and to place those who do not conform to this conception outside the realm of normalcy, and perhaps even humanity. "By stressing the point that there are no innate or inherent intellectual or moral differences between races . . . empiricists have provided a methodology which leads to toleration."[14] The arguments of Bracken, Popkin, and Chomsky notwithstanding, "[t]he Cartesian theory of the human mind provides no logical barrier to formulating a theory of racial or sexual inferiority."[15]

At the level of generality at which this debate developed, it is difficult to say which "side" has the better arguments. On the one hand (and as the essays in this volume bear out), it would seem that the three main philosophers usually classed as "empiricists" have much more to answer for with regard to race than the three "rationalists." Locke participated in the slave trade in various ways, Berkeley owned slaves, and Hume produced one of the first clear statements of a racist (or racialist) doctrine. By contrast, Descartes, Spinoza, and Leibniz seem not to have stated clearly racialist or racist sentiments, nor to have engaged in activities that were associated with such sentiments. However, if we focus on philosophical doctrines, matters become more ambiguous. It is true that the moral universalism of rationalism appears inhospitable to racism. But in the first place, the moral doctrines of at least some of the empiricists are equally universalist. Second, as George Fredrickson has pointed out, the universalist and egalitarian character of much of modern thought may have been one of the contributing factors in the development of racist ideas.[16] Where hierarchy or inequality is presumed, little justification for it is needed, but where equality is presumed, inequality requires justification—and separate categories among humans, or between humans and subhumans, may serve this purpose.

Yet engaging these issues at this level of generality has severe limitations. The debate involves broad claims about "Cartesianism" (rather than about Descartes), and, worse still, about "empiricism" and "rationalism," categories that obscure important differences among philosophers classified together, and perhaps similarities between those classified apart. Furthermore, claims about these categories risk ignoring many of the interesting questions related to race that are specific to a particular philosopher. Rather than focusing on whether "empiricism" facilitates racism, perhaps we should ask whether, say, Berkeley's empiricism (or, simply, his philosophy) facilitates racism, and whether Locke's or Hume's does. These questions might not have the same answer, and asking them separately enables us to consider evidence that might be relevant to one but not to another. In short, the debate we have been considering might be better conducted at a greater level of specificity, giving attention to each philosopher rather than relying on broad categories. This suggests that the question of race and modern philosophy is best addressed by considering specific philosophers, and by focusing on the particular issues raised in their philosophy (and perhaps in their biography) with regard to race.

Despite this, some scholars have suggested more recently that it is nevertheless accurate to say that modern philosophy as a whole (or at least major schools of thought within it) is deeply racist. For example, in *Racist Culture*, David Theo Goldberg argues that modern liberalism is inherently racist, because liberalism and racial ideas developed together and shaped each other. According to Goldberg, "[b]y working itself into the threads of liberalism's cloth just as that cloth was being woven, race and the various exclusions it licensed became naturalized in the Eurocentered vision of itself and its self-defined others, in its sense of Reason and rational direction." Even today, Goldberg argues, race serves "as a boundary constraint upon the applicability of moral principle." He adds that Chomsky and Bracken "are on firm ground" in stating that empiricism facilitates racism but parts company with them in holding that rationalism is equally guilty of this. The charge of facilitating racism "tugs at the very heart of the Enlightenment's rational spirit."[17]

Emmanuel Eze has also suggested that race is central to the Enlightenment. His collection, *Race and the Enlightenment*, collects excerpts from the writings of major Enlightenment thinkers that demonstrate their attention to matters of race and in some cases is able to show the racist or racialist character of their thought. In another work, Eze uses passages such as these and, focusing on Hume and Kant, argues that their racism is not merely a contingent and detachable feature of their thought but is deeply rooted in their philosophical doctrines.[18]

In *The Racial Contract*, Charles Mills argues that one of the main devices of modern political philosophy, the social contract, is despite its universalist appearance racially coded. The actual social contract was a contract among whites, and the content of the agreement was to exclude and exploit nonwhites. In the course of developing this argument, Mills makes a number of charges against the social contract theory of Hobbes, Locke, Rousseau, and Kant. In each case, according to Mills, the philosopher understood the parties to the contract to be white Europeans, whereas non-Europeans either were incapable of participating in the contract or were simply excluded so that whites need not be constrained in their actions toward nonwhites.[19]

The work of Goldberg, Eze, and Mills, among others,[20] poses a challenge to the traditional understanding of modern philosophy. As usually taught, modern philosophy appears far removed from such issues as race, slavery, and colonialism. Yet according to these authors modern philosophy not only is related to these developments but actually facilitated them. So again we return to the question of whether modern philosophy is racist or racially coded and whether thoroughgoing reevaluation of it is required in light of these charges.

|||

In any discussion of race and racism in modern philosophy, two dangers must be avoided: anachronism and lack of conceptual clarity. The former is a danger because many of the concepts and presuppositions that we use for thinking about these issues today may not have existed (or may not have been as widespread) in a given period of the past. To call, say, a seventeenth-century figure a racist may be to impute to him a position that had not yet been articulated. Hence, the interesting question regarding a modern philosopher on matters of race is not simply whether he was a racist. Rather, we must ask what specific doctrines he endorsed, what other suppositions—explicit or implicit—seem to lie in the background of his thought, and whether his thought lent itself to the subsequent development of racist ideologies. Sensitivity to context and nuance, rather than a rush to attach a label, should be the hallmark of this kind of research.

The problem of conceptual clarity is perhaps more difficult because, even if anachronism is avoided, the fact remains that at any given point in time, there is surprisingly little consensus about the meaning of such words as *race* and *racism*. In the public arena today, these words are perhaps used more often as rhetorical weapons than as tools for clarifying issues or arguments. Yet even among philosophers, whose job it is to do the latter, there is no universal agreement. Part of the problem is that since ordinary language does not provide precise definitions, any philosophical definition of these key concepts must be, to at least some extent, stipulative. Still, one virtue of even a stipulative definition is that it captures some of the features of how the word is ordinarily used. Which features to pick out is open to debate, and different philosophers, who agree on the need for greater conceptual clarity than ordinary language provides, disagree on how this is best achieved.

One well-known attempt to achieve clarity on these matters is the effort by Anthony Appiah to distinguish between racism and racialism and then to distinguish between two kinds of racism.[21] Racialism, on Appiah's understanding, is the "belief that there are heritable characteristics, possessed by members of our species, that allow us to divide them into a small set of races, in such a way that all the members of these races share certain traits and tendencies with each other that they do not share with members of any other race." As such, racialism is the belief in a "racial essence." While this view is mistaken, according to Appiah, it presents "a cognitive rather than a moral problem" because the issue is not a normative one—how people are to be treated—but "how the world is."[22]

Moral issues come to the fore, however, with racist doctrines, because these do involve how people are appropriately treated. Racist doctrines generally endorse different treatment of people identified with different races, but Appiah distinguishes between two kinds of reasons for this treatment. For the *extrinsic* racist, "the racial essence entails certain morally relevant qualities"; that is, the extrinsic racist believes that people in different racial categories exhibit different characteristics, and these justify differential treatment. Extrinsic racism, then, rests on empirical claims whose successful rebuttal should undermine the extrinsic racist's racism. The *intrinsic* racist, on the other hand, does not rest her racism on empirical claims. She believes that "each race has a different moral status," and "no amount of evidence" will suffice to undermine her views.[23] She simply prefers members of some race(s) (usually her own) over others, but does not base this preference on morally relevant or empirically observable characteristics. In this way, Appiah says, the intrinsic racist is like someone who prefers her own family members simply because they are *her* family members.

I agree with Appiah that we must distinguish between racism and racialism, and between the moral and the empirical claims associated with each. However, there seem to be difficulties with Appiah's approach. Since both racialism and extrinsic racism involve empirical claims, the distinction between them rests on whether those claims involve "morally relevant qualities," that is, whether racial differences justify different treatment. Appiah mentions honesty, courage, and intelligence as examples of morally relevant qualities, but it is not clear how or in what ways these are morally relevant. For example, in what ways is it just to treat some people differently because of their inferior or superior intelligence? It would seem preferable if our conceptual distinction between racism and racialism did not rest on a substantive moral view about which qualities are morally relevant.

Another way of putting this point is that if the extrinsic racist is right that the characteristics on which she focuses are morally relevant, and right about the *way* they are relevant, then her basic moral position might not be objectionable. She could be wrong in associating these characteristics with certain races, but this is the same kind of error that the racialist makes—a cognitive, not a moral, one. So the extrinsic racist combines two positions: associating certain morally relevant characteristics with certain races (an empirical proposition) and advocating different treatment based on these characteristics (a normative proposition). If the latter proposition is not in itself objectionable (since the characteristics are *ex hypothesi* morally relevant), it is difficult to see what is morally, rather than empirically, wrong with the extrinsic racist's position—except insofar as it is objectionable to misapply a basically sound moral principle.

This suggests that the crucial distinction to be made here is between two propositions. The first is that there are races that differ in certain characteristics, an empirical position shared by racialists and extrinsic racists. The second is that members of different races are justly treated differently, a moral position shared by the extrinsic racist and the intrinsic racist. The key feature of racism that distinguishes it from racialism is its endorsement of different—usually worse—treatment of people according to race.

This way of distinguishing racism from racialism is suggested by the approach to these matters that Jorge Garcia takes.[24] Garcia states that "what we have in mind when we talk of racism is no longer simply a matter of beliefs." Rather, racism is best thought of as "rooted in the heart." Garcia's proposal "is that we conceive of racism as fundamentally a vicious kind of racially based disregard for the welfare of certain people . . . on account of their assigned race. . . . Racism, then, is something that essentially involves not our beliefs and their rationality or irrationality, but our wants, intentions, likes and dislikes." This way of thinking of racism accounts for why racism is always wrong. As "a form of disregard" or "ill-will," it is wrong for the same reason that any kind of disregard or ill will is wrong.[25]

Garcia's approach also captures the distinction between moral claims and empirical claims about race. If racism is essentially ill will or disregard, then it is distinct from (though, of course, often related to) empirical beliefs about whether races exist and, if so, what characteristics they have. Hence Garcia's account is compatible with Appiah's suggestion that racialism, as distinct from racism, involves empirical claims about the world, and that if these claims are wrong, this is "a cognitive rather than a moral problem."

Of course, the relation between our empirical and our normative beliefs is not as simple as this account would seem to suggest. If one probes the attitudes of someone who believes in the inferiority of some races on some characteristic, one is very likely to conclude that this person is not merely a racialist but also a racist. In fact, if someone insists on maintaining racialist beliefs in the face of overwhelming evidence to the contrary, this in itself is evidence of racism. According to Garcia, "merely voicing an opinion that members of R_1 [a certain race] are inferior (in some germane way) will count as racist (in any of the term's chief senses, at least) only if, for example, it expresses an opinion held from the operation of some predisposition to believe bad things about R_1s [members of that race], which predisposition itself stems in part from racial disregard."[26] Yet despite the common connection between racism and racialism, it is worth preserving the distinction between them. This allows scientists, for example, to argue about empirical matters without worrying about being called racists, and it also allows us to correct mistaken racialist beliefs without moral condemnation. In the case of genuine racism, moral condemnation is appropriate, but in some cases the problem may be simply mistaken beliefs about the world.

There are many questions left unanswered by this brief account. For example, some might object to the individualist nature of this view, as it sees racism as fundamentally about individuals' beliefs and feelings. However, Garcia argues that his account can accommodate and explicate nonindividualist forms of racism such as institutional racism.[27] More difficult, perhaps, is the notion of "cultural racism," which, some have argued, has come to replace traditional forms of racism. Cultural racism, as the name suggests, focuses on culture rather than biological race, but it is often associated with the same attitudes that came with "old" racism. Whether cultural racism is a form of racism or a form of ethnocentrism is a complex issue that I cannot settle here. The important point that emerges from this discussion, however, is that the distinctions I have sketched, or something like them, are essential for thinking clearly about matters of race.

||||

The volume opens with Timothy Reiss's treatment of Descartes's silences on slavery and race. Descartes had little to say on either subject, and his silences appear odd once Reiss places Descartes in his context. Descartes lived much of his adult life in Holland, which was a major slave trader at the time, and Descartes's "teachers' teachers" included thinkers who had debated the propriety of conquest and slavery extensively. So Descartes must have been aware of the growing slave trade and the philosophical debates to which it gave rise, and yet he remained silent, except for using the figure of a slave in his *Meditations*. His references to slaves in this work are vehicles for Descartes to discuss issues of free will, but they leave no doubt as to the humanity of the slave. Reiss concludes that there are no grounds for thinking Descartes supported slavery but that his silence on the issue remains troubling.

Barbara Hall then takes up the case of Hobbes. Hall points out that human equality is the fundamental assumption of Hobbes's account of the state of nature, yet she also reminds us that "the savage people in . . . America" is Hobbes's example of this state. While this may not necessarily reflect a racial view, Hall argues, it certainly shows that Hobbes thought Native Americans to be less developed than Europeans. Hobbes's views on conquest are also disturbing, according to Hall, because Hobbes believed that Europeans had a "perfect right" to capture "insufficiently populated" lands. Hobbes also discussed slavery and argued that a slave has a right to kill his master but that in exchange for ending this state of enmity the slave might consent to being a servant. Hall concludes that Hobbes would have nothing to say against the African slave trade and would have endorsed the conquest of the "New World," and that therefore, despite the lack of direct evidence for racism in Hobbes, his philosophical positions on these issues warrant considering him as a racist.

The two chapters that follow argue that the metaphysics of Spinoza and Leibniz are incompatible with racism. For Spinoza, Debra Nails reminds us, every existing thing is a mode of existence, a manifestation of a single substance. Things are individuated by their tendency to cohere in a certain way, but in this sense, a race cannot simply be defined into existence—a brake against racial oppression, according to Nails. Indeed, from the perspective of Spinoza's metaphysics, it is unclear in what sense races can be said to exist at all, except as a matter of "rational voluntary association." When discussing the case of Jews, Spinoza—himself a Jew who was expelled from the Amsterdam Jewish community for his unorthodox views—denies any transcendent status to this group of individuals. Hence for Spinoza, the very idea of a race is without foundation, undercutting any rational basis for racism or racialism.

Though Leibniz is often cited as one of the first to use the word *race* in its modern sense, Peter Fenves argues that it is a mistake to view him as an advocate of the idea. Rather, Leibniz mentions race in passing, but does not endorse the idea or even dwell upon it. Early in his career, however, Leibniz did say that non-Christians were not humans but beasts and recommended aggressive war upon them. Furthermore, Leibniz conceived a bizarre plan to kidnap young, non-European boys and train them into a fierce army for such a war. Still, Leibniz's mature philosophy makes the idea of race highly problematic. If in reality there are only monads, then any classification of individuals must be justified. Nowhere does Leibniz endorse racial classification, and Fenves argues that there is reason to think he would not endorse it. The mature Leibniz denies that non-whites (or specifically "Australians") are not humans and says that they are able to be converted to Christianity, which is open to all rational animals. Hence Leibniz's metaphysics and his theology mitigate against racialism.

It was mentioned above that the three empiricists have much to answer for with regard to race, and the following three chapters bear this out. Robert Bernasconi and Anika Maaza Mann detail Locke's involvement in the African slave trade and in the writing of *The Fundamental Constitutions of Carolina*, which sanctioned slavery. Can Locke's complicity with racialized slavery be reconciled with his political theory? Some commentators have answered no, but Bernasconi and Mann argue that we must interpret the political theory as being consistent with Locke's actions. Though on a literal reading Locke's just war theory of slavery would not sanction the hereditary institution of slavery, the authors argue that this does not show that this was not its intended purpose, or its effect. In fact, some did use Locke's theory to justify slavery. We cannot know for certain how Locke saw the relation between his just war theory of slavery and his support for racialized chattel slavery, but in any case the latter is strong evidence of Locke's racism.

Berkeley participated in slavery too—by owning slaves. William Uzgalis details Berkeley's efforts to found a college in Bermuda that would educate indigenous people and convert them to Christianity, and it was while he lived in Rhode Island waiting for funding for his college that Berkeley owned slaves. Berkeley was motivated by missionary zeal, and, Uzgalis argues, he is clearly guilty of ethnocentrism—presupposing the superiority of his own culture and religion. However, Berkeley is not guilty of racism, because he did not believe in the inherent or irremediable inferiority of non-Europeans. Another reason that Berkeley had no quarrel with slavery is his rather conservative political views. He embraced the doctrine of passive obedience, which supports submission to existing authority and institutions. In the end it is not racism but Berkeley's religious and political views that explain Berkeley's approval of slavery.

Hume had no direct dealings with slavery, but he was among the first to explicitly state a racist, or at least racialist, doctrine. In my chapter on Hume, I focus on this statement, which appears in a footnote to his essay "Of National Characters." My main argument is that though the footnote itself is quite troubling, it does not have some of the implications that some scholars have drawn from it. It does not show, for example, that Hume was committed to a polygenetic theory of human origins, or that he supported slavery—in fact, he explicitly states his disapproval of slavery elsewhere. More important, the footnote does not show that Hume's whole philosophy is somehow racially coded, and attempts to demonstrate that it is have failed. Still, the footnote remains, showing that Hume himself believed in the inferiority of nonwhites, or at least of blacks. Here the contrast with Berkeley is instructive with regard to the contingent relation between views on slavery and on race: Berkeley was a nonracist who endorsed slavery, and Hume was a racialist who did not.

Unlike Berkeley and Hume, Rousseau embraced neither slavery nor racialism, according to Bernard Boxill's chapter. Boxill's argument focuses on The Discourse on the Origins of Inequality, whose talk of "natural man" has led some to suspect Rousseau of racist sentiments. Boxill argues that the Discourse has neither racist presuppositions nor racist implications. While it is true that Rousseau believed some non-Europeans to be at an earlier stage of cultural development than Europeans, he explained this difference by reference not to innate racial differences but rather to differences in environment. (It could also be added that for Rousseau the kind of cultural development that European society had achieved was a mixed blessing at best.) In addition, and in contrast to Kant, Rousseau held a nonteleological vision of history, so while, according to Boxill, Kant's views potentially justify "the Europeanization of the world," Rousseau's do not.

As foreshadowed in Boxill's discussion, Kant's views may have some troubling implications in matters of race, and this worry is only confirmed by Charles Mills's chapter. Mills begins by differing with the general approach often taken to modern philosophers who both defend universalist ethics and express racist sentiments. Rather than seeing the latter as contradicting the former, we should see the racist sentiments as qualifying the universalism. In Kant's case, Mills argues, this means that Kant's views on the inferiority of nonwhites show that he intends his universal moral theory to apply only to white Europeans—that only these count as "persons" for Kant. Mills argues that any attempt to detach Kant's racial views from his philosophy, or to view them as peripheral, simply presupposes an answer to the very question at issue. Mills suggests that a nonracist "Kantianism" may be possible, but this should not be mistaken for Kant's own philosophy.

Like Kant, Hegel expressed some clearly racist views, and his whole philosophy is infamously Eurocentric. In his chapter, Michael Hoffheimer focuses on Hegel's philosophy of religion to show the importance of race in Hegel's overall social and political philosophy. Hoffheimer demonstrates that early on Hegel absorbed the racial and cultural prejudices of his day, particularly the anti-Turk and anti-Islamic views. Hegel also absorbed the racial classifications of Kant and Blumenbach, and in his later work he increasingly relied upon race to categorize various religions. Through all of the changes in the particular features of his views, a constant theme in Hegel's work on religion is the superiority of Christian Europe over non-European peoples; only the former are capable of freedom and of being governed by law. Hence, race—and the religious and cultural differences associated with it—is central to Hegel's moral and political philosophy.

Although John Stuart Mill is often seen as a progressive thinker on issues of difference—particularly gender equity questions—Anthony Bogues argues in his chapter that Mill was not as enlightened on race as some have thought. Bogues places Mill in the context of Victorian political thought, which exhibits a consensus on the importance of character and "civilization." Mill participated in this consensus, which led him to view many non-European societies as less developed than European ones. So while Mill was the "good guy" in his debate with Carlyle—rejecting the latter's contentions that blacks are naturally inferior and that slavery is justified—Bogues argues that Mill remained within the mindset that saw European civilization as superior. As a result, Bogues interprets the Mill-Carlyle debate as being between two participants who agree more than they disagree with each other. The disagreement is over the form that European colonial rule should take, not over its fundamental propriety. These limitations in Mill's thought are reflected in his provisos in On Liberty and in Considerations on Representative Government that liberty and self-government are not appropriate for "backward" societies.

Marx agreed with Mill that European civilization is superior, and with Hegel that history itself, in a strict sense, takes place mainly in European society. Despite this—and despite some racist remarks in his private letters—Richard Peterson argues that Marx should not be seen as a racist thinker. Rather, the most notable feature of Marx's views on race is the extent to which Marx left race untheorized. Though Marx (and later Marxists) saw race as a barrier to working-class solidarity, he did not examine it as an independent source of oppression. In addition, Marx's relation to anti-Semitism is complex. Marx himself came from a Jewish family (his father converted so that he could practice law), and Marx was the object of anti-Semitic attacks. Yet at the same time Marx sometimes seems to be anti-Semitic, because, Peterson explains, he adopted the conventional association of Judaism with commercial activity. In any case, Peterson argues, the fundamental problem with Marx's relation to race is not that Marx was racist but that he failed to account for the complex relations between race and class and for the importance of racial identity.

In the final chapter, James Winchester examines Nietzsche's views on race. Against those who have charged that Nietzsche was a racist, Winchester shows that his relation to race is far too complex to be captured by this label. Although Nietzsche made some disturbing remarks on this score, he also departed from conventional racial thinking of his day by claiming, for example, that Jews constituted a strong race and Germans a mixed and weak one. These views, among others, do show that Nietzsche was a racialist—he believed that races were real and had great causal significance in shaping thought and culture. This view, combined with his assessment of the German and Jewish races, led Nietzsche to recommend "mixing" of the two in order to strengthen the German race. While Nietzsche sometimes thought in racial terms, his use of racial ideas was neither consistent nor well worked out.

I do not attempt to draw any overall conclusion from the chapters of the volume. There are far too many issues in play here, far too much complexity to allow for that, and my brief summaries do not begin to capture the subtlety of the arguments. Furthermore, there are many issues—of both interpretation and substance—on which the contributors to the volume disagree. It would therefore be a mistake to attempt to bring the discussion to a neat conclusion. It also would be a mistake to pretend that any of the arguments contained here is the last word. Rather, the goal of the volume is to assess the state of the discourse on race and modern philosophy and to contribute to this important set of discussions. If the chapters that follow do this—both individually and collectively—we will consider it a success.

NOTES

1. John Immerwahr and Michael Burke, "Race and the Modern Philosophy Course," *Teaching Philosophy* 16 (1993): 21–34.

2. Ivan Hannaford, *Race: The History of an Idea in the West* (Baltimore: Johns Hopkins University Press, 1996).

3. Bernard Boxill, Introduction to *Race and Racism*, ed. Bernard Boxill (Oxford: Oxford University Press, 2001), 1–42.

4. George M. Fredrickson, *Racism: A Short History* (Princeton: Princeton University Press, 2002).

5. See Harry M. Bracken, "Essence, Accident, and Race," *Hermathena* 116 (1973): 81–96; Bracken, "Philosophy and Racism," *Philosophia* 7 (1978): 241–60.

6. Richard H. Popkin, "The Philosophical Basis of Eighteenth-Century Racism," *Studies in Eighteenth-Century Culture* 3 (1973): 245–62; Popkin, "The Philosophical Basis of Modern Racism," in *The High Road to Pyrrhonism* (San Diego: Austin Hill, 1980), 79–102; Popkin, "Hume's Racism," in *High Road*, 251–66; Popkin, "Hume's Racism Reconsidered," in *The Third Force in Seventeenth Century Thought* (Leiden: E. J. Brill, 1992), 64–75.

7. Noam Chomsky, *Reflections on Language* (New York: Pantheon, 1975), 123–34.

8. Bracken, "Essence," 93.

9. Popkin, "Philosophical Basis of Eighteenth-Century Racism," 246.

10. Chomsky, *Reflections*, 132.

11. John Searle, "The Rules of the Language Game" [review of Chomsky's *Reflections on Language*], *Times Literary Supplement*, September 10, 1976, 1120.

12. Searle, "Rules," 1120.

13. Kay Squadrito, "Racism and Empiricism," *Behaviorism* 7 (1979): 105–15.

14. Ibid., 110.

15. Ibid., 112.

16. Fredrickson, *Racism*, 64–70.

17. David Theo Goldberg, *Racist Culture: Philosophy and the Politics of Meaning* (Oxford: Blackwell, 1993), 10, 28. Goldberg continues this line of thought in *The Racial State* (Oxford: Blackwell, 2002).

18. Emmanuel Chukwudi Eze, *Race and the Enlightenment* (Oxford: Blackwell, 1997); Eze, *Achieving Our Humanity: The Idea of the Postracial Future* (New York: Routledge, 2001), chaps. 2, 3.

19. Charles W. Mills, *The Racial Contract* (Ithaca: Cornell University Press, 1997), 64–72.

20. There are too many works on philosophy and race to cite them all here, but some notable examples not yet cited include Julie K. Ward and Tommy L. Lott, eds., *Philosophers on Race: Critical Essays* (Oxford: Blackwell, 2002); Robert Bernasconi and Tommy L. Lott, eds., *The Idea of Race* (Indianapolis: Hackett, 2000); Robert Bernasconi, ed., *Race* (Oxford: Blackwell, 2001); Robert Bernasconi with Sybol Cook, eds., *Race and Racism in Continental Philosophy* (Bloomington: Indiana University Press, 2003); Lucius T. Outlaw Jr., *On Race and Philosophy* (New York: Routledge, 1996); Leonard Harris, ed., *Racism* (Amherst, NY: Humanity Books, 1999); H. F. Augstein, ed., *Race: The Origins of an Idea, 1760–1850* (Bristol: Thoemmes Press, 1996); Susan E. Babbitt and Sue Campbell, eds., *Racism and Philosophy* (Ithaca: Cornell University Press, 1999); Lawrence Blum, *"I'm Not a Racist, But . . .": The Moral Quandary of Race* (Ithaca: Cornell University Press, 2002); Michael P. Levine and Tamas Pataki, eds., *Racism in Mind* (Ithaca: Cornell University Press, 2004).

21. Kwame Anthony Appiah, "Racisms," in *Anatomy of Racism*, ed. David Theo Goldberg (Minneapolis: University of Minnesota Press, 1990), 3–17.

22. Ibid., 4–5.

23. Ibid., 5–6.

24. Jorge L. A. Garcia, "The Heart of Racism," in *Racism*, ed. Harris, 398–434.

25. Ibid., 399–401.

26. Ibid., 408.

27. Ibid., 404.

| 1 |

Descartes's Silences on Slavery and Race

TIMOTHY J. REISS

Although many have accused Descartes of philosophical liability for modern racist attitudes, Descartes said nothing of race—not at least in any modern sense—or, directly, of slavery. This reticence dictates that on issues of slavery, Descartes, alone of the philosophers in this collection, be approached obliquely. This chapter's four parts respond to this need. The first notes briefly what "race" could mean in Descartes's time and how he has been accused of condoning what it became later. The second scans Descartes's education and life context to show what he knew of ideas and practices of slavery (and "race"), and ends with his use of slavery to frame his thinking in the *Meditations*. Fully to understand this use requires knowing old and recent debates on slavery and race. The third part details these earlier ideas, facts, and disputes, focusing on American and African enslavements and a threefold effort to justify them by nature, sin, and just war. Probing what Descartes was getting at in light of debates to which he had access and could be reacting raises questions whose answers may offer new understanding of what could be meant by terms like "race," "barbarian," or "savage." The oblique approach also makes clear the need to distinguish legal, philosophical, and theological thought from commercial, colonial, and imperial interests, however fiercely they engaged one another. This part unearths the parameters of a particular history established for later argument, even as it prefaces this chapter's own narrower last part, returning to Descartes to argue how he used the legal tra-

Debate with Patrick Feeney in a 1998 graduate class stirred this chapter's research. His fine case that study of Descartes drew a blank on its matter has nagged. I thank Stanley Corngold, Martin Elsky, Andrea Goulet, John Hill, Marie-Hélène Huet, Vicki Kahn, Marcia Norton, Nell Painter, Francesca Sautman, Adam Sutcliffe, Stephanie Smallwood, and publics at Princeton, the University of Illinois, Urbana-Champaign, the CUNY Graduate Center, and the Bay Area Early Modern Group for feedback, Joe Valente for his useful critique, Doris Garraway at Northwestern for making me rethink an argument, Michel Beaujour and Kate Stimpson for their remarks, Ngugi wa Thiong'o for his judicious advice, Tim Hampton for his fruitful reading. I especially thank Patricia Penn Hilden for mending syntax, thought, and argument, and Andrew Valls for his valiant, generous, and mostly successful efforts to shorten a very long chapter. Translations are mine.

dition and these recent conflicts to cement important elements of his thinking, and to suggest reasons for his silences.

RACE, HISTORY, AND DESCARTES DEFENDANT

Assertions about race and slavery in Descartes need qualifying. Early modern Europeans did not use "race" to denote visible physical identity or to mark "biologically determined ethnic inequality."[1] Race meant lineage, clan, species, or "residents of a particular environment." People saw physical difference, especially skin color, but not as tagging "great divisions of human beings."[2] The biblical story of common human ancestry prevailed into the seventeenth century, still setting parameters to debate Native American origins. Nor had slavery and ethnicity been tied. In ancient Greece slaves were Greeks or "barbarians," aliens speaking other tongues. In Rome they came from across the empire. Medieval European slaves were mainly other Europeans. Their status was legal, not essential or natural. To later sailors and settlers like Amerigo Vespucci (1454–1512) and Gonzalo Fernández de Oviedo (1478–1557), the difference between master and slave was religious: slaves were heathens, subject to "cristianos," Christians. Nearly four centuries of transatlantic slave trade, starting in 1502, inexorably tied slavery and race. Descartes, writing in the not-so-early years of the Middle Passage, might have addressed either. He named race never and slavery twice. Why? Does his silence say anything serious about how and when slavery and race became—could become—grave moral issues? About how and when slavery became racialized? Do two exceptions to this silence matter for construing his apparent indifference?

His virtual silence and seeming indifference have not stopped people from taxing him and some putative "Cartesianism" with spawning modern Western philosophical apologia for slavery and racism or, conversely, from praising both for having treated everything human except mind as purely accidental, making all facets of body, including sex and skin color, insignificant. This last view explains why a woman, the princess Elisabeth, became his chief philosophical collaborator. Descartes's indifference to external social categories also drove him to train artisans and peasants into admired mathematicians, prompting Maxime Leroy to see him as a protosocialist.[3]

Among those blaming Descartes for a philosophical validation of slavery and racism, many are as angry as Joan Dayan, who finds the 1685 *Code noir*, regulating French colonial slavery, unthinkable without him. After the *Discours de la méthode* and *Meditations*, the *Code* was "the nasty belch that follows a meal of pure thought." "The thinker of Descartes' *Meditations* in 1640 set the stage for the 1685 edict of Louis XIV. These two texts show how the making of enlightenment man led to the demolition of the unenlightened brute, how the thinking mind's destructive or generative proclivities dominated a passive nature or servile body." Descartes's quest for his essence, in the first Meditation's thought experiment of self-dismemberment, enabled later arguments that those supposed to lack thought—black ivory, "pieces of the Indies," or African "ebony wood"—could be "bought, bartered, and sold, . . . figured as heads of cattle, coins, parcels of land, pieces of furniture." For these, being without thought, "no amount of amputation, torture, or disfiguring can matter."[4] According to Dayan, then, objectifying racialized others resulted from claims of mind's control of body and body's lack of thought. Despite the *Code*'s stated intention to make slavery *less* onerous for its victims, "to help them in their needs,"[5] these basic "Cartesian" warrants rendered it inevitably and fundamentally oppressive.

The *Code* is certainly glacially instrumentalist in its (actually failed) effort to govern treatment, behavior, punishment, habits, nourishment, lives, and deaths of slaves, who were their master's entire property and treated in fact as if they had lesser minds. It is silent on such colonial realities as "the number of lashes a slave could receive [or] the length of the workday."[6] But whether such views and practices had anything to do with Descartes is a serious question, whatever later people may have done with what they called Cartesianism. It is serious because Dayan's words, however unfair to Descartes's actual work, echo wide understanding in the writing of many decolonized peoples that it was Cartesianism, and so Descartes himself, that encouraged an instrumental control of the "other" of which racialized slavery was a limit case.[7]

|||

EDUCATION, TRADE, AND TRAVEL

Descartes's silences may be as telling as anything he might have said. He could have been unaware of neither slavery nor visible ethnic variety, as facts and, in the first case, as a topic of tangled legal, philosophical, and theological debate. Trained at the Jesuit College of La Flèche from 1606/7 to 1614/15, and at the University of Poitiers Law Faculty for one or two years, he later explored free will and freedom, *générosité*, friendship, and collective bonds in general.[8] For him freedom was opposed not to slavery or servitude but to abstractions like license or ignorance or to realities like prison (the last less different than appears). But his Jesuit teachers' teachers, from Aristotle through Aquinas to the Coimbran commentators, to Luis de Molina (1535–1600) and Francisco Suárez (1548–1617), were never silent on slavery. They followed tradition in taking it as a fact of the human condition. It was vital in Francisco de Vitoria's (1483–1546) and Domingo de Soto's (1494–1561) work at

Salamanca on law in general and Spain's legal duties to the indigenous peoples of the Americas in particular. It was crucial in the fierce debates between Juan Ginés de Sepúlveda (1490–1573) and Bartolomé de Las Casas (1484–1566). On all these, Descartes's Jesuit teachers were groomed. But Descartes knew much of this directly, telling Marin Mersenne (1588–1648) in 1639 that he carried Aquinas's *Summa theologica* with him everywhere, or twice recalling a year later that he was raised on the Coimbrans.[9] He had had the run of La Flèche's library, which would have held more of these writings. He knew their general picture of human nature and relations, including slavery, whether or not he knew particular cases illustrating it, such as African or Indian. Even here, he had reason to be informed, for Las Casas deeply marked his admired Michel de Montaigne (1533–92).

In all this, whether involving conditions of Indians, Africans, or others, slavery was a legal, philosophical, and theological issue having nothing to do with race. Its link was to "barbarian," "savage," or "heathen," words, we shall see, signaling inferiority of mind or culture, or absence of Redemption, rather than ethnic identification.

Whatever philosophy's take on slavery, material conditions where Descartes lived cast it otherwise. He was in Holland in 1618–19, settled there in 1628, and stayed until 1649. During this time, the United Provinces became Europe's great entrepôt, its fleets forging a global trade. Their slave trading began, illegally, in the late sixteenth century. A much-told event befell in 1596, when "a Dutch privateer brought a hundred and thirty slaves he had captured on a Portuguese ship to the province of Zeeland." The burgomaster of Zeeland's capital, Middelburg, "held that they could not be kept or sold as slaves and so they were freed." "Others captured at sea," Allison Blakely adds, "were given control of captured ships or were put ashore on the nearest land."[10] But as American plantation trade grew, so did Dutch slaving, notably during the Twelve Years' Truce with Spain (1609–21). By the 1640s, the Dutch West India Company, founded as the truce ended, was the main European slaver. Slaves were then its chief, and by the 1550s and 1660s its near-exclusive, trade,[11] after which the English took over.

In a 1631 letter to his friend Jean-Louis Guez de Balzac (1597–1654), Descartes extravagantly praised Dutch business and the *commodités* it fetched from Europe and the Indies. Above all, he admired the bustling port of Amsterdam, where he then lived, and its hectic trade. Opposing what he found to be Holland's calm atmosphere to the chaos reigning elsewhere, he noted that everyone's single-minded focus on trade and profit left him serene. He got "pleasure" watching the ships "come in, bringing us abundance of all that the Indies produce and everything rare in Europe," yielding every commodity he could desire (AT 1:203–4).[12] Descartes repeated these views in ending the third part of the *Discours* in 1637:

Just eight years ago . . . this desire [for privacy] made me resolve to move away from all places where I might have acquaintances and move here, to a country where the long duration of war [the eighty years' revolt against Spain] has established such orders that the armies maintained here seem to serve only to make people enjoy the fruits of peace with the more security and where, among the mass of a very busy people more careful of its own business than curious of others', without lacking any of the comforts found in the most populous cities, I have been able to live as solitary and retired as in the most remote deserts [les desers les plus escartez]. (AT 6:31)

These Dutch traders, profiting from European and West and East Indian business, still at war with Spain, had by now long shared in the slave trade supplying Europe's American colonies.

Indeed, when Descartes wrote this, paintings, architectural decor, shop signs, and theater all stressed the fact—especially in Amsterdam.[13] In his 1615 *Moortje* (Little Moor), Gerbrand Adriaensz Bredero, fitting moralizing affect to law, cried: "Inhuman practice! Godless knavery, / That men sell men into chattel slavery." Bredero's protest still let him give "his lover a black girl as a gift."[14] Not only art bespoke the trade. So did the many Africans, brought directly or via the Caribbean, and mixed-blood people, some maybe from those freed in Middelburg in 1596 with no way to leave, others consequent on sixteenth-century slave markets in Antwerp.[15] Africans were also in England in large numbers from the 1570s, mostly as domestic servants, entertainers, and prostitutes.[16] By century's turn, Elizabeth was urging edicts to remove them from the country.[17] If so visible in England, how much greater their presence in the United Provinces, where the trade was already substantial? Africans and mixed bloods were part of the bustle into whose "Desers . . . ESCARTEZ" Descartes solidly placed his name and being.[18]

Unlike many of his contemporaries, Descartes was impervious to the lure of the Americas. He wrote in deep sorrow to Denis Mesland (1616–72) in late 1645 or early 1646, after this stout partisan of his had been exiled (apparently for that reason) to Canada, where he was "to convert the savages." He would, he added, be sadder still "if I were not here in a land where every day I meet many people who have come back from the Antipodes" (AT 4:345). Among these was his relative Étienne Charlet (1570–1652), one of his teachers at La Flèche and, later, Jesuit Provincial of France (AT 4:585). Descartes's consolatory letter signaled the constant marine circulation at the source of the wealth whose acquisition he had so praised in the letter to Balzac.

The second part of the *Discours*, Peter Hulme offers, sent the same signal as it argued that wide discord among thinkers showed that "one man" was more apt to find "truths that are a bit hard to find." For "the same man, with the same mind, raised from childhood among French or Germans, becomes different from what he would be if he had always lived among Chinese or Cannibals" (AT 6:16). Since all, in his Montaigne-like phrase, had "as much [reason] as we, or more," the difference showed that to find agreed truths just required a model enabling right use of reason. Still, if French, Germans, Chinese, and cannibals were labeled as equally rational peoples, the geography pitted a center against east and west extremes. On this map, discovery needed one person to find the right model, as Columbus sailed without guide to the Caribbean. Francis Bacon (1561–1626) used this image in the frontispiece of his 1620 *Instauratio magna*, picturing a ship passing the Pillars of Hercules into the Atlantic, a precursor on the horizon, leaving the Old World's both real and imaginative limits.[19] Bacon always tied natural-philosophical research and Europe's maritime expansion.[20] Descartes knew Bacon's works the *Novum organum* and *De augmentis scientiarum* (1623),[21] but he had already used the maritime image in the publicity for his 1616 law theses' defense. Rejecting humanist learning for legal science, he said that his training had led to "the vast waters of the sciences and all the rivers that flow from them so plentifully."[22] Search for a set of rules for the discovery of the truth in all areas of knowledge in these waters was the core of the first part of the *Discours*. In 1616 he assumed the law would give those rules. By 1619 he was sure to find them in mathematics, long thought fundamental to navigation, discovery and conquest of territories, spread of religion, growth of commerce, defeat of enemies, and indeed a conqueror's moral virtue.[23] Descartes's awareness of global expansion and trade is conspicuous. So is his sense of living at its center.

These circumstances may make his silence on slavery seem the odder—even more, maybe, considering his admiration for Montaigne and that writer's echo of Las Casas. But silence was not total. Ending the first Meditation, positing the existence of an evil genius (AT 7:22) and the need to suppose himself with no body and concentrate only on thinking, he wrote:

But this is an arduous endeavor, and a certain laziness leads me back to customary habits of life. No otherwise than a prisoner, who was enjoying imaginary liberty in sleep, when s/he then starts to suspect s/he is sleeping, fears to be woken and conspires with the pleasant illusions as long as possible; just so I readily fall back into old opinions and fear to be shaken from them, lest arduous labors follow peaceful repose and I then have to work not in the light but among the inextricable darkness of the difficulties now raised. (AT 7:23)

In Claude Clerselier's French, approved by Descartes, "prisoner" became "slave," the rest staying virtually the same—except for naming it a dream: "And just like a slave who was enjoying an imaginary freedom in sleep, when he starts to suspect that his freedom is only a dream, fears to be woken, and conspires with his pleasant illusions so as to be deceived longer, so I fall back . . ." (AT 9:18). The model is the usual ancient and contemporary one of the captive enslaved by a conqueror, which Descartes could find recently in Suárez or Hugo Grotius (1583–1645), anciently in Justinian, and about everywhere in between.

| | |

SLAVERY AND RACE IN LAW, PRACTICE, AND DEBATE

Fully to grasp the weight of the slave/captive equation and the centuries-long tradition it grounded, we need to follow some of its aspects from its ancient origins, not only in Justinian, but from long before in Aristotle, the thinker whose authority remained paramount everywhere (including the philosophical part of Descartes's education), although it was opposed on this issue by nearly all the sixteenth-century teachers named earlier. We also need to recall that after he left La Flèche, Descartes trained in the law and defended theses on Roman testamentary law. He knew Justinian in detail.

The *Institutes* and *Digest* were categorical on the slave's legal status. After opening by distinguishing between humans according to their status as free or slave, the *Institutes* elaborated:

> [F]reedom is a natural faculty, by which people are called free, to do what is open to one, unless forbidden by force or law. But slavery is an institution of the law of nations [*iuris gentium*], by which one is subjected to another's dominion against nature. And slaves are so called because generals order captives to be sold, and in this way they manage to save, and not kill, them; so they are also called *mancipia*, because taken from enemies by hand. Too, slaves are either born or made. They are born from our *ancillis*; they are made either by the law of nations, that is, by captivity; or by the civil law, as when a free person, more than twenty years old, suffers to sell him or herself for a share of the price.

Slavery was an institution of the law of nations by which one was subjected to another's dominion against nature. The *Digest* echoed these terms verbatim, adding their earlier sources.[24] Slaves were made by the law of nations; their conduct and condition fell under the civil law. Neither the law of nations nor civil law had anything to do with their human status under natural law.

These precepts counter what many think a main ancient view: Aristotle's belief that slaves were inferior *by nature*. But he often contradicted himself, differentiating at least twice between slave qua slave and slave qua human. Speaking of friendship as between equally virtuous humans, he said that if master and slave could not be friends insofar as one was tool and property of the other, as humans they could. Asking whether a slave could enjoy the happy life, he again distinguished: "no one assigns to a slave a share in happiness, except as he grants him also a share in human life [*ei mê kai biou*]."[25] The word for slave here, *andrapodon*, named a war captive. In his longest discussion as to whether there were natural slaves, Aristotle thought nature "would have liked" clearly to distinguish minds and bodies of free and slave, but admitted that it had not. Those who held that slavery was no natural condition because a slave was so only by brute force might thus be right.[26] The whole passage is a muddle, betraying ideological rather than philosophical aims. With others, Robert Schlaifer notes that Aristotle could contradict himself on this matter in the space of a sentence.[27] It is hardly surprising that this idea of slaves' natural inferiority virtually vanished in philosophy after Aristotle.[28]

With trade growing in Africa and invasion of the Americas, explorers, raiders, traders, and settlers certainly *wished* other peoples to be less than human. A remark by the Scottish theologian John Major (1469–1550) in 1512 to the effect that inhabitants of the Antilles were Aristotle's natural slaves may have prompted a few Spanish (and Portuguese) apologists adopt the idea again.[29] Those on the spot had a harder time. Vespucci, startled as he was by unknown habits and life ways, brutal as he and his fellows often were, noting native people's comeliness and dignity, often praised their warmth and gentleness, their building skills, their many languages (key sign of reason), and wrote of them in his 1502 letter to Lorenzo de' Medici as "rational." Still, noting their lack of clothes (justifying it by climate) and barbarous sexual and eating habits, he echoed a far more influential writer than Major. This was Giles of Rome, Aegidius Romanus (c. 1243–1316), whose 1285 *De regimine principum* was used for centuries in universities, religious orders, and courts, "studied as a textbook in every European court and noble household" in the fifteenth century, and was "the most immediate source of the political theory and even of the rules of government of" Portuguese kings.[30]

Taking a cue from Thomas Aquinas (1225–74), who used Justinian to differ from Aristotle but applied a Christian twist in saying that while humans were naturally free, by sinning they could fall into the "slavish state of the beasts," Giles enlarged on what divided humans from beasts, giving four criteria. (1) Humans cultivate and prepare their animal and vegetable food sources. (2) They make clothing to cover their nudity from weather and other people, not having feathers or fur. (3) They avoid danger from afar, using their hands, Aristotle's "organ of organs," to guard against foes, making and using weapons and tools of self-defense, not having horns, fangs, claws, or special agility. (4) They have speech and knowledge, by which to learn, and live in well-ordered society and community.[31] Later, he gave three criteria for civilized society. (1) It aims to better its people—a duty of ruler and ruled alike. So "it is requisite in a right government that a good citizen be a good man." (2) In this order, "the government's and city's safety" depends on obedience to king and laws. *Pace* some, this "obedience" is not "servitude but freedom." "For, since beasts are of a servile nature, so the more one accedes to a bestial nature, the more one is naturally a slave. To be a criminal and zealous seeker of war, a disturber of the peace, or to live without curb or law is, according to the Philosopher's maxim and Homer's dictum, to be a beast rather than a human. So those who do not observe the laws, who refuse to obey their kings and superiors, are rather beasts than humans, and are consequently slaves rather than free." (3) This obedience to kings and observance of laws produce civil peace and tranquility and "abundance of external things," including civil relations, health, wealth, and all other goods.[32]

Moderns have paid Giles little attention despite his centrality to later debates. We shall see that another of his works made these criteria even more serviceable to later traders and settlers seeking justification for theft and rapine—gave, indeed, a way used by all such writers to define peoples as collectively inferior or superior. Sixteenth-century philosophers and theologians, however, were unconvinced. They, and at least one "economist," observed that those deploying the arguments were far from disinterested. We must keep these discordant interests in mind when considering ideas of race and slavery, and how efforts to justify them readily slid from nature to sin to just war.

One of Descartes's best-known near predecessors, Jean Bodin, began discussion on the first of these in his 1576 *Six livres de la république* by saying that in his day "the whole world is full of slaves, except for a small part of Europe," and that every slave was either natural, "born of a slave woman," that is, "or made by the right of law, or by crime," or one who sold, wagered, or voluntarily put himself into slavery. The idea that the slave "by nature" is one born into slavery, not one with a servile soul, was un-Aristotelian. Bodin derided the view that some were "naturally made to serve and obey, others to command and rule." "Jurists," he joked (he being one), "who pay less heed to philosophers' disquisitions than to public opinion, hold that slavery is directly against nature, and do all they can to uphold freedom."[33] In book 1, chapter 5, he rejected at length Aristotle's idea of natural slavery, inveighing, indeed, against *all* slavery. Slavery, Erasmus had said earlier, typically echoing Justinian, was "pitiable and dishonourable" and "imposed upon nature," "since nature created all men free."[34] These arguments reacted to Aristotle's general authority rather than to his idea of natural slaves, and maybe to some of the partisan writers just mentioned, for very few thinkers adopted the idea and, if we believe Bodin, even fewer among the general public. If by 1576 the idea was more prevalent, it was perhaps because philosophers and lawyers, like Vitoria in a famed 1537 lecture on Americans' rights and his pupil Soto in his 1553 De iustitia et iure, a vital jurisprudential work known across scholarly Europe, had taken seriously settlers and traders who had, for obvious advantage, found the idea serviceable. Columbus had from the start shipped Americans to Spain as slaves and planned a large traffic that Queen Isabel stopped. Similarly, Vespucci told in a private 1500 letter how he had sent 232 Americans seized by force as slaves to Castile, although in the published version of 1504–5, he told of taking prisoners in a war fought at the request of peoples whom the others had been attacking.[35] This version made the slaves fair captives ("prigioni schiavi") in just war, not victims of the earlier tale's casual ferocity.

Vespucci thus avoided a need to argue natural inferiority, simultaneously showing why others found just war and related claims handy, since most agreed that Indians were free humans. Even the most tentative claim of natural slavery, let alone of "rights" it gave conquerors, lost all conviction once the Spanish empire went beyond the Caribbean into urbanized Mexico. But just as Giles gave useful criteria for distinguishing barbarism from civilization, so he gave grounds, if not for natural slavery, at least for "natural" dominion. In his influential De ecclesiastica potestate (1301), he wrote that all creatures were in a hierarchy descending from God, all superiors having "dominium," lordship, over all inferiors. Those recognizing and accepting Christ's redemption were "worthy of eternal inheritance," then of worldly possession, and superior to those who had not accepted it. Unredeemed original sin made one unworthy of eternal inheritance and so of any dominion or possession. So, too, did one's own sin, such that a believer who had possessed justly could be justly stripped of dominion. Whoever did not accept God's dominion was unworthy to possess or have dominion over anything, and did so only by usurpation and injustice.[36] The argument validated Christians' title to the Americas and their inhabitants, if it could be shown that indigenous peoples had willfully refused redemption and accepted sin. It also justified war against them. So the chronicler of the first Portuguese West African voyages, Gomes Eanes de Zurara (c. 1405–1473/74), justified enslaving black Africans by their legacy of the sin and curse of Ham. He added to this legacy the fact that "they lived in perdition of souls and bodies . . . : of souls, because they were pagans, without the clarity and light of holy Faith; and of bodies, because they lived like beasts, with none of the order of rational creatures, for they knew not at all what was bread or wine, nor covering of cloth, nor accommodation in a house;

and what was worse was their great ignorance, so that they had no knowledge of the good, simply living in bestial sloth." The list came directly from Giles, whose *De regimine* Zurara indeed later named as a source.[37]

Vespucci, Oviedo, and others emphasized Indians' sinfulness—and, in Oviedo's case, their forgetting redemption in the past and refusing it in the present. Vitoria and his followers had to answer. In his official *Historia* of Spain in the Americas (1535), Oviedo, landowner and crown official, was painstaking, seeking like Zurara to make assurance doubly sure. Certainly, he wrote in the "Proemio" to the second book, Spain's right was secured by "the donation and apostolic title that the Supreme Pontiff made of these Indies to the Catholic Kings, Ferdinand and Isabel, and their successors in the kingdoms of Castile and León," but these lands were already Spain's in antiquity. They were the Hesperides islands, named after Hesperus, twelfth king of Spain, who ruled "1658 years before our Redeemer was clothed in our human flesh," "before the Savior of the world was born."[38] This claim of ancient possession was and is much criticized, but Oviedo was right to see that the papal donation alone gave no title. As Las Casas observed in his *Historia de las Indias*, it authorized only preaching the Gospel, christianizing the indigenous peoples, and saving their souls.[39]

But Oviedo repeated *Redemptor* and *Salvador* for cause, saying that the apostles Paul and James had spread the Gospel in the Americas, and that "if news of the Holy Gospel has been cultivated and brought here from Castile in our day, it does not mean that from the day of the apostles these savage peoples did not know of Christian redemption and the blood our Redeemer Jesus Christ spilled for humankind; rather is it to be thought that these generations and Indians of these regions had now forgotten it." The Bible says the Gospel was spread across the world, "so these Indians already had news of gospel truth and cannot feign ignorance of it." That they did so proved "their incapacity and evil inclinations." The very "air of the land" bred discord, for which "sin and many others that teem among them, God has forgotten them for so many centuries." This was a reason why Indians "were divided up and entrusted [*encomendados*]" by Columbus to "Christians."[40] Christians' sins had much wronged Indians but had acted as the scourge of God, who gave "divine approval for their removal from the earth, [punishing] the great, ugly, and wicked sins and abominations of these savage and bestial peoples"—and so he went on.[41] Oviedo iterated these ideas at length in book 5, whose "Proemio" explained that the book's aim was to clarify "that this fault [of the Indians] and punishment is principally founded in the crimes and abominable customs and rites of this people . . . from which may easily be gathered God's justice and how merciful he has been with this race [*generación*], waiting so many centuries for them to mend their ways. For no creature is unaware that there is an all-powerful God."[42] If Indians were knowingly and willfully living in sin, then Spaniards, by papal and historical title and duty to God and Church, had legal, historical, and theological dominion and grounds for just war against Americans. Again we see Giles's footprints.

Vitoria addressed these questions about Americans' nature and ownership of their lands and whether this ownership could be as easily abrogated as Oviedo urged by displacing the issue from civil or nation law (involving historic Spanish dominion or papal donation) to natural law. He denied that they were unredeemed sinners, "slaves by nature," bestial, or irrational. So they could be owners. Even were they sinners, they would still be in "God's image by [their] inborn nature, that is, [their] rational powers," and no more lose natural dominion than would sinful Europeans[43]—an issue Oviedo skirted by making the latter God's scourge. In Indians, as in all humans, God had set the rules of divine *ratio*, just as an architect, said Soto in his *De iustitia*, "used a set of drawings."[44] Indians, said Vitoria, had full use of will and reason and could not by nature belong to others. "Such slavery is a civil and legal condition, to which no man can belong by nature."[45] If neither nature nor sin voided Indians' human rights, no war against them on such grounds could be alleged just; nor had Indians ever harmed the Spanish. So Vitoria argued, awkwardly for the Spanish crown, that there was no victor's right of possession over occupied land, and that while Indians might *agree* to Spanish presence, rule could not justly be imposed on them. At most the Spanish could be tutors to raise the Indians from barbarism to civilization, provided the latter so accepted them. Vitoria was by no means alone, others arguing that no kind of conquest gave aggressors rights over defeated peoples, some arguing by the mid-fifteenth century that the Spanish might owe Indians restitution. In his bitter contest with Las Casas in the 1550s, Sepúlveda, like Oviedo, and again recalling Giles, wrote of Indians as hostile to natural law, living without rulers and laws, committing human sacrifice and cannibalism, and so fair prey of the first "civil" person to encounter them, their sinfulness and savagery justifying war the others rejected. One trouble, as even Oviedo granted—settler, conqueror, and laudatory historian as he was—was that Christians were no less sinful: that they were God's scourge did not lessen Spaniards' guilt for depredations and savagery toward Indians or temper their loss of humanity.[46]

Although Soto, writing simultaneously with Sepúlveda, began his *De iustitia* by seeming to adopt Aristotle's view that a "person can have ownership of another person as much by natural law as by the law of nations," humans being divided by nature to rule or serve, he in fact agreed with Vitoria. Following Justinian, he reviewed the kinds of slavery allowed under nations' and civil law, concluding that the first slavery, that of nature, was not slavery at all: the diverse talents it named meant that the more favored must not treat the less "as if they were his property, but . . . as free and independent beings in their own use and purpose, instructing them in mores, for example, and teaching them."[47] Among these thinkers, even so fleeting a concession to Aristotle's view was rare. The rule in these years was increasingly to reject the theory of natural slavery. Las Casas began his *Historia* by saying that Indians were as rational as others, "being of far better judgment and sustaining a far better polity and government than many other peoples [*naciones*] who vaunt themselves and scorn them." In his *Apologética*, he held Indians fully rational: "all nations of the world are humans, and of all humans and every one of them there is no other definition than that they are rational; all have their intellect, their will [*voluntad*] and their free will insofar as they are made in the image and semblance of God."[48] Well known in manuscript, these works were not printed for 300 and 350 years, but the view was shared by these thinkers and surely absorbed by those they taught.

In 1569, shortly before Bodin's *République*, the Dominican Tomás de Mercado (before 1530–1576) rejected Roman law's three licit conditions for slavery: capture in a just war, criminal punishment, and a father's sale of his child. Mercado's *Suma de tratos y contratos* was another much-read work, said by later members of his order to embody its views. One remark implies that he was writing in the 1550s, coevally with the debates just indicated. He called the African slave trade "not only wrong but deplorable and wretched." All three Roman conditions were now illicit, he explained, being in practice "mixed with an infinite number of false and unjust ones, effected by trickery, violence, force and theft." The trade was "*bestial y brutal,*" one of whose two parties was "tricked or tyrannically captive or forced." Blacks were treated more cruelly by "Christians" than Christians were when captured by Turks. In law the trade was licit, but given "the reality in truth of what happens, it is a mortal sin and merchants who deal in bringing blacks from Cape Verde [the departure point for West African slaves] live in an evil state and great danger." Given, too, the misery of Africans living "one or two thousand leagues from their own land," no solution is better than to "give up" the trade.[49] Mercado devoted a chapter to advancing this view of the African slave trade but knew that the Spanish colonies could not function without it and gave an earlier chapter (chapter 7) to slaves' value and just price.[50] Usually seen as radically hostile to the trade, he equivocated. Bartolomé de Albornoz, in his 1573 *Arte de los contratos*, faulted him and, treating the same conditions for "the slave trade in blacks of Africa," rejected all slavery.[51] The parameters in his work were still those of Roman law and just war, as they were in the Portuguese Fernão de Oliveira's (1507–81) blazing censure of 1555. Like Mercado, he accused traders of getting slaves by savage violence and damned his compatriots as "inventors of so evil a trade, never practiced or heard of among humans . . . buying and selling peaceable free men as one buys dumb animals, oxen, horses, and such. They are poked, driven, herded, taken, tested, and picked with as much disdain and force as a slaughterhouse butcher shows to cattle in a stockyard."[52]

Descartes would not have known all these, although the debates and views unquestionably pervaded Montaigne. Descartes certainly would have breathed in their attitudes and known some of the writings expressing them. He could also have read the Jesuit José de Acosta's (1540–1600) influential *Historia natural y moral de las Indias*, first issued in 1590, with four French-language editions by 1616. Acosta, too, held that Indians, like all humans, had "reason and prudence." In his "Proemio" he remarked that he had divided his work in two, a first part treating the physical surroundings of the Indians, "the works of nature," a second their actions and mores, the works, he repeated Las Casas, "of their free will."[53] Descartes certainly knew Suárez, the greatest Jesuit teacher and thinker, who was adamant that natural slavery did not exist, although he held that natural law logically assured obedience under the law of nations. For as to "captivity and slavery," it was clear that "if it is licit for one to reduce another to captivity or slavery, even if by coercion of the second, yet by that very fact the latter has to obey and not resist, since there can be no war that is just on both sides." Like war, slavery fell fully under nations' law, since "it was not necessary by simple natural reason."[54] Rather, "freedom from slavery is a natural property of man and so is usually said to be by the law of nature. Yet a man can deprive himself of it by his own will, or even for a just cause be deprived of it and reduced to slavery." This was pure Justinian. Just as slavery, especially of war captives, "was introduced by nations' law," so it could "be repealed by custom."[55] Captivity and slavery were constraints under nations' and civil law. The just war question was vital: it was apropos of just war that Mercado wrote of abuses so grave that one should not engage in the slave trade and that Oliveira and Albornoz rejected slavery out of hand, denying that even just war justified slavery of people by nature free.

Save the last three, perhaps, these were Descartes's teachers' teachers. His notions of the ties of reason, will, and free will and their generality in humans came from them. Perhaps, too, Soto supplied the major simile for God and the lone thinker of the method in the *Discours*: an architect planning a city or house (AT 6:11–15, 22). Nowhere in this tradition, save Soto's self-canceling case, was the slave qua slave treated as falling under the law of nature. By the mid-sixteenth century, theologians and philosophers had thoroughly discredited any idea that original sin justified slavery or any essential distinction among peoples. The slave was made by nations' and civil law. By nature's law, all humans were the same. That was why, very early, Vespucci changed his tale of slave taking to adjust it to the just war validation. The idea that there was no natural slavery grounded the Salamanca debates (Vitoria, Soto, and their colleagues and pupils) over Indians' rights that the Spanish crown had to defend.

Nor did this tradition use "race" in any sense of biologically determined ethnic inequality. Its writers used terms like *negros* usually only to identify, often prefacing discussion of possible wrongs (see note 65 below). Acosta held "Ethiopians" to be as rational as all humans, their present "barbarism" (like Indians') due to environment. Even Oviedo implied as much, while the Salamancan Dominicans and their "successor" Jesuits were clear that there was no nature, original sin, or, for some, even war able to make things otherwise. In the final chapters of his *Apologética*, Las Casas recapped Indians' rationality, then ran over the four meanings of the term "barbarous." The first denoted an utter lack of humanity: "ferocity, disorder, deviation, degeneracy of reason, justice, good mores and human kindness"; the second, use of a different language or want of the kind of learning familiar to the person using the word; the third, lack of social and political order and rational habit; the fourth, absence of "true religion and Christian faith." The last was double: one naming those refusing redemption, another those never having heard of it. Thus considering both Aristotelian and Aegidian claims about nature and sin, Las Casas concluded that only in this last sense, separating pagans from Christians, could Indians be called barbarous.[56] The same, as others diversely observed, applied to Africans. This is not to say that racism did not circulate in popular speech or act. It did. It seems to have been a small issue in philosophical debate.

| | |

DESCARTES, TRADITION, AND LIMITS OF NEW THOUGHT

Descartes would have known much of the theoretical debate. He must have heard cruder attitudes circulating in the north as in the south, whatever their shamefaced ambivalence. But they signaled an anticommunal cutthroat social future that he, like his Jesuit teachers, would have envisaged with boundless dismay. It opposed all he understood as the "concordant" civil society whose new ethical foundations he sought. Thus it was the long tradition of slavery under the law that he used to end the first Meditation. His captive slave was inhibited in the use of his body, the master's tool, but not in his inherent rights ("his" because Descartes was the imagined slave). At issue was the slave's ability to control his body, closing his sense organs to avoid a possible evil genius's traps. As Jacques Lezra says of this passage: "A slave being, very exactly, someone who no longer owns the organs of his or her body, and who is thus incapable of making intentional decisions that concern them, the possibility of initiating doubt by choosing to cover eyes, ears and so on is immediately in question."[57] Descartes used the slave's person and status to sap the possibility of doubt. But what were the "pleasant illusions" that the Meditation ascribed to its slave? Well, here they would become the will enabling these operations, whose actual existence he established in the fourth Meditation. Will played the role of the natural rights that the slave never lost, however limited his civil rights. The first Meditation's closure led to establishment of God's existence (as architect of the natural law), of human will and free will, of control over reasons, senses, and action, and of the assertion in the fourth Meditation that true freedom is knowledge and will to act in accordance with what natural law prescribes.

Descartes there insisted that it was "only the will, or freedom of choice, that I experience within me to be so great that I can grasp the idea of none greater; so much so that it is above all through the will that I understand myself to bear some image and likeness of God" (AT 7:57). He virtually equated God, will, and the ground of truth. Their equation came not just from will's being the power to act, but from its basis in God's truth, whose certainty grounded the willful soul for right action in the world. Descartes repeated the idea in the *Passions de l'âme*, while studying self-control and relations with others via the concept of "generosity."[58] For "the will, *or free will*," he wrote in the fourth Meditation,

> consists simply in that we can do or not do (that is, affirm or deny, pursue or flee), or rather, simply in that we are brought to an affirming or denying, a pursuing or fleeing what is proposed to us by the intellect in such a way that we sense we have been determined to it by no external force. For me to be free, I do not need to be able to be moved two ways, but on the contrary, the more (I) lean in one direction, whether because (I) understand evidently that truth and goodness lie in it or because God so disposes my inmost thoughts, the more (I) choose more freely. Neither divine grace nor natural knowledge ever diminishes freedom, but rather increases and confirms it. (AT 7:57–58)

To be able to choose between "indifferent" possibilities was "the lowest level of freedom." To lack constraint was just anarchic license: "not at all perfection of will, but defect of knowledge, or some negation: for if I always saw clearly what is true and good, I should never ponder over what is to be chosen or judged; and so although I would evidently be free, I could never be indifferent" (AT 7:59). Will made one do what one knew as right and true under God's reason: divine and natural law. I recall a radiant phrase translating an ancient Chinese critic's remark on the *Book of Poetry* as being essentially characterized by "freedom from undisciplined thought." "Freedom from undisciplined thought" exactly catches Descartes's idea here, freedom from Montaigne's *branloire perenne*, in the world no less than the mind.[59] This was what Jesuits like Acosta said that right conversion would do for the Indians: discipline all facets of human life subject to "free will."

Descartes held all humans to be by nature free and equally rational, as Las Casas, Acosta, Suárez, and their teachers argued: "as much reason as we, or more," said Descartes. The nature of divine and human will compelled people along rational paths, in the image of his captive slave. That image led Descartes to an ethics of disciplined freedom that took him to the brink of a new conception of community, reliant on ruled operations of generosity—defined as proper awareness of the power of one's will and reason joined to like awareness of everyone else's, these forging a duty to help make and maintain a certain mutual community.[60]

Descartes *began* the *Meditations*: "Opportunely on this day, I have thus rid the mind of all cares, I have obtained for my mind secure leisure, I am quite alone, I shall work seriously and freely at a general overthrow of my opinions" (AT 7:17–18). This leisure (*otium*) is "opposed to and made possible by the *negotium* [business] that characterizes Amsterdam, where 'on this day' he is writing the *Meditations*."[61] The feel of being here, now, in a real place—his Amsterdam sitting room—is basic to the first Meditation's work to reject the senses' immediate evidence. Is it a stretch to think that this place, which remained background noise hampering even provisional efforts to cut himself from it, both elicited the captive/slave idea and paralleled the barrier that figure epitomized to the very possibility of radical doubt? Amsterdam's material presence snarled efforts to divide thinking and matter, as one of its businesses—slavery—signaled the vast difficulty of *choosing* to bracket the senses. The issue is no metaphorical one of being "enslaved" by the senses. It is the harder one, flagged by interjection of slavery's material reality, of being unable to rule the senses because having no *right* to do so. Like all human faculties they were of God (once shown no evil genius). So it mattered that human and divine wills be equivalent. Only so could humans, "by nature" (we shall see), control their own reasons and actions.

In the captive/slave analogy, here, perhaps lay the ghost of an Aristotelian claim about the natural slave, insofar as it corresponded to some simile of "enslavement" to the senses. This ghost was resolved by a quasi-counter-Aristotelian claim ("counter," as to the idea of natural slavery) that rightly ordered reason *did* avoid such enslavement, *did*, the *Meditations* showed, both benefit from bracketing the senses and learn the necessary habits of mind to order and use them to obtain knowledge and, argued the *Passions de l'âme*, to practice generosity toward oneself and others. The issue of legal right over one's body bore on humans' relation to nature and to God (whether true or malign), and was resolved, in the third and fourth Meditations, into matters of free will and determinism. Too, while

Descartes granted humans only imperfect reason, he ascribed their liability to error to the distance between that imperfection and their perfection of will, in which attribute alone humans had as much as God: a point made in the *Meditations*, and reiterated in the *Principia* and the *Passions*.

Did Descartes exclude any humans from this rational ability to willfully control senses, reason, and action? The thought of himself as prisoner/slave and where it leads suggests not, as do many of his relations in actual life. But another case is telling, especially in the context of Descartes's mature thought and later years. In 1642, he added a long polemic to the second edition of the *Meditations*, protesting the "quibbles" of the new seventh Objections by the Jesuit Pierre Bourdin. Taxing Pierre Dinet, Jesuit Provincial of France, with what he took as a global Jesuit attack, he cited others from even before 1641 by the Dutch Gysbert Voetius (1589–1676), rector of the University of Utrecht and ardent Gomarist, whose faith entailed the absolute need of God's grace for salvation and sharp limits on human will. Publication of Descartes's remarks incited Voetius to have Martin Schoock (1614–69), a protégé now teaching at Utrecht, write out and publish his criticism of Descartes's doctrine. This spurred a fierce book-length reply, published as the *Epistola ad Voetium* in 1643. The quarrel was serious, up to a charge of heresy against Descartes. In its course, he was censured by the Utrecht burgers. Final settlement needed the French ambassador's intervention. Its effects continued to a last publication by Descartes in 1648. How gravely he took it is shown in three long writings over nearly six years, when he was publishing the *Meditations* and the *Principia* and their French versions and finishing the *Passions de l'âme*: by a man who, as many observe, sought ardently to protect his time and privacy. Apart from philosophy, theology, science, and education, at stake were also the nature and ease of Descartes's life in Holland, about which we have already seen enough. All this suggests that in the *Epistola* he chose his words and arguments with care.

Besides science, tradition, and authority, Voetius fretted most over Descartes's insisting on the power of human will, and so apparent autonomy from God and from knowledge of God. Refuting Voetius's attack that his showings of God's existence "have no value save for those who already know he exists, since they rely wholly on our innate ideas," Descartes held: "i[I]t is to be noted that all things whose knowledge is said to be set in us *by nature* are not therefore expressly known by us; but are just such that we can know them by the powers of mind itself without any sense experience" (AT 8B:166). The natural idea of God needed activating by willful reason. He recalled a familiar passage in Plato's *Meno*, where, "by questioning a [slave] boy on the elements of geometry and so working it that this [slave] boy draws certain truths from his own mind that he had not earlier known to be there, he manages to show them to be in his memory" (AT 8B:167; *Meno*

82b–86b). "Knowledge of God," Descartes ended, "is of this kind." The assertion is knotty. Descartes did not explicitly call the boy a slave, although Plato did. Descartes says that the knowledge drawn out was "by nature." By now in our analysis, this resonates. The "drawing out" was akin to Salamancan ideas of training the Indian child. However this may later have been tuned to Anglo-Saxon desires of expansionist Manifest Destiny ("Kill the Indian and save the Man"), for Descartes it marked a process common to all humans and assumed a shared natural reason. He could have used many examples.[62] Voetius was targeting crucial arguments of the *Meditations*: relations of human reason, will, and God. Descartes may not have sought out the *Meno* passage: he no doubt had it in memory. At the least it implies that slave and free were not categories he found usefully distinctive when talking of what it was to be a rational human. Or rather, the *idea* of the slave was especially useful to get at truths of *all* human nature, especially those of will, free will, and reason.

Whatever else this passage shows, it asserts that the slave boy possessed the same soul as any other human. As a whole, the dialogue concerns the question as to whether virtue is innate or learned, and reaches the conclusion that it is neither, but a gift of divine grace. This fact matters in the letter's context: Descartes was reminding Voetius that his accusations muddled issues and that humans' natural abilities to will, reason, know, and act did not contradict the fact or possibility of God's grace. They were separate facets of divine and human acts and relations. We, maybe, could ask whether that fact about virtue meant that the slave might not lack it. If so, it would inevitably constrain all humans, slave or free, since this gift of grace would have nothing to do, exactly, with the nature of the soul per se. In its own context no less than that in which Descartes sets it, the *Meno* passage implies the shared natural will and reason of human beings.

Where does this leave us? I return to the questions with which I began. For Descartes, the slave of the legal tradition gave a way to imagine the willful rational nature of all humans and the disciplined freedom it entailed. That took him toward what, in the "Lettre-Préface" to the 1647 *Principes de la philosophie*, he called the final goal of philosophy and all his scientific studies: "I mean the highest and most perfect moral system, which, presupposing a complete knowledge of the other sciences, is the ultimate level of wisdom" (AT 9B:13–14). This system would establish public "gentleness and harmony," permit discovery of ever "higher" truths, and set "perfection of life" in private and public "concord" (AT 9B:18, 20). This society was founded not on cohabitation of individual willful agents, but on a personhood seen as itself "communal." Had he lived to clarify his new moral system, maybe real slavery would have risen over the horizon. As it was, slavery fell under the earlier *morale par provision*, living for the present by known social norms. Here, the slavery Descartes alluded to was no moral issue. Nor did it involve philosophical issues of, for example, mental difference. It concerned a strictly *civil* condition: the captive as slave. Unlike Zurara and other not-disinterested chroniclers, Descartes and other major thinkers also ignored the biblical curse of Noah on the race of Ham, blackening them and setting them in Africa—a tale that, Benjamin Braude convincingly shows, was also not fixed before these years.[63] Descartes's slave was not racialized. The *idea* of a particular kind of slavery gave Descartes an important way to rethink issues of will, reason, and freedom and to approach a different ethic of community.

How does this notion of slavery affect the issue of race? Slavery as a philosophical issue had never involved race (although race may be incipient in the proposal, most notoriously made by Las Casas, to replace Indian slavery with African).[64] *That* involvement resulted from facts on the ground, facts of actual trade that philosophy did not yet face. West European slavery until the late fifteenth century involved mainly east Europeans. A few Africans came via the Sahara. Only as the Portuguese began to ship many people from the African west coast to Lisbon in the second half of the fifteenth century did this arrangement start to change. Even so, there was little impact on attitudes, Zurara being an early exception. Certainly, slaves were reckoned a commodity. *Pace* James Walvin, that was not synonymous with "sub-human."[65] In the 1550s, John Hawkins took Africans as "merchandise," but Walvin agrees that language tended until much later to use "legal fictions" papering over legal and commercial realities.[66] Ideas of African slaves enshrined in the *Code noir* were not new. But earlier slaves were also treated as property and commodity. They were not thereby "sub-human": they were *civil* slaves, *natural* humans.

What was new, and maybe did make a difference, was growing miscegenation in European colonies in the Americas, particularly as it contravened a Spanish tradition of *limpieza de sangre*, purity of blood, important in the Peninsula since at least the mid-fifteenth century, and playing a role in the expulsion of the Jews in 1492 and the Moors in 1608–12. This tradition had been accompanied by a discourse of ethnic vituperation since the late Middle Ages. By the second half of the sixteenth century ethnic mixing in the Iberian colonies of America had produced ever more complex counting of blood quanta, reckoning levels of mixture between Spanish, Creoles, Indians, and Africans. The more intricate of these may have been other than number games, making economic counters of the most valuable transatlantic merchandise, but they had small effect on daily local practice. Still, by the 1570s up to ten names signifying different proportions were routinely used to establish education, taxation, legal rights, civic and military participation, and so on. Such spectra were calculated on a principle setting Europeans at one end and Africans at the other, graded by real degrees of freedom and slavery and supposed degrees of barbarism and civilization: by century's end, too, by the growing popular cultural and commercial link between skin color and slavery.[67]

Even so, something other than ethnicity seems to have been the first issue, the body being a pretty useless indicator for even simple counting. The calculations were used at first mostly for lineage distinctions: who was at the upper end of colonial life and would benefit from most rights, who at the lower. Here it is useful to bear in mind the captive/slave equation. Moved by Las Casas and others, Charles V had forbidden Indian slavery (as had Isabel earlier, and as Pope Paul III did in the 1537 bull *Sublimis Deus*). Royal edicts were often not followed three thousand miles off; they still held that defeated indigenous peoples were not captive and not slave. Africans' status was other: they were captives *and* slaves, at a time when in philosophers' and theologians' minds these conditions were morally and legally acceptable. At first, blood quanta spectra ranged between freedom and captivity/slavery, not between white and black. That was why Indians and mestizos of varying degrees fell on the spectras' "upper" half: they were not captives in a just war. Africans were (or were readily believed to be so on the seller's warrant),[68] and they and their mulatto offspring fell accordingly on the spectras' "lower" half. Of course, such spectra once in place, white/black could readily become a metaphor for freedom/captivity. From there, it was no great leap to make the equation a reality and find justifying arguments.

By 1589, the *criollo* Juan Suárez de Peralta took color to mark those fit to be slaves. Like other colonials he resented edicts against enslaving Indians, saying that if blacks could be slaves, as they were of government officials of all ranks and churchmen of every level, "bishops, priests and even friars," so could Indians, for the only difference was that blacks were "of deeper color and darker." Otherwise, "both are idolaters, both eat human flesh, although this case is worse among the Indians . . . , and both are accustomed to be sold or sell others." He ended this chapter by asserting the injustice of "taking the slave from his owner, if he held him with just title."[69] Color, here, marked those satisfying Giles's criteria for the barbarian. These changes in language and fact were more widespread by the 1630s and 1640s, the very time, too, when as a result of the huge growth of Middle Passage trade, African chattel slavery was replacing older forms of slavery in the Atlantic world.

The two comments Descartes *did* make on slaves suggest first that he made no difference between them and any other humans—as humans. This is indicated by their internal structure of argument and by the fact that both were part of his developing thought on human will and freedom. His general silence on slavery shows accord with his teachers and the tradition as to its being a civil condition, however appalling.[70] It may also show awareness of changing conditions on the ground that now set Mercado's ethical horror against colonial economic need, awareness of expanding African trade, and that overseas practice of which Aimé Césaire remarked that it was neither

> evangelization, nor a philanthropic enterprise, nor a desire to push back the frontiers of ignorance, disease, and tyranny, nor an attempt to extend the rule of law. . . . The decisive actors here are the adventurer and the pirate, the wholesale grocer and the ship owner, the gold digger and the merchant. . . . I find that hypocrisy is of recent date; that neither Cortez discovering Mexico from the top of the great teocalli, nor Pizarro before Cusco (much less Marco Polo before Cambaluc), claims that he is the harbinger of a superior order; that they kill; that they plunder; that they have helmets, lances, cupidities; that the slavering apologists come later.[71]

Sensitivity to these conditions would set them under Descartes's new *morale*, in progress at his death. His silences imply they were not yet issues—not in European debate outside Iberia. There, and in Iberia's western colonies, they were now unavoidable. Descartes was perhaps the last major thinker able to implicate philosophy in them without taking reality to have transformed philosophers' moral obligations—who could be neither a Las Casas nor an apologist. Had he lived to write the ethics that he said in 1647 was the final aim of all his study and thought, he would have had to face realities directly. To treat them in an organon, a physics, a metaphysics, or even a psychology (one taking all humans, qua humans, to be alike) was out of place. His philosophical successors could not avoid these new forms of slavery and race, already crucial in everyday life, snakes whose multiplying made them willy-nilly require philosophers' and others' attention. Then, if speaking could be for or against, silence was necessarily complicit.

NOTES

1. Edith Hall, *Inventing the Barbarian: Greek Self-Definition through Tragedy* (Oxford: Clarendon Press, 1989), ix.

2. Karen Ordahl Kupperman, "Presentment of Civility: English Reading of American Self-Presentation in the Early Years of Colonization," in *Constructing Race: Differentiating Peoples in the Early Modern World*, ed. Michael McGiffert, *William and Mary Quarterly*, 3rd ser., 54.1 (1997): 193; cf. Emily C. Bartels, "*Othello* and Africa: Postcolonialism Reconsidered," in McGiffert, 47.

3. Maxime Leroy, *Descartes social* (Paris: Vrin, 1931).

4. Joan Dayan, *Haiti, History, and the Gods* (Berkeley: University of California Press, 1995), 204.

5. *Code noir, touchant la police des Iles de l'Amérique* [Versailles, March 1685], in *Recueil général des anciennes lois françaises, depuis l'an 420, jusqu'à la révolution de 1789,* ed. MM. [Athanase-Jean-Léger] Jourdan, [Alphonse-Honoré] Taillandier et Decrusy, and [François-André] Isambert, 29 vols. (Paris: Berlin-le-Prieur et Plon, 1812–33), 494.

6. Doris Lorraine Garraway, *The Libertine Colony: Creolization in the Early French Caribbean* (Durham: Duke University Press, forthcoming), chap. 6.

7. Timothy J. Reiss, *Against Autonomy: Global Dialectics of Cultural Exchange* (Stanford: Stanford University Press, 2002), 184–218.

8. *Générosité* is not generosity. Descartes used the word in a sense perhaps closest to English "magnanimity." We will see it again; suffice it to say here that it involves reason, will, self-knowledge, and relations with and behavior toward others. It is in Descartes's sense that the English word *generosity* will be used later to transcribe the French.

9. René Descartes, *Œuvres,* ed. Charles Adam and Paul Tannery, new ed., 11 vols. (1964–76; rpt. Paris: Vrin/C.N.R.S., 1996), 2:630; 3:185, 251. All future references to this standard edition are directly in the text in the customary scholarly form of AT followed by volume and page.

10. Allison Blakely, *Blacks in the Dutch World: The Evolution of Racial Imagery in a Modern Society* (Bloomington: Indiana University Press, 1993), 4; cf. Cornelis Ch. Goslinga, *The Dutch in the Caribbean and on the Wild Coast, 1580–1680* (Assen: Van Gorcum, 1971), 340–41.

11. Goslinga, *Dutch in the Caribbean,* 345, 353.

12. Such remarks were clichés about French trade, too. Montaigne had talked in 1580 of bringing medicinal "guaiacum, sarsaparilla and china-root" from the Americas (*Œuvres complètes,* ed. Albert Thibaudet and Maurice Rat [Paris: Gallimard, 1962], 752) and before 1585, another favorite of Descartes, the poet Pierre de Ronsard (1524–85), wrote a preface for his national epic, the *Franciade,* where he noted "how, in our harbors and ports, merchandise sought in far-off America is retailed everywhere" (*Œuvres complètes,* ed. Gustave Cohen, 2 vols. [Paris: Gallimard, 1950], 2:1028: I thank Tim Hampton for this reminder).

13. Blakely, *Blacks in the Dutch World,* 51ff.

14. Ibid., 171–72; cf. Goslinga, *Dutch in the Caribbean,* 339.

15. Jan Albert Goris, *Étude sur les colonies marchandes méridionales (portugais, espagnols, italiens) à Anvers de 1488 à 1567: Contribution à l'histoire des débuts du capitalisme moderne* (Louvain: Librairie Universitaire, Uystpruyst, 1925), 31ff.; Goslinga, *Dutch in the Caribbean,* 341.

16. Peter Fryer, *Staying Power: The History of Black People in Britain* (London: Pluto, 1984), 8.

17. James Walvin, *The Black Presence: A Documentary History of the Negro in England, 1555–1860* (1971; rpt. New York: Schocken, 1972), 12, 64–65; Edward Scobie, *Black Britannia: A History of Blacks in Britain* (Chicago: Johnson, 1972), 8.

18. Jacques Lezra, *Unspeakable Subjects: The Genealogy of the Event in Early Modern Europe* (Stanford: Stanford University Press, 1997), 124. Does it matter that Isaac Beeckman (1588–1637), Descartes's closest friend in 1618–19, was a well-placed Middelburg educator, certainly acquainted with the slave ship case, to whom Descartes's letters in 1619 concerned military affairs and navigational aids?

19. Francis Bacon, Lord Verulam, *The Works*, ed. James Spedding, Robert Leslie Ellis, and Douglas Denon Heath, new ed., 7 vols. (London: Longmans [et al.], 1875–79), 1:119; Peter Hulme, "The Spontaneous Hand of Nature: Savagery, Colonialism, and the Enlightenment," in *The Enlightenment and Its Shadows*, ed. Peter Hulme and Ludmilla Jordanova (London: Routledge, 1990), 18–21. This dramatic frontispiece has been endlessly glossed.

20. Timothy J. Reiss, " 'Seated between the Old World and the New': Geopolitics, Natural Philosophy, and Proficient Method," in *Bacon and The Advancement of Learning*, ed. Catherine C. Martin and Julie R. Solomon. Forthcoming.

21. Descartes cited the *Novum organum* as a model in Jan. 1630, Dec. 23, 1630, and May 10, 1632, letters to Mersenne (AT 1:109, 195–96, 251), and apparently the *De augmentis scientiarum* in a May 19, 1635, letter to Jacob Golius (1596–1667) (AT 1:318, 321).

22. "La licence en droit de Descartes: Un placard inédit de 1616," ed. Jean-Robert Armogathe, Vincent Carraud, and Robert Feenstra, *Nouvelles de la République des Lettres* (1988–II): 126–27.

23. I trace this thread in other writings, source of some of these remarks: "Calculating Humans: Mathematics, War, and the Colonial Calculus," in *Arts of Calculation: Quantifying Thought in Early Modern Europe*, ed. David Glimp and Michelle R. Warren (New York: Palgrave Macmillan, 2004), 137–63; cf. Reiss, *Knowledge, Discovery, and Imagination in Early Modern Europe: The Rise of Aesthetic Rationalism* (Cambridge: Cambridge University Press, 1997).

24. Justinianus, *Corpus iuris civilis*, ed. Paul Krueger and Theodor Mommsen, 2 vols. (Berlin: Weidmann, 1872–88) vol. 1: *Institutiones* 1.3.1–4; *Digesta* 1.5.3–5. The word *ancillis* names slaves who are members of "our" household.

25. Aristotle, *Nicomachean Ethics* 1161a35–b8, 1177a7–10. The second passage is often translated as if it asserted that a slave could not be granted this share.

26. Aristotle, *Politics* 1254a18–55b8.

27. Robert Schlaifer, "Greek Theories of Slavery from Homer to Aristotle," in *Slavery in Classical Antiquity: Views and Controversies*, ed. Moses I. Finley (1960; rpt. with bibliographical supplement, Cambridge: Heffer; New York: Barnes & Noble, 1968), 121–22.

28. G. E. M. de Ste. Croix, *The Class Struggle in the Ancient Greek World from the Archaic Age to the Arab Conquests* (Ithaca: Cornell University Press, 1981), 418; "Slavery and Other Forms of Unfree Labour," in *Slavery and Other Forms of Unfree Labour* (London: Routledge, 1988), 28–29.

29. Anthony Pagden, *The Fall of Natural Man: The American Indian and the Origins of Comparative Ethnology*, 2nd ed. (Cambridge: Cambridge University Press, 1986), 38–39.

30. Charles F. Briggs, *Giles of Rome's De regimine principum: Reading and Writing Politics at Court and University, c. 1275–c. 1525* (Cambridge: Cambridge University Press, 1999), 51–52; Peter Russell, *Prince Henry "the Navigator": A Life* (New Haven: Yale University Press, 2000), 16; Joachim de Carvalho, "Sobre a erudição de Gomes Eanes de Zurara. Notas em torno de alguns plágios deste Cronista," in Estudos sobre a cultura portuguesa do século XV, vol. 1 ([Coimbra]: Por ordem da Universidade, 1949), 99.

31. Giles of Rome, *De regimine principum libri III*, ed. Hieronymus Samaritanius (Rome: Apud B.

Zannettum, 1556; facs. rpt. Aalen: Scientia Verlag, 1967), 214–18 (bk. 2, pt. 1, chap. 1). The Aquinas citation is from *Summa theologiae* 2a.2ae.64.2, the Aristotle from *De anima* 432a2–3.

32. Giles, *De regimine*, 547–50 (3.2.34).

33. Jean Bodin, *Les six livres de la république*, ed. Christiane Frémont, Marie-Dominique Couzinet, and Henri Rochais, 6 vols. (Paris: Fayard, 1986), 1:85–86, 88.

34. Desiderius Erasmus, *The Education of a Christian Prince*, trans. Neil M. Cheshire and Michael J. Heath, with *Panegyric for Archduke Philip of Austria*, trans. and ed. Lisa Jardine (Cambridge: Cambridge University Press, 1997), 24, 40.

35. Américo Vespucio, *El nuevo mundo: Cartas relativas a sus viajes y descubrimientos, textos en italiano, español e inglés*, ed. Roberto Levillier (Buenos Aires: Editorial Nova, 1951), 118, 120, 228.

36. Giles of Rome, *De ecclesiastica potestate*, ed. Richard Scholz (1929; rpt. Aalen: Scientia Verlag, 1961), 53, 75–80, 93, 96; *On Ecclesiastical Power*, trans. Arthur P. Monahan (Lewiston, NY: Edwin Mellen Press), 78, 108–15, 131, 137 (bk. 2, chaps. 4, 8, 10, 11).

37. Gomes Eanes de Zurara, *Crónica de Guiné*, ed. José de Bragança, [new ed.] (Barcelos: Livraria Civilização, 1973), 85 (chap. 16), 126 (chap. 26), 243 (chap. 56).

38. Gonzalo Fernández de Oviedo, *Historia general y natural de las Indias*, ed. Tudela Bueso, 5 vols., Biblioteca de Autores Españoles 117–21 (Madrid: Atlas, 1959), 1:13a, 19a, 20a (bk. 2, chap. 3).

39. Bartolomé de Las Casas, *Historia de las Indias*, ed. Miguel Angel Medina, Jesús Angel Barreda, and Isacio Pérez Fernández, vols. 3–5 in *Obras completas*, gen. ed. Paulino Castañeda Delgado (Madrid: Alianza Editorial, 1994), 3:344; cf. 339.

40. Oviedo, *Historia general* 1.30b, 31a (2.7); 1.52b (2.13); 1.66b (3.6).

41. Ibid., 1.67a–69b (3.6).

42. Ibid., 1.111a.

43. Francisco de Vitoria, *Political Writings*, ed. Anthony Pagden and Jeremy Lawrance (Cambridge: Cambridge University Press, 1991), 239, 242.

44. Pagden, *Fall*, 67.

45. Vitoria, *Political Writings*, 249–51.

46. Sabine McCormack sees growing despondency in Oviedo's texts and manuscripts, as violence and failure imbued Spain's American and European endeavors alike (personal exchanges, September 4 and 7, 2002).

47. Domingo de Soto, *De iustitia et iure libri decem* / *De la justicia y del derecho en diez libros*, facsimile ed., trans. Marcelino González Ordóñez, intro. Venancio Diego Carro, 10 vols. in 5 (Madrid: Instituto de Estudios Políticos, 1967–68), 2:290a. The earlier citation is from 288b–89a, both bk. 4, qu. 2, art. 2.

48. Las Casas, *Historia*, 3:339; Las Casas, *Apologética historia sumaria*, ed. Vidal Abril Castelló, Jesús A. Barreda, Berta Ares Queija, and Miguel J. Abril Stoffels, vols. 6–8 in *Obras completas*, gen. ed. Paulino Castañeda Delgado (Madrid: Alianza Editorial, 1992), 7:536.

49. All citations and references since the last note are from Mercado, *Suma* 230–38 (bk. 2, chap. 21) (1571 ed., bk. 1 in that of 1569).

50. Ibid., 229–39, 109–10.

51. Bartolomé de Albornoz, "De la esclavitud," in *Obras escogidas de filósofos*, ed. Adolfo de Castro, Biblioteca de Autores Españoles 65 (Madrid: Rivadeneyra, 1873), 232a.

52. Fernão de Oliveira, *Arte da guerra do mar* [1555], pref. Quirino da Fonseca, intro. Fernando Oliveira do Botelho de Sousa (Lisbon: Arquivo Histórico da Marinha, 1937), 24.

53. José de Acosta, *Historia natural y moral de las Indias*, ed. José Alcina Franch (Madrid: Historia 16, 1987), 438:6.1, 54: Proemio.

54. Francisco Suárez, *Tractatus de legibus, ac deo legislatore in decem libros distributus* [1612] / *Tratado de las leyes y de dios legislador en diez libros*, facsimile ed., trans. José Ramón Muniozguren, intro. Luis Vela Sánchez, 6 vols. (Madrid: Instituto de Estudios Políticos, 1967–68), 1:186a (bk. 2, chap. 18, sec. 5), 1:190b (bk. 2, chap. 19, sec. 8).

55. Ibid., 2:205b (bk. 3, chap. 3, sec. 7, 4:783a (bk. 7, chap. 4, sec. 6).

56. These quotations: *Apologética* 8.1576, 1583; the whole discussion: chaps. 263–67 and Epilogue.

57. Lezra, *Unspeakable*, 95.

58. AT 11.445–47 (§§ 152–54). And see note 8 above.

59. Liu Hsieh, *The Literary Mind and the Carving of Dragons*, trans. and ed. Vincent Yu-chung Shih (bilingual ed.; Taipei: Chung Hwa, 1970), 43. These two paragraphs come from Timothy J. Reiss, *Mirages of the Selfe: Patterns of Personhood in Ancient and Early Modern Europe* (Stanford: Stanford University Press, 2003), 485–86.

60. Reiss, *Mirages*, 469–518.

61. Lezra, *Unspeakable*, 100.

62. Six years earlier, Descartes had in fact written to Mersenne that grace had no more to do with reason's choice of the good and the doing of it than being a man or a woman had to do with good sense's making one an "*honnête homme*" (end of May 1637: AT 1:366).

63. Benjamin Braude, "The Sons of Noah and the Construction of Ethnic and Geographical Identities in the Medieval and Early Modern Periods," in *Constructing Race*, ed. McGiffert, 103–42. Noah's curse was widespread in medieval and early modern Arab commentaries on the trade in non-Muslim sub-Saharan African slaves, but while presumably known in Muslim Spain, these were unknown (and untranslated) elsewhere in Europe.

64. This, too, needs interpreting in the context of the war-captive legal tradition, which by the mid-sixteenth century did not consider Indians to be captives in a just war, but did (or wanted to) see Africans as such. Oliveira and Albornoz denied even so much, but Vitoria tried to mark a difference, writing in a 1546 (?) letter about Portuguese slave traffic on the Guinea coast that if those traded were already enslaved (in just war), no injustice was done, but that if they had been tricked into capture by the Portuguese, lured by prospects of a different trade, their enslavement was illicit (*Political Writings*, 334–35). Interestingly, Pagden and Lawrance, in a note, have Vitoria use the word *blacks* here: so they translate a pronoun *ellos* which in fact refers to "*esclavos.*" The term *negros* is actually in an undated explanation by Miguel de Arcos, Dominican Provincial of Andalusia, among whose pa-

pers the letter was found (Vitoria, *Relecciones sobre los Indios y el derecho de guerra* [with two letters and two other short texts] [Buenos Aires: Espasa-Calpe Argentina, 1946], 27–29). Arcos's use of the term was to identify and in no way pejorative.

65. "Even by the late sixteenth century British commercial practice, and the legislation defending that commerce, were actively treating the African as a form of sub-human; a species of property, or a simple commodity." Walvin, *Black Presence*, 10.

66. James Walvin, *Black and White: The Negro and English Society, 1555–1945* (London: Allen Lane, Penguin Press, 1973), 38.

67. See Reiss, "Calculating," 155–56.

68. See Vitoria's letter mentioned in note 64.

69. Juan Suárez de Peralta, *Tratado del descubrimiento de las Indias (Noticias históricas de la Nueva España)*, ed. Teresa Silva Tena (Mexico City: Dirección General de Publicaciones del Consejo Nacional para la Cultura y las Artes, 1990), 77, 78.

70. When Lord Chief Justice Mansfield settled the famous case of James Somerset by denying his colonial owner a right to seize and ship him to Jamaica for sale, he called on "positive law," which "in a case so odious as the condition of slaves must be taken strictly." Somerset could not be taken from England, since "tracing the subject to natural principles, the claim of slavery can never be supported here. The power claimed by this return was never in use here: or acknowledged by the law" (full verdict in Folarin O. Shyllon, *Black Slaves in Britain* [London: Oxford University Press for the Institute of Race Relations, 1974], 108–10). Shyllon says that Mansfield was just following "mediaeval common law" (121, 123). He was not. He appealed to positive law and natural principles. This case, capping Granville Sharp's persistence in seeking a clear legal test of slavery in England, was the first legal success of the English antislavery movement. One might see Descartes and the Somerset case as bookends to two centuries in which even the law accepted racist arguments (they were not bookends to philosophical argument or popular claim).

71. Aimé Césaire, *Discourse on Colonialism*, trans. Joan Pinkham (New York: Monthly Review Press, 1972), 10–11.

| 2 |

Race in Hobbes

BARBARA HALL

In this chapter I examine the question of whether Thomas Hobbes, considered the founder of modern political philosophy, was a racist. One naturally expects the political or moral theorist to embody the principles she espouses—be they noble or ignoble. And, when she does not, one tends (correctly or incorrectly) to discredit not only her but her argument also. For even though the truth or merit of a theory is logically severable from the theorizer herself, proof of an inconsistency between the words and the acts of an individual tends to diminish her in some respects. It is with this perspective in mind that I examine whether Thomas Hobbes, whose political theories advanced the ideals of justice, equality, and natural freedom, believed that certain peoples were inherently less equal and free than others.

The question "Is X a racist?" is a very difficult one to answer. The term "racist" is ambiguous. Thus, my co-worker and I may both agree that the boss is a racist, yet upon examination, it might well be that we have widely varying notions of what a racist actually is. Compounding this difficulty is the fact that the whole notion of biological race and racial classification is founded upon principles that science has long maintained are untenable. This latter concern poses no real problem, however, since there is little controversy regarding the notion that race *does* exist as a socially constructed phenomenon. Thus, it is still valid to maintain that Y is a member of race S or that some person X is or is not a racist.

As to the problem of ambiguity, I shall take a generalist approach. My aim is to determine whether or not Thomas Hobbes maintained any beliefs about the subordinate status or worth of certain people based on their racial designation. If he harbored any such beliefs, they would represent an inconsistency between his actual beliefs and his egalitarian ideology. I offer no technically sound definition of the terms "racist" or "racism." Rather, I give what I believe to be the least common denominator in the common usage of the terms: I define "racism" as the view that some groups of people are inherently intellectually, culturally, or socially superior or inferior to other groups owing to some biological or genetic characteristic they do or do not possess. By extension, a racist is anyone who holds such views. I shall begin by examining Hobbes's early years for the possible germination of racist ideas.

||| |

EARLY HOBBES

Soon after graduating Oxford in 1608, Thomas Hobbes was hired by Lord Cavendish, Earl of Devonshire, as a tutor for his son William.[1] Hobbes and the younger Cavendish were about the same age and became friends and companions as well as teacher and student.[2] This relationship lasted for twelve years. One of William's financial investments was in the Virginia Company. In 1606, the Virginia Company (officially designated as "The Treasurer and Company of Adventurers and Planters of the City of London for the First Colony of Virginia") received a charter from English monarch James I to establish England's first permanent settlement in the New World—Jamestown. The company was founded as a profit-making venture, and it solicited for investors to become members of the company by purchasing shares.[3] The bitter misfortunes besetting these first English settlers are well documented in the history of the Jamestown colony.[4] Unable to return a profit, the company was dissolved in 1624. Hobbes had a relatively short four-year involvement with the Virginia Company. It occurred when he was still a fairly young man of thirty-four and not yet the political thinker he was later to become. Hobbes became a shareholder in the Virginia Company when William gave him one share on June 19, 1622.[5] Hobbes's single share most likely precluded him from exercising any great influence on important decisions regarding the direction and purpose of the company. However, there are two reasons why Hobbes should not be relieved of moral responsibility with respect to the business dealings of the Virginia Company. The first is that Cavendish did have substantial holdings in the company, and the relationship between him and Hobbes was such that one would be naïve to presume that Hobbes would have had absolutely no influence upon his thinking.[6]

Secondly, even if Hobbes had minimal dealings with the Virginia Company and his one share was merely a token, one may hold that an individual is still morally responsible for any deliberate support he gives to a morally questionable venture. Thus, culpability arises from the *fact* of the support more than from the degree of it. (So, for instance, those who looked the other way during Nazi atrocities may be less morally compromised than the storm troopers, but the "scales of iniquity" teeter unbalanced rather than tip over.) Therefore, if any Virginia Company business involved the slave trade, then Hobbes is to some degree morally answerable whether he owned one share or one thousand shares. So, did the company have any ties to the burgeoning market in human flesh?

As I stated earlier, the Virginia Company's goal was to establish a profitable settlement in the New World. Although the members of the company realized that there would be a very great need for laborers in order for the venture to become profitable, at this point in time the British were ambivalent about slave labor. They relied instead on the labor of indentured servants. There were several reasons for this. One was that the Spanish, who had settlements to the south, relied heavily on the labor of enslaved Africans. The British, having a great enmity for the Spanish, felt that "if that's what the Spanish do, we shouldn't do that, we'll do it differently. And, in fact, our English heritage demands that we do it differently, to prove that we're better than those enslaving Catholics."[7]

A second reason was that the Jamestown settlers were too poor to invest in slaves or servants. They did, however, make use of whatever help came their way. Thus, "when a Dutch ship shows up in the Chesapeake in 1619 with several dozen Africans whom they were unable to sell in the West Indies, they're bought and put to work in Jamestown, just the way indentured servants [from England] were being bought at the docks and put to work."[8]

Though the lot of the Virginia Company settlers was a difficult one, there is nothing to indicate that African slave labor was ever utilized during the eighteen years the company was chartered. Thus, the only known avenue by which Hobbes might have been directly linked to the slave trade (the Virginia Company) yields no such conclusion.[9] Of course the fact that Hobbes's business dealings with the company do not reveal ties to the slave trade suggests nothing regarding any racist views he may have possessed then or later come to harbor. Absent indications of a direct connection between Hobbes and the slave trade, one must look to the ideas he expressed in his works if one is to uncover evidence of racist dogma.

|||

HOBBES ON RACE

Hobbes wrote virtually nothing concerning race. In his seminal treatise *Leviathan* he presented his hypothesis concerning the development of civilized man. When he described the state of nature and the "solitary, poor, nasty, brutish and short" lives of its denizens, reason would lead one to assume that he was advancing a generalized theory about the social and political evolution of mankind en bloc. He seemingly did not purport to describe the condition of only *some* groups of humans, or to provide a view of how only *some* societies came about while allowing that others possibly evolved through totally different means.[10] For if he had meant to suggest this, then his theory's application would be limited and dubious without some parameters or criteria to demarcate and justify its restricted application. Assuming then that Hobbes meant for his thesis to be a broad hypothesis about the progression of man from a condition of unrestricted barbarism to one of civil subjugation, he articulated what he took to be the standard for almost all, if not all, peoples. Hobbes began chapter 13 with the following statement:

> Nature hath made men so equall, in the faculties of body, and mind; as that though there bee found one man sometimes manifestly stronger in body, or of quicker mind then another; yet when all is reckoned together, *the difference between man, and man, is not so considerable, as that one man can thereupon claim to himselfe any benefit, to which another may not pretend, as well as he.* [11]

Here, Hobbes articulated what can only be taken to be an expression of the fundamental equality of all men and the basic superiority of none. If Hobbes did in fact presume some qualitative differences between peoples regarding their capacities for advancement, then he was being unnecessarily disingenuous in making this claim. Certainly, he could have equally well put forth the thesis that some peoples do in fact have inferior or lesser capacities than others. At this point in history, a view such as this would likely have provided welcome confirmation to nascent ideas supporting slavery and New World conquest.

But perhaps Hobbes did make just such a claim! A bit further down in this same chapter 13 of *Leviathan* Hobbes wrote:

> It may peradventure be thought, there was never such a time, nor condition of war as this [every man against every man]; and I believe it was never generally so, over all the world: but there are many places, where they live so now. For the savage people in many places of *America*, except the government of small Families, the concord whereof dependeth on natural lust, have no government at all; and live at this day in that brutish manner, as I said before. Howsoever, it may be perceived what manner of life there would be, where there were no common power to feare; by the manner of life, which men that have formerly lived under a peacefull government, use to degenerate into, in a civil Warre. [12]

As a philosopher interested in the presociety state of man, it is surprising that Hobbes wrote so little concerning those groups whom Europeans considered the "uncivilized" peoples of the Americas and other non-European regions. This particular reference to the peoples of the Americas represents his most concrete description. And, not coincidentally, it is to this section that accusations of Hobbesian racial bigotry refer.

This particular paragraph has led to several interpretations of Hobbes's stance regarding the state of nature. Some individuals have interpreted Hobbes's words as indicating that the state of nature was not a description of an actual state of mankind but instead a rhetorical fabrication or a heuristic device to convey to people the necessity for an authority figure.[13] The problem with this view is that Hobbes specifically refers to areas wherein there are actual "savages" toiling in the state of nature. Thus Hobbes apparently does make distinctions between groups of peoples concerning the origins of their societies. His description of life in the state of nature illustrates that such a condition represents man in his least evolved state. And Hobbes is clearly suggesting that such a horrible state did not exist in all parts of the world; some societies experienced a superior form of development—the state of nature was merely symbolic for them.[14] This was not true, however, for the "savages" in America. As Charles Mills writes:

> The non-European state of nature is thus *actual*, a wild and racialized place that was originally characterized as cursed with a theological blight as well, an unholy land. The European state of nature, by contrast, is either hypothetical or, if actual, generally a tamer affair, a kind of garden gone to seed, which may need some clipping but is really *already* partially domesticated and just requires a few modifications to be appropriately transformed—a testimony to the superior moral characteristics of this space and its inhabitants.[15]

Mills continues:

> So a nonwhite people, indeed the very nonwhite people upon whose land his fellow Europeans were then encroaching, is his only real-life example of a people in a state of nature. . . . [T]here is a tacit racial logic in the text: the lit-*eral* state of nature is reserved for nonwhites; for whites the state of nature is *hypothetical*. . . . [W]e know that whites are too rational to allow this to happen to *them*. So the most notorious state of nature in the contractarian literature—the bestial war of all against all—is really a *nonwhite* figure, a racial object lesson for the more rational whites whose superior grasp of natural law will enable them to take necessary steps to avoid it and not have to behave as "savages."[16]

Mills understandably interprets Hobbes's use of the term "savages" as pejorative. Historically, the savages have all been Africans or Native Americans or other dark-skinned non-European people. There are savages and then there are respectable, cultured folks. Traditionally, this latter group has been Anglo-Saxon. So Mills correctly assumes that any group to which the appellation "savage" has been applied is not a group that is viewed as desirable by most individuals.

Anyone wishing to deny that Hobbes has cast aspersions on the natives in America must present evidence that his use of the term "savage" reflected no disapproval. This is what Tommy Lott attempts to do:

Hobbes's view of the "savage people in many places of America" mentioned in *Leviathan* was based on ethnographic accounts available to him. But his use of terms such as "barbarian" and "savage" was influenced more by his study of the classics. . . . His reference to the Native Americans as "savages" suggests a presocial paradigm of rugged individuals living outside of civil association. He sometimes employed the term "savage" to indicate a relationship between social dissolution and the presocial condition, specifically that the social dissolution of a civil war is a return to the presocial condition. That this "natural condition" lurks beneath the artificial bond of political obligation supplies the major thrust of his argument for absolute sovereignty.[17]

He continues:

Hobbes does not use racial concepts or terms such as "negro" and "african" in a negative fashion to imply inferiority. . . . [H]e uses the term "savage" generally to refer to groups of people that have not developed a civil society. When he refers to Native Americans in this regard, sometimes he includes the ancient Germans and the early inhabitants of other "civil countries" in the same statement. The best reason for believing the dichotomy of "savage" and "civil" with which Hobbes operated was not racialized is his appeal to these historical and contemporary examples to provide corroborating evidence of his view of human nature—a view he applies universally.[18]

Lott claims that Hobbes's "savages" are not racially determined. For him, Hobbes's use of the word seems to be essentially value neutral. The term represents a "natural condition." And certainly if European peoples can be savages, then there is no reason for believing that Hobbes's use of the term in reference to Native Americans is racially motivated. Nevertheless, the term, even if not racially motivated, is laden with negative connotations.

Savages are not simply different from people in society. They are less developed. They are lesser. Hence, they are worse and so represent an unenviable group. Thus, the fact remains that Hobbes thought Europeans were superior. This view may not reflect a racist ideology, but it does smack of an uncomfortable bias. The focus on the terminology of Hobbes, however, does not shed any light on the real problem—that Hobbes presumed that some European societies did not evolve from the wretched and lowly state of nature, while at the same time he took for granted that peoples whose social development did not mirror the Europeans' were examples of people in a real state of nature. As Matthew Kramer states:

A credible reading of the words [quoted] would take them to imply that a sheer hell of chaotic and relentless war did precede the founding of civil institutions, but that that dreadful plight did not emerge everywhere. . . . [The] quoted words might suggest that ruthless conflicts of everyone against everyone have clearly not turned up at the origins of *all* schemes of civil life; certain schemes may originate from the occupying of lands by people who very smoothly work together, perhaps as the colonial agents of a strong mother country.[19]

So, the question remains, why did Hobbes distinguish between Europeans and non-Europeans and then decide that the societies of the former may well have not arisen from such a depraved state of nature while the peoples in the latter groups were, even at that time, still lingering in such a state? Was his attitude based on a barely disguised racial bias upon which he formulated his views regarding social evolution?

Lott attempts to address Hobbes's belief in the retarded societal growth of non-Europeans and the reasons for it. He quotes a passage from Hobbes's *Elements*, in which he claims Hobbes denies that European development in the arts and sciences indicates their superiority over the "inhabitants of divers places in America."[20] According to Lott, "[t]here is an important reason Hobbes explains this difference in terms of social development and environmental influences rather than in terms of greater intelligence."[21]

The state of nature for Hobbes, Lott argues, represents a point on the social evolutionary scale—one through which all humanity came and one into which human societies shall one day again dissolve. It may be debatable whether Hobbes believed that the state of nature (a representation of man in his least developed state) existed for all human societies but at different times for each, or whether some societies were so "civilized" that it was difficult for him to imagine them as ever having been as lowly as the different groups of non-Europeans appeared to him to be. What does seem to be clear, though, is that if Hobbes was not expressing his prejudice against non-European peoples in claiming that they and not Europeans were products of the state of nature, then his theory is, as I suggested at the beginning of this section, limited and dubious—for he does not offer any justifications that warrant such a view. Perhaps Hobbesian racial bias may be more apparent in his views on conquest.

| | |

HOBBES ON CONQUEST

It would not be difficult to suggest that Hobbes's imperialist beliefs were not based on the assumption that the conquered peoples were lesser humans than their conquerors. There is no suggestion that he subscribed to the view that conquest was mandated by the inability of culturally, socially, and intellectually inferior natives to be self-governing, while colonization and resource appropriation benefited not just the conquerors but also the hapless indigenous population. And Hobbes did not sheath his views in the guise of religious beneficence.[22]

Racism, however, need not always be affirmative in nature. One need not always do or take some action X to demonstrate a racist attitude or disposition. Sometimes one may demonstrate such an attitude or disposition by one's failure or inaction. With this in mind, let us examine Hobbes's views on conquest.

According to Hobbes, conquest is mandated by physical necessity: overpopulation. Lands are to be targeted based on the sparseness of their populations and the vastness of their territories. This view reflected the basic European attitude regarding the settlement of the Americas. Colonies in the New World were justified and even mandated given the European perspective of these "new" lands and their inhabitants.

This mandate held (1) that the Americas were unclaimed and available territories; and (2) that European nations were entitled (if not divinely obliged) to lay claim to these areas. For example, the British crown had claimed the Virginia territory, so Virginia Company shareholders took for granted that they were entitled to it and all of its resources. The Jamestown settlers had no qualms about occupying and securing the region from the natives who were living there. Noel Malcolm writes:

> For a colonial company the most important theoretical issue was, of course, that of legitimizing the settlement and appropriation of land. The simplest argument was that the colonists held their territory by right of conquest. This appears to have been the official view of James I. . . . [However, some individuals] did not recognize that any right or title was to be gained by conquest alone. . . . Although the Virginia Company emphasized, in all its public pronouncements, the importance of its work in the conversion of Indians, its members were reluctant to claim that this was sufficient to justify conquest. . . . [I]n the end, no extensive attempt at a solution to the problem of legitimation was ever offered by the Virginia Company; there was a tendency to regard the actual colonization as a fait accompli and to justify its continuation on the grounds of converting infidels.[23]

The fervor with which these beliefs would be put into practice throughout the New World indicates that the Europeans did not deny the basic property rights of the native peoples so much as they denied them basic human rights. And there is no evidence that Thomas Hobbes found the Virginia Company's venture morally problematic. Indeed, not only was Hobbes was not troubled by the notion of imperial conquest but he viewed it as right and necessary at times. In *Leviathan*, Hobbes gave what he believed was a justification for the conquest and colonization of foreign lands:

> The multiple of poor, and yet strong people still encreasing, they are to be transplanted into Countries not sufficiently inhabited: where neverthelesse, they are not to exterminate those they find there; but constrain them to inhabit closer together, and not range a great deal of ground, to snatch what they find; but to court each little Plot with art and labour, to give them their sustenance in due season. And when all the world is overcharged with Inhabitants, then the last remedy of all is Warre; which provideth for every man, by Victory, or Death.[24]

The only "insufficiently" populated countries known to Hobbes and others at the time were the lands in the New World. Hobbes is blatantly advocating what Hannah Arendt calls his "philosophy of power."[25] The European nations had a perfect right, according to Hobbes's theory, to capture these "insufficiently populated" lands and to push the native inhabitants onto whatever undesirable land was left. This scenario could be a script for the southeastern Indians' Trail of Tears and every other territorial usurpation imposed on the native population by the U.S. government.

The passage advocates a virtually total lack of respect for the sovereignty of independent nations in the face of an overcrowded and more powerful aggressor nation. Hobbes seemed to view sovereign nations essentially as provisional events—colonies in waiting. Lest we forget, though, Hobbes did not view the lands in the Americas as nations at all, sovereign or otherwise. They were not nations because there was no (recognizable European) form of government in these lands.[26] And there was no government because the populations had not evolved to rise up out of the state of nature. This attitude, seen in light of the increasing European and particularly British predilection for conquest, does not cast Hobbes in a favorable, egalitarian light. He did not accept the notion that the inhabitants of New World territories had a right to exist as independent and self-determined entities; he thought they were not advanced enough.

But the question I am addressing is whether Hobbes was a racist—whether he believed in the inherently inferior status of certain peoples based on their genetic heritage. So far it has been somewhat plausible to suggest that though Hobbes thought that non-Europeans were "savages" (in essence, because they did not mimic European society), that some Europeans were probably never savages, and that savages were rightfully subject to the will and force of conquering (presum-

ably European?) nations, it is still possible that his beliefs were not racially motivated. The final area of Hobbesian exposition to which we should turn in order to
examine whether he held racist views is the area of slavery.

| | |

HOBBES ON SLAVERY

Slavery represents conquest: the conquest of the individual. And Hobbes recognized this. He did not put into writing his views of the African peoples or the
transatlantic slave trade into which they were forced. However, in discussing the
conqueror's dominion over the conquered he did shed light on his views regarding slavery.

In discussing the difference between a servant and a slave Hobbes says:

> Dominion acquired by Conquest, or Victory in war is that which some writers
> call Despotical . . . which signifieth a *Lord* or *Master*; and is the Dominion of
> the Master over his Servant. And this Dominion is then acquired to the Victor,
> when the Vanquished, to avoyd the present stroke of death, covenanteth either
> in expresse words, or by other sufficient signes of the Will, that so long as his
> life, and the liberty of his body is allowed him, the Victor shall have the use
> thereof, at his pleasure. And after such Covenant made, the vanquished is a
> Servant, and not before; for by the word *servant* . . . is not meant a Captive,
> which is kept in prison, or bonds, till the owner of him that took him, or
> bought him of one that did, shall consider what to do with him: (for such men,
> (commonly called Slaves,) have no obligation at all; but may break their bonds
> or the prison; and kill, or carry away captive their Master, justly:) but one, that
> being taken, hath corporeall liberty allowed him; and upon promise not to run
> away, nor to do violence to his Master, is trusted by him.[27]

Paradoxically, a slave is captured by force but is *made* only by consent. According
to Hobbes, a slave is someone over whom no other person can have any legitimate authority, and this is by definition. Legitimate authority can be conferred
only via the consent of the conquered person to accept the dominion of the conqueror. However, once consent is given, that person ceases to be a slave and becomes a servant. Thus, no slave can consent to serve another, for when or if he
does he can no longer be called a slave. The notion of a voluntary slave is contra-
dictory. Hobbes's views on slavery may seem somewhat confusing because of his
manner of distinguishing between a slave and a servant. A slave is someone
whom a conqueror captures in his conquest of a foe. Hobbes states that the conqueror should either kill this person or keep him imprisoned. For though he had
the power to capture and imprison the slave, he has no power that the slave need

respect. Thus, the slave may and actually *must* constantly attempt to escape and/or kill his captor. The irony and source of confusion stems from the fact that though the conqueror gains power over the death of the enslaved, he has no power over the life of the enslaved, absent the latter's choice to bestow it upon him.

According to Hobbes, the slave cannot acquiesce to his condition for a moment. He cannot indicate that he values his life, because if he does, he has thereby implicitly promised service to the master for sparing his life and he is a servant. At the same time, Hobbes believes that a slave may voluntarily surrender his natural right to freedom and become a servant. What this involves is the slave's implicit or explicit agreement to do the bidding of the captor. What the slave barters with is his life, since the captor already "owns" his death. The "deal" the captive makes is to give to the conqueror his life as a servant. Hobbes states:

> There are but three ways only, whereby one can have a dominion over the person of another. . . . The second is, if a man taken prisoner in the wars, or overcome, or else distrusting his own forces (to avoid death) promises the conqueror or the stronger party his *service*, that is, to do all whatsoever he shall command him. . . . Now he that is thus tied, is called *a servant*; he to whom he is tied, a Lord.[28]

The conqueror is entitled to do as he wishes with the slave qua slave and with the slave-turned-servant. The difference for the slave-turned-servant is that he has consented to relinquish his freedom and he now has no rights vis-à-vis his captor, certainly no right to try to escape.

> The "servant" had no rights whatsoever and was obliged to obey every command of his lord. For disobedience he might even be killed with impunity. He could be sold or conveyed as his master wished.[29]

As a slave, he was entitled, no, obligated to exhaust all means of escape to regain his freedom. Why? Because freedom is the natural state of man and if it is not voluntarily surrendered, then no laws can restrict a man's attempt to free himself from involuntary bondage.[30]

Hobbes's position on slavery might justifiably be used both in the defense of slavery and in an argument opposing the institution. While Hobbes condemns the unnaturalness of involuntary bondage, he also denies the existence of involuntary servitude. Thus, he sees a right and duty of the enslaved to fight and even kill to regain his freedom. At the same time, he views any slave who ceases to fight or struggle for however long as voluntarily surrendering his or her freedom forever and becoming a servant.

Hobbes's view of just who can be considered a slave and who a servant is almost mechanically rigid. In the context of the African slave trade, one may rightfully claim that because Africans were forcibly enslaved, Hobbes would contend that they had the right to employ whatever means they felt necessary to regain their freedom. But, there is a problem. Hobbes's involuntary slave literally had only two choices: to fight or to die. Any hint of submission to the captor would be taken as a capitulation of the slave's freedom. Hobbes was insensitive to human need and the survival instinct that could easily have mandated employing trickery or false, ostensible subservience to bide time and assess options for escape. And certainly Hobbes would (could) not have understood the vast majority of Africans who, kidnapped from their homes and brought to an alien land, having familiarity only with their captors, did not choose to die, but certainly did not choose to be slaves, and had no choice but to submit to the will of their captors.

Hobbes's view of slavery and enslavement was incredibly facile and unsophisticated. He would most likely have pronounced African enslavement to be a system of voluntary service. It was voluntary for those individuals who did not fling themselves over the sides of slave ships and voluntary for those individuals who, terrorized, dazed, and in shock, obeyed the directions of their captors to leave the ships in chains and step up to the auction block. But does all of this make Hobbes a racist?

| | |

HOBBESIAN RACISM

Hobbes was not a racist in the startling manner of some philosophers such as John Locke or Immanuel Kant. There were no obvious or glaring inconsistencies between his writings and his life. But, as I stated earlier, not all racism or racial prejudice is affirmative or obvious in nature. Sometimes individuals harbor beliefs and preferences that when viewed in their totality, rather than individually, suggest prejudice. And sometimes individuals further racist aims by failing to confront racist institutions or policies and practices as surely as if they had positively acted to enforce them.

Thomas Hobbes wrote about the natural freedom and equality of men during a time in which the African slave trade and the European conquest of the New World were in their embryonic stages. The evidence I have examined in this chapter indicates that he said little directly for or against these trends and that he likely would have sanctioned the former while justifying the latter. In spite of explanations or excuses to the contrary, such a person can justifiably be termed a racist.

NOTES

1. Noel Malcolm, "Hobbes, Sandys, and the Virginia Company," in *Great Political Thinkers*, vol.2: *Hobbes*, ed. John Dunn and Ian Harris (Cheltenham, UK: Elgar, 1997). He did not become the Earl of Devonshire until a decade after this.

2. A. P. Martinich, *Hobbes: A Biography* (Cambridge: Cambridge University Press, 1999), 19, 27–28.

3. There were two ways a person could become a member of the company. Those who wished only to invest money in the company could invest as "Adventurers" (stockholders). Individuals who traveled to the colony and lived there were designated as "Planter" members and given one share of stock each. http://ukonline.co.uk/lordcornell/va/via.html.

4. See, for instance, Carl Bridenbaugh, *Jamestown, 1544–1699* (New York: Oxford University Press, 1980).

5. Malcolm, "Hobbes, Sandys," 262. The consensus was that Cavendish's gift was made not so much out of friendship for Hobbes as in an attempt at "vote packing." Voting at shareholders' meetings was done on the basis of one man, one vote. Someone with one hundred shares carried no more weight than someone with one share. There was a bitter ideological divide among shareholders regarding the direction of the company, and Cavendish could depend upon Hobbes's support when issues came to a vote.

6. Hobbes would accompany and sometimes stood in for Cavendish at company meetings. Ibid.

7. See comments by Peter Wood, www.pbs.org/wgbh/aia/part1/1i3054.html, the PBS website for "Africans in America."

8. Wood, www.pbs.org/wgbh/aia/part1/1i3053.html.

9. In this respect, Hobbes was hardly on a par with John Locke who held quite profitable investments in the Royal Africa and the Bahamas Adventurers Companies, both of which operated as transatlantic slave-trading companies.

10. I shall discuss the debate regarding this point momentarily.

11. Thomas Hobbes, *Leviathan*, ed. C. B. Macpherson (London: Penguin, 1968), 183 (chap. 13) (emphasis added).

12. Ibid., 187.

13. Matthew H. Kramer, *Hobbes and the Paradoxes of Political Origins* (New York: St. Martin's Press, 1997), 64–66.

14. Superior because not having the state of nature is superior to having it.

15. Charles W. Mills, *The Racial Contract* (Ithaca: Cornell University Press, 1997), 46–47.

16. Ibid., 66.

17. Tommy L. Lott, "Patriarchy and Slavery in Hobbes's Political Philosophy," in *Philosophers on Race: Critical Essays*, ed. Julie K. Ward and Tommy L. Lott (Oxford: Blackwell, 2002), 71.

18. Ibid., 72.

19. Kramer, *Hobbes and the Paradoxes of Political Origins*, 65.

20. Thomas Hobbes, *The Elements of Law, Natural and Politic*, chap. 13, para. 3.

21. Lott, "Patriarchy and Slavery," 72.

22. For a thoughtful examination of the imperialist mind-set, see Charles Mills's *Racial Contract*.

23. Malcolm, "Hobbes, Sandys," 366–68.

24. Hobbes, *Leviathan*, 387 (chap. 30).

25. Hannah Arendt, *Origins of Totalitarianism* (Cleveland: World, 1958), 143. This is basically the view that "might makes right"—that power is and ought to be the only justification necessary for acts.

26. There is evidence that Hobbes, in fact, was aware of governing bodies among some tribes in America.

27. Hobbes, *Leviathan*, 255 (chap. 20).

28. Thomas Hobbes, *De Cive or The Citizen: Philosophical Rudiments concerning Government and Society*, in *Man and Citizen*, ed. Bernard Gert (Indianapolis: Hackett, 1991), 205–6.

29. David Brion Davis, *The Problem of Slavery in Western Culture* (Ithaca: Cornell University Press, 1966), 117.

30. The notion that one can be forced or obliged to pursue what is natural to one is somewhat oxymoronic.

| 3 |

Metaphysics at the Barricades
Spinoza and Race

DEBRA NAILS

Spinoza is simultaneously the philosopher who speaks least of race and racism—dead long before the systematic development of the social institution of racism in eighteenth-century Germany[1]—and the philosopher who provokes the deepest and most difficult philosophical questions about race: What is race? Does race *exist*? What is and what *ought* to be the right of a race? Can imposed differential treatment of a race be justified? Because the reader is required to infer the answers from Spinoza's several texts, the pursuit of his positions can be baffling and frustrating.[2] And that task is complicated by at least two further problems: (1) his two political treatises are not entirely compatible with one another, the later one abandoning his earlier notion of social contract,[3] and (2) the contemporary secondary literature on the political works has been steering in recent years away from consensus toward anarchist and global democratic readings on the one hand, and classical liberal readings on the other.

In the brief treatment of Spinoza on race that follows, section 1 provides some biographical and historical context. Section 2 recounts in schematic form how Spinoza is interpreted in influential recent work on his political theory. My aim in these first two parts is to equip readers with the overview and tools necessary to investigate further and independently the topic of race in Spinoza. The so-called *philosopher's philosopher* is as difficult as he is iconoclastic, but no philosopher repays study so richly, and his views are no less to be reckoned with now than they were when he first set them out. My own view of Spinoza on race, sketched in sections 3 and 4, takes an unusual path through the material: I privilege Spinoza's ontology rather than his political theory. It is his ontology, I argue, that undermines all forms of racism while preserving the right of a race to do what is within its power.

Friends and strangers have been generous with their suggestions and clarifications. I have attempted to identify their help where I used it below; but William Levitan, Dick Peterson, Andrew Valls, and Win Wilkinson sprinkled their help throughout.

||

LIFE AND TIMES

Baruch de Spinoza (1632–1677)[4] spent his life entirely in cities of the Dutch republic, now The Netherlands, perhaps the most tolerant and free of Europe's cities at the time.[5] Of Amsterdam, Spinoza wrote approvingly in the *Theological-Political Treatise*:

> Take the city of Amsterdam, which enjoys the fruits of this freedom, to its own considerable prosperity and the admiration of the world. In this flourishing state, a city of the highest renown, men of every race[6] and sect live in complete harmony; and before entrusting their property to some person they will want to know no more than this, whether he is rich or poor and whether he has been honest or dishonest in his dealings. As for religion or sect, that is of no account, because such considerations are regarded as irrelevant in a court of law; and no sect whatsoever is so hated that its adherents—provided that they injure no one, render to each what is his own, and live upright lives—are denied the protection of the civil authorities.[7]

The description may have been more or less accurate when Spinoza published it in 1670,[8] but had not long been so; and Amsterdam, while more progressive than other cities of the republic, found its policies of tolerance under constant attack from the Calvinist consistory of the Reformed Church.[9] Thus the Jewish community there, primarily Marrano Jews whose ascendants had fled the Inquisition in Spain and Portugal, but many of whose religious practices had been affected by forced conversions and proximity to Roman Catholicism, were always on their guard, self-policing their community to prevent any appearance of sacrilege or scandal that might draw the unwelcome attention of authorities. Jews were not subject in the Dutch republic to such "blood purity" laws[10] as had prevented even *conversos*—Jews who had converted willingly or not to Christianity—from attaining offices of authority in their home countries, but some of the guilds were still closed to Jews, and isolated acts of discrimination were not unknown. However, Jewish expertise in trade and connections with the Spanish and Portuguese colonies in the New World ensured for the Jews of Amsterdam, including Spinoza's merchant family, a share in the great Dutch prosperity of the seventeenth century.[11]

Spinoza himself, however, had been cast out of that community by the age of twenty-three; he was subjected to a *cherem* (banning) by the Jewish community of Amsterdam on July 27, 1656, for his "wrong opinions and behavior," the "horrible heresies which he practiced and taught, and . . . monstrous actions which he performed"—and in which he persisted although the rabbis "tried various means and promises to dissuade him from his evil ways." Spinoza's *cherem* was more virulent in its terms than any other of which we have records: "Cursed be he by day, and cursed be he by night, and cursed be he when he lies down, and cursed . . . [etc.]. We order that nobody should communicate with him orally or in writing, or show him any favor, or stay with him under the same roof, or come within four ells of him, or read anything composed or written by him."[12] Nevertheless, Spinoza remained a citizen of the Dutch republic. He enjoyed the right to live wherever he chose and to associate with anyone; early biographies name among his companions political radicals, freethinkers, an ex-Jesuit, and Christians, especially Mennonites.[13]

Spinoza could not, however, speak or publish his radical views without real danger of persecution. To remain out of the light of public scrutiny, he chose privacy and poverty over a professorship offered to him by the University of Heidelberg,[14] and insulated himself further by writing almost entirely in Latin, the language of scholars, previously used by both Galileo and Descartes in their efforts to avoid censorship; so only one of Spinoza's works, *Principles of Cartesian Philosophy*, was published in his lifetime under his name. When he published the subversive *Theological-Political Treatise*, he did so anonymously and with false information substituted for the place and name of the publisher, Johannes Rieuwertz, a close friend whose life and liberty would have been as much at risk as the author's.[15] The treatise was condemned by the States of Holland in 1673, and a few months before Spinoza died in February of 1677 the Synod of the Hague ordered an inquiry into its authorship.[16] As Spinoza's correspondence attests, he was wary of allowing his written words to be shared outside his circle of friends; he sometimes warns them to beware of inadvertently sharing even his opinions with particular individuals, Leibniz, for example.[17]

Such caution was fully warranted by the era's bigotry. Jews were viewed not only as having a separate religion but as being a separate race or birth-group (*natio*).[18] Spinoza did not discuss the institution of African slavery that spread in other parts of the world during his lifetime, with one exception: his last work, the unfinished *Political Treatise*, breaks off as he initiates a discussion of women and slaves as unsuited for democracy while under the domination of husbands and masters. Where that discussion might have led is lost to us.[19]

Apart from religious cum racial bigotry, Spinoza lived among political upheavals, wars, and oppression, making political matters urgent and unavoidable for the philosopher and many of his closest associates and correspondents— however dangerous the discussion of such matters might prove. And dangerous it was: Spinoza's associates suffered imprisonment, torture, state execution, and gory mob violence.[20]

SPINOZA'S POLITICAL THEORY

To situate Spinoza in the context of seventeenth-century political thought, it is best to begin with the philosopher's own statements, and first of all with his 1674 letter to Jarig Jelles: "With regard to political theory, the difference between Hobbes and myself, which is the subject of your inquiry, consists in this, that I always preserve the natural right in its entirety, and I hold that the sovereign power in a state has right over a subject only in proportion to the excess of its power over that of a subject. This is always the case in a state of nature."[21] It is crucial to note Spinoza's view that right (jus) and power (potentia) are coextensive, for that will prove to be the key to Spinoza's current prominence in Europe as a political philosopher. Spinoza argues that "whatever an individual thing does by the laws of its own nature, it does with sovereign right, inasmuch as it acts as determined by nature, and can do no other"; he admits no "distinction between men and other individuals of nature" (TTP 16, par. 3). With this statement, the necessity of examining Spinoza's metaphysics, rather than his political theory, should be clear: *no distinction between men and other individuals of nature*. Thus there is no reason *a priori* to take the citizen, or the state, or the worker, or the cell, or the race, class, or gender to be one's fundamental unit of analysis across a variety of contexts; for to take any of these—or some other—as fundamental is to distort the interconnections among them that are characteristic of them. Human beings exist as parts of ever more encompassing systems, and yet are themselves contexts in which other individuals (viruses, freckles) are embedded. Yet our human distinctions are not merely arbitrary, for some inhibit, and others promote, our ability to persevere in existence (conatus).[22] What is a person? A web of relations. A race? A web of relations.[23]

Before I spell that out in detail, I promised background, and there is more than one significant beginning to Spinoza's contemporary importance as a political philosopher. The first, Spinoza as precursor to views that culminate in Karl Marx, starts with Ludwig Feuerbach's "recognition that 'God, or Nature' was far more thoroughgoing in its elimination of every form of transcendence and ideality than the work of many self-described materialists,"[24] and is explored by interpreters Louis Althusser, Pierre Macherey, and Etienne Balibar.[25]

The second beginning has been more fruitful, still owing much to Marxian analysis, but emerging from the focus of Michel Foucault and Gilles Deleuze on *power*, culminating in the influential works of Antonio Negri, who finds in Spinoza a "metaphysics carried to the front lines of the political struggle," and "the transfer of a religious and metaphysical foundation into a humanistic and revolutionary project."[26] Right as power in the sense Negri advances has brought in its wake other bold attempts to derive from the philosophy of Spinoza political advice for the day.[27] Thus one recent expositor of Spinoza's political theory has declared that the one inalienable right of the individual is to "criticize, protest, dissent, rebel," for this is Spinoza's lesson for people of color in the United States in these times of antiterrorism.[28] It is his lesson for us all. Another commentator has used power relations in Spinoza to explicate class;[29] and there have been other, incompatible approaches to Spinoza's political theory as well—nationalist, classical liberal.[30]

I regard the political treatises as tainted with the detritus of the brief life of an outcast spent in constant struggle against religious and secular authorities. The inconsistencies that send commentators in so many directions are the lingering but superficial marks of Spinoza's ardently lived life—political theory begotten of politics. There is more to gain from a theory of race born of a philosophy of nature.

| | |

SPINOZA'S METAPHYSICS

According to part 1 of Spinoza's *Ethics*, where the ontological argumentation is complete, there is only one substance, i.e., one independent cause of itself, and there is *nothing but* the one substance.[31] Some innocuously call the one substance "nature," while the superstitious and ignorant understand the laws of nature to be the laws of God. Substance, according to Spinoza, expresses itself continually in ways or *modes* that are, put rather poetically, the face of the universe, the ever-changing present. We are ourselves modes of substance, *ways* in which substance is manifested, and we encounter other modes of substance (e.g., a crystal, a cat, Andrew Valls, the British monarchy, the Milky Way)—some of which are conscious of themselves, and all of which exist in relation to one another—throughout our lives. Furthermore, we encounter *nothing but* substance in its modes, for there is nothing else. Lest Spinoza be mistaken for a materialist or physicalist, it cannot be overemphasized that substance is mind as well as body for these are identical under the aspect of eternity (*sub specie aeternitatis*). Puny human beings, lacking the ability to apprehend substance under its infinite attributes, must be content to conceive a finite mode—a coffee cup, say—now under the attribute of thought, now under the attribute of extension. But thought and extension, mind and body, are identical, despite the persistent existential experience of difference: the human incapacity to conceive a mode under both attributes at once is the human inability to attend to mind and body simultaneously in consciousness.[32] The inadequacy of human apprehension, however, should not be confused with a limitation by fragmentation of substance itself. As Spinoza puts it succinctly, "a mode of extension and the idea of that mode are one and the same thing, expressed in two ways" (E2p7s).

Let us pause now to consider the coffee cup, a Spinozian individual, before proceeding to the more complex individual that is race.[33] Mine is a cylindrical green cup, less than half full of a rich brown espresso with an aroma reminiscent of darkest chocolate; as I lift it, I am struck by its heaviness, and by the hardness and coldness of the rim compared to the hot liquid within; yum. What I have just described in terms of perception is a finite mode of substance conceived under the attribute of extension, the cup as a body. But wait. The coffee that was in the cup a moment ago is now a part of the conscious individual that is Debra Nails (who is herself a veritable colony of individuals: cells, bacteria, organs, etc.), and the cup is empty, yet I still experience it as cylindrical, green, heavy, hard, and cold; and beyond these merely experiential facts, it has exact dimensions, density, rest mass, and reflects particular wavelengths of light. I suspect that it is a glazed clay cup, but I cannot be certain about that without violating the integrity of the cup, scraping off its glaze to examine its composition. That integrity of the individual, its tendency to remain a cup, displacing rather than integrating itself with the air around it, is what Spinoza calls *conatus*. An individual, for Spinoza, is that which has a natural disposition to cohere in existence, so each molecule of my cup is likewise an individual. The sense in which the set of coffee cups from which mine comes is an individual is far less clear—for the sense in which the set exhibits a disposition to remain a set is far less clear than is the sense in which the cup sitting by my computer exhibits a disposition to remain a cup. We will see in a moment just how a race of people differs from a set of matching coffee cups.

The mind of my coffee cup—though it sounds peculiar in English—is the idea of the extension of my cup, i.e., the set of true formal mathematical expressions describing the cup, as we might say *corresponding* to its density, mass, and other properties. Because the order and connection of ideas is the same as the order and connection of things (E2p7), the mind of the cup, i.e., the cup conceived under the attribute of thought, i.e., the idea of the cup, is exactly as essential to the mode of substance that is my cup as its being an extended thing. The cup is precisely and irreducibly both—under alternating descriptions.[34] The mind of the cup is different from my mind as I contemplate my cup, of course; and the idea of the cup, its mind, is different from *my* idea of the cup. My idea of the cup is itself a mode of substance that is in no sense green or cylindrical, but my idea can nonetheless be conceived under the attribute of extension, as a brain state, and under the attribute of thought, as a mental state.[35]

The story becomes more complex *sub specie aeternitatis*, for I am bound to consider the history and the future of my cup—under the attributes of both extension and thought: its recent origins in the clay of western China and its eventual disorganization into bits of crushed landfill, its ultimate origin in the Big Bang and its eventual disposition, its relations to other elements, to people, to the laws of nature, and to space time, including multiple dimensions—its relation, that is, to substance itself and thus to all the modes of substance, past, present and future.

To speak curiously again, but not incorrectly, my cup has exactly as much *right* to exist as it has *power* to persevere (*conatus*) against the onslaught of heavier and sharper objects, the effects of my clumsiness, and the pressures of style to exchange mugs for dainty teacups. That *right* and *power* are coextensive is the crux of Spinoza's political philosophy, as we saw in section 2. And that brings us at last to race.

|||

SPINOZA AND RACE

What is race? Race is a finite mode of substance—a web of relations—that, like any other finite mode, has exactly as much *right* to exist as it has *power* to persevere. Race can be apprehended under the attribute of thought, i.e., exhaustively described by the laws of nature as expressed in a set of mathematical descriptors; and apprehended under the attribute of extension, i.e., perceived. The descriptors are to the race as the mind is to the body—the expression in idea of what is physically perceptible. To exist qua individual, a race must itself have *conatus*, the power to persevere in existence; and, because *conatus* is necessarily a capacity internal to any individual (from bacterium to binary star system), a race depends for its continued existence on the free identification and participation of its members—where "free" carries its own complex of epistemological requirements. A race cannot be *defined* into individuality and then perpetuated by external factors—not for Spinoza. Rational voluntary association is the only legitimate form of solidarity.[36] Thus one of the potentially oppressive uses of race is precluded—at least metaphysically.

Although a race is an individual, it is not much like an individual person (just as my set of cups does not seem to be an individual in quite the same way that this particular cup seems to be). What about a school of fish?[37] Uncontroversially, each fish in the school has *conatus*. But the school too has *conatus*, a tendency to remain in formation against attempts to separate its members from one another—though the school has no consciousness of its "desire to persevere" (a stone likewise has *conatus* without consciousness of *conatus*). Moreover, any *school of fish* has more individuality than a group of randomly selected fish from different bodies of water thrown together in a tank. Whereas a person has a mind that is complex and is conscious of its own existence, a race (like a state) can be severally conscious of the existence of the whole but has no distinct consciousness of its own.[38]

Whereas a person can choose to identify with a race or to assimilate into some broader population, a race cannot determine its own future, cannot choose anything at all, and therefore cannot be free.[39] When a race, for example, adopts or forbids—encourages or discourages—some attitude or practice, it must do so as a collectivity through its members: even if accomplished through such institutions as exhortation, isolation, peer pressure, role modeling, or threat of violence, it is the individual persons comprised in the individual race who reason, if they reason, and they who choose. It is only they who can be free, except by loose analogy, for we do sometimes speak of the emancipation of a race, by which we mean the absence of the oppression of its members by another political or social entity.

Like a state, a race has a history and a future: Egypt under the pharaohs had a future, an existence in our present—in history books, imaginations, ruins, and among archaeologists—long after the citizens, laws, and other institutions had disappeared. Under the attribute of extension, these are the ancient state's present existence. Might we not say, then, that a race could after all be generated externally in the same way that a state might establish a colony that develops over time into a fully mature state in its own right? Imagine rounding up all the philosophers, or all the redheads, and announcing that they are a separate race. Like a colony that grows into a state, the redheads might come to view themselves as a race. But, for Spinoza, there is no individual state and no individual race until each has *conatus* to unify and preserve it. Now, the "race" of redheads does, in a sense, constitute an abstract individual thing and to that extent does exhibit *conatus*, but it is based on a very tenuous connection, very easily broken, and so the tendency of this artificial race to cohere is very weak, while the history, culture, and kinship relations among a natural group of people, as well as their free participation in the group, establish a much stronger cohesion; hence we are justified in thinking of this group as an entity in a different way from the way in which we think of a group designated through some arbitrary common feature.

Spinoza's case in point is his account of the Jews, i.e., his biblical criticism in the first fifteen chapters of the *Theological-Political Treatise*. Its ideas outraged and appalled his Amsterdam Jewish community and the Calvinists of the Dutch republic precisely because it was a naturalistic chronology of a people, describing the Jews' literature and narrative history while utterly denying the very possibility of the supernatural. Spinoza's story described the commonalities that enabled and encouraged individual Jews to adhere to one another as a race, and by the same stroke denied anything whatsoever that the Jews can arrogate to themselves above other nations. As to their continued existence for so many years when scattered and stateless, this is in no way surprising, since they have separated themselves from other nations to such a degree as to incur the hatred of all, and this not only through external rites alien to the rites of other nations but also through the mark of circumcision, which they most religiously observe.[40]

Despite Spinoza's criticism of the Jews, and despite the problem that freedom is unavailable to races, transient needs can be served by the identification of individuals as a race: like a sports team that gathers periodically to practice and play, and then disbands into a variety of other human roles, observing rules, uniforms, and a sense of *conatus* as a team only once a week, a Spinozian individual, like Theseus's ship, has no fixed existence in space time.[41] For Spinoza, the primary transient usefulness of race is exactly the usefulness of all other collaborative efforts; that is, individuals enjoy increased power and right through banding together into a collective; he says in the *Political Treatise*, "If two men come together and join forces, they have more power over nature, and consequently more right, than either one alone; and the greater the number who form a union in this way, the more right they will together possess."[42] It is because this is so that education in sympathy and reason is a central concern of Spinoza's greatest work, the Ethics.

The final question I set out at the beginning of the chapter was whether the external imposition of the differential treatment of races, bias, could be justified under Spinoza's political system. Fortunately, the answer to this question is as simple as the question of just what constitutes a race is difficult. The simple answer is no: racial bias is a species of bias, and all bias is for Spinoza a refusal of the counsel of reason; and reasoning validly from true premises is the business of all persons who would be free. The fact that no one can abrogate one's right or power to any exercise government or other authority ensures a continuing adhesion to the values of *freedom* and absolute *democracy* as Spinoza defines those terms and develops their meaning in his political theory. Spinoza may well have envisioned a global direct democracy denying rigid individuality to all states and to all races, including the human race,[43] but that vision was neither for his present nor for ours.[44]

In the end, is Spinoza's view of race just an interesting footnote to the history of modern philosophy, or does it offer something of permanent importance to the discussion of race?[45] The latter. Spinoza takes issue at the most fundamental ontological level with claims that race exists independently, claims that will, a century later, fuel the rise of the physiological basis for modern racism. In our day, those same arguments from ontological principles are naturally deployed against the concept of group consciousness, against the organicist notion of collective social entities, and thus against the very idea of the black experience, or the mind of the ancients—in the sense those expressions are now used. There is no collective consciousness, according to Spinoza, only the consciousness of persons. Experiences, beliefs, and reasons for action differ across any group of people, so "race" can only be a vague term for analysts and racists to use in describing various social constructions.

NOTES

1. Ancient "proto-racism" has recently received a magisterial treatment in Benjamin Isaac, *The Invention of Racism in Classical Antiquity* (Princeton: Princeton University Press, 2004), which, despite its catchy title, assiduously avoids the claim that Greeks and Romans had a modern notion of race. One of the best and most accessible descriptions of the rise of racism in the West—the development of the biological or physiological basis for race—is Stephen Jay Gould's *The Mismeasure of Man* (1981; New York: Norton, 1996); also of great value in telling the story of racism, especially its prominence in eighteenth-century Germany, is the succinct account in Martin Bernal, *Black Athena: The Afroasiatic Roots of Classical Civilization*, vol. 1: *The Fabrication of Ancient Greece, 1785–1985* (London: Free Association Books, 1987), 201–23.

2. Of principal importance for the discussion of race are the *Ethics*, the *Theological-Political Treatise* (TTP), and the *Political Treatise* (PT), all in Spinoza, *Complete Works*, trans. Samuel Shirley et al., ed. Michael L. Morgan (Indianapolis: Hackett, 2002). All translations used herein are those of Shirley.

3. Alexandre Matheron, "Le problème de l'évolution de Spinoza du *Traité Theologico-Politique*," in *Spinoza: Issues and Directions. The Proceedings of the Chicago Conference*, ed. Edwin Curley and Pierre Françoise Moreau (New York: Brill, 1990), 258–70. See also Matheron's "The Theoretical Function of Democracy in Spinoza and Hobbes," and Etienne Balibar's "*Jus-Pactum-Lex*: On the Constitution of the Subject in the *Theologico-Political Treatise*," which goes further to deny that Spinoza's philosophy is systematic—both in *The New Spinoza*, ed. W. Montag and T. Stolze (Minneapolis: University of Minnesota Press, 1997), 212–13 and 171, respectively. Osamu Ueno argues that Spinoza's break with Hobbes, in particular Hobbes's view that men transfer their rights in the formation of a social contract, had occurred already in Spinoza's *TTP*, where it is rather *power* that is transferred; see "Spinoza et le paradoxe du contrat social de Hobbes. 'Le reste,' " *Cahiers Spinoza* 6 (1991): 269–95.

4. A large number of spelling variants appears even in extant documents bearing the philosopher's name and those of his family: Spinosa, de Spinosa, D'Espinosa, Despinosa, Espinoza, de Espinosa, et al. As for his given name, he would originally have had the Hebrew name Baruch, but—in a time when most Marrano Jews had one or more aliases used in trade, for Amsterdam's burgeoning economy hosted merchants of many languages—he would also have been known as Bento, from the Portuguese spoken in the family, and also as Benedict and Benedictus among his circle of friends. Spinoza's preserved letters are signed in a variety of ways. Many questions about Spinoza's background and times are answered in Steven Nadler's satisfying biography, *Spinoza: A Life* (Cam-

bridge: Cambridge University Press, 1999), which places Spinoza's life within the context of European Jewry. For extant documents and brief historical explanations, see A. M. Vaz Dias, W. G. Van der Tak, et al., *Spinoza Merchant and Autodidact = Studia Rosenthaliana* 16.2 (1982); for Spinoza's complete correspondence, see *Complete Works*.

5. While Venice, for example, had a far larger and more established Jewish community than did the Dutch republic, it was a community confined to a ghetto—not the case in Amsterdam.

6. The usual Latin word for race is *gens*. The more common term in Spinoza is *natio*, which is used here; it means literally a being born or birth, hence breed, stock, race, kind, or species; and, in a more restricted sense, a race of people or nation. In ecclesiastical Latin, when opposed to Christians, both terms refer to heathens.

7. TTP 20, par. 14. Simon Schama, *The Embarrassment of Riches* (Berkeley: University of California Press, 1988), 595–96, notes that the situation was very different indeed for the Romanies, i.e., Gypsies, during the same era. They were not tolerated outside fairs and sideshows and were afforded no rights and no residence within the Dutch republic. It is sometimes suggested that Spinoza's praise of Amsterdam may have been exaggerated in consideration of his audience.

8. Citing H. W. Blom and J. M. Kerkhoven, "A Letter concerning an Early Draft of Spinoza's Treatise on Religion and Politics?" *Studia Spinozana* 1 (1985): 371–77, Nadler (*Spinoza*, 133, 170) describes Spinoza as writing the TTP from 1665, having perhaps composed an earlier version of, or notes about, the biblical portions earlier, perhaps in the late 1650s.

9. See Nadler, *Spinoza*, 23–26, 74–75, 140–41.

10. Spinoza, *Complete Works*, 425 n. 6. Such laws are evidence that Jews were considered a separate race in some countries, Spain for example, in the sixteenth and seventeenth centuries.

11. See Schama, *Embarrassment*, 587–95 (esp. 590–91) for a multifaceted account of the lives of the Jews in Amsterdam, set in a broader context of seventeenth-century Dutch culture, for the monetary and eschatological reasons behind such tolerance as the Jews enjoyed. A more statistically oriented account of that history, notable for its treatment of the Dutch economy under empire and thus its involvement with slavery in the colonies, mostly later, is provided by Jonathan Israel, *The Dutch Republic: Its Rise, Greatness, and Fall, 1477–1806* (Oxford: Clarendon, 1995), chap. 35. For purposes of this chapter, much of the history of the period is drawn from Schama, *Embarrassment*, and from biographies of Spinoza mentioned elsewhere in these notes.

12. Trans. R. Mendes-Flohr in Vaz Dias and Van der Tak, *Spinoza Merchant*, 164, 170. See Nadler, *Spinoza*, chap. 6. It is quite likely that the content of the biblical exegesis later to make up the first fifteen chapters of the TTP was already becoming known to those close to Spinoza around the time of his banishment. The Jewish *cherem*, although usually translated "excommunication" by analogy to the Roman Catholic tradition, involved a number of curses as well as prohibitions on others in the community from associating with the person cast out.

13. The earliest biographies were collected into J. Freudenthal, *Die Lebensgeschichte Spinozas in Quellenschriften, Urkunden und Nichtamtlichen Nachrichten* (Leipzig: Von Veit, 1899), but a number of documents have come to light in recent years that address details omitted there. A useful guide to

recent sources is Hubertus G. Hubbeling, "Spinoza's Life: A Synopsis of the Sources and Some Documents," *Giornale critico della filosofia italiana* 8 (1977): 390–409, followed by several works by Wim Klever published since 1987; see especially Klever's "Spinoza's Life and Works," in *The Cambridge Companion to Spinoza*, ed. Don Garrett (Cambridge: Cambridge University Press, 1996), 13–60.

14. *Complete Works*, letter 47; cf. Nadler, *Spinoza*, 311–14.

15. *Principles of Cartesian Philosophy Demonstrated in the Geometric Manner* had been published by the same Rieuwertz in 1663, to which had been appended Spinoza's own *Metaphysical Thoughts*. Spinoza's *Short Treatise on God, Man, and His Well-Being*, written in Dutch, was not published in his lifetime, nor was his *Hebrew Grammar*; and Spinoza entreated Jarig Jelles in 1671 not to allow the translation of the TTP into Dutch (*Complete Works*, letter 44).

16. *Complete Works*, ix–xx; cf. Nadler, *Spinoza*, 322, for more detail and slight variations of the relevant dates.

17. To Simon De Vries in 1663, Spinoza says, "I should like you and all our acquaintances not to communicate my opinions to him" of Johannes Casearius, who was at the time living in the same house with, and being tutored by, the philosopher (*Complete Works*, letter 9). More famously, following some correspondence with the philosopher Gottfried Wilhelm Leibniz in 1671, Spinoza refused in 1675 the earnest request of Ehrenfried Walther Tschirnhaus, a young nobleman known to Spinoza, that Leibniz be granted permission to read the manuscript copy of the *Ethics*: "I think it imprudent to entrust my writings to him so hastily. I should first like to know what he is doing in France, and to hear our friend Tschirnhaus's opinion of him after a longer acquaintance and a closer knowledge of his character" (letter 72 to Georg Hermann Schuller, who had written to Spinoza on behalf of Tschirnhaus).

18. Margaret Gullan-Whur, *Within Reason: A Life of Spinoza* (New York: St. Martin's, 1998), 45, 328, uses "race" as a near synonym for "religion" when she attributes to Spinoza poignant later writings addressing racial oppression; the passages she cites, TTP 4 and 5, address what would now be called religious oppression. The later PT likewise names oppressive practices.

19. See PT 11.3–4. Spinoza's several discussions of slavery (e.g., TTP 16, par. 11; *Ethics* 4) refer to the enslavement of one who lives rather by pleasure than by reason. But see Matheron's "Femmes et serviteurs dans le démocratie spinoziste," in *Speculum Spinozanum*, ed. Siegfried Hessing (Boston: Routledge & Kegan Paul, 1977), 368–86.

20. Among the better known: Henry Oldenburg, Secretary of the Royal Society, was imprisoned in 1667 for "dangerous desseins and practises," presumed to include his correspondence with Spinoza during the second Anglo-Dutch War (Nadler, *Spinoza*, 260–61); Adriaan Koerbagh, whose views on religion, published in the vernacular Dutch, bore witness to the close attention he had paid to Spinoza's *Ethics* and TTP, was tortured, then died in prison in 1669 (ibid., 264–69); in August of 1672, the brothers Cornelis and Johan de Witt were killed and literally torn to pieces by a mob (ibid., 305–6); and Spinoza's Latin tutor from the years 1654–58, Franciscus Van Den Enden, an ex-Jesuit, was hanged for plotting against Louis XIV in 1674 (ibid., 106–7). Cf. Gullan-Whur, *Within Reason*, 214–23, 247–49.

21. *Complete Works*, letter 50. Shirley, the editor, notes connections to *Ethics*, pt. 4, scholium to proposition 37 (E4p37s11 in the common notation, used below) and to TTP 16.

22. My colleague Matt McKeon poses the question, What sort of condition is *conatus*? Necessary? Sufficient? Both? Neither? There is a direct sense in which the answer has to be "both" (E3p7 with E2def2), but the question is more interesting and challenging than I can pursue here, for it points to the difference between the physical concept of cohesion and the metaphysical concept of *conatus* in Spinoza's event ontology; the latter is more comprehensive.

23. This paragraph echoes "A Human Being Like Any Other: Like No Other," *Philosophical Forum* 18.2–3 (1986–87), 124–36, my attempt to use Spinoza's ontology to support women's resistance to apartheid and its feeder institutions such as individualism and capitalism in South Africa.

24. See Warren Montag's introduction to Etienne Balibar, *Spinoza and Politics* (London: Verso, 1998; originally published in French in 1985), p. ix. Montag goes on to say that "in declaring God to be the immanent cause of the world, Spinoza rejected not only every dualism of spirit and matter, but also the dualisms of unity and diversity, of the temporal and the eternal." It is Montag who suggests Engels was "speaking as a Spinozist rather than as a Marxist when he defined materialism as the effort to 'conceive nature just as it is, without any foreign admixture,' " in *Ludwig Feuerbach and the End of Classical German Philosophy* (Moscow: Progress Publishers, 1969), 36. Montag has far more to say about the reception of Spinoza among Marxists than I can present here.

25. See Louis Althusser's "The Only Materialist Tradition, Part I: Spinoza," in *New Spinoza*, ed. Montag and Stolze, 3–19; Althusser describes Spinoza as a detour in his own path to Marx (3). Althusser also wrote on Spinoza in his *Essays in Self-Criticism* (London: New Left Books, 1976; originally published in French in 1974), but it is perhaps more significant that Althusser's formidable *Reading Capital* (London: New Left Books, 1970; originally published in French in 1965) employed Spinoza's method of textual critique. See also Macherey's *Hegel ou Spinoza* (Paris: François Maspero, 1979).

26. Antonio Negri, *The Savage Anomaly: The Power of Spinoza's Metaphysics and Politics*, trans. Michael Hardt (Minneapolis: University of Minnesota Press, 1991; originally published in Italian in 1981), 122 and 215. Negri offers much interesting commentary on the secondary literature surrounding Spinoza's political philosophy in his "*Reliqua Desiderantur*: A Conjecture for a Definition of the Concept of Democracy in the Final Spinoza," in *New Spinoza*, ed. Montag and Stolze, 219–48, prefiguring his important collaboration with Hardt in *Empire* (Cambridge: Harvard University Press, 2000). See Foucault's *The Archaeology of Knowledge* (New York: Pantheon, 1972; originally published in French in 1969). Deleuze wrote much on Spinoza, but most important is his *Expressionism in Philosophy: Spinoza*, trans. Martin Joughin (New York: Zone Books, 1990; originally published in French in 1968).

27. If right were simply identical to power, then we would be back with Thrasymachus and Socrates in Plato's *Republic*: might makes right. But identity is not their relation, nor can one justify the other. Rather, right and power are coextensive, as argued by Edwin Curley in "Kissinger, Spinoza, and Genghis Khan," in *Cambridge Companion*, ed. Garrett, 321–22.

28. E. San Juan Jr., "What Lessons about Race and Ethnicity Can We Learn from Spinoza?" *Lens-grinder Journal* 1.1 (2002), http://www.tlgjournal.com/Articles/TLGVol1No1Art-01PV.htm, accessed October 23, 2002. San Juan follows the linguistic use of Gullan-Whur, *Within Reason*, in his identification of passages about race and ethnicity. An expanded version of his Internet article appears as *Spinoza and the Terror of Racism* (Sheffield: Sheffield Hallam University Press, 2002).

29. Marin Terpstra, "An Analysis of Power Relations and Class Relations in Spinoza's *Tractatus Politicus*," *Studia Spinozana* 9 (1993): 79–105.

30. A particularly broad approach is taken by David Freeman, "Spinoza on Self-Consciousness and Nationalism," *History of European Ideas* 16.4–6 (1993): 915–20. Best known is the reactionary work of Leo Strauss; see both *Spinoza's Critique of Religion* (New York: Schocken, 1965), and "How to Study Spinoza's Theologico-Political Treatise," in *Persecution and the Art of Writing* (Glencoe: Free Press, 1952), 142–201. Advocating a liberal democratic interpretation of Spinoza is Lewis Samuel Feuer, *Spinoza and the Rise of Liberalism* (Boston: Beacon, 1958), joined recently by Steven B. Smith, *Spinoza, Liberalism, and the Question of Jewish Identity* (New Haven: Yale University Press, 1997).

31. Spinoza's geometrical method implies that, given the definitions and axioms of part 1, one can derive all its propositions. His ontological argument for the existence of substance appears at E1p1–11.

32. This is a difficult Spinozian concept, one that even the secondary literature cannot be counted on to represent accurately; it remains common to see Spinoza misleadingly described as holding a theory of *parallel* attributes. A classic and accessible account of Spinoza's theory of the identity of the attributes is Marx Wartofsky, "Action and Passion: Spinoza's Construction of a Scientific Psychology," in *Spinoza: A Collection of Critical Essays*, ed. Marjorie Grene (New York: Doubleday, 1973), sections 1–4. Michael Della Rocca, in a series of stunning advances on the topic, has made it more difficult for parallelism to be attributed to Spinoza. See his "Causation and Spinoza's Claim of Identity," *History of Philosophy Quarterly* 8.3 (1991): 265–76; "Spinoza's Argument for the Identity Theory," *Philosophical Review* 102.2 (1993): 183–213; and "Spinoza's Substance Monism" in *Spinoza: Metaphysical Themes*, ed. Olli Koistinen and John Biro (Oxford: Oxford University Press, 2002), 11–37.

33. In the matter of Spinozian individuals, my position has been influenced by conversations with Joe VanZandt; by Matheron's *Individu et communauté chez Spinoza* (Paris: Éditions de Minuit, 1969); and by Jeffrey Bernstein's "The Ethics of Spinoza's Physics," *North American Spinoza Society Monograph* 10 (2002), 3–19.

34. Donald Davidson attempted to preserve the identity while developing the view that there is an incommensurability of human apprehension between ideas and the things of which they are the ideas—referring to E2p7; see "Spinoza's Causal Theory of the Affects," in *Desire and Affect: Spinoza as Psychologist; Papers Presented at the Third Jerusalem Conference*, ed. Yirmiyahu Yovel (New York: Little Room, 1999), 95–111.

35. It is notoriously difficult to articulate what Spinoza means by the idea of a particular idea, i.e., an idea conceived under the attribute of thought. Since further exposition would lead us far

from Spinoza and race, I shall not attempt it. But this much is clear: we humans cannot simultaneously apprehend the attributes of thought and extension, even if we determine intellectually that they are identical.

36. I thank Ralph Dumain, who gave me this formulation upon reading an early draft; I could not have said it better.

37. To temper Matheron (*Individu et communauté*), Steven Barbone offers this useful example in "What Counts as an Individual for Spinoza?" in *Metaphysical Themes*, ed. Koistinen and Biro, 89–112. Barbone denies the "global *conatus*" of the school (100), which I affirm following Matheron (42). Consistently, Barbone appears to deny that the state has a mind, whereas in my view Spinoza would deny only independent *consciousness* to the mind of the state, the citizens of which are conscious. My objection in principle to labeling states and races "quasi-individuals," as Barbone suggests (following Lee Rice, "Individuation in Leibniz and Spinoza," *North American Spinoza Society Monograph* 8 [1999]: 19–33), is that all inanimate objects would similarly lose their status as individuals—and that would be incompatible with Spinoza's text.

38. See Bill Lawson, "Social Disappointment and the Black Sense of Self," in *Existence in Black*, ed. Lewis Gordon (New York: Routledge, 1996), 149–56.

39. Freedom for Spinoza consists in self-determination. The will always and without exception acts from necessity, i.e., under constraint (E2p32). That is, for any action there is a determinate cause or causes, each of which is similarly constrained by cause. But we label those actions "free" the causes of which are our own *reason* (in Spinoza's restricted sense of that term).

40. TTP 3, pars. 19–21. Spinoza continues, "The Chinese . . . too, religiously observe the custom of the pigtail which sets them apart from all other people, and they have preserved themselves as a separate people for so many thousands of years that they far surpass all other nations in antiquity."

41. See E2p13le4. There is a weak sense (under the attribute of extension) in which modes of substance persist, i.e., under the guarantee of the conservation of matter and energy; but that does not imply that an individual qua individual endures, much less that it is eternal; when there is no *conatus*, there is no longer an individual properly so called. So long as an individual mode of substance endures in space-time, its mind expresses the actual existence of its body; with the destruction of the individual's body, the eternal part remains: "we assign to the human mind the kind of duration that can be defined by time only in so far as the mind expresses the actual existence of the body, an existence that is explicated through duration and can be defined by time. That is, we do not assign duration to the mind except while the body endures (E2p8c)" (E5p23). Thus Spinoza makes explicit for human beings what I extrapolate for individuals more generally. On this point, Joe Van-Zandt has been especially helpful.

42. PT 2.13. The tension between the TTP and the PT can be seen in the two quotations of this paragraph, demonstrating again the problems one faces philosophically when working strictly from Spinoza's political works. A better strategy is to find what follows from the ontological and epistemological work.

43. "Spinoza denounced any understanding of humanity as an *imperium in imperio*. In other words, he refused to accord any laws to human nature that were different from the laws of nature as a whole. Donna Haraway carries on Spinoza's project in our day as she insists on breaking down the barriers we pose among the human, the animal, and the machine. If we are to conceive Man as separate from nature, then Man does not exist. This recognition is precisely the death of Man" (Hardt and Negri, *Empire*, 91).

44. Negri (*Savage Anomaly*, 21) says as much in the last sentence of his first chapter: "Spinoza's philosophy is truly a timeless philosophy: Its time is the future!"

45. My colleague Bill Lawson pushed me relentlessly on this issue and I am indebted to him for not giving up.

| 4 |

Imagining an Inundation of Australians; or,
Leibniz on the Principles of Grace and Race

PETER FENVES

Leibniz has an ambiguous position in the history of racial "science." The vision that informs all of his major philosophical speculation runs counter to classificatory systems that depend on the idea of a generational series, for all substances are independent of one another. Only for this reason does the creator of these substances need to establish harmony among them in advance of their creation. This independence is doubly important for all self-conscious monadic substances: any common trait that can legitimately be ascribed to them must be well founded not only in the principles of nature but in those of grace as well. Race scarcely seems to be among the traits conducive to the principles of grace. Nevertheless, Leibniz's name is often found in lists of those who were early proponents of a racial system of human classification. This chapter explores the source of this ambiguity.

The entire chapter requires a caveat, however: Leibniz's writings are so vast, his interests so wide, his thought so intricate, and his influence at once so pervasive and so shallow that everything I propose here must remain preliminary. There is as yet no complete edition of his works, and many of the texts that would have to be reviewed for an adequate account of his conception of race—in particular, his immense series of historical, chronological, and genealogical studies— are available only in rare volumes or are still stored away in various archives. Many of the sentences in this chapter are therefore accompanied by a silent addendum: "to my knowledge."

| | |

A MISREPRESENTATION

Leibniz has little to say about the question of race, and yet, strangely enough, it is not uncommon to find his name among the list of earlier proponents of a new, racial division of human species. For it is often said that Leibniz concurs with— and gives credence to—the novel representation of supranational distinctions that François Bernier first proposes in his essay "A New Division of the Earth, by the

Different Species or Races of Man" (1684).[1] Leibniz was doubtless familiar with Bernier's anonymously published contribution to the *Journal des Sçavants*, since his work also appeared in the pages of this important organ of the early Enlightenment. And there is no doubt that Leibniz vaguely remembered having perused Bernier's essay, which is often identified as the first use of the term *race* as a technical term of anthropological speculation. On January 29, 1697, Leibniz writes the following to Johan Gabriel Sparwenfeld, a Swedish scholar with whom he conducted an extensive correspondence about the genesis and structure of Slavic languages: "If it is true that the Calmucs as well as the Moguls and the Tartars of China depend on the Grand Lama in matters of religion, it is possible that this says something about the relation among their languages and the origin of these peoples. It is simply that the size and constitution of their body is so different among them. I remember reading somewhere (but I cannot recall where)"—the reference is doubtless to Bernier's essay, which appeared thirteen years earlier—"that a certain voyager divided human beings into certain tribes, races, or classes [*tribus, races, ou classes*]. He assigned a particular race to the Lapps and Samoyeds, a certain to the Chinese and neighboring peoples; another to the Negroes, still another to the Cafres or Hottentots. In America there is a marvelous difference between the Galibis or Caribbean, for example, who have a great deal of value and just as much spirit, and those of Paraguay, who seem to be children or youths all their lives." To this Leibniz immediately adds: "This does not prevent all the human beings who inhabit the globe from being all of the same race [*tous d'une meme race*], which has been altered by the different climates, as we see animals and plants changing their nature and becoming better or degenerating."[2]

Unlike the vast majority of Leibniz's correspondence, his letter to Sparwenfeld was published relatively soon after it was written—in 1718, to be exact, in a collection of miscellaneous papers entitled *Otium hanoveranum*. Johann Friedrich Blumenbach read this rather inconspicuous volume and incorporated certain passages from Leibniz's letter into the last version of his *De generis humani varietate nativa* (1795).[3] Blumenbach's intention is unmistakable: he wishes to name Leibniz as a forerunner of his own scientific program of racial anthropology. Leibniz's philosophical program by Blumenbach's time may have lost some of the prestige it once enjoyed; but the distaste for "essays in theodicy," which found its most famous expression in Voltaire's travesties of philosophical optimism, did not destroy Leibniz's reputation altogether; on the contrary, he was still considered a preeminent scholar, mathematician, and scientist. And his philosophical speculation was by no means a mere curiosity, especially after the publication of the *New Essays in Human Understanding* in the second half of the century. By naming Leibniz as his predecessor, Blumenbach could therefore present himself in very good company indeed: the co-inventor of the infinitesimal calculus could also be seen as a co-inventor of the scientific theory of race. And Blumenbach's identification of Leibniz as his precursor was not without effect. Scholars to this day have followed suit, as they cite certain passages from his letter to Sparwenfeld as evidence that Leibniz ratified the "new division" of the human species into different "species or races."[4]

Blumenbach, however, misrepresents the explicit intention of Leibniz's letter. Not only does the later scholar take it out of its context—which is perhaps understandable, given its appearance in *Otium hanoveranum*[5]—but he fails to emphasize the degree to which Leibniz remains wary of Bernier's proposal, even as he vaguely recalls its outlines. Instead of ratifying Bernier's "new division," Leibniz mentions it only in passing, while encouraging the addressee of the letter to direct his attention to a completely different terrain of scholarship, namely the field of world-historical linguistics. In other words, human language—not "tribe, race, or class"—is under discussion from beginning to end. And this is scarcely surprising, since Leibniz initiated the correspondence with Sparwenfeld in order to acquaint himself with the newest research into Old Church Slavonic, the first modern lexicon of which the Swedish resident of Moscow was then in the process of preparing. Immediately after his uncertain recollection of Bernier's essay, Leibniz proposes that Sparwenfeld seriously pursue a project with which a certain Father Thomassin has recently toyed, namely the project of producing a detailed account of "the harmony of languages by relating them all to Hebrew." The result of this would be the demonstration "that the human genus [*le genre humain*] derives entirely from Adam" (A, 4, 1:545). Leibniz, in short, asks a well-respected scholar to do what an amateurish priest cannot: establish a scientifically valid defense of monogenesis by undertaking "the grand and beautiful enterprise" of demonstrating the inner unity of apparently unrelated languages. In comparison with this project, Bernier's proposal is hardly worth discussing, even if he mentions it in passing. Thus does Leibniz forget the new "science" of racial anthropology immediately after he recalls its initial expression.

|||

AN IMMODEST PROPOSAL

The harmony of human languages is one of the dominant motifs of Leibniz's thought. But it is, of course, not the sole motif. Nor is the metaphysical doctrine of the "preestablished harmony" between the soul and the body, which Leibniz first announces in an essay published in the *Journal des Sçavants*, the title of which is strangely reminiscent of Bernier's "New Division": "A New System of the Nature and Communication of Substances" (1695). In most circumstances Leibniz tends to emphasize agreement over disagreement and harmony over discord, going so far as to assert that "I have found that most of the sects are right in a good part of what they assert, but not so right in what they deny."[6] Polemic, in other words, is not to his liking. And to this effect, as a longtime jurist and some-time diplomat, he sought to recreate a unified Christian order. From this perspective, his interest in Sparwenfeld's inquiries into the history of Slavic languages is readily comprehensible: Sparwenfeld's inquiries into Old Church Slavonic might help identify and thereby alleviate the metaphysical-linguistic misunderstanding around which the schism between Western Catholicism and Eastern Orthodoxy originally formed. If this schism can be repaired, so, too, can the one internal to the Western church.

Yet Leibniz's lifelong aversion to polemics did not prevent him from recommending war—indeed, urging that real war be waged against those whom he considered enemies of the Christian-European order. Leibniz may have dedicated himself to the project of "perpetual peace." Kant, of course, borrowed this famous term and its corresponding joke—"it lies only in the graveyard"[7]—from his predecessor. But war could still be, for him, a means of peace. For the sake of re-unifying and securing European Christianity, Leibniz offers Louis XIV an unsolicited proposal under the modest title *Consilium Aegyptiacum* (1671). The primary purpose of this "Egyptian Plan" is to divert Catholic France's imperial aspirations away from Protestant Holland and direct them toward the Turkish "barbarians" (Leibniz's term), who control Egypt, "the Queen of the East." There is no doubt that Leibniz was disturbed by the contradiction between humanistic universalism, which would recognize no rationale for aggressive warfare, and Christian particularism, which can identify a reason for war in the rightness of the Christian cause. Indeed, this contradiction was so disturbing to Leibniz that he resolved it in a particularly brutal manner. Non-Christians are nothing but nonhumans: "The following saying of a wise man is right," Leibniz admonishes Louis, "that a powerful and wise monarch is like the guide of the whole human race [*generis humani*]: that he is not only *philhellena* [friend of the Greeks] nor *philoromaion* [friend of the Romans] but *philanthropon*. And his war is not against human beings but against beasts (that is, barbarians), and not for the purpose of massacre but to defend his interests" (A, 4, 1:379).

This representation of the non-Christian world as a bestiary in the conclusion to the *Consilium Aegyptiacum* is not an isolated aberration, moreover. It receives a particularly virulent exposition and expansion in a brief addendum to this plan, which was first published in 1931 and has yet to receive much critical attention.[8] The addendum is even more audacious than the *Consilium*, since it is, as it were, a universalization of the particularism that gives shape to the latter. And this particularism no longer has anything to do with religious doctrine; instead, it is based solely on physiological characteristics. Leibniz does not use the term *race*, which is hardly surprising since it has no exact Latin equivalent; but as a young jurist and would-be diplomat—he was only twenty-five at the time of its composition—he presupposes a racially defined division of the globe, according to which the rulers of Europe have a right to dominate the original inhabitants of the other continents. The title of the addendum to the *Consilium* says as much: "A Method to Institute a New, Invincible Militia That Can Subjugate the Entire Earth, Easily Seize Control over Egypt or Establish American Colonies" (A, 4, 1:408). In 1671, for the first time in the history of philosophy, Leibniz explicitly proposes the principle of reason: "*nihil est sine ratione*" (nothing is without a reason)[9] (G, 4:232). And in the very same year Leibniz proposes a "method" (*modus*) for global conquest. This coincidence could scarcely be an accident, as the principle itself implies. Not only does the addendum to the *Consilium Aegyptiacum* demonstrate that the aggressive war it proposes is only the beginning; it also indicates that the imperative of method is intimately associated with certain imperial ambitions.

Paul Ritter, the editor of the volume of Leibniz's *Sämtliche Schriften* in which the addendum to the *Consilium Aegyptiacum* appears, dubs it—without any evidence—a mere "fantasy," although it is no more fantastic than the *Consilium*, which Leibniz certainly proposed in deadly earnest.[10] At any rate, here in brief is the new method of planetary conquest: take possession of a relatively large island like Madagascar; expel its current inhabitants; bring slaves from "barbarian" regions like "Africa, Arabia, America, and New Guinea, etc." (A, 4, 1:408); keep only the young males around twelve years old; suppress any independence of will that they might manifest; and form them, finally, into expert soldiers who so completely submit themselves to their European-Christian masters that they lose all concern for their own welfare, with the result that they will terrify all potential enemies of the new *imperium*. Leibniz leaves no doubt about the peoples and places from which the twelve-year-old boys will be stolen, since, after naming "Africa, Arabia, America, and New Guinea," he proceeds to produce a more detailed list: "Without any distinction Ethiopians, Nigerians, Angolians, Caribbeans [*Cannibals*], Canadians, Hurons can be used" (A, 4, 1:408). And immediately after having produced this second list of potential captives, Leibniz exclaims: "What a fine bunch of semibeasts [*Pulchrum concilium semibestiarum*]" (A, 4, 1:408)—with no indication, however, of how such a hybrid could come into being. Nor, indeed, does Leibniz indicate the criterion by which human being should be distinguished from beast.

The absence of a criterion for the distinction between human being and beast is no small matter in this context, moreover, for Leibniz cannot use the criterion upon which philosophers have traditionally relied—that human beings "have logos," whereas beasts do not. The imperial plan depends entirely on the ability of the youthful captives to speak in a reasonably effective manner; otherwise, they could not follow complex military orders. And the principle of division that will make the captives into members of well-defined and well-trained military companies is entirely linguistic: the militia is to be divided into "as many classes as nations, that is, languages" (A, 4, 1:408). What distinguishes the various peoples he names, in other words, is not a racially but, rather, a linguistically defined nationality. And as Leibniz emphasizes, it is absolutely essential that national-linguistic distinctions remain in place. Speakers of one language should not be able to communicate with speakers of another; otherwise, all of the captives might collectively recognize themselves as captives and violently liberate themselves from their European masters. This, then, is the central motif of the new method of world domination: "Take care lest troops of diverse languages ever get used to one another and thereby understand one another" (A, 4, 1:408). Leibniz's many plans for the development and deployment of a universal language assumes a less brilliant hue in light of this violent recommendation: the ability to translate one language into another is not only a scientific desideratum; it is also—and perhaps primarily—a means of mastery. The absolute master, who, as such, exercises control over the entire planet, can translate all human languages into his own. Those whom this master controls, by contrast, can understand only their own captive kind.

Leibniz goes even further in the same direction, moreover, as he completes his preliminary exposition of the principles of selection with the following directions: "The same things must be guarded against among men of the same language" (A, 4, 1:408). Although all captives must be able to speak, they cannot be allowed to exercise this capacity for the very same reason that members of different nations are prohibited from communicating with one another. The activation of linguistic capacities, Leibniz subtly suggests, is always in league with liberation. What, after all, would the captives more urgently discuss among themselves than their accounts of captivity—and strategies for regaining their freedom? And this emancipatory power of language is irrepressible and ubiquitous. Leibniz does not explicitly say so; but even as he contemptuously calls the captives "semi-beasts," he recognizes that they are not fit "by nature" for slavery: if they ever get the chance to speak with one another, they are sure to revolt—and perhaps form themselves into a counter-European-Christian army. Leibniz sees only a single measure against this threat: the captives must be made into philosophers, which is to say, into human beings who are *least* in need of language, inasmuch as they can intuit what everyone else knows only by means of symbols. Leibniz thus concludes his preliminary exposition of the composition of the invincible militia in the following manner: "Let a Pythagorean taciturnness be introduced among them; let them be permitted to say nothing among themselves except when necessary or when ordered" (A, 4, 1:408). Whether Leibniz was conscious of the irony contained in this recommendation cannot be known; but in any case this much is clear: the reference to Pythagoras, the first philosopher-mathematician, suggests that the inventor of the infinitesimal calculus and the author of the proposal for planetary conquest recognizes, perhaps against his will, that the "semi-beasts" whom he plans to form into an invincible militia could outsmart their master and become a new breed of Pythagoreans.

And from the perspective of Leibniz's mature thought, which culminates in the famous "Monadology" (1714), this method of terrestrial conquest appears even stranger still. The soldiers whom he envisages appear as the very models of monadic individuality: none can directly communicate with each other; all communication is mediated by their master, who, as he forms the militia, makes sure that no direct communication is ever required. This is to say, in monadological terms, all "windows" are closed.[11] And yet both monads and members of the invincible militia are so well coordinated that they act in perfect harmony nevertheless. The military monasticism Leibniz proposes is, in effect, monadic: none of the soldiers is affected by the sight of their enemies; such is the source of their strength. And none is affected by their own plight; such is the force of their isolation. Leibniz may have had only an inkling of the metaphysical principles that would give direction to his later work; but the addendum to the Consilium Aegyptiacum anticipates—in a perverse form, to be sure—the vision of the ultimate structure of reality that Leibniz would seek to capture.

| | |

RACE AND MONADS

To my knowledge, Leibniz never again proposes—or even alludes to—the imperial project that finds expression in the addendum to the Consilium Aegyptiacum. Once Louis XIV invaded Holland rather than Egypt, the Consilium Aegyptiacum was in any case a moribund document, and Leibniz soon turned against the imperial-minded king, whom he would sarcastically call "the most Christian War God."[12] Yet the addendum to the Consilium Aegyptiacum cannot simply be dismissed as a mere aberration. The list of potential captives corresponds in large part to Leibniz's geopolitical imaginary, which accords a certain superiority to the civilizations at the far ends of the Eurasian landmass: Western Europe and China. Leibniz took an interest in the work of Sparwenfeld for precisely this reason: the lands inhabited by the Slavic peoples are a bridge between the two extremes. A careful study of Slavic languages could therefore prove to be an indispensable element not only of a reunited Christendom but of a European-Chinese synthesis.[13] What Leibniz did not have at his disposal and, as his correspondence with Sparwenfeld indicates, made no efforts to develop was a theory of race that would provide a physiological basis for a geopolitics of historical languages. As Leibniz explains in numerous places, languages are not only means of communication but also archives of knowledge. A more developed language is therefore a sign that greater levels of knowledge have been collectively achieved. Never perhaps is this thought more succinctly expressed and more closely linked to an outstanding political problem than in the following passage of a short text probably written in the 1680s entitled "Einige patriotischen Gedanken" (Some Patriotic Thoughts):

> I am of the opinion that the nations [Nationen] that develop and perfect their languages thereby have a great advantage in sharpening their intellect. For one must affirm that words are not only signs with which we can reveal our intentions to others but also signs with which we can speak with ourselves, in our interior, and consider what experience shows. And the better or more convenient and clearer the signs, the better the intellect can operate; in this way, one can calculate better with the numerals currently used than Roman numerals. . . . Therefore, when striking and well-differentiated words are common in a language, many good thoughts and insights are, as it were, available to the mind. (A, 4, 3:362–63)

That one language and system of notation is superior to another does not by itself mean the nation that speaks this language enjoys the same political or legal superiority. The virtues of the German language, which Leibniz champions in "Einige patriotischen Gedanken" and elsewhere,[14] do not make the Germanic nation superior to neighboring ones. And for this reason, linguistic superiority remains a puzzle. A language can be superior to others, even if everything articulated in this language is below the level of things articulated in inferior ones. The paradigmatic case of this enigma is, again, German: "And I must often confront the astonishing fact that so many bad books currently appear in the German language" (A, 4, 3:363). As far as I have been able to discover, Leibniz never sought to resolve this enigma with reference to a physiological quality like "race." This does not mean, however, that he was entirely unfamiliar with the term. In its conventional sense, as a synonym for kind or species, especially of the human variety, it appears in his French texts and letters. But to my knowledge, Leibniz defines the term only once. It appears in the notes he appended to John Wilkins's Essay towards a Real Character and a Philosophical Language (1668). Following Wilkins's principles of division, Leibniz elucidates and defines a wide range of words—from the most general terms in Latin (*aliquid*, *nihil*, and *res*) to specific grammatical connectives in English. Of particular prominence are fifty or so words for "mixed relations pertaining to discrete quantities," including the relations among things or phenomena (as opposed to relations among words or times); the last of these terms is *race*, for which Leibniz proposes the following elucidation: "*Race, genus, Geschlecht*, generational series. *Genealogy* is the explication of this series."[15] Leibniz does not so much define as translate *race*—first into Latin and then into German. Neither translation helps much, however, since the Latin and German words are even more equivocal than the French and English ones. "Generational series," by contrast, is relatively univocal: a "racial" relation is causal; more exactly, to use the term *race*, one must be able to identify a class whose members generate other elements who are capable of the same action.[16]

Nowhere in his notes to Wilkins's treatise does Leibniz worry about the field of application in which the causal term *generation* is valid; but in at least one place in these extensive notes Leibniz—perhaps for the first time—introduces a term that would render any use of *race* unacceptable in a strictly metaphysical context, namely, *species monadica*. As "the absolute lowest species," each *species monadica* must be "an individual" (A, 6, 4:31–32). The only generative series in which a "monadic species" can enter is that of its creator, who, for its part, transcends the series simply because it is, by definition, not an element of the class it creates. And if the world is ultimately composed of the infinite complex of "monadic species," as Leibniz will argue again and again, in various different manners and with a series of corresponding terms, then the following conclusion is inevitable: the concept of race is not applicable to reality. In reality, there are no species other than monadic ones, which, as such, allow for only a single member. The causal character of racial terms makes race illegitimate within the parameters of a strict logical-metaphysical exposition. Things do not cause other things to happen. God is the sole cause in the strict sense of the term, which is to say, all things are of the same race, and each thing is its own species. In short, everything in the strict sense of the term *thing* is a *species monadica*, and these species owe their origin to a single cause, whose serial calculus rules out the possibility that two things are, in reality, of the same kind.

Such is a brief outline of Leibniz's metaphysics, which doubtless undergoes considerable alterations of terminology and emphasis but which nevertheless retains a single vision: reality is composed of the best possible complex of compossible "monadic species." None of this is meant to suggest, however, that Leibniz is uninterested in grounding the various kinds, classes, and orders to which human beings can legitimately be said to belong; on the contrary, his wide-ranging juridical, political, and diplomatic efforts, including the *Consilium Aegyp-*

tiacum, are concerned with nothing else. The question at every turn, however, is this: given that, in reality, there are only "substantial forms" or "monads," each of which is a "monadic species," under what condition is it justifiable to use a term for a higher species, which is to say, a species that has more than a single member? "Human" is justifiable because all those who can be thus predicated belong to a realm from which merely natural things are excluded, namely, that of "grace." The term "Christian" is justifiable, moreover, inasmuch as it distinguishes those who accept their inclusion in the realm of grace from those who do not. Social and political predicates can be justified accordingly—as marks of membership in the institutions through which the realm of grace establishes terrestrial equivalents. Such is the case with "national" predicates—German, French, English, and so forth—that are removed from Christian doctrine. That the *respublica Christiana* is divided into different nations is not only acceptable; it is in keeping with the principles of divine justice, which demands difference as an indispensable feature of unity.[17] Leibniz can thus present himself as a German patriot, whose loyalty to his fatherland largely consists in opposing French expansion on the European continent, on the one hand, and in championing the usefulness of the German language for the sciences and arts, on the other. Just as the highly diversified political and social predicates by which Christianity establishes its earthly institutions are justifiable, so, too, are the national predicates through which the peoples of the Christian republic are distinguished for the greater glory of God. And the composition of the Christian republic does not preclude loyalty to the particular land in which one happens to be born; on the contrary, as he writes at the end of "Einige patriotischen Gedanken," "I am of the opinion that everyone, from the prince down to the peasant, is required to perform some martial service for the fatherland whenever it is necessary" (A, 4, 3:365).

The question remains, however, whether *race* is one of the class-terms by which human beings can be divided—whether, in other words, it is legitimate to describe individual members of the species in terms of subspecial yet supranational "generational series." As far as I have been able to discover, Leibniz never poses this question in so many words; only in his vague reminiscence of Bernier's essay does he even enter into its vicinity, and even here he hesitates over the appropriate class-term: whereas Bernier oscillates between *species* and *race*, Leibniz cannot decide whether the term in question should be *tribe*, *race*, or *class*. At any rate, as the correspondence with Sparwenfeld indicates, Leibniz takes an interest in this question only insofar as it is posed within the same theological-political context as his many reflection on, and defenses of, a diverse yet unified *respublica Christiana*. He may say nothing in his letter to Sparwenfeld about the realm of grace; but it motivates his entire correspondence, to say nothing of his specific plea for a scientific argument for monogenesis. As for a neutral, non-political-theological justification for the application of the term *race*—or any equivalent term—there is, to my knowledge, none in his enormous literary corpus. What Blumenbach wanted from Leibniz is nowhere to be found.

| | |

AN INUNDATION OF "AUSTRALIANS"

And there is good reason to suppose that the mature Leibniz would have positively rejected any proposal in the direction of a neutral term for subspecial and supranational "generational series." A rarely cited passage in the *New Essays* (written around 1703) indicates as much. At issue in this passage is not the question of race per se but, rather, in Locke's words, "the frequent Production of Monsters, in all Species of Animals, of Changelings, and other strange Issues of humane Birth."[18] For Locke, the existence of hybrids is sufficient proof that any system of classification expresses only the nominal essence of things: class-terms have nothing in principle to do with the real essences of the things classified. Leibniz, by contrast, argues that the existence of supposed "monsters" or "changelings" is merely an indication that the "lowest species" has not yet been determined. And this indetermination extends further than is generally supposed. What we call gold, for example, may turn out to be in reality two substances, each of which deserves a different name. This immensely complex problem cannot be discussed here, of course; it is among the most controversial elements in contemporary arguments about "naming and necessity." But the motivation for Leibniz's uncompromising critique of Locke's account of the "strange Issues of humane Birth" is nevertheless clear from the start: the assault on real essences does damage to the definition of the human being as a rational animal. And once damage is done to this definition, the fundamental distinction between the realm of nature and that of grace begins to totter in turn.[19] Nowhere is this underlying motivation for Leibniz's critique of Locke more in evidence than in the following passage, which suddenly adopts the term *race* and reads as though it were the vengeful inversion of the scenario for world conquest that Leibniz had proposed some thirty years earlier:

> All that can be said about these general propositions is that if we take the human being as a lowest species and restricted to the race of Adam [*race d'Adam*], then one will absolutely not have any properties of the human being that one calls *in quarto modo* or that can be predicated of him in a reciprocal or simply convertible proposition, unless it is predicated provisionally, as in the

saying: *the human being is the only rational animal.* And by taking the *human being* for those of our race, the *provisional* [proposition] consists in understanding in advance that he is the only rational being among the animals that are known to us; for it could happen that some day there would be other animals that have everything in common with all the human beings who have ever lived, but who have a different origin. It is as if imaginary Australians inundated our countries [*C'est comme si les Australiens imaginaires venaient inonder nos contrées*]: it is likely that some way would be found of distinguishing them from us. But if this is not the case, and supposing God had forbidden the mingling of these races [*le melange de ces races*] and that Jesus Christ had redeemed only our own, then it would be necessary to try to make artificial marks to distinguish the races from one another. No doubt there would be an inner difference, but since it could not be made recognizable, one would have to rely solely on the *extrinsic denomination* of birth, and one would try to accompany it with a durable artificial mark that would provide an *intrinsic denomination* and a permanent way of distinguishing our race from theirs. (A, 6, 6:400–401)

To this remarkable scenario, for which there is no corresponding passage in Locke's *Essay on Human Understanding*, Leibniz immediately adds a caveat: "These are all nothing but fictions, for we have no need to resort to this kind of differentiation, since we are the only rational animals on this globe" (A, 6, 6:401).[20] "Australians" will not inundate "our countries," and if something like this comes to pass, they can be converted to Christianity and therefore enter into "our race." As he turns his gaze toward Africa and the Americas, Leibniz momentarily names "New Guinea" (A, 4, 1:408) as one of the places from which a Europeans prince could capture adolescent boys for incorporation into his invincible militia. In the scenario of the *New Essays*, however, Australia attains a certain prominence: it functions as Europe in reverse—with one major difference: nowhere does Leibniz imagine that the Australians will use Europeans as captives for the purpose of global domination. Instead of being invaders, they are migrants, who, so it seems, merely wish to settle in Europe—and can be allowed to do so, since they are, despite their foreignness, capable of conversion to Christianity.[21]

All of this *must* be fictitious, however; otherwise, the "catholic" character of Christianity comes under suspicion. Unless all those who appear to be human beings can in principle be saved—regardless of the doctrinal principle that, as Leibniz states in the *Theodicy*, "the elect are only very few"[22]—there can be no *principles* of grace. And if grace is as unprincipled as the term suggests, then suspicions will likewise be cast on the universality of the principle of reason. Not only does Leibniz's political theology therefore demand that the term *race* be applicable to human beings only insofar as it is synonymous with *species*; so, too, does the principle of reason. The fiction of Europe inundated by Australians is nevertheless fully warranted, for, as Leibniz proceeds to explain, philosophy cannot fail to invent counterfactual possibilities—in this case, the possibility of an unredeemable "race"—for the purpose of clarifying its fundamental concepts:

> These are all nothing but fictions. . . . Nevertheless, these fictions allow us to gain knowledge of the nature of ideas, of substances, and of general truths about them. But if the human being is not taken for the *lowest species*, nor as the species of rational animals of the race of Adam, and if, instead of all this, the word meant a genus common to several species—to which only a single known race now belonged but to which others could still belong, distinguishable either by birth or by other natural marks, as, for example, by the imaginary Australians [*feints Australiens*]—then, I say, there would be *reciprocal propositions* about this genus, and current definitions of the human being would not be *provisional*. (A, 6, 6:401).

The fiction of Australians inundating the shores of Europe is of service to philosophy only insofar as it is a logical possibility—which, however, happens to be impossible for strictly theological reasons: it would render Christianity into a local doctrine, applicable only to a segment of the rational animals on earth. Logical and theological possibility part ways at the intersection of Europe and Australia, so to speak. Yet, as Leibniz recognizes at the conclusion of this reflection on "racial" counterfactuals, there is one further element of philosophical analysis that he has entirely ignored—the element of history. A consideration of historical change makes his entire discussion of provisional propositions itself provisional. With respect to the definition of gold Leibniz has nothing to worry about: gold is nonhistorical. This is not true of races, according to Leibniz, as he uneasily concedes in the concluding sentence of his discussion. And with this inconclusive conclusion he changes the topic: "I have been supposing up until now that the race does not degenerate or change; but if the same race were to develop into another species, one would be all the more obligated to have recourse to other marks and intrinsic or extrinsic denominations, without relying on the race [*sans s'attacher à la race*]" (A, 6, 6:402).

This last phrase, which is uncharacteristically ambiguous, points in two diametrically opposed directions: on the one hand, toward a racial "science" in which corporeal marks (both natural and artificial) express special distinctions that can serve as the basis for the schematization of both history and geography; and on the other, toward the only satisfactory solution to the problem of classification, from Leibniz's perspective—namely, the metaphysical proposition that each individual is a lowest species. According to the "Discourse on Metaphysics," which first lays out the elements of his mature philosophical program, "[i]t is not true that two substances can be exactly alike and differ only numerically, *solo numero*, and what St. Thomas says on this point regarding angels and intelligences (that among them every individual is a lowest species) is true of all substances" (G, 4:433). In order to assure the ordered relation among these singular, "angelic" substances, Leibniz happily appeals to the Christian idea of a divine kingdom in which everything enjoys its rightful place. Such is the nature of divine goodness. The assault that Kant's *Critique of Pure Reason* launches on Leibnizian metaphysics leaves scarcely no room in the "land of truth" for the vision of each substance as a lowest species. And in the same stroke this critical assault makes room for systems of anthropological classification, in which races function as the lowest biological species—or more accurately, as the lowest self-sustaining generative series of organic beings. The fact that Kant champions the new division of rational beings on the surface of the earth is therefore far from surprising: this division is a transformation—and travesty—of the monadological vision he effectively destroys.[23]

NOTES

1. François Bernier, "Nouvelle division de la terre, par les différentes espèces ou races d'hommes qui l'habitent, envoyée par un fameux Voyageur à Monsieur *** à peu près en ces termes (24. 4. 1684)," *Journal des Sçavants* 12 (1685): 148; T. Bendyshe's translation of Bernier's essay (1863–64) has recently been republished in *The Idea of Race*, ed. Robert Bernasconi and Tommy L. Lott (Indianapolis: Hackett, 2000), 1–4.

2. Leibniz, *Sämtliche Schriften und Briefe*, ed. Preußische [later, Deutsche] Akademie der Wissenschaften (Darmstadt and Leipzig: Reichl, 1923–), I, 13:544–45; hereafter, A. All translations are my own. For a presentation of Sparwenfeld's lexicon and a brief account of his life, see Ulla Birgegård, *Johan Gabriel Sparwenfeld and the Lexicon Slavonicum: His Contribution to the Seventeenth-Century Slavonic Lexicography* (Uppsala: Almqvist & Wiksell Tryckeri, 1985), esp. 85–96 (for a discussion of his correspondence with Leibniz).

3. Johann Friedrich Blumenbach, *De generis humani varietate nativa* (Göttingen: Vandenhoek and Ruprecht, 1795), § 83.

4. See, for example, Antje Sommer's entry "Rasse," in *Geschichtliche Grundbegriffe*, ed. Otto Brunner, Werner Conz, and Reinhard Koselleck (Stuttgart: Klett-Cotta, 1972–), 4:142–43; see also the brief remarks of Robert Bernasconi in "Who Invented the Concept of Race? Kant's Role in the Enlightenment Construction of Race," in *Race*, ed. Robert Bernasconi (Oxford: Blackwell, 2001), 12–13.

5. For a description of the appearance of the letter in the *Otium hanoveranum*, see the editorial apparatus to the Akademie edition; A, 1, 13:545.

6. Leibniz, *Die philosophischen Schriften*, ed. C. J. Gerhardt (1875–90; rpt. Hildesheim: Olms, 1978, 3:607; hereafter, G.

7. See the preface to his *Codex Iuris Gentium*, which has been ably translated in Leibniz, *Political Writings*, ed. and trans. Patrick Riley (Cambridge: Cambridge University Press, 1988), 165–76.

8. One of the very few analyses of this fragment can be found in Marcelo Dascal, "One Adam and Many Cultures: The Role of Political Pluralism in the Best of Possible Worlds," in *Leibniz and Adam*, ed. M. Dascal and E. Yakira (Tel Aviv: University Publishing Projects, 1993), esp. 390–91.

9. See the twenty-fourth (and last) axiom of the "Fundamenta praedemonstrabilia" of Leibniz's treatise of 1671, *Theoria motus abstracti seu Rationes Motuum universales, a sensu et Phaenomenis independentes* (G, 4:228–32).

10. See Paul Ritter's brief description of the fragment in his introduction to the Akademie edition (A, 4, 1:xxvi). Ritter indicates that the Janissaries and Mamelukes (accounts of which Leibniz had studied) were at the forefront of his mind during the composition of the *Consilium Aegyptiacum*. In the margins to the addendum, Leibniz refers to "A Relation of Pico Teneriffe" in Thomas Sprat's *History of the Royal Society*, which describes the corporeal hardening of the Guanchen; see *History of the Royal Society of London* (1667; rpt. St. Louis: Washington University Press, 1958), 200–213.

11. As Leibniz famously proposes in the so-called "Monadology," "Monads have absolutely no windows through which anything could enter or leave" (G, 6:606).

12. See the treatise of this title translated in *Political Writings*, 121–45

13. For Leibniz's efforts in this regard, see *Writings on China*, ed. and trans. Daniel J. Cook and Henry Rosemon Jr. (Chicago: Open Court, 1994).

14. See, for example, the remarks in the lengthy preface to Leibniz's own edition of Mario Nizolio's *De veris principiis et vera ratione philosophandi contra pseudophilosophos* (A, 6, 2:414) and, most famously, in "Ermahnung an die Teutsche ihren Verstand und Sprache besser zu üben" (generally dated in the early 1680s) and "Unvorgreifliche Gedancken, betreffend die Ausübung und Verbesserung der Teutschen Sprache" (after 1697); readily available versions of the edition published by Paul Pietsch (with modernized spelling) can be found in Leibniz, *Unvorgreifliche Gedanken, betreffend die Ausübung und Verbesserung der deutschen Sprache, Zwei Aufsätze*, ed. Uwe Pörksen (Stuttgart: Reclam, 1983). For Leibniz's inquiries into the German language—as well as Leibniz's other linguistic researches—see the remarkable study of Sigrid von Schulenburg, *Leibniz als Sprachforscher*, ed. Kurt Müller (Frankfurt am Main: Klostermann, 1973).

15. A, 6, 4:34. It is unclear whether *race* in these notes should be understood as an English or French word. Of course, Leibniz knew French much better than English, but in the seventh category of "Transcendental Relations of DISCONTINUED QUANTITY or Number" Wilkins offers the following set of terms: "SERIES, *Rank, Row, Class, Successive, Chain, Course, Race, Collateral, Concatenation, Alphabet*" (*An Essay Towards a Real Character and a Philosophical Language* [London: Gellibrand, 1668], 34).

16. After working for several decades on the history and genealogy of the House of Brunswick without arriving at a satisfactory result (at least in his own estimation), Leibniz was well aware of

the immense empirical difficulties of establishing a reliable account of a "generational series" whose elements are human beings. A fuller investigation into the theme of Leibniz and race would have to analyze in detail the methods that he developed in order to initiate, conceptualize, and present his groundbreaking historical and genealogical inquiries.

17. For an inquiry into Leibniz's conception of the *respublica christiana*, see Patrick Riley, *Leibniz' Universal Jurisprudence: Justice as the Charity of the Wise* (Cambridge: Harvard University Press, 1996), 236–60.

18. John Locke, *Essay on Human Understanding*, ed. Peter Nidditch (Oxford: Oxford University Press, 1975), 418 (book 3, chap. 3, § 17).

19. Nicholas Jolley emphasizes the degree to which Leibniz's motivation for refuting Locke's conception of essence lies in his desire to secure the concept of the human being as rational animal; he does not discuss the further motivation—to secure the realm of grace as a sphere in its own right; see Jolley, *Leibniz and Locke: A Study of the New Essays on Human Understanding* (Oxford: Clarendon Press, 1984), 144–45.

20. Every other use of the term race in the *New Essays* is preceded by the adjective *human*.

21. It is not out of the question that, when writing of "Australians" in this context, Leibniz has in mind the Jews, about whose legal status he writes extensively in "Judenschaft zu Frankfurt" (A, 4, 3:44–60): the Jews in Frankfurt, as Leibniz would doubtless have known, were forced to wear distinctive marks on their clothing, and it was by no means clear to everyone in Christendom that they were capable of redemption. Leibniz's complicated relationship to Judaism and the Jews of his time is the subject of another study.

22. Leibniz, *Essais de Théodicée*, ed. J. Brunschwig (Paris: Garnier-Flammarion, 1969), 435 (section 56).

23. As I have tried to indicate elsewhere, as Kant completed his critical project, he began to withdraw from the racial "science" he began to develop in the 1770s. At the very least he was much less inclined to use the term *race*; see Fenves, *Late Kant: Towards Another Law of the Earth* (London: Routledge, 2003), 101–5.

5

The Contradictions of Racism

Locke, Slavery, and the *Two Treatises*

ROBERT BERNASCONI & ANIKA MAAZA MANN

Locke was heavily involved in the slave trade, both through his investments and through his administrative supervision of England's burgeoning colonial activities. He invested in "The Company of Royal Adventurers in England Trading into Africa" when in 1663 it received the charter that gave it a monopoly in the slave trade on the West African coast.[1] By 1665 one quarter of the company's trade was in slaves, and in 1667 it claimed to be delivering six thousand slaves to the plantations each year.[2] Even if that number is exaggerated, the true number of transported slaves remains considerable. Locke was also one of the original subscribers to the company that succeeded the Royal Adventurers in 1672, the Royal African Company, which in the first sixteen years of its existence would transport almost ninety thousand slaves.[3] In the same year, Locke became a merchant adventurer by investing in a new company trading with the Bahamas.[4]

Moreover, few Englishmen who had not visited North America and the Caribbean knew more about the extent, nature, and impact of slavery than Locke. He was the secretary for the Lords Proprietors of Carolina from 1668 to 1675, and during most of that time he was also one of eleven members of the Council of Trade and Plantations, which met on average twice a week.[5] In June 1673 he was appointed secretary to the council and served in that role until, in 1676, the council was formally disbanded. He also would have learned about the colonies as secretary to Sir Anthony Ashley Cooper, the first Earl of Shaftesbury. Finally, between 1696 and 1701 Locke was one of only seven members on the Board of Trade and Plantations, or, according to its proper title, "His Majesty's Commissioners for promoting the trade of this Kingdom and for Inspecting and Improving His Plantations in America and elsewhere."

The attempt to reconcile Locke's involvement in the slave trade with his reputation as a philosopher of liberal freedom has a long history, beginning shortly after the abolition of the slave trade, and for that reason cannot simply be dismissed as the product of the recent fashion for so-called political correctness, as some academics want to do. Already in 1807 John Towill Rutt issued a defense of

Locke against the charge of supporting slavery.[6] Rutt denied that there was a "syllable respecting Negro slavery" to be found in Locke's works, with the exception of *The Fundamental Constitutions of Carolina*, and, against John Adams's criticisms of this text, he excused it as the work of a thirty-year-old new to political theory.[7] Since Rutt, scholars have been increasingly inventive in their efforts to resolve the contradiction between the Locke who profited from slavery and the Locke who, as a theorist of natural rights, would be appealed to by opponents of slavery.

The contradiction is highlighted by the opening lines of the first of Locke's *Two Treatises of Government*: "Slavery is so vile and miserable an Estate of Man, and so directly opposite to the generous Temper and Courage of our Nation: that 'tis hardly to be conceived that an *Englishman*, much less a *Gentleman*, should plead for't."[8] Locke's readers are faced with the problem of how he could have been so intimately involved in promoting an activity that he apparently knew to be unjustified. To be sure, this is not an unusual phenomenon, for conscious evildoing is commonplace, and self-deception and hypocrisy are even more widespread. Nevertheless, the tradition of Locke as a promoter of ideas that are a theoretical resource against oppression is so strong that some are reluctant to see him in another light. How could the father of these natural rights, in the name of which, according to a familiar story, the slaves were subsequently to be freed, have himself been involved in the slave trade? In this chapter we find some of the recent attempts by scholars to resolve the contradiction to be far more perplexing than the contradiction itself. We argue that, instead of trying to resolve the contradiction, philosophers should recognize it as evidence of his racism. He was concerned with the freedom and prosperity of Englishmen, and he was not troubled if they were gained at the expense of Africans in much the same way that, at the time of the American Revolution, white Americans were concerned with what they considered to be their own slavery and not with that of their black slaves.

In this chapter, we argue for four major claims. First, we insist that, because Locke was writing at a time when the form of slavery to be adopted by the new colonies had not yet been settled, his proposals in *The Fundamental Constitutions of Carolina* and elsewhere must be understood, not as a reflection of established norms about how slaves should be treated, but as playing a role in establishing those norms. Locke was one of the principal architects of a racialized form of slavery whose severity was by no means predestined. Second, although some recent commentators have highlighted the ways in which the *Two Treatises* must be read, not only in its domestic context, but also in its colonial context, we believe that these readings do not give sufficient weight to the fact that a defense of colonialization in the American context was also a defense of slavery, for the simple reason that slavery was judged to be indispensable to the profitability of the new American

colonies. Locke was well aware that the colonists were convinced that the colonization of North America could not be sustained without slave labor, that Africans
were the best source of slave labor for this purpose, and that the higher purpose
served by the agricultural development of North America necessitated a constant
supply of slaves. Third, although scholars have recently recognized that the argument in the fourth chapter of the Second Treatise, that one could legitimately enslave prisoners of war because they had deprived themselves of the right to live,
does not authorize the specific form of chattel slavery practiced in North America at
that time, the limitations of this argument for that purpose were widely ignored by
Locke's contemporaries. We argue that the fact that this argument does not fit the
form of slavery that was taking shape in the North American colonies is not ir-
refutable evidence that Locke did not introduce it with the intention of bolstering
the existence of slavery. Finally, we are disturbed by the ease with which some commentators excuse Locke of racism or minimize its significance. To be sure, there is
something artificial in the application of this word to a man who lived at a time
when the races were seen in very different terms than has been the case in the last
two centuries. But to advocate, administer, and profit from a specifically racialized
form of slavery is clear evidence of racism, if the word is to have any meaning at all.

| | |

LOCKE AS AN ARCHITECT OF THE NEW RACE-BASED SLAVERY

The frequently heard defense that someone was a "child of his time" is inappropriate if it is used to excuse someone of views that were contested at the time. Although there is little evidence of outright opposition to slavery in Locke's time,
there were those, particularly among the Quakers, who not only criticized the way
that slaves were treated but also argued for them to be given their freedom after
some years of service.[9] In light of this position The Fundamental Constitutions of Carolina should be regarded as a significant document. This text was the blueprint
provided by the Lords Proprietors of Carolina as to how they wanted Carolina organized. They intended that a copy of the Fundamental Constitutions be kept by the
register of every precinct and that every adult over seventeen be required to sign it
or be deprived of the right to hold property.[10] Locke's role in the authorship of the
Fundamental Constitutions can almost certainly not be determined with precision
now, although we do know that already two years earlier he had been involved in
writing a pamphlet advertising the plantations at Cape Fear.[11] However, the evidence is clear that Locke took particular interest in the way the document described the rights of masters over their slaves.

Although it appears that the document was not written in Locke's handwriting, as was once widely supposed, J. R. Milton, the scholar who is most fre-

quently cited as the authority on the question of the document's authorship, has identified Locke's handwriting among the corrections made to an early draft.[12] Because Milton lists the changes that were not made in Locke's hand, it can be concluded that Locke was responsible for one particularly significant change. In the draft, article 101 read: "Every freeman of Carolina shall have absolute Authority over his Negro Slaves, of what opinion or Religion so ever."[13] Locke changed the phrase "absolute Authority over his Negro Slaves" to read "absolute power and Authority over his Negro Slaves."[14] In other words, at a time when the way that slaves were to be treated was still being debated, the document placed no limits on the way slaveowners could mistreat their slaves, with the exception of guaranteeing them religious freedom.

Even without the evidence of Locke's handwriting, we might suspect that Locke was responsible for this change. The distinction between authority and power is already found before the *Fundamental Constitutions* in the form of a distinction between *potestas* and *potentia* in a Lockean text from the early 1660s.[15] Later, in the *Two Treatises of Government* the phrase "absolute power" was also used by Locke in his discussions of slavery to refer to the power of life and death (1T § 51 and 2T § 135). This notion of absolute power was central to Locke's understanding of the basis of slavery: slaves had forfeited their natural rights (2T § 178), including their right to life (2T § 23). It was a view Locke developed at a theoretical level in the Second Treatise against James Tyrell's position in *Patriarcha non Monarcha* that there was a kind of contract for slavery that denied slave owners the right to kill their slaves.[16] But Locke's view in the Second Treatise was consistent with that he had introduced into *The Fundamental Constitutions of Carolina* in 1669, when he gave to the freemen of Carolina absolute power over their African slaves, and thus the right to kill their slaves with impunity.

In 1669 it was by no means clear what form slavery would ultimately take in North America, or how harsh it would be. Because there were no slaves in Carolina at this time, William Uzgalis has speculated that article 101 was, like some of the first slaves themselves, imported from Barbados. He has suggested that Sir John Colleton may have been responsible for the stipulation about absolute power, on the grounds that Colleton, like other Barbados planters, would not have wanted to renounce existing rights they had over their slaves.[17] However, there is no basis for the claim. Indeed, Peter Colleton, Sir John Colleton's son, congratulated Locke on having "so great a hand" in writing the *Fundamental Constitutions*.[18] Furthermore, we have not found any evidence that the planters in Barbados legally had been given the power of life and death over their slaves. So far as we are able to tell, it was not until 1688, and then only after a report of a slave conspiracy, that the legal issue was addressed in Barbados, at which time the legislature mandated a fine for anyone who "wantonly or cruelly kills his own slave."[19]

There is no clearer indication of the fact that slavery in the colonies was still searching for its form than the effort made in the 1690s to control some of the most extreme excesses. At that time Locke himself was also involved in writing proposals that were more restrictive than those espoused in *The Fundamental Constitutions of Carolina*. In 1698, Locke, on behalf of the Board of Trade, drafted instructions for Governor Francis Nicholson of Virginia encouraging him "to get a law pass'd restraining of Inhumane Severities . . . towards Slaves, and that Provisions be made therein that the willful killing of Indians and Negroes may be punished with Death, and that a fit penalty be imposed for the maiming of them."[20] Although this seems to suggest that Locke may have revised his position on the power that belonged to a slave owner, we have no way of knowing whether the change was primarily from strategic or from philosophical reasons. In any event, the necessity for such provisions highlights the extreme severity of *The Fundamental Constitutions of Carolina*, and in 1690 Carolina adopted a law to regulate the treatment of slaves, whereby anyone who killed a slave was liable to three months' imprisonment.[21] However, this does not mean that slaves were beginning to gain protection of the law. In 1691 Virginia created a law according to which slaves found hiding from their owners or concealing those who were could by killed by any means by anyone, with provision also being made to compensate the owner with four thousand pounds of tobacco.[22]

The other important provision relating to slavery in the *Fundamental Constitutions* was the provision stating that slaves would be free to practice religion. Although this might appear to be a significant concession, in the colonial context it was in fact the opposite. Many Europeans had come to be persuaded that Christians should not enslave other Christians. It was for this reason, and not because of doubts as to whether they had souls, that the baptism of slaves was controversial.[23] Indeed, there is some evidence that enslaved Indian Americans and Africans were freed before the 1660s on the grounds that they had been baptized.[24] Hence the significance of the fact that alongside article 101 of the *Fundamental Constitutions*, which specified that slaves could be "of what opinion or Religion soever," was the proviso, "But yet, no Slave shall hereby be exempted from that civil dominion his Master has over him, but be in all other things in the same State and condition he was in before."[25] It marked a decisive step toward the new race-based slavery, as indicated by the specific reference to "Negro slaves."[26]

This issue continued to be controversial for some time, but the position set out in the *Fundamental Constitutions*, which was eventually adopted by the colony, succeeded in reconciling the interests of the slave owners with those of the missionaries. This is confirmed by a book published in 1680 by Morgan Godwyn, a former student of Locke.[27] Even though Godwyn was under no illusion about the cruel and inhumane way in which the African slaves were treated, he was more concerned to harmonize the interests of the planters, who needed slaves, with those of the churches, whose task was to save souls, than to care for the conditions under which the slaves lived.[28] Indeed, in an effort to reassure the planters further, he later wrote a tract that portrayed the slave as more interested in baptism than freedom.[29]

That Locke at the end of his life was fully in agreement with Godwyn's position is clear from *A Paraphrase and Notes on the Epistles of St. Paul*. When Locke read Saint Paul's call "Let everyman abide in the same calling wherein he was called" (Corinthians 7:20) as saying that "Christianity gives not anyone any new privilege to change the state or put off the obligations of civil life which he was in before," to his contemporaries this would have evoked the ongoing debate on the legitimacy of the continued enslavement of slaves who had converted to Christianity.[30] Locke continues, "Wert thou called being a slave, think thy self not the less a Christian for being a slave: but yet prefer freedom to slavery if thou canst obtain it."[31] The reconciliation of Christianity with the enslavement of baptized Africans was the decisive step in turning Europe into a society whose wealth was based on African slaves, and it was only when the alliance between the churches and the colonial interest was broken that slavery could be abolished. It is arguable that it was the shift to interpreting the Bible as a document opposed to slavery, rather than the introduction of a theory of natural rights, that had the most impact on eventually bringing about the abolition of slavery. If so, then Locke, as one of the authors of the *Fundamental Constitutions*, should be given a different role in the history of slavery than that usually accorded to him. Commentators often like to highlight references to Locke in the abolitionist literature, but the defenders of slavery also cited Locke as one of their authorities.[32] Indeed, one of the defenses of American slavery offered on the eve of the Civil War was that it was not as harsh as the form of slavery defined by Locke in terms of "absolute and arbitrary power" and so it could be argued that "in this sense there is no such thing as a slave in the United States."[33]

| | |

COLONIALISM AND SLAVERY

According to the interpretation dominant among Locke scholars since Peter Laslett's work in the 1950s, the larger purpose of the *Two Treatises of Government* is to be found in English domestic politics and specifically in Shaftesbury's circle.

However, there have recently been a number of studies highlighting the colonial context.[34] We argue that just as English domestic politics should not be separated in Locke's thought from colonialism, they cannot be separated from the question of slavery either. Locke's *Two Treatises* was a manifesto for a political group that had long seen its power and wealth tied to the conditions of North America. For a member of Shaftesbury's circle like Locke, the two activities, colonizing the east coast of North America and trading in slaves, were intimately linked.

This can be shown by examining how Shaftesbury pursued his interests in these two areas. Soon after the Restoration in 1660, Sir Anthony Ashley Cooper, the first Earl of Shaftesbury, was appointed as one of ten members of a council whose task was to supervise the colonies in North America.[35] At the very same time that Shaftesbury became involved in supervising the colonies, he was investing in a new company, the Royal Adventurers into Africa, and when in 1672 the Royal Adventurers was replaced by the Royal African Company, we find four of the eight Proprietors of Carolina, including Shaftesbury, among its directors.[36] Shaftesbury took a special interest in the American colonies, particularly in Carolina, which he described as his "darling."[37] However, the colonies in America suffered not only from a profound labor shortage but also from a climate that made the importation of African slaves essential if the colonies were to be financially beneficial. In 1663 the Company of Royal Adventurers had informed the king that "the very being of the plantations depends upon the supply of negro servants for their works."[38] We thus agree with Michael Seliger that there is a connection between slavery and colonialism, although we depart from him on historical grounds when he says that "Locke's justification of slavery and of colonial conquest are in full harmony with the opinions and practices of his time."[39] Just as Locke must be seen as an innovator at a time when the practice of slavery had not yet found its dominant form, he must also be cast as an advocate at a time when there was great ambivalence in England about the wisdom of establishing colonies in America.[40]

| | |

JUSTIFICATIONS OF SLAVERY

Although Locke in the first sentence of the First Treatise proclaimed himself an opponent of slavery, he proceeded in the fourth chapter of the Second Treatise to rehearse a long-standing justification for slavery. This justification of slavery did not allow for the ultimate degradation of hereditary slavery, but it did legitimate an extraordinarily harsh form of slavery, according to which the slave owner held the power of life and death over his slaves, thereby, as we have seen, evoking the formulation of *The Fundamental Constitutions of Carolina*, that "slaves . . . are by the right of nature subjected to the absolute domination and arbitrary power of their masters" (2T § 85).

Is it possible to determine for sure whether Locke had African slaves in North America in mind when he wrote chapter 4 of the Second Treatise and limited slavery to prisoners captured in a just war? Recent interpretations tend to highlight the fact that Locke placed significant limitations on the conditions under which someone might legitimately be enslaved. Specifically, Locke limited slavery to those who have forfeited their lives "by some Act that deserves Death" (2T § 23). Later in the Second Treatise Locke specified that "we call Slaves . . . Captives taken in a just War" (2T § 85; see also § 172). This seems to exclude both non-combatants and the offspring of slaves, which appears to rule out hereditary slavery of the kind that had taken shape in the plantations of America at that time. James Farr claims that when Locke wrote the Two Treatises, "the slaves of Africa and America were out of sight and out of mind."[41] However, at a general level this claim cannot be sustained. In addition to a number of references to America and Native Americans, there are also references to the power and absolute dominion West Indian planters had over their "Slaves bought with Money" (1T §§ 134 and 135).[42]

Although a reading of the fourth chapter of the Second Treatise that takes Locke at his word has to acknowledge, as some commentators have done, that it does not fit chattel slavery in North America, it would also have to acknowledge that were Locke's ideas on slavery to have been put into practice they would have allowed for the reintroduction of slavery into Christian Europe. Indeed, given that Europe was torn by wars, the supply of slaves would have been extensive. This implication could be avoided only if one assumes the principle that Christians should not enslave their fellow Christians, thereby highlighting the significance of the discussion of the impact baptism had on the slave's status, and the exception concerning Negro slaves. Our point here is that those commentators who emphasize that a literal interpretation of the chapter does not fit the African slave trade have to consider what the implications would have been had the chapter's principles been literally applied in Locke's day.[43] Thus, one is forced to reintroduce reference to the historical context. That is to say, one has to offer a reading of the text that is consistent with ways in which it might have been read at the time.

Both Jennifer Welchman and Uzgalis have recently challenged the consensus according to which the fact that Locke's justification of slavery as presented in the Second Treatise did not extend to the children of slaves, because it was expressly limited to the combatants captured during a war, was taken to mean that Locke cannot therefore have intended this account to be applied to the African slave trade. However, their responses could not be more different. According to Welchman, "hereditary slavery is fundamental to Locke's conception of right,"[44] whereas, according to Uzgalis, the fact that Locke excluded hereditary slavery means that we must read Locke's account as an attack on the form of slavery that he had earlier helped to develop in the colonies.

Welchman's argument that Locke's theory could accommodate the form of chattel slavery that Europeans were in the process of inventing has two parts. In the first part she argues that because sub-Saharan Africa was by Locke's standards in a state of nature, and because anyone who in the state of nature had assaulted another or tolerated an assault could legitimately be enslaved by anyone else by virtue of the executive right of the law of nature, then the action of enslaving Africans could be understood as a legitimate exercise of that right. Furthermore, once ownership of the slave was established, then the captive could be bought and sold. This much of Welchman's interpretation is consistent with Locke's discussion of slavery, but the use to which she puts it is difficult to reconcile with Locke's overall argument and the way Africa was conceived of at that time. Her claim that Locke would have seen the failure of Africans to establish a civil authority capable of preserving their rights by entering into a social contract as a forfeiting of their natural rights suggests that she has converted the Lockean state of nature into the Hobbesian state of war.[45] To be sure, Locke's state of nature from time to time threatens to pass into a state of war, but accounts of Africa at the end of the seventeenth century do not present it as in a permanent state of war, as later accounts attempted to do. Furthermore, the distinction between the state of nature and the state of war is crucial to Locke's theory. It is by specifying that property and money can develop in the state of nature that he meets the condition Shaftesbury's party required: that one can change the ruler without property reverting to the sovereign.

However, the second aspect of Welchman's argument is the more original and more important part. It is here that she suggests that Locke can account for hereditary slavery. Locke is clear that it is legitimate only to enslave combatants. One cannot enslave the wife or child of a combatant simply because of their relationship to the combatant.[46] Welchman proposes that the children of someone already enslaved are not born free because she reads Locke as dividing the human species, after the introduction of slavery, into two ranks: right-bearing human persons and non-right-bearing human property. "The term 'man' no longer denotes any human being, but only those human beings who are persons. Children born to non-persons are neither the children of men nor entitled to claim rights natural to men."[47] In support of this reading she points to the passage where Locke proclaims that "Creatures of the same species and rank . . . should . . . be equal one amongst another" (2T § 4). The reference to rank would be redundant if all members of species were of the same rank. Nevertheless, this is not enough to reconcile Locke's theory with the historical reality, as Welchman attempts to do.

Even in its early years, the slave trade in Africans was manifestly not confined to captives of just wars. The records of the companies in which Locke invested provide details of the slaves transported from Africa that are not consistent with this possibility. For example, in the seven-month period before March 1664, during which the Royal African Adventurers provided Barbados with 3,075 slaves, of the 2,261 of which we have the details, only 1,051 were adult men. The rest were mainly women, of which 56 were girls.[48] Only half of the slaves whom the Royal African Company transported were adult males.[49] These numbers are important because they speak directly to Welchman's denial of "a serious contradiction between Locke's principles and contemporary slavery."[50] She concedes that capturing and enslaving both women and children would have contradicted Locke's theory, if any of them were noncombatants, and that it was likely that some of them were. She thus resorts to saying that the contradiction becomes a contradiction in practice and not a contradiction in principle. However, the direct enslavement of women and, above all, children undermines her attempt to show that "the historical facts about slavery" were consistent with Locke's theory.[51]

By contrast, Uzgalis argues that Locke's discussion of slavery in the *Two Treatises* excludes chattel slavery and so is to be understood as a rejection of the enslavement of Africans as it had come to be practiced in his time and partly under his direction.[52] The problem is that there is no supporting evidence for this interpretation and a great deal that runs counter to it. Indeed, the fact that Locke had helped to administer slavery in the English colonies and that he had financially benefited from it through his investments suggests the contrary. Uzgalis asks us to believe that Locke underwent some kind of silent conversion during his time of exile, but Locke seems to have made no effort by his words or actions to draw attention to this alleged conversion. The fact is that at the end of his life Locke in his *A Paraphrase and Notes on the Epistles of St. Paul* dismisses the idea that the baptism of slaves entails granting them liberty, which refutes the idea that Locke underwent a late conversion on the question of slavery.

However, the decisive difficulty that Uzgalis's interpretation cannot overcome is the fact that Locke was heavily involved in the administration of the colonies in the last years of his life, when, even though he had not officially been involved in the administration of colonial affairs for over twenty years, he was included as an expert. Uzgalis dismisses Locke's activity as a member of the Board of Trade by describing him as "a sick old man."[53] However, the facts of Locke's involvement do not allow this to be offered as an excuse. Although he would usually be away for more than half of each year, he attended 372 meetings in less than five years. The additional workload in terms of reading reports was enormous, but however reluctant Locke might initially have been to take on this onerous burden, he was from the outset one of the board's most important members.[54] According to Peter Laslett, Locke controlled the board in its formative years, worked out its policy, and dictated its decisions.[55] He was involved in detailed questions of the administration of Virginia. It is true that Locke was ill during much of this time, but he was anything but idle.

Uzgalis's decontextualized reading of chapter 4 is not confined to the idea that Locke was an early abolitionist. He argues that Locke produced a justification for Africans to enslave at least some Englishmen, that Locke claimed that those who had been unjustly enslaved had a legitimate right to enslave "their tyrannical masters, be these black African slave traders, officers or sailors on slave ships, or plantation owners or their minions."[56] Elsewhere Uzgalis employs the phrase "combatants and government officials" to describe this group of people.[57] But that raises the question as to whether, on Uzgalis's interpretation, Locke has not articulated a theory according to which Locke himself could have been justly enslaved, as one of the architects, administrators, and, as an investor, beneficiaries of this system. And yet Uzgalis still wants to say that Locke "knew" that his theory of slavery was incompatible with the Atlantic slave trade as conducted in his time and that he intended his account as a rejection of it.[58] This interpretation amounts to a reductio ad absurdum of all efforts to apply a literal reading of Locke's text to the Atlantic slave trade without taking account of how the English perceived the slave trade in Locke's time. Rather than explaining why Locke offered an account of slavery in the Second Treatise that was not an account of the form of slavery adopted by the colonists, Uzgalis succeeds only in making the enigma more enigmatic.

What then is one to make of the fact that the classical defense of slavery in terms of prisoners taken in war did not fit the reality of slavery in his time? The crucial point to recognize is that many of Locke's contemporaries continued to justify the African slave trade by reference to this theory. Initially there was some concern about how the slaves were acquired. Richard Baxter insisted in *A Christian Directory* that it was a "heinous sin, if men buy negroes or other slaves of such as we have just cause to believe did steal them by piracy, or buy them of those that have no power to sell them."[59] Although first published in 1673, this was written between 1664 and 1665. Even more significant is the fact that the "Body of Liberties" established by Massachusetts in 1641 enacted that "There shall never be any bond slaverie, villinage or captivitie amongst us unles it be lawfull captives taken in just wares, and such strangers as willingly selle themselves or are sold to us."[60] Locke in the Second Treatise would have objected to the second provision, but the reference establishes the point that the classical justification of slavery was still current at that time. Indeed, a few years later, the General Court of Massachusetts came out explicitly against "ye heinous & crying sinn of man stealing" and ordered that everyone unlawfully taken from New Guinea should be returned there.[61]

Reference to captives taken in a just war provided only a limited defense of slavery. As people became accustomed to the large numbers of Negro slaves and the profits they produced for their owners, the emancipatory force of the argument was lost. When Samuel Sewall, in what is widely held to be the first anti-slavery tract published in North America, attacked the just-war argument, he did so, not by questioning its applicability to the enslavement of women and children, but by questioning the justice of just wars: "Every War is upon one side Unjust. An Unlawful War can't make lawful Captives."[62] William Bosman, in his influential study *A New and Accurate Description of the Coast of Guinea*, originally published in Dutch, emphasized that the Kingdom of Aquamboe on the Gold Coast sold prisoners of war to the Europeans, as if in an effort to establish the continued relevance of the argument to the ongoing slave trade.[63] John Atkins, in 1735, confirmed that the argument was still current as a justification for the slave trade and set out to refute it, as well as the claim that slaves were bought, not for economic reasons, but by Christians wanting to preserve them from sacrifice and cannibalism and bring them to a better life. Against the claim that the slaves were captives taken in war, Atkins insisted: "By War for the most part is meant Robbery of inland, defenceless Creatures, who are hurried down to the Coast with the greater Cruelty, as it is from a contented, tho' a very poor Life."[64] This shows that the argument was still current.

We are therefore forced to conclude that, in spite of its unsuitableness for the task, the argument that captives taken in a just war could legitimately be enslaved was widely used in the seventeenth and eighteenth centuries to defend chattel slavery in North America. Even though Locke knew more about slavery than most of his contemporaries, that does not give us a reason to believe that he did not share the widespread tendency of his contemporaries to justify slavery in their own minds as if the slaves had been captured in a just war. Indeed, it is impossible to defend Locke against the charge of racism by insisting that he knew that many of the slaves in North America had not been legitimately captured. Given his involvement in the administration of the slave trade, he would have been obliged to point out the inappropriateness of the argument. As Robin Blackburn has pointed out, the Board of Trade had the right to object to the slave laws being enacted in the colonies but chose not to do so.[65]

As a number of commentators have noted, Locke was the last major political theorist to justify slavery, which is curious for a man with a reputation for promoting freedom.[66] The presence of this argument in the Second Treatise, while consistent with Locke's overall position, cannot be explained by reference to the need to justify a right to revolution under appropriate circumstances, which is what most commentators dwell on when explaining the shape of the *Two Treatises*. One needs an explanation of why Locke includes in the Second Treatise a legitimation of slavery that gave the slave owner the power of life and death over his slaves. The fact that he had already sought to secure that power for slave owners in America suggests a reason. Throughout his life Locke acted as if enslaving Africans was justified, but we find only one attempted justification of slavery in his writings. Did he have another justification? Did he, like many of his contemporaries, extend the argument beyond its limits? Or did he think that slavery did not need to be justified? In any other author's work the appearance of a chapter justifying slavery, written by a man known to have invested in the slave trade, would not raise problems of interpretation. Why should one make an exception in Locke's case when we are unwilling to suppose that all the people who used this argument were closet critics of the system then in operation? The fact that it is not a good argument for the purpose does not establish that the argument was not intended for that purpose, even when one is reading the works of a major philosopher. Racists often use bad arguments: it is the only kind they have.

| | |

LOCKE'S RACISM

Finally, we turn to the question of Locke's racism. Although the term "racism" is not a precise one, particularly when applied to late-seventeenth-century England when the notion of race did not yet have its modern meaning, we are puzzled by the attempts of some scholars who argue that one could be involved with the administration of a race-based system of slavery, profit from it, and yet not be a racist. The fact that Locke was not troubled by the contradiction between his political ideals and the chattel slavery from which he profited is prima facie evidence of racism, given that slavery was organized along racial lines. Whether he did not see the contradiction or whether he simply considered it to be unimportant does not affect our claim. Insofar as we have succeeded in relating Locke's philosophical writings to Shaftesbury's circle, with its interests in colonialism and the African slave trade, then we believe we have rendered less plausible some of the ways in which philosophers have sought to resolve the contradiction that arises because of Locke's failure to apply his theory of natural rights to Africans. In addition, because Locke belonged to the circle that helped to shape the specific form in which the institution of chattel slavery took root in North America, we consider the charge of racism to be more serious than it would be if he had simply inherited these institutions.

Farr introduced into the secondary literature on Locke an unfortunate distinction between strong and weak racism, which has been widely adopted by subsequent commentators. His proposal was that Locke could legitimately be considered a strong racist only if there was an explicit theory about hereditary inferiority to support the accusation. He concluded that since Locke did not develop such an account, then Locke the theorist cannot be considered racist (in the strong sense), although Locke the man may have held prejudicial views toward Africans. But that is to operate with a bizarre and restricted definition of strong racism. One consequence of this claim seems to be that only a theorist can be a strong racist, which would exonerate all but the philosophically inclined. Racism is not confined to theory. In our view, Locke's investment in the slave trade is more damning than would be "the embarrassing caricatures of black people" that we agree are not found in his works.[67] To try to separate Locke the political theorist from Locke the secretary of the Board of Trade does violence to the kind of political thinker Locke was and wanted to be remembered as being.[68]

Locke supported the organization of slavery along racial lines. The fact that it does not seem to have occurred to him that his justification of slavery, if it had been applied according to the letter of his text, could have led to the enslavement of Englishmen is evidence that he was unable to conceive of English men, women, and children being denied the rights that were denied to the African slaves. There is further evidence of the racialization of slavery beyond the provision in The Fundamental Constitutions of Carolina for the baptism of Negro slaves. At the end of 1671, the Lords Proprietors instructed the governor and Council of Carolina that "Noe Indian upon any occasion or pretense whatsoever is to be made a slave without his owne consent to be carried out of our country."[69] These instructions were recorded in Locke's handwriting. The significance of this demand is even greater insofar as it ran counter to the dominant tendency of that time. Indeed, it was a policy that South Carolina would subsequently abandon.[70] The fact that Shaftesbury's party, and presumably Locke himself, supported the enslavement of Africans, but not of Native Americans, confirms that they favored the new racialized system of slavery that was only then taking shape. By the same token, Locke and Shaftesbury seem to have been concerned that Native Americans should not be mistreated, long before Locke turned his attention to protecting African slaves from mistreatment.[71]

Addressing the hypocrisy of a nation that heralds the tenets of the Declaration of Independence, while simultaneously supporting chattel slavery, Frederick Douglass asked, "What to the slave is the 4th of July?"[72] In the same vein, we want to ask philosophers who consider Locke to be a champion of liberty, "What to the slave is the *Two Treatises*?" As long as principles of freedom and independence are applicable only to white Americans, and not blacks, then, as Frederick Douglass states, "America is false to the past, false to the present, and solemnly binds herself to be false to the future."[73] Philosophers who ignore the extensive evidence of Locke's racism and yet still cling to the misguided notion that Locke intended his principles of liberty to be applied universally to all "men" not only are being false to the past and false to present efforts to shed light upon the history of the racism of Western philosophy, but they are also being false to the future, insofar as efforts to establish a society free from racist institutions will be thwarted until there is greater honesty about the past.

NOTES

1. Hugh Thomas, *The Slave Trade* (London: Picador, 1997), 199. So far as we are aware, Thomas is the only commentator to have mentioned Locke's investment in this first company, so it is possible that this is an error.

2. Ibid., 198–99, and George Frederick Zook, *The Company of Royal Adventurers Trading into Africa* (New York: Negro Universities Press, 1969), 82.

3. K. G. Davies, *The Royal African Company* (New York: Atheneum, 1970), 58n. Thomas, *Slave Trade*, 202.

4. Maurice Cranston, *John Locke* (London: Longmans, Green, 1957), 155–56.

5. George Beer, *The Old Colonial System* (London: Macmillan, 1932), 1:249.

6. J. T. Rutt, "Defense of Locke against Lord Eldon," in *The Reception of Locke's Politics*, ed. Mark Goldie (London: Pickering and Chatto, 1999), 4:391–94.

7. Ibid., 393. Locke was, of course, actually thirty-seven years old at the time when *The Fundamental Constitutions of Carolina* were written.

8. John Locke, *Two Treatises of Government*, ed. Peter Laslett (Cambridge: Cambridge University Press, 1988), 141. We follow the convention of giving references to paragraphs of the *Two Treatises*. 1T refers to the First Treatise and 2T the Second Treatise. For a sketch of responses to the contradiction that shows the state of the question in 1990, see Wayne Glasser, "Three Approaches to Locke and the Slave Trade," *Journal of the History of Ideas* 51 (1990): 199–216.

9. William Summer Jenkins, *Pro-Slavery Thought in the Old South* (Gloucester, MA: Peter Smith, 1990), 7.

10. David Duncan Wallace, *The History of South Carolina* (New York: American Historical Society, 1924), 1:65.

11. Louise Fargo Brown, *The First Earl of Shaftesbury* (New York: Appleton, 1933), 154–55.

12. J. R. Milton, "John Locke and the Fundamental Constitutions of Carolina," *Locke Newsletter* 21 (1990): 111–33. See also Celia McGuinness, "The Fundamental Constitutions of Carolina as a Tool for Lockean Scholarship," *Interpretation* 17 (1989): 127–43.

13. Article 101, "The Fundamental Constitutions of Carolina," *North Carolina Charters and Constitutions, 1578–1698*, ed. Mattie Erma Edwards Parker (Raleigh, NC: Carolina Charter Tercentenary Commission, 1963), 164.

14. See Robert Bernasconi, "Locke's Almost Random Talk of Man," *Perspektiven der Philosophie* 18 (1992): 296. Even if the fact that the change was made in Locke's handwriting does not have the significance we have given to it or if subsequent research shows it is not in fact Locke's handwriting, it is significant Locke did not disown the clause, as he did the ninety-sixth article. See Edward McCrady, *The History of South Carolina under the Proprietary Government, 1670–1719* (New York: Macmillan, 1901), 104.

15. John Locke, *Essays on the Law of Nature*, ed. W. von Leyden (Oxford: Oxford University Press, 1970), 182–88.

16. David Wootton, "Introduction," *John Locke: Political Writings* (London: Penguin, 1993), 83–84.

17. William Uzgalis, " 'An Inconsistency Not to Be Excused': On Locke and Racism," in *Philosophers on Race: Critical Essays*, ed. Julie K. Ward and Tommy L. Lott (Oxford: Blackwell, 2002), 98.

18. *The Correspondence of John Locke*, ed. E. S. Beer, (Oxford: Oxford University Press, 1976), 1:395.

19. Statute 82. Cited by John Poyer, *This History of Barbados from the First Discovery of the Island in the Year 1605 till the Accession of Lord Seaforth, 1801* (London: J. Mawman, 1808), 132.

20. Quoted by James Farr, " 'So Vile and Miserable an Estate': The Problem of Slavery in Locke's Political Thought," *Political Theory* 14.2 (1986): 269. Whether this means that Locke acknowledged what A. John Simmons has called "the right not to be cruelly degraded" or whether this policy was for entirely different reasons, which do not reflect a shift in Locke's philosophical views, is not clear. See A. John Simmons, *The Lockean Theory of Rights* (Princeton: Princeton University Press, 1992), 196.

21. *Statutes of South Carolina*, vol. 7, p. 363. Cited by Alan Watson, *Slave Laws in the Americas* (Athens: University of Georgia Press, 1989), 74.

22. "An Act for Suppressing Outlying Slaves," April 1691, in William Walker Hening, *The Statutes at Large; being a Collection of All the Laws of Virginia* (Philadelphia: Thomas Desilver, 1823), 3:86.

23. The baptism of slaves confirms that Africans were regarded as human beings with souls, contrary to the thesis proposed by Clarence Sholé Johnson, *Cornel West and Philosophy* (New York: Routledge, 2003), 170. Robert Bernasconi has addressed this issue in more detail, addressing also the relevant passages of Locke's *Essay concerning Human Understanding*, in "Locke's Almost Random Talk of Man," 302–15.

24. Edmund S. Morgan, *American Slavery, American Freedom* (New York: Norton, 1975), 331–32, and Meron L. Dillon, *Slavery Attacked: Southern Slaves and Their Allies, 1619–1865* (Baton Rouge: Louisiana State University Press, 1990), 18–20. In 1732 the solicitor-general and the crown's attorney were still combating the idea that being baptized was inconsistent with the state of slavery: see "Anniversary Sermon before the Society for the Propagation of the Gospel," *The Works of George Berkeley*, ed. A. A. Luce and T. E. Jessop (London: Thomas Nelson, 1955), 7:122.

25. Article 98, "Fundamental Constitutions of Carolina," in *North Carolina Charters*, 150.

26. It is also significant that in spite of the idea of freedom of religion, in 1671 a letter from Shaftesbury, Carteret, and Colleton distinguishes between Christians and Negroes. A. S. Salley, ed., *Records of the Secretary of the Province and the Register of the Province of South Carolina, 1671–1675* (Columbia: Historical Commission of South Carolina, 1958), 12.

27. Cranston, *John Locke*, 71–72.

28. Morgan Godwyn, *The Negro's and Indians Advocate, Suing for Their Admission into the Church* (London, 1680), 40–41. Locke had a copy in his personal library. See John Harrison and Peter Laslett, *The Library of John Locke* (Oxford: Oxford University Press, 1965), 144.

29. Morgan Godwyn, *Trade preferr'd before Religion and Christ made to give a place to Mammon: Represented in a Sermon Relating to the Plantations* (London: B. Took, 1685), 5.

30. John Locke, *A Paraphrase and Notes on the Epistles of St. Paul*, ed. Arthur W. Wainright (Oxford: Oxford University Press, 1987), 201.

31. Ibid.

32. For example, "Charters and Constitutions of South Carolina," *De Bow's Review* 20 (1856): 344, and "North Carolina," *De Bow's Review* 2 (1851): 32.

33. Rev. Samuel Seabury, *American Slavery Distinguished from the Slavery of English Theorists* (New York: Mason Brothers, 1861), 42.

34. James Tully, "Rediscovering America," *An Approach to Political Philosophy: Locke in Contexts* (Cambridge: Cambridge University Press, 1993), 137–76, and Barbara Arneil, *John Locke and America* (Oxford: Oxford University Press, 1996). For a defense of the conventional interpretation against them, see Stephen Buckle, "Tully, Locke, and America," *British Journal for the History of Philosophy* 9, (2001): 245–81. It is our view that reference to the slavery question could have helped Tully and Arneil explain more than they did without this reference, and so would have made Buckle's position harder to sustain. This is the upshot of our interpretation of the fourth chapter of the Second Treatise.

35. W. D. Christie, *A Life of Anthony Ashley Cooper, First Earl of Shaftesbury, 1621–1683* (London: Macmillan, 1871), 1:249.

36. McCrady, *History of South Carolina*, 357.

37. E. E. Rich, "The First Earl of Shaftesbury's Colonial Policy," *Transactions of the Royal Historical Society*, 5th ser., 7 (1957): 47–70.

38. Elizabeth Donnan, *Documents Illustrative of the History of the Slave Trade to America* (New York: Octagon Books, 1969), 1:164. Confirmation that a planter could not manage without Negro slaves

was later provided by Smeal Wilson, in a way that is entirely in keeping with Locke's conviction developed in chapter 5 of the Second Treatise that land without labor is virtually useless. See Constantine George Caffentzis, *Clipped Coins, Abused Words, and Civil Government* (Brooklyn: Autonomedia, 1989), 142.

39. M. Seliger, *The Liberal Politics of John Locke* (New York: Frederick A. Praeger, 1968), 122.

40. Arneil, *John Locke and America*, 90–95.

41. Farr, " 'So Vile and Miserable an Estate,' " 285.

42. See further Seymour Drescher, "On James Farr's 'So Vile and Miserable an Estate,' " *Political Theory* 16 (1988): 502–3.

43. Farr, " 'So Vile and Miserable an Estate,' " 276.

44. Jennifer Welchman, "Locke on Slavery and Inalienable Rights," *Canadian Journal of Philosophy* 25.1 (1995): 81.

45. Ibid., 79.

46. Seventeenth-century literature on Africa highlighted the existence of women combatants, and on Locke's theory those women could have legitimately been enslaved. However, this does not serve as an explanation of all enslaved women, because he specifies "wife and child" (2T § 183).

47. Welchman, "Locke on Slavery," 80.

48. Zook, *Company of Royal Adventurers*, 82. See also the evidence amassed by Farr, " 'So Vile and Miserable an Estate,' " 276.

49. Davies, *Royal African Company*, 299.

50. Welchman, "Locke on Slavery," 80.

51. Ibid., 78.

52. William Uzgalis, " ' . . . The Same Tyrannical Principle': Locke's Legacy on Slavery," in *Subjugation and Bondage*, ed. Tommy L. Lott (Lanham, MD: Rowman and Littlefield, 1998), 56.

53. Ibid., 65.

54. I. K. Steele, *Politics of Colonial Policy: The Board of Trade in Colonial Administration* (Oxford: Oxford University Press, 1968), 15, 21–28, 173–76, and 178–79.

55. Peter Laslett, "John Locke, the Great Recoinage, and the Origins of the Board of Trade: 1695–1698," *William and Mary Quarterly*, 3rd ser., 14 (1957): 368–402.

56. Uzgalis, " ' . . . The Same Tyrannical Principle,' " 54.

57. Ibid., 53.

58. Ibid., 56.

59. Richard Baxter, *A Christian Directory, The Practical Works*, vol. 1 (Ligonier, PA: Soli Deo Gloria Publications, 1990), 463.

60. *The Colonial Laws of Massachusetts, Reprinted from the Edition of 1660* (Boston: Rockwell and Churchill, 1889), 53.

61. Mary Stoughton Locke, *Anti-Slavery in America* (Gloucester, MA: Peter Smith, 1965), 14. See also Donnan, *Documents Illustrative*, 3:7–8.

62. Samuel Sewall, *The Selling of Joseph: A Memorial*, ed. Sidney Kaplan (Northampton: University of Massachusetts Press, 1969), 14. We thus give this passage a different significance from the one James Farr gave it. See " 'So Vile and Miserable an Estate,' " 275.

63. William Bosman, *A New and Accurate Description of the Coast of Guinea* (London: James Knapton, 1705), 70.

64. John Atkins, *A Voyage to Guinea, Brazil and the West-Indies* (London: Caesar Ward and Richard Chandler, 1735), 176.

65. Robin Blackburn, *The Making of New World Slavery* (London: Verso, 1998), 265.

66. For example, David Davis, *Slavery and Human Progress* (Oxford: Oxford University Press, 1984), 107.

67. Farr, " 'So Vile and Miserable an Estate,' " 278.

68. Peter Laslett, "Locke as Founder of the Board of Trade," in *A Locke Miscellany*, ed. Jean S. Yolton (Bristol: Thoemmes Press, 1990), 127–36.

69. "Temporary Laws to be added to Instruction to Ye Governor and Council of Carolina." Quoted by Arneil, *John Locke and America*, 126.

70. George M. Stroud, *A Sketch of the Laws Relating to Slavery in the Several States of the United States of America* (Philadelphia: Kimber and Sharpless, 1827), 11–15.

71. Arneil, *John Locke and America*, 130.

72. Frederick Douglass, "What to the Slave is the Fourth of July?: An Address Delivered in Rochester, New York, on 5 July 1852," *The Frederick Douglass Papers*, ed. John W. Blassingame, ser. 1, vol. 2 (New Haven: Yale University Press, 1982), 359–88.

73. Ibid., 369.

6

Berkeley and the Westward Course of Empire
On Racism and Ethnocentrism

WILLIAM UZGALIS

We tend to think of George Berkeley as the philosopher who propounded the doctrine of immaterialism and as one of the three great British empiricists along with Locke and Hume. But Berkeley was also an official of the Anglican Church, eventually becoming a bishop. As a student at Trinity College, Dublin, Berkeley encountered the Society for the Propagation of the Gospel in Foreign Parts (SPG) and learned about Anglican missionary work in America. Early in his career in the church, from about 1721 on, Berkeley began considering moving to America. Berkeley wrote and published a proposal to build a college in Bermuda in order to improve missionary work. He actually voyaged to America and lived in Newport, Rhode Island, for some three years (1729–31) while he waited in vain for the money to found his college. While in Newport, Berkeley visited the villages of the indigenous people. He also owned slaves. In considering Berkeley's views on race, I will follow Berkeley's progress in his efforts to found a college in America. Starting with H. M. Bracken's essay "Essence, Accident, and Race" and Richard Popkin's "The Philosophical Basis of Modern Racism," scholars have attempted to find in the works of European philosophers explicit racist theories that justify the ill treatment of Africans slaves and indigenous peoples around the world. In these terms my examination of Berkeley leads to two conclusions. The first is that we should distinguish between racist and ethnocentric ways of thinking in the eighteenth century. The second is that Berkeley is a clear example of the latter. Since Berkeley was an official of the Anglican Church, I begin by considering the relation of that church and its missionaries to the colonies.

| | |

THE ANGLICAN CHURCH, BERKELEY, AND THE COLONIES

Berkeley was an Anglican official. Anglicanism was the state religion in England. It was instituted by Henry VIII, reinstituted by Elizabeth I, and continued during the reign of the Stuarts with a significant interruption during the Commonwealth period. One need only remember that the Puritans and other religious dissenters were fleeing the religious repression of the Anglican Church both before the English Civil War and after the Restoration to realize that the church might not be as strong in the New World as it was at home. Still, it had its proponents in the eighteenth century, even in Puritan New England.

Thomas Bray founded the Society for the Propagation of the Gospel (SPG) in London in 1701. It was, in Edwin Gausted's words,

> Anglicanism's formal response to the growth of dissent and irreligion . . . in Britain's colonies abroad. No bishop of the Church of England resided in America, and no bishop residing in England had responsibility only for America. Almost causally, the Bishop of London had his diocese somewhat enlarged to include the foreign plantations, but neither special funds nor additional personnel nor appropriate ecclesiastical machinery augmented his already heavy duties. A sprawling mission field ready for harvest, the colonies called out (or so it seemed to loyal churchmen in England) for more laborers to bring that harvest in: to convert the Indian and the black, to reform the morals and fill the minds of the whites, to provide clergy and fill churches, to distribute good books and inculcate sound doctrine—in short to save England's colonies for England's Church.[1]

The society had made efforts to convert black slaves and indigenous people before Berkeley came along. There were a number of ambitious programs for the Christianization of American slavery during this period carried on by a number of different religious sects such as Quakers and Moravians as well as the SPG. They were a reaction to a dramatic increase in the slave trade. But the efforts of the SPG were significantly larger than those of Quakers or Moravians. The SPG was officially supported by the Church of England and could thus count on support from the government. Nonetheless these efforts had been and continued to be largely unsuccessful. The chief reason for this was the indifference or open hostility of the American colonists.[2] On occasion, the money to be made by the use of slaves corrupted even the Society for the Propagation of the Gospel. Codrington College in Barbados was the most notable example of such a failure.[3] Berkeley discovered the scheme for Codrington College in Barbados in his researches in Trinity College library. This may well have been what suggested the idea of a college in America to him in the first place.[4] When he came to propose his own college, however, Berkeley wanted nothing to do with Barbados.[5] What brought Berkeley to make the proposal for a college in the colonies?

There are two factors that brought Berkeley to his interest in America: missionary zeal on the one hand, and dissatisfaction with the state of Europe and even of Great Britain on the other. The Society for the Propagation of the Gospel had a branch in Dublin. Berkeley heard a good deal from the missionaries about America and the work of a missionary in America. Berkeley saw Europe and England as in moral decline. Berkeley the philosopher was a leader in a conservative religious reaction to the new science and the mechanical philosophy. Berkeley held that the dualism of Descartes and Boyle, Locke and Newton was as dangerous as the materialism of Hobbes. Dualism and materialism alike lead to skepticism and atheism and these in turn to immorality. As for England, the South Sea Bubble had burst, rocking the nation. In response, Berkeley had written his *Essay towards Preventing the Ruin of Great Britain*. Berkeley saw a Britain beset by moral decline. At the most despairing point in the essay, Berkeley wrote, "The final period of our State approaches," though he then went on to suggest sensible measures for reform. Berkeley saw America as the place of the next Golden Age. The last three stanzas of Berkeley's "Verses on America" go:

> There shall be sung another Golden Age,
>   The Rise of Empire and of Arts,
> The Good and Great inspiring epic Rage,
>   The wisest Heads and Noblest hearts.
>
> Not such as *Europe* breeds in her decay,
>   Such as she bred when fresh and young.
> When Heavenly Flame did animate her Clay,
>   By future poets shall be sung.
>
> Westward the course of Empire takes its Way,
>   The four first Acts already past.
> A fifth shall close the Drama with the Day,
>   The World's great Effort is the last. (W, 7:370)

Berkeley saw himself as playing a role in the development of this Golden Age in the West. His utopian vision failed, but his involvement with the American colonies reveals that his aim was to bring religion and civilization through education to America.

In 1722 Berkeley published his proposal for the foundation of St. Paul's College in Bermuda. The proposal was aimed at raising money and public support for the project. The conversion of the indigenous people was so important an aspect of the proposal that it appeared on the title page. The conversion of slaves was added later. Berkeley's remarks in the course of the proposal reveal fairly clearly his attitude toward both the indigenous peoples of the Americas and Afro-American slavery. They are, therefore, worth considering in some detail.

In the first paragraph of the proposal Berkeley notes that in spite of English efforts at propagating the Gospel around the world, it is "acknowledged, that there is at this Day, but little Sense of Religion, and a most notorious Corruption of Manners, in the English Colonies settled on the Continent of America, and the Islands." He then continues: "It is also acknowledged, that the Gospel hath hitherto made but a very inconsiderable Progress among the neighboring Americans, who still continue in much the same Ignorance and Barbarism, in which we found them a hundred Years ago" (W, 7:345). These are the evils that Berkeley is proposing to remedy by the foundation of St. Paul's College in Bermuda, which is to produce a supply of worthy clergymen to reform the morals of the colonists and "a like constant Supply of Zealous missionaries, well fitted for propagating Christianity among the Savages" (W, 7:345).

It may be worth considering here why Berkeley uses the word *savage* so regularly in describing the indigenous peoples of the Americas. He writes:

[N]o part of the Gentile World are so inhumane and barbarous as the savage Americans, whose Chief Employment and Delight consisting in Cruelty and Revenge, their Lives must of all others, be most opposite, as well to the Light of Nature, as to the Spirit of the Gospel. Now to reclaim these poor Wretches, to prevent the many Torments and cruel Deaths which they daily inflict on each other, to contribute in any sort to put a stop to the numberless horrid Crimes they commit without Remorse, and instead thereof to introduce the Practice of Virtue and Piety, must surely be a Work in the highest Degree becoming every sincere and charitable Christian. (W, 7:345)

Berkeley held that there were various difficulties in converting the indigenous peoples of the Americas. Even able missionaries from England will find it difficult to convert the native peoples "if we consider the difference of Language, their wild Way of Living, and above all, the great Jealousy and Prejudice which Savage Nations have towards Foreigners, or Innovations introduced by them" (W, 7:346). Later in the proposal Berkeley adds: "that the savage Indians, who live on the Continent, will not suffer their children to learn English or Dutch, lest they should be debauched by conversing with their European Neighbors" (W, 7:350).

Berkeley's solution to this dilemma is to propose teaching indigenous people in his seminary.

[T]he children of Savage Americans, brought up in such a Seminary, and well instructed in Religion and Learning, might make the ablest and properest Missionaries for spreading the Gospel among their Countrymen; who would be less apt to suspect, and readier to embrace, a Doctrine recommended by Neighbors or Relations, men of their own Blood and Language, than if it were proposed by Foreigners, who would not improbably be thought to have designs on the Liberty or Property of their Converts.

The young *Americans* necessary for this Purpose, may in the Beginning, be procured, either by peaceable Methods from those savage Nations, which border on our Colonies, and are in Friendship with us, or by taking captive the Children of our Enemies. (*W*, 7:346–47)

It is notable that Berkeley is ready to use whatever means necessary to accomplish this goal, even if this means capturing "the Children of our Enemies." This seems to be a characteristic of Berkeley as a missionary.[6] Berkeley wants native children under ten years of age "before evil habits have taken a deep root; and yet not so early as to retain their Mother Tongue, which should be preserved by Intercourse among themselves" (*W*, 7:347). They would be thoroughly grounded in Religion and Morality along with "a good Tincture" of other learning—rhetoric, history, practical mathematics, and perhaps medicine. Berkeley suggests that if the seminary could send forth eight or ten such missionaries each year, the world would quickly see a positive effect from this effort.

Berkeley goes on to remark that it would not require much expense "to subsist and educate" the indigenous missionaries in a "plain simple Manner, such as might make it easy for them to return to the coarse and poor Methods of Life in use among their Countrymen" (*W*, 7:347). Later he says, "Ten pounds a year, would (if I mistake not) be sufficient to defray the expenses of a young *American* in the College of *Bermuda*, as to Diet, Lodging, Clothes and Education" (*W*, 7:359).

Toward the end of the proposal, Berkeley takes up various objections that might be made to it. One of these is that given the difficulties of converting people at home, "no Success can be expected among Savages abroad" (*W*, 7:355). Berkeley's response is to note that there is a considerable difference between error and ignorance. He continues:

Whereas, the Savage *Americans*, if they are in a state purely natural, and unimproved by Education, they are also unincumbered with all that Rubbish of Superstition and Prejudice, which is the Effect of a wrong one. As they are less instructed, they are withal less conceited and more teachable. And not being violently attached to any false System of their own, are so much the fitter to receive that which is true. Hence it is evident that success abroad ought not to be measured by that which we observe at home (*W*, 7:356)

At home there are all of those other systems to which people are violently attached, while the indigenous peoples of the America are unencumbered by such rubbish. This clearly suggests that Berkeley does not consider the possibility that there may be native religions that might compete with Christianity.[7]

Berkeley next considers the objection that "this Scheme has already been tried to no Purpose." His reply is that his scheme has never been tried because no Native American has ever been given a thorough education in religion and morality. He goes on to discuss the general capacity of the indigenous people for education:

> That they show as much natural sense as any uncultivated Nations: That the Empires of Mexico and Peru were evident proofs of their Capacity, in which there appeared a Reach of Politics, and a Degree of Art and Politeness, which no *European* people were ever known to have arrived at without the Use of Letters or of Iron, and which perhaps some have fallen short of with both these Advantages. (W, 7:356–57)

Grasping Christianity and being civilized are certainly within the capacity of the indigenous peoples of the Americas. But there is one final difficulty that is indeed serious. Berkeley continues:

> It must nevertheless be acknowledged a difficult Attempt, to plant Religion among the *Americans,* so long as they continue their wild and roving Life. He who is obliged to hunt for his daily Food, will have little Curiosity or Leisure to receive Instruction. It would seem therefore the right Way to introduce Religion and civil Life at the same Time into that Part of the World: either attempt will assist and promote the other. Those therefore of the young Savages, who upon Trial are found less likely to improve by academical Studies, may be taught Agriculture, or the most necessary Trades. And when Husbandmen, Weavers, Carpenters, and the like, have planted those useful Arts among their savage Countrymen, and taught them to live in settled Habitations, to canton out their land and till it, to provide vegetable Food of all Kinds, to preserve Flocks and Herds of Cattle, to make convenient Houses, and to clothe themselves decently: This will assist the spreading of the Gospel among them; this will dispose them to social Virtues, and enable them to see and feel the Advantages of a religious and civil Education. (W, 7:359)

Clearly this is a much more invasive and culturally destructive proposal than merely the teaching of Christianity alone. Here we see the typical prejudice of agricultural people against hunting and gathering people. Here we also see again the willingness to use almost any means to bring about a conversion to Anglican Christianity.

The last passage clearly displays Berkeley's religious ethnocentrism. The indigenous people are barbarians who commit "numberless horrid Crimes . . . without Remorse." Presumably Europeans were doing nothing like this to one another! There is no hint that the native peoples might have things to teach Englishmen, or that they have their own religion or religions that are sufficient for their own purposes. Here we have some of the worst attitudes of universalizing religions. On the other hand, it is reasonably clear that Berkeley is not advocating the destruction of these peoples or the seizure of their lands. Their culture is another story. Insofar as it interferes with their conversion to Christianity, Berkeley would like to see it changed. In a better world, the indigenous peoples are going to go on living where they are, but they will become Christians, and more civilized. Is this kind of ethnocentrism racist?

||||

RACISM AND ETHNOCENTRISM

In his essay "The Philosophical Basis of Modern Racism" Richard Popkin defines *liberal racism* as "making the best of the European experience the model for everyone, and the eventual perfection of mankind consisting in everyone becoming creative Europeans."[8] It seems clear that on this definition Berkeley is a liberal racist, in the company of Father de Las Casas and the Abbé Grégoire. Still, one might wonder whether "liberal racism" really is a form of racism at all. According to Popkin the characteristic feature of modern racism is that it seeks to show that one group of people is rendered *permanently inferior* to some other group by factors such as biology and climate.[9] Popkin's modern racism requires a reason, or an account, or a theory that explains the permanent inferiority of one group to another.[10] *Liberal racism* supposes a cultural inferiority that is, at least in principle and perhaps in practice, reversible. *Liberal racism* does not fit the definition of modern racism that Popkin himself gives.

Let us consider another account of racism. James Farr holds that *strong racism* provides an empirical account or a theory to explain the inferiority of one group to another and a moral theory to justify enslavement or other ill treatment of that inferior group.[11] Berkeley clearly thinks indigenous people less civilized than Europeans. But does he hold that people of color ought to be treated worse than Europeans because they are less civilized? The answer is clearly negative. In believing that indigenous people ought to be led to accept Anglican Christianity, Berkeley is supposing that this is a benefit. Berkeley thinks a European education would improve indigenous minds. He thinks that living like Europeans and giving up hunting for farming would make indigenous peoples more civilized. He sees these as benefits to be conferred. These considerations strongly suggest that we should distinguish ethnocentrism from racism. Both of these attitudes are morally objectionable but for quite different reasons. Popkin's concept of liberal racism conflates the two.

We can go farther. H. M. Bracken in "Essence, Accident, and Race" suggests that there is a connection between empiricism and racism. He includes in his account of racism "the doctrine which a group may articulate in order to justify their oppressing another group by appealing to some putative flaw in the human essence, in recent times usually interpreted as the biological constitution of the oppressed group."[12] He focuses on Locke and Hume in particular as examples of empiricist philosophers who were interested in controlling other peoples. He thinks both of them articulated racist views with this aim in mind.[13] Bracken contrasts the immaterial Cartesian soul with more empirical accounts of the self and argues that the Cartesian view provides a modest brake against racism. The immaterial Cartesian soul, after all, has no skin color, while empiricists tend to think bodies more important in defining persons. It is fairly clear that Bracken's thesis about the relation of empiricism to racism, weak though he claims that relation is, is quite implausible. Bracken (a fine Berkeley scholar) gives Berkeley only a brief mention, but it is reasonably clear that he believes Berkeley is a racist. He mentions Berkeley among a list of philosophers and scientists from the eighteenth and nineteenth centuries with racist views. Of the Irish philosopher he says: "Berkeley supported slavery but he rejected the specific difference thesis."[14] This means that Berkeley did not hold that other peoples were inferior in that they were lacking some feature or features that belonged to the human essence. He was a racist in Bracken's view because he supported slavery. It is worth noting that Berkeley was surely a more radical empiricist than Locke was. Yet the chief connection that Bracken alleges to hold between empiricism and racism is completely absent in Berkeley. Perhaps because he concedes that Berkeley did not accept the specific difference thesis, Bracken also makes no mention of the fact that Berkeley's account of the soul was as immaterialist as that of Descartes. But this fact makes it clear that Bracken's modest bar to racism is as available to empiricists as to rationalists.[15]

On the other hand, Bracken claims that "racism . . . runs counter to the three major religions that have dominated the west . . . because they are universalistic."[16] Bracken is surely right about this. Since Berkeley's chief motivation is religious, we would expect him not to be a racist, and we would expect his thought to run counter to racism. We will find confirmation of this when we consider Berkeley's visit to America and his reflections on it. Still, what Bracken completely fails to see (or at least say) is that the ethnocentrism fostered by such universalistic religions can be just as damaging to indigenous peoples and their cultures as racism. Missionaries, after all, had their own reasons for wanting to control people. Berkeley illustrates this point nicely. This again shows that we ought to carefully distinguish racism from ethnocentrism and note the ill effects produced by each of them.

Still, Bracken is claiming that Berkeley is a racist simply because he supports slavery.[17] This would clearly be true if Berkeley had given an account that justifies slavery in the way that Popkin, Farr, and Bracken himself say characterizes racist thought. But Berkeley gives no such an account. Berkeley does not support or justify slavery on this basis at all. He simply accepts it as part of the conditions under which a missionary works. Given the Christian acceptance of slavery, it seems that Bracken should either change his view about the relation of universalizing religions to racism, or he should not call Berkeley a racist for adopting the view of the Anglican Church to slavery. Let us turn to the portion of Berkeley's proposal that deals with the conversion of black slaves.

In 1724 Berkeley became aware of a bequest of nine hundred pounds by Sieur Abel Tassin D'Allone (the private secretary to William III) for the conversion of Negroes in the British plantations. Berkeley's friend Percival tried to get this money assigned to Berkeley's college. Writing to Berkeley, Percival pointed out to him that the he must "oblige himself to instruct a certain number of Negro Children that shall be offer'd him, that it may appear we come as near answering the Intent of the Donor as we possibly can." Berkeley in return pledged "to enter into any obligation to maintain and educate such Blacks" as Percival would decide.[18] The bequest never came into Berkeley's hands, for the executor of it, Thomas Bray, was quite skeptical about Berkeley's plans.

In the second edition of the proposal for St. Paul's College, Berkeley added a paragraph concerning the conversion of black slaves. He thought the clergy in America inadequate. One piece of evidence of this was the

small Care that hath been taken to convert the Negroes of our Plantations, who, to the Infamy of England, and Scandal of the World, continue Heathen under Christian Masters, and in Christian Countries. Which could never be, if our Planters were rightly instructed and made sensible, that they disappointed their own Baptism by denying it to those who belong to them: That it would be of Advantage to their Affairs, to have Slaves who should *obey in all Things their Masters according to the Flesh, not with Eye-service as Men-Pleasers, but in singleness of heart as fearing God:* That Gospel Liberty consists with Temporal Servitude; and that their Slaves would only become better Slaves by being Christians. (*W*, 7:346)

From this quotation it is perfectly plain that Berkeley accepted the legitimacy of Afro-American slavery. Indeed, he is arguing that Christian baptism would make the slaves better slaves! Still, black slaves were people, and people in urgent need of conversion to Christianity. How was the conversion of black slaves to be achieved? The answer is that Berkeley's college in Bermuda would produce a steady stream of worthy clergymen. These clergymen would reform the character of the plantation owners, and this in turn would lead these men to convert their slaves. In addition, Berkeley was perfectly willing to educate Negro children to achieve the same effect among black slaves as his Native American missionaries were supposed to achieve amongst their peoples. Berkeley's attitude toward black slaves was quite similar to his attitude toward the indigenous people of America—both groups were badly in need of conversion. Still, while it is plain that Berkeley's only interest in black slaves was to confer what he regarded as the supreme benefit on them, this does not explain Berkeley's acceptance of slavery. Before turning to that question, however, we should consider Berkeley's visit to America and what he learned from it.

||

BERKELEY IN AMERICA AND AFTERWARD

When Berkeley went to America, he went not to Bermuda but to Newport, Rhode Island. At the time, Berkeley was the highest-ranking Anglican official to visit the colonies. Rhode Island was one of the strongholds of Anglicanism in the colonies, and Newport was a populous trading port. Berkeley bought a large farm that was intended to provision the college in Bermuda once it was established. Berkeley waited for the news that the British government had allocated the twenty thousand pounds that he had been promised. In the meanwhile, Berkeley wrote *Alciphron*, preached in the local church, and held meetings with clergymen from all around. Berkeley also crossed the bay to visit the parish of James McSparran, and it was presumably here that he and his party visited the Narragansett Indians. Berkeley apparently visited them a number of times. It has sometimes been suggested that Berkeley learned of tar water from the Narragansett.[19] But this apparently is not the case.[20]

Berkeley also bought slaves and followed the directions of the bishop of London that slaves on the plantations in the colonies should be baptized.[21] Gausted notes: "In October, 1730, he purchased three slaves; in the following Winter in

Whitehall he carefully instructed them, and on June 11, 1731, 'Dean Berkeley Baptized three of his negroes, 'Phillip, Anthony and Agnes Berkeley.' "[22] Presumably, Berkeley as the highest-ranking Anglican official in America was providing a model of how the church thought slaves should be treated.

Eventually, Berkeley learned that the funds that he was waiting for would not be appropriated. He returned to England, where he preached a sermon before the Society for the Propagation of the Gospel. In that sermon Berkeley makes the point that it is the duty of Christians to try to convert non-Christians. He considers and replies to various objections to engaging in missionary work. In doing this he describes the terms on which missionary work proceeds in the modern world: "It is Power against Weakness, Civility against Barbarism, Knowledge against Ignorance, some or another, if not all of these Advantages, in the present Times, attending the Progress of the Christian Religion, in whatever part of the World Men shall attempt to plant it" (W, 7:119–20).

Turning to Rhode Island, Berkeley describes the condition of the native inhabitants:

> The native *Indians*, who are said to have formerly been many Thousands, within the Compass of the Colony, do not at present amount to One Thousand, including every Age and Sex. And these are either all Servants or Labourers for the *English*, who have contributed more to destroy their Bodies by the Use of strong Liquors, than by the use of any means to improve their Minds or save their Souls. This slow Poison, jointly operating with the Small-Pox, and their Wars (but much more destructive than both) hath consumed the *Indians*, not only in our Colonies, but also far and wide upon our Confines. And having made Havoc of them, it is now doing the same thing to those who taught them this odious Vice. (W, 7:121)

Clearly, Berkeley was appalled by the treatment the Indians received from the English colonists. Berkeley holds that what the English colonists should be doing to the native Indians is improving their minds and saving their souls, not destroying them with alcohol.

He then turns to the religious situation of black slaves and the attitudes of the colonists toward both slaves and the indigenous people:

> The Negroes in the Government of *Rhode Island* are about half as many more than the *Indians*; and both together scarce amount to a seventh Part of the whole Colony. The Religion of these people, as is natural to suppose, takes after that of their Masters. Some few are baptized; several frequent the different Assemblies; and far the greater Part none at all. An ancient antipathy to the

Indians, whom it seems, our first Planters (therein as in certain other Particulars affecting to imitate *Jews* rather than *Christians*) imagined they had the right to treat on the foot of *Canaanites* or *Amelkites*, together with an irrational Contempt of the Blacks, as Creatures of another Species, who had no right to be instructed or admitted to the Sacraments, have proved a main Obstacle to the Conversion of these poor People. (*W*, 7:121–22)

Berkeley finds the prejudices against the indigenous peoples of the Americas and black slaves offensive and irrational, and the actions taken on the basis of such prejudice cold, un-Christian, and objectionable. Berkeley also notes that the planters have "an erroneous notion, that the being baptized is inconsistent with the State of Slavery." Berkeley reports that he asked the king's attorney and the solicitor general to provide an opinion on this subject. They provided a signed document with the opinion that slavery and baptism are consistent with one another. This was then, according to Berkeley, published in Rhode Island and "dispersed throughout the plantations" (*W*, 7:122). Berkeley is also much more insistent on the importance of converting dissenters at home than he had been before his visit to America. This change in point of view probably is related to seeing the degree of dissent in the colonies and its effects on Anglican affairs.

Berkeley goes on to recommend that colonists should intermarry with the native peoples:

It must be owned, our reformed Planters, with respect to the Natives and the Slaves, might learn from those of the Church of *Rome*, how it is their interest and duty to behave. Both *French* and *Spaniards* have intermarried with *Indians*, to the great Strength, Security and Increase of their Colonies. They take care to instruct both them and their Negroes in the *Popish* Religion, to the Reproach of those who profess a better. They have also Bishops and Seminaries for Clergy; and it is not found that their Colonies are worse Subjects, or depend less on their Mother-Country, on that Account. (*W*, 7:122)

I would take this as one piece of evidence that shows that while clearly ethnocentric, Berkeley was not a racist. Berkeley's strong rejection of the actions of the colonists toward the indigenous people and their attitudes toward slaves, along with his suggestion that the colonists intermarry with the Indians, shows that there is not only a difference between ethnocentric attitudes and racists attitudes but a clear conflict between them. This also gives us good reason to distinguish them.[23]

How much, if at all, did Berkeley's views change as a result of going to America and encountering actual slaves and native inhabitants? The sermon to the SPG suggests that Berkeley became aware of the prejudices of the colonists and their actions toward the native inhabitants of the Americas. He clearly disliked the prejudices and condemned the actions and saw these as the chief obstacles to the conversion of the indigenous peoples. It appears that while he was previously aware of the views of planters about African American slaves, he rejected those prejudices and took action to convince the planters that baptism and the civil state of slavery were not incompatible. His attitude toward the American clergy and missionaries became much less critical and much more supportive. Clearly he came to view conversion of dissenters at home as more important than he had before he left. Still, certain basic attitudes remained the same. While Berkeley regarded Native Americans as people who deserved to be converted to Christianity, he also regarded them as the most uncivilized of barbarians. While he regarded black slaves as people who deserved to be converted, he raised no questions about the institution of slavery and the slave trade. He was comfortable enough with the institution of slavery to buy and own slaves while he lived in Rhode Island. So why did Berkeley accept the institution of slavery?

|||

SLAVERY, THE CHURCH, AND BERKELEY'S POLITICAL PHILOSOPHY

With the contract to carry slaves from Africa to Spanish America, the English slave trade had taken off. English ships would end up carrying a quarter of all those Africans transported to the New World in the entire course of the transatlantic slave trade. Eighty percent of these were transported during the period from 1700 to 1850.[24] By the 1720s the slave trade was approaching its zenith in England. The English colonies, both on the mainland and in the West Indies, had finally developed economies that worked, and many of these employed slave labor. Much of the wealth that was flowing into England thus depended in one way or another on slavery. In 1725 John Houstoun described it as "the hinge on which all the trade of this globe moves."[25] Still, slavery was controversial. As Englishmen learned what slavery in the colonies was all about, some of them came to oppose it. Dr. Johnson, we are told, gave a toast to the next slave revolt in the West Indies at an Oxford party.[26] There was an English antislavery movement in Berkeley's era, although historians date the real drive to end slavery as beginning in 1770. We can probably reasonably ask why Berkeley belonged to those who supported slavery or simply accepted its legitimacy. Why was he not part of the antislavery movement?

Berkeley's place in the Church of England and the position of the church and its missionaries in respect to slavery provide the largest part of the answer. As David Brion Davis notes: "British missionaries and philanthropists regarded the Negro slave as a man possessing an immortal soul, but the institution of slavery they accepted without question."[27] There are clear reasons why the church and its missionaries held this position. Christianity grew up during the life of the Roman Empire. Christianity had come to terms with slavery long before the advent of the transatlantic slave trade. The Anglican Church was a state church, and the state was profiting from the slave trade. Had its missionaries opposed the institutions of Afro-American slavery, they would have received far less cooperation in the conversion of slaves from planters or colonists than they did receive. They would very likely have come into conflict with the government. As it was, planters were not particularly interested in having their slaves educated so that they could learn about religion. Planters were quick to blame slave revolts on the influence of preachers on their slaves. Nor were they eager to give slaves the Sabbath to worship. This interfered with work. The position of the church and its missionaries on slavery was practical, given their position and what they were trying to do. But in adopting this position, they acquiesced in what we have come to regard as an inhumane, immoral, and racist economic system. Presumably they did not share our evaluation of the system. They regarded it as both legal and moral and happily in the national interest.

Berkeley's political philosophy provides another illuminating if less important part of the answer. Berkeley's early political philosophy (like his metaphysics and epistemology) contrasts strongly with that of Locke. In the *Second Treatise of Government* Locke develops an analogy between the relation of a tyrannical king and his subjects and that of a master and his slaves.[28] It is possible we may learn at least something about Berkeley's attitude about slavery by contrasting his attitudes concerning the obedience subjects owe to their king and the conditions under which revolution is legitimate with those of Locke.

In the *Second Treatise of Government* Locke distinguishes between legitimate and illegitimate slavery. Chapter 4 of the Second Treatise gives his carefully circumscribed account of legitimate slavery. Legitimate slavery happens only as a result of a war in the state of nature. The aggressors in such a war have a settled intention to violate the rights of others to life, liberty, health, and property. If the victims of such aggression win the war and capture the aggressors, they have legitimate absolute power over the aggressors. This means they have the right to either kill or enslave them. Should the victims choose to let the aggressors live and use them for their own purposes, this would be legitimate slavery. On the other hand, a state of illegitimate slavery occurs if the unjust aggressors win the war and attain illegitimate absolute power over their victims. The point of all this is to make it clear that the claims of monarchs to be able to systematically violate the rights of their subjects to life, liberty, health, and property amount to illegitimate slavery. Ultimately this analogy between tyranny and illegitimate slavery plays a role in Locke's argument that under certain conditions it is legitimate for subjects to rebel against and kill tyrannical rulers. Locke does not explicitly develop the implications of the analogy for African American slavery, yet it is clear that Locke's theory would condemn its institutions and practices as illegitimate.

Berkeley published an essay in 1712 called "Passive Obedience" dealing with the issues of the obedience of subjects to their rulers and rebellion. The doctrine of passive obedience was not Berkeley's creation. This doctrine had been repeatedly appealed to by Anglican divines in the seventeenth century, particularly in rejecting rebellion against James II. As A. A. Luce notes, when Berkeley wrote his essay, "the advocacy of passive obedience was toiling in its last campaign." As Luce explains it, passive obedience "faces in two directions: against resistance to the ruler, because loyalty is a duty of conscience, and against absolute positive obedience to him, because conscience has other duties as well" (W, 6:5). In respect to the issue of resistance to the ruler, Luce continues, "[t]he end of society is the good of its members; the fundamental rational means thereunto is subjection to an accredited ruler or ruling body; therefore, the subject has no rational right to resist such an authority" (W, 6:6).

Berkeley's doctrine is that one must obey an accredited ruler or ruling body. This clearly leaves open the question as to how to determine who the rightful ruler or ruling body is. Berkeley addressed this issue in a letter of 1709: "When I consider what the difference is between a king *de jure* and a king *de facto*, I cannot easily find it." He goes on to say that when the English line is examined, "we are forced to place the right of kings in the consent and acquiescence of the people." William the Conqueror had as much right to England, Berkeley tells us, as a robber does to your purse. So it can only be the "consent and acquiescence of the people" that could make William a legitimate ruler. He dismisses heredity as a basis for the right of kings, remarking: "[I]t seems to me a kingdom is not a property but a charge; it is not therefore necessary that it go by the same rule as an estate or goods or chattels" (W, 6:6). Private property is not a charge, and this suggests that owners of private property have even more control over their property than a king does over his kingdom. Since Berkeley nowhere raises the question of the legitimacy of enslavement of Africans, the implications for chattel slavery are fairly clear: slave revolts would never be legitimate.

It is worth noting some Lockean objections to the doctrine of passive obedience that Berkeley considers and rejects. One is that self-preservation is the first law of nature, so presumably when a king threatens one's life (illegitimately), one has the right to resist. Berkeley claims that no negative precept may be broken to observe a positive one—that is, evil may not be committed to produce good. Another objection is that nonresistance would be slavery. Berkeley's answer in Luce's summary is this: "No; no more than is the subjection of our passion to reason, this and civic obedience being the condition of our humanity" (W, 6:9). Berkeley is here rejecting Locke's analogy between tyranny and illegitimate slavery. But what of the consequences of nonresistance? Are there not exceptional circumstances under which rebellion is right? Berkeley's response is that there are none. Rebellion is a sin, and a sin can never be right. If exceptional oppression should occur, the ruler's ministers would be morally obliged not to execute his decrees, that is, they would engage in passive obedience. We may wonder whether Berkeley's doctrine of passive obedience would allow passive resistance in the form in which Gandhi or Martin Luther King practiced it. On the one hand, insofar as the passive resister is willing to suffer the penalties for breaking the laws, his or her actions would fall within the doctrine of passive obedience. But still, passive resistance on the part of the people, and not simply ministers, might amount to more resistance than Berkeley would be willing to tolerate. It is certainly clear that the doctrine of passive obedience does not allow any violent rebellion. Whether Berkeley still held these views when he came into contact with African slaves is not clear. But if he continued to hold them, their emphasis on authority and his views about property might well explain to some degree why Berkeley would not have found slavery a particularly troubling concept.

||

CONCLUSION

Berkeley was not a philosophical racist. He propounded no theory to explain or justify the ill treatment of one group by another. He was an ethnocentric Christian missionary. He regarded Europeans as civilized while viewing the indigenous people of the Americas largely as savage barbarians. He would have welcomed the destruction of Native American cultures insofar as this might aid in the conversion of these people to Christianity. He wanted to see them give up the life of hunters for a settled agricultural way of life. He referred to such a change as the civilizing of the indigenous people. Berkeley had no conception that there were religions of indigenous peoples, much less that these might be genuine competitors with Christianity. Berkeley, along with other officials of the Anglican

Church, accepted the institution of slavery without question. Berkeley was comfortable enough with slavery to buy slaves in Rhode Island and educate them and baptize them. In his capacity as the highest-ranking Anglican official in the colonies, he was providing a model of how slaves should be treated. Berkeley's political philosophy with its emphasis on submission to authority and the rejection of Locke's analogy between tyranny and illegitimate slavery simply reinforced the legitimacy of African American slavery.

If we find ourselves disappointed with Berkeley, we might consider that we live on the other side of a great moral sea change that came about slowly during the course of the eighteenth and nineteenth centuries. We regard chattel slavery as utterly immoral. We have come to see much of the treatment of indigenous peoples by European colonial powers around the world as racist, ethnocentric, and immoral. This indictment includes much of the work of Christian missionaries. Berkeley lived on the other side of that great change in morality. To us he may appear blind to the evils of slavery and insensitive to the cultural riches of indigenous people. These charges seem even more compelling when we consider that there were other people at the time who regarded slavery as immoral and were vastly more sensitive to the cultural riches of indigenous people. The charges may gain additional force when we consider that Berkeley was a philosopher of the first water, for we expect that (at least to some degree) philosophers will transcend the assumptions and prejudices of their own time and culture. On the whole, I think these expectations on our part are unrealistic. Berkeley was not only a philosopher; he was an official of the Anglican Church and a missionary. His attitudes and his rhetoric reflect the views of the institutions to which he belonged. His political philosophy was consistent with those attitudes. His failures are the failures of the church government to which he belonged. On the other side, even if Berkeley held a really destructive form of religio-ethnocentrism, he was appalled by the treatment of the indigenous people of the Americas. He rejected colonial prejudices against both blacks and native peoples as non-Christian. He advocated a policy of interracial marriage with Indians both to increase the strength of the colonies and to break down the prejudices that prevented the conversion of indigenous people. His religious focus and ethnocentric views were in conflict with the racist views of the colonists. His utopian efforts would have included both indigenous peoples and black African slaves. Still, it has to be admitted that Berkeley played a role, even if a minor one, in the westward course that the British Empire was taking in the first half of the eighteenth century. Its way included the destruction of the indigenous population and their cultures and the use of Afro-American slaves throughout the colonies.

NOTES

1. Edwin S. Gausted, *George Berkeley in America* (New Haven: Yale University Press, 1979), 4.

2. David Brion Davis, *The Problem of Slavery in Western Culture* (Ithaca: Cornell University Press, 1966), 110–15.

3. Ibid., 219–22.

4. John Wild, *George Berkeley* (New York: Russell & Russell, 1962), 289.

5. For Berkeley's rejection of this site for his college, see *The Works of George Berkeley Bishop of Cloyne*, ed. A. A. Luce and T. E. Jesop (London: Thomas Nelson & Sons, 1955), 7:349 (hereafter, *W*).

6. Here we might well wonder if Berkeley is implicitly displaying racial prejudice. Would he advocate kidnapping of children from other groups, e.g., French Catholics? And if he would not, how would he justify it in the one case and not the other? Would such a justification not have to be racist? Since it is clear that Berkeley's answer would be in purely cultural terms, this would not fit Popkin's account of modern racism, though perhaps it might fit some other definition of racism that both takes differences in culture more seriously than Popkin does in defining racism, and is willing to ignore intent in assessing the damage that one culture inflicts on another. This would, I think, take us outside the realm of philosophical racism.

7. In this respect Berkeley's attitude is in sharp contrast with the attitudes of Locke. Locke draws an explicit analogy between the indigenous peoples of the Americas and dissenters at home, and objects to the seizure of property and the violation of other rights of both groups on grounds of religion. See John Locke, *A Letter Concerning Toleration in Focus*, ed. John Horton and Susan Mendus (London: Routledge, 1991), 38.

8. Richard Popkin, "The Philosophical Basis of Modern Racism," in *The High Road to Pyrrhonism*, by Richard Popkin, ed. Richard A. Watson and James E. Force (San Diego: Austin Hill Press, 1980), 89.

9. Ibid., 85.

10. It is worth noting at this point that some would take the accounts of racism given by Popkin, Bracken, and Farr as too demanding. There are scholars who hold that simply using the language of "civilization" and "barbarism" is enough by itself to convict someone of racism. I would simply remark that the distinction to be drawn here between racism and ethnocentrism suggests that this is a mistaken view. Both kinds of thinking use this kind of language, so more is required in either case to tell us what kind of thinking is involved.

11. James Farr, " 'So Vile and Miserable an Estate': The Problem of Slavery in Locke's Political Thought," *Political Theory* 14.2 (1986): 278.

12. H. M. Bracken, "Essence, Accident, and Race," *Hermathena* 116 (1973): 81.

13. See William Uzgalis, " ' . . . The Same Tyrannical Principle': Locke's Legacy on Slavery" in *Subjugation and Bondage: Critical Essays on Slavery and Social Philosophy*, ed. Tommy L. Lott (Lanham, MD: Rowman and Littlefield, 1998), 49–79; and William Uzgalis, " 'An Inconsistency Not to Be excused:' On Locke and Racism," in *Philosophers on Race: Critical Essays*, ed. Julie K. Ward and Tommy L.

Lott (Oxford: Blackwell, 2002), 81–100. In these papers I present what I take to be a nonracist reading of Locke. Hume is a racist, but I think it is very likely that this is in spite of, and not because of, his empiricism.

14. Bracken, "Essence," 83.

15. Bracken's argument for dualism suggests that an antiracist could not argue her case on empirical grounds. This is, I would argue, clearly false.

16. Bracken, "Essence," 83.

17. There are those who suppose that accepting Afro-American slavery is prima facie evidence of racism. Of course there were people who were racists and accepted Afro-American slavery as a consequence. However, it seems clear to me that one can find cases of people who accepted slavery without being racist (I would put both Locke and Berkeley in this class); and that one can find cases where people reject slavery but are clearly racist, e.g., Hume and Lincoln's first postmaster general, Montgomery Blair. Thus the acceptance or rejection of Afro-American slavery by itself was neither a necessary nor a sufficient condition for being a racist in the eighteenth and nineteenth centuries. This should make us at least cautious in treating it as evidence for racism.

18. Gausted, *George Berkeley in America*, 98–99.

19. Tar water was a concoction of fir or pine tar boiled up in water. It was supposed to be drunk by the glassful as a cure for small pox, and Berkeley regarded it as a medical panacea. His last published work *Siris: A Chain of Philosophical Reflexions and Inquiries concerning the Virtues of Tarwater, and divers other subjects connected together and arising one from another*, began with a discussion of the virtues of tar water and the best means of manufacturing it.

20. Gausted, *George Berkeley in America*, 173–75.

21. David Humphreys, *An Historical Account of the Incorporated Society for the Propagation of the Gospel in Foreign Parts* (New York: Arno Press & The New York Times, 1969), 250–75.

22. Ibid., 94.

23. There is certainly the possibility that this passage reveals that Berkeley is a racist in respect to Black Africans in a way in which he is not toward American Indians. There is no suggestion of intermarriage with Black slaves here, only of providing religious instruction. But is this because they are black or because they are slaves? We don't have enough information to answer this question.

24. Peter Hogg, *Slavery: The AfroAmerican Experience* (London: British Library, 1979), 9.

25. Ibid., 4.

26. Davis, *Problem of Slavery*, 413.

27. Ibid., 218.

28. Uzgalis, " ' . . . The Same Tyrannical Principle,' " 49–50.

| 7 |

"A Lousy Empirical Scientist"

Reconsidering Hume's Racism

ANDREW VALLS

David Hume presents a difficult case study in the relation between race and philosophy. On the one hand, Hume's main philosophical doctrines are devoid of any racist or racialist overtones. On the other hand, however, there are a few remarks in his writings that do raise concerns. The most striking of these is an infamous footnote in which Hume says he is "apt to suspect" the inferiority of nonwhites (and, in a revised version, blacks specifically) to whites. The other main passage is in the Enquiry concerning the Principles of Morals, which some have read as an endorsement of the ill treatment of "Indians" at the hands of Europeans.[1] As with other philosophers, these remarks raise the question of whether the whole of Hume's philosophy is somehow racially coded, whether these remarks reflect something deep within his thought. In the case of Hume, I argue in this chapter, there is no warrant for the conclusion that they do. Hume's prejudiced remarks, I suggest, are not deeply rooted in his philosophy; on the contrary, Hume's philosophical views provide the resources to explain and correct Hume's own racialism.

Hume's philosophy is committed to the universality of human nature and the (rough) equality of human beings. The universality of human nature is a fundamental methodological presumption of the whole of Hume's philosophy, and especially of his Treatise of Human Nature.[2] Hume's views on human equality are not as fundamental to his thought, but he nevertheless explicitly affirms the equality of human beings on more than one occasion.[3] Hume's views on race, especially what he says in the footnote, are not an outgrowth of his philosophy but rather depart from his main philosophical commitments.

A portion of this chapter was presented at the meeting of the Pacific Division of the American Philosophical Association, Pasadena, California, March 25–28, 2004, and at the meeting of the Hume Society in Tokyo, Japan, August 2–6, 2004. I thank those who participated in the discussions in these two forums, and I thank Ann Levey for her valuable comments at the latter. I also thank Frederick Whelan, James Fieser, Kaveh Kamooneh, William Uzgalis, Geoff Sayre-McCord, and Paul Farber for their insights and comments on an earlier draft of the essay.

The chapter proceeds as follows. I first examine the footnote that has been the subject of so much attention, and I argue that Hume presents a very strong racialist thesis that may reflect racist sentiments. At the same time, however, I argue that some of the charges leveled against Hume on the basis of the note are unfounded. I then briefly examine his revision of the footnote and review recent debates about its meaning and the reasons for the change. Following this, I discuss three attempts to connect the footnote to Hume's broader philosophical doctrines, and I argue that all of these fail. Leaving the footnote behind, I turn my attention to the Enquiry passage that has troubled some readers, and I attempt to show that it has none of the racist implications that some have drawn from it. Hume's disturbing remarks on race, then, do not reveal anything deep about his philosophy, and others of his remarks that have been seen as racist or racialist in fact do not betray such attitudes.

|||

THE FOOTNOTE

The footnote that has attracted so much attention from scholars appears in his essay "Of National Characters."[4] The main argument of this essay is that culture and social environment—what Hume calls "moral causes"—play a greater role in shaping national character than climate and geography ("physical causes"). This argument was presented mainly in response to Montesquieu, who argued in favor of the predominance of physical causes. Hume's position in this debate is very consistent with his general philosophical views, which, while presuming a fundamental uniformity of human nature, also emphasize the crucial role of conventional rules and established practices in shaping the character of a society.

Given these features of Hume's philosophy, it is surprising that he presents us with the following note to his argument in "Of National Characters":

> I am apt to suspect the negroes, and in general all the other species of men (for there are four or five different kinds) to be naturally inferior to the whites. There never was a civilized nation of any other complexion than white, nor even any individual eminent either in action or speculation. No ingenious manufactures amongst them, no arts, no sciences. On the other hand, the most rude and barbarous of the whites, such as the ancient GERMANS, the present TARTARS, have still something eminent about them, in their valour, form of government, or some other particular. Such a uniform and constant difference could not happen in so many countries and ages, if nature had not made an original distinction betwixt these breeds of men. Not to mention our colonies, there are Negroe slaves dispersed all over EUROPE, of which none

ever discovered any symptoms of ingenuity; tho' low people, without education, will start up amongst us, and distinguish themselves in every profession. In JAMAICA indeed they talk of one negroe as a man of parts and learning; but 'tis likely he is admired for very slender accomplishments, like a parrot, who speaks a few words plainly.[5]

What is Hume claiming here? He is clearly asserting that whites are superior to nonwhites in "action" and "speculation," and in other qualities used in the "arts" and "sciences." There are many characteristics Hume may have had in mind, but for the sake of simplicity, let us assume that Hume believed whites to be superior to nonwhites in intelligence. Intelligence would no doubt loom large in any account of the kinds of characteristics of which Hume is speaking. Even if Hume had in mind other characteristics, such as creativity, the argument I present below—which focuses on intelligence—could be applied to other characteristics equally well.

Hume claims that nonwhites' inferiority is both "natural" and "original." Aaron Garrett has argued that by "natural" here Hume should be understood to mean uniform or regular, a sense that is compatible with an artificial, that is, conventional difference.[6] If this is so, then calling the difference between whites and nonwhites natural does not mean that it is irremediable; it could be a matter of cultural development. However, the use of the word "original" is more disturbing, because for Hume this term refers to features of human nature that are inherent, prior to the operation of physical or moral causes, and irremediable. Hume's use of the term "original," therefore, strongly implies basic differences among human beings that cannot be overcome.

Even more disturbing, perhaps, is the phrase "nor even any individual eminent either in action or speculation." This is a much stronger claim than the one that whites as a group are superior to nonwhites as group. We can imagine two overlapping normal distributions, such as that presented by Richard Herrnstein and Charles Murray, asserting that one group's distribution of some quality, in this case intelligence, is higher on a scale than another's.[7] Notice, however, that this is compatible with the view that there are eminent individuals among the supposedly inferior group. These are the individuals who constitute the right-hand "tail" of their distribution, which might place them above the average of the supposedly superior group. By asserting that there are no eminent individuals among nonwhites, then, Hume is making a very strong claim. It is not merely that whites as a group are superior to nonwhites as a group, but that the differences are so great that the right-hand tail of the distribution of nonwhites is such that not a single nonwhite individual qualifies as eminent. This means that the distributions are quite far apart and that the nonwhite distribution does not extend beyond, or not much beyond, the middle of the white distribution. This is why Hume must, in the last sentence of the footnote, dismiss even a single example of an eminent nonwhite: it would falsify his claim.[8]

Is this view racist? In common parlance, it certainly is, as many see any claim that asserts the superiority of one race over another as racist. However, in the introduction to this volume, I argued that this kind of view is not necessarily racist, that it is better characterized as racialist. I agree with Jorge Garcia that something beyond a belief about races is required to call a view or an individual racist. In particular, we should understand racism as "a racially based disregard for the welfare of certain people . . . [or] a hatred, ill-will, directed against a person or persons on account of their assigned race."[9] If this is a correct understanding of racism, is it fair to call Hume's view—and Hume himself—racist? It would seem that, based on the evidence of the footnote alone, the answer to this question is no. While it is true that Hume asserts racial superiority as an empirical thesis, he never says or implies that whites are morally superior (that their interests are more worthy of consideration) or expresses ill will toward nonwhites. If this is correct, then casual assertions that Hume is racist, based on the footnote alone, are too quick. At the very least, those like Richard Popkin who make this assertion owe an account of their understanding of racism, as opposed to racialism.[10]

Still, one could argue that the assertion of racial superiority, even in the absence of an explicit expression of other sentiments, is evidence of ill will, at least under circumstances where the evidence seems not to support the empirical thesis of racial superiority. That is, when there is evidence that the racialist doctrine is false—or when the available evidence is ambiguous—one might suspect that the individual asserting the racialist doctrine is in fact racist. The willful assertion of racialism in the face of contrary evidence may reasonably be taken as evidence of racism.

Is it fair to suspect that Hume was racist, in light of his explicit statements, combined with our knowledge of the evidence that was available to him at the time? Is his racialist assertion of the willful sort, stated in the face of countervailing evidence? Here scholars disagree. According to Popkin, "Hume's racist contention was disproven in his own day by empirical evidence that he must have known about. . . . Hume's view had been empirically falsified in his own time, and . . . he must have known this. . . . If Hume genuinely expressed himself on the difference between the races on the basis of empirical investigation and induction, then he was a lousy empirical scientist."[11] Annette Baier and Robert Palter are more generous toward Hume. Baier suggests that "we should give credit to [Hume's] tentativeness in making any generalization, [and] his respect for such empirical evidence as he had."[12] Palter says that the footnote is "scholarly in its motivation" but that the scholarship is "flawed, being based on what Hume should have recognized as some extremely weak inductions."[13] Still, Palter argues that despite Popkin's recitation of evidence of nonwhite, and particularly black, accomplishments available to Europeans in the mid-eighteenth century, "it seems that really impressive instances of individual Negro intellectual achievement in England did not appear until the 1780s."[14]

Popkin's position seems much more plausible. Hume surely must have known about some of the many impressive achievements of nonwhite societies throughout the world. And the fact that Hume goes out of his way to dismiss contrary evidence of an eminent Jamaican suggests that he is determined to maintain his racialist thesis in the face of such evidence.[15] Also, many of Hume's contemporaries came to the opposite conclusion as Hume. James Ramsey,[16] James Beattie,[17] Lord Kames,[18] François Xavier Swediaur,[19] and Lord Monboddo[20] all came to the opposite conclusion on the issue of racial superiority, based on essentially the same evidence available to Hume. So we cannot attribute Hume's racialism merely to the poor state of the evidence that he had at the time. It seems that Hume was determined to maintain his racialism, in the face of countervailing evidence and alternative interpretations of it.

On the whole then, we can conclude that Hume held a very strong racialist view, so strong that he denied the possibility of even a single eminent nonwhite individual. We can also, I believe, be justified in thinking that Hume harbored racist sentiments, because he maintained his thesis about white superiority in the face of contrary evidence.

To be fair to Hume, however, we should be clear about what the footnote does *not* say. Many of the charges that have been leveled against Hume on the basis of the footnote go far beyond what he says there, and what he says anywhere. The two main charges that I think are unjustified are that he supported slavery and that he maintained a polygenetic position on human origins.

The charge that Hume supported slavery has been made by Emmanuel Eze and Eric Morton. Eze suggests that Hume might have written the footnote "as a statement of principled philosophical position on the debate current at the time in England and America about whether or not the Negro is a legitimate 'article of trade.' "[21] Elsewhere, Eze is more direct when he asserts: "For Hume the Negro was, in the language common at the time, a legitimate 'article of trade.' "[22] Similarly, Morton has stated that "[t]he desire to exploit other people and continents inclined European thinkers to accept the idea that some men are by nature slaves, especially since the idea was acceptable to a man as important as David Hume."[23] These charges are unfounded, and they ignore Hume's explicit arguments against slavery in his essay "Of the Populousness of Ancient Nations."[24] There Hume criticized slavery as worse than political tyranny and pointed out its bad effects on all involved in it—slave and slaver-master alike. As Eugene Miller points out, in his arguments against slavery "Hume anticipates the arguments of many in Britain and America who agreed with him in opposing slavery."[25] So the suggestion that Hume supported slavery or that he wrote the footnote to lend support to the practice is not tenable.

The second unfounded charge against Hume based on the footnote is that Hume endorsed—if only "implicitly"—the polygenetic theory of human origins. This theory holds that racial differences among human populations are explained by the different evolutionary origins among the races. The polygenetic view has been associated with the most virulent forms of racism, because it denies a common origin for all humans. The idea that Hume endorsed this theory was first asserted by Popkin[26] and has since been repeated many times by others.[27] The main evidence for this claim is Hume's use of the word *species* to refer to the different races of humankind. But Hume also uses the terms "kinds" and "breeds," and he seems to use them interchangeably. This is meager evidence on which to hang the claim that Hume supported polygenism. Aaron Garrett has pointed out, "Hume offers no theory of race other than [the footnote], so it is also quite possible that he had not thought matters through as to what form the distinction between black and other humans takes."[28] Furthermore, though polygenism came to be associated with racism in the nineteenth century, the two are not necessarily related and were not strongly connected in the eighteenth century. As Robert Wokler points out, Lord Kames believed in separate origins of some races but explicitly denied the racial superiority of whites.[29] So the evidence that Hume endorsed polygenism is very slim, and even if he did, that view is not necessarily related to racism.[30]

On the whole, then, it is clear that Hume expresses a strong version of racialism in his infamous footnote, and, in light of the evidence available to him at the time, one can reasonably conclude that he stubbornly maintained his position in the face of countervailing evidence, raising the very real possibility of racist motivation. However, the charge that Hume supported slavery is utterly false, and the evidence that he embraced polygenesis is extremely weak.

| | |

THE REVISIONS

For the final, posthumous edition of the essay "Of National Characters," Hume revised the footnote. The main substantive revision is to the first two sentences.

For convenience, I reproduce the original version of the opening sentences, and then give the revised version:

> I am apt to suspect the negroes, and in general all the other species of men (for there are four or five different kinds) to be naturally inferior to the whites. There never was a civilized nation of any other complexion than white, nor even any individual eminent either in action or speculation.

> I am apt to suspect the negroes to be naturally inferior to the whites. There scarcely ever was a civilized nation of that complexion, nor even any individual eminent either in action or speculation.[31]

What does this change amount to? In a sense, Hume has weakened his claim by no longer asserting that all nonwhites are inferior to whites and instead claiming that only blacks are inferior. The substitution of "scarcely ever" for "never" could also be seen as a weakening. Nevertheless, the main conclusions I came to in the previous section hold true for the revised version of the footnote: Hume continues to assert a very strong version of racialism by not only claiming overall group inferiority but also denying the existence of even a single "eminent" individual among blacks.[32]

Why did Hume make the change? This question has given rise to some controversy, and the story of recent discussions of it is a story of how a plausible hypothesis, once asserted, lives on even after it has been seriously called into question. In his 1992 article "Hume's Revised Racism," John Immerwahr pointed out that scholars like Popkin were working with the original, not the revised version of the note. The unrevised version appeared in the old standard edition of Hume's essays edited by Thomas Hill Green and Thomas Hodge Grose,[33] but the revised version became widely known with the publication of the new standard edition edited by Eugene Miller.[34] Immerwahr suggested that Hume revised the footnote in order to respond to the criticism of it leveled by James Beattie in a work published in 1770 attacking Hume's philosophy.[35] Beattie devotes the bulk of his book to discussing the doctrines Hume advanced in the *Treatise*, but toward the end he spends several pages attacking Hume's ideas on race asserted in the footnote.[36] Beattie makes several criticisms of Hume's footnote, but the one to which Immerwahr draws attention focuses on the empires of Peru and Mexico as evidence of "eminence" among nonwhite peoples.[37] Immerwahr argues that Hume narrowed the scope of his assertion of inferiority from all nonwhites to only blacks in order to get around the evidence presented by Beattie, and supports this claim by citing a letter that Hume wrote to his editor that refers to Beattie's criticisms.[38]

Immerwahr's thesis about why Hume revised the footnote has been pretty well refuted by Aaron Garrett.[39] Garrett points out that there is no evidence that Hume had Beattie's criticisms of the footnote in mind when he revised the footnote or when he referred to Beattie in his letter. The letter asks that an "Advertisement" be placed at the beginning of one of the volumes of the final edition of Hume's works. The advertisement asks that the reader consider Hume's *Enquiries*, rather than his *Treatise*, as containing his definitive philosophical doctrines. Garrett suggests that Hume did this in order to blunt the force of Beattie's (and Reid's) criticisms, which were directed at the *Treatise*. There is no mention of the footnote in either the letter or the advertisement. Indeed, the advertisement was to be added to a volume of the new edition that did not even contain the essay in which the footnote appears. Rather, it was to be added to the volume containing the *Enquiries*. Garrett suggests that there are any number of reasons why Hume might have revised the footnote and that we will probably never know the reason(s) for certain, but that in any case we have no reason to think that it had anything to do with Beattie.

Despite Garrett's article, other scholars have picked up on the Immerwahr thesis, which seems to have taken on a life of its own. Morton advances the thesis,[40] and Eze does so three times,[41] though neither author gives Immerwahr credit for it. It may be that these authors' failure to cite Immerwahr reflects an impression that what he asserted is now conventional wisdom or common knowledge. In light of Garrett's convincing arguments, however, one cannot plausibly assert the Immerwahr thesis without providing further evidence to support it.

Two final points should be made about Hume's revision, points that Immerwahr makes and about which he is surely right. First, Immerwahr notes that the fact that Hume took the trouble to revise the footnote suggests that it was not merely a "casual addition," as Popkin asserted in one of his earlier treatments of it.[42] Rather, Immerwahr says, "Hume's racism was deliberate and considered."[43] As Popkin himself recognized after he discovered the revision, Hume "was no innocent, just dropping a casual prejudiced remark amongst the gentlemen after dinner."[44] This suggests that Hume scholars must take the footnote seriously and that any attempt to understand its relation to his general philosophical doctrines must begin with the assumption that the ideas contained in it reflect his considered views.

Second, however, the revision shows even more clearly that there is no reason to think that Hume was committed to polygenism. I argued above that the evidence that he endorsed the polygenetic thesis is very weak and depends on placing great emphasis on Hume's use of the word *species*, despite the fact that he seems to use it interchangeably with the words *kinds* and *breeds*. Immerwahr points out that in the revision Hume "drops the [purported] polygenetic language."[45] If the note was ever any reason to believe that Hume endorsed the polygenetic account of the origins of humankind, then in light of the revision we can conclude with Immerwahr that "Hume's commitment to polygenesis appears to have been either non-existent or superficial. It is most likely that he originally used the term 'species' in a casual and non-technical way."[46]

| | |

THE FOOTNOTE AND HUME'S PHILOSOPHY

There have been several attempts to relate the footnote to Hume's philosophical works and thereby impute racism to some aspect of Hume's overall philosophy. All of these attempts, I believe, fail to establish any such connection. Indeed, as others have pointed out, Hume's philosophy contains the resources to understand and correct the view Hume expressed in the note.

Eric Morton seems to be of two minds on the relation of the note to Hume's philosophy. On the one hand, and most prominently, he argues that Hume's racism is deeply connected to Hume's philosophy. In discussing the footnote, Morton asserts that "[t]his example of racism seriously impugns Hume's theories of human nature" and that "Hume's racial prejudice . . . forced him to reconsider his original idea of the universality of human nature."[47] On the other hand, however, Morton admits that Hume's footnote is incompatible with his broader philosophical commitments. As Morton correctly points out, an overwhelming theme in Hume's philosophical work is the universality of human nature. Indeed, Morton does not provide any evidence that Hume did reconsider his ideas on human nature in light of his views on race. Rather, he says that "Hume contradicted himself."[48] If the footnote is simply incompatible with Hume's theory of human nature, it is difficult to see how one impugns the other.

A different problem confronts Morton's account of the note's relation to the essay in which it appears. He states: "The contention of Hume's essay that moral causes determine national character is a flawed epistemological premise. This contention is an example of how Hume's theory of knowledge is driven by Hume's racism and the built-in racism in his philosophical worldview."[49] Yet Hume's racism, as advanced in the footnote, is emphatically not grounded in his argument in the essay that human differences are the result of moral causes. Rather, Hume makes an exception to the general thesis of the essay, maintaining that these differences are not "moral" (i.e., cultural) but rather "natural" and "original." Hence Morton's contention that the footnote shows the racism of Hume's emphasis on moral causes is mistaken: the argument in favor of moral causes, if applied to all human differences, would imply a nonracialist position.

The problem, again, is not that Hume's philosophical theses are racist but rather that he departs from them by carving out an exception in the footnote.

Eze's attempts to ground Hume's racialism in his philosophy are no more successful.[50] Eze claims that the footnote "is rooted both in Hume's epistemology and in his political thought," and he answers "Yes" to the question "Was Hume's theory of human nature racist?"[51] Eze relies on Hume's distinction between perception and reasoning to argue that his racism is deeply embedded in his theory of human nature. Hume says that "[a]ll kinds of reasoning consist in nothing but a *comparison*," but that reasoning proper takes place only when at least one of the objects being compared is not present to the senses; when both are present, "we call this perception rather than reasoning" because this involves "a mere passive admission of the impressions thro' the organs of sensation."[52] Eze asserts without argument that for Hume blacks are capable only of perception and not of reason. In this respect, he further states, for Hume blacks are like animals. Eze concludes that "for Hume the mental capacity of Negroes as a race—which is to say, the level of their humanity—is more nearly animal than white."[53]

Hume's discussions of animals are particularly odd choices for Eze to rely upon in advancing his argument that Hume's theory of human nature is racist.[54] For in these sections, Hume is at pains to emphasize the essential *similarity* between human mental life and that of nonhuman animals. He writes—in a direct refutation of Eze's contention that for Hume animals do not possess reason— that "beasts are endow'd with thought and reason as well as men."[55] Similarly, he writes that "[t]he *causes* of these passions [pride and humility] are likewise much the same in beasts as in us," and he maintains "not only that love and hatred are common to the whole of sensitive creation [that is, to both humans and nonhuman animals], but likewise that their causes, as above-explain'd, are of so simple a nature, that they may easily be suppos'd to operate on mere animals."[56] In all of these places, Hume is relying on the similarity between animals and humans to further support his account of human mental life. He explains: " 'Tis usual with anatomists to join their observations and experiments on human bodies to those on beasts, and from the agreement of these experiments to derive an additional argument for any particular hypothesis."[57] Since Hume saw the mental life of humans and nonhuman animals as essentially the same, and since he explicitly states that animals are possessed of reason, Eze's position is unsupported. Hume could not have believed that blacks are inferior to whites because their mental life was "more animal than white," since for Hume animal mental life is essentially the same as that of humans—white or black.

The fact that Hume believed that animals were possessed of reason does not, of course, prove that he did not hold racist or racialist views.[58] Though animals have reason, Hume held that "[m]en are superior to beasts principally by the superiority of their reason: and they are degrees of the same faculty, which set such an infinite difference betwixt one man and another."[59] By the same token, Hume might have believed that nonwhites, though possessed of reason, are inferior to whites in the degree to which they possess reason. In this sense, Hume's views on the universality of human nature might appear to be compatible with racialism, just as his views on the similarity of animals are compatible with "species-ism."

Several points should be made about this. First, Hume's assertion on the inferiority of nonwhites is incompatible with Hume's views, asserted several times throughout his writings, on the rough equality of human beings. Hume writes that "men" are "nearly equal" in "bodily force, and even in their mental powers and faculties, till cultivated by education."[60] Second, there is an important disanalogy between Hume's view on the degree to which animals possess reason and any view he might have had on the inferior degree of reason possessed by nonwhites. After all, Hume's position that nonhuman animals share many aspects of human mental life did not lead him to write a *Treatise of Animal (Human and Nonhuman) Nature*. Hume's whole philosophy is committed to a greater degree of universality among humans (and he never denies that nonwhites or blacks are human) than exists between humans and nonhuman animals. Finally, an account of Hume's racialism based on nonwhites' inferior reason is not Eze's account. Eze's account holds that for Hume, animals do not have reason, and that nonwhites are like animals in this respect. This account is clearly mistaken.

Eze is also mistaken when he claims that the footnote "was on numerous occasions publicly defended by Hume against criticisms."[61] I know of no evidence to support this, and Eze provides none. The only piece of evidence that he does supply seems to be an error. Eze claims that the letter in which Hume called Beattie "a bigotted silly fellow" was published in the *London Chronicle*.[62] It is true that part of this letter did appear in that publication (June 12–14, 1777), but the published portion is a paragraph on British colonialism in America, not the part about Beattie.[63] Moreover, even if it were true that the part of the letter discussing Beattie were published, the publication of an originally private letter would hardly constitute "numerous" or "public" defenses of the footnote. As we have seen, the letter in which Hume refers to Beattie does not refer to the footnote.

Finally, let us consider Popkin's position on the relation between Hume's philosophy and the footnote. Like Morton, Popkin seems to be of two minds about what this relation is, and I wish to endorse one tendency we find in his analysis and reject the other. On the one hand, Popkin often writes as if Hume's footnote were a product of his overall philosophy. He writes that Hume's racialism is "intimately related to his thought," that in the footnote Hume is "applying his method of historical experimental reasoning," and that "Hume's racist views . . . are consonant with his analysis of human nature."[64] All of this suggests that Hume's racialism is an outgrowth of his general philosophical doctrines, that it is a correct or natural extension of his overall philosophy. Yet, on the other hand, Popkin also writes as if the footnote were incompatible with Hume's overall philosophy or an incorrect, or very poor, application of his general thought. He writes: "It seems to me that all theories of knowledge and theories of human nature, especially in the period from the Renaissance to the Enlightenment, are theoretically non-racist," and he does not exclude Hume from this characterization.[65] Furthermore, as I noted above, Popkin says that "Hume's racist contention was disproven in his own day by empirical evidence that he must have known about," and that "Hume's view had been empirically falsified in his own time, and that he must have known this."[66] These remarks suggest that the footnote is not of a piece with Hume's overall philosophy, but rather that Hume erred in the application of his philosophical principles to the available evidence. Again, the problem with the footnote is not that it is a valid extension of Hume's universalist theory of human nature, but rather that he departs from that theory. It is in making the exception for nonwhites, and then for blacks, that Hume errs.

Indeed, as Popkin himself and others have noted, Hume's philosophy contains the resources to explain and correct his racialist footnote.[67] All of these authors refer to the section of the *Treatise* entitled "Of Unphilosophical Probability" in which Hume gives an account of the very sort of prejudice that he himself exhibits in the footnote. Hume writes:

> A fourth unphilosophical species[68] of probability is that deriv'd from *general rules*, which we rashly form to ourselves, and which are the source of what we properly call PREJUDICE. An *Irishman* cannot have wit, and a *Frenchman* cannot have solidity; for which reason, tho' the conversation of the former in any instance be visibly very agreeable, and of the latter very judicious, we have entertain'd such a prejudice against them, that they must be dunces or fops in spite of sense and reason. Human nature is very subject to errors of this kind; and perhaps this nation as much as any other.[69]

Hume goes on to explain that this error occurs when circumstances lead us to mistake the accidental or contingent for the essential, and that "[w]e may correct this propensity by a reflection on the nature of those circumstances."[70] This suggests, as Popkin says, that Beattie, in his response to Hume's footnote, shows himself to be a better Humean than Hume himself was in this matter.[71] Beattie pointed out that Hume's evidence for his strong assertions was very inadequate and that at the same time Hume ignored contrary evidence.

There is a final way in which the footnote marks an important departure from Hume's general philosophical commitments. In discussing the "original" features of human nature, Hume violates his own methodological premise in the *Treatise*, where he emphasizes that the only evidence that we have in analyzing human nature is our observation, which can reveal certain regularities but does not tell us about the most fundamental features. He states that "any hypothesis, that pretends to discover the ultimate original qualities of human nature, ought at first to be rejected as presumptuous and chimerical."[72] A little later Hume claims that "I pretend not to explain [the] *original* qualities of human nature."[73] By his own admission, then, Hume's assertion of an original difference among races "ought . . . to be rejected as presumptuous and chimerical."

So the footnote, in either its original or its revised form, is incompatible with both Hume's general philosophy and the thesis that he advances in the essay in which it appears. The universality of human nature is a fundamental assumption of Hume's philosophy, yet here he seems to violate his own principles. As John Werner has noted, the footnote also "is not consistent with Hume's usual respect for the dignity of man."[74] And in the context of the essay "Of National Characters," again the trouble is not that Hume is correctly applying an essentially racist thesis, but that, as historian David Brion Davis has noted, "the one eighteenth-century writer who had some understanding of the relation of character to cultural and situational environment failed to extend his insights to the Negro."[75] All of this points to the conclusion that, while Hume clearly asserts a strong racialist thesis, he had to depart from his philosophical commitments to do so.

| | |

IS HUME A HOBBESIAN?

There is one other passage in Hume's writings—this one in a key philosophical work, the *Enquiry concerning the Principles of Morals*—that has given some scholars concern that Hume would be inclined to justify ill treatment of nonwhites. Here is the passage:

> Were there a species of creatures intermingled with men, which, though rational, were possessed of such inferior strength, both of body and mind, that they were incapable of all resistance, and could never, upon the highest provocation, make us feel their resentment; the necessary consequence, I think, is that we should be bound by laws of humanity to give gentle usage to these creatures, but should not, properly speaking, lie under any restraint of justice with regard to them, nor could they possess any right or property, exclusive of such arbitrary lords. Our intercourse with them could not be called society,

which supposes a degree of equality; but absolute command on the one side, and servile obedience on the other. Whatever we covet, they must instantly resign: Our permission is the only tenure, by which they hold their possessions: Our compassion and kindness the only check, by which they curb our lawless will: And as no inconvenience ever results from the exercise of a power, so firmly established in nature, the restraints of justice and property, being totally useless, would never have place in so unequal a confederacy.

This is plainly the situation of men, with regard to animals; and how far these may be said to possess reason, I leave it to others to determine. The great superiority of civilized Europeans above barbarous Indians, tempted us to imagine ourselves on the same footing with regard to them, and made us throw off all restraints of justice, and even of humanity, in our treatment of them. In many nations, the female sex are reduced to like slavery.[76]

The passage has made some commentators worry about the implications of Hume's philosophy for women and nonwhites (as well as animals): "In this passage Hume maintains that gender and race can determine whether one has a right to just treatment. Race and gender are important for Hume's theory of justice because his theory at least apparently privileges the strong, and race and gender indicate contrasting degrees of strength. Benevolence, not justice, is the source for virtuous treatment of the weak."[77] I think that this interpretation is mistaken, and that if it were correct, Hume would be, in this single passage, rejecting almost everything else that he says about justice.

To understand the meaning of this passage, we must begin by examining the context in which it appears, which is part 1 of section 3, "Of Justice," in the Enquiry.[78] This section is devoted to describing what have come to be called "the circumstances of justice."[79] Hume's account of justice—in both the Treatise and the Enquiry—begins with the idea that certain empirical conditions in the world and certain facts about human nature give rise to the idea of justice, which for Hume is the complex set of rules that regulates property. In arguing that certain conditions are necessary for the idea of justice to arise, Hume asks us to imagine the world as otherwise than it is, and argues that under these other, counterfactual conditions there would be no place for justice. For example, he writes, "Let us suppose that nature has bestowed on the human race such profuse abundance of all external conveniences, that . . . without any care or industry on our part, every individual finds himself fully provided with whatever his most voracious appetites can want." Under these circumstances, "the cautious, jealous virtue of justice would never once have been dreamed of." This is intended to show that limited abundance—scarce resources—is one condition that gives rise to the idea of justice. Where there is overabundance, there is no need for rules determining what belongs to whom. Hume makes a similar point about human generosity. "Again; suppose, that, though the necessities of the human race continue the same as at present, yet the mind is so enlarged, and so replete with friendship and generosity, that every man has the utmost tenderness for every man . . . it seems evident, that the use of justice would, in this case, be suspended by such an extensive benevolence." Hence limited benevolence in human nature is another precondition for justice.[80]

Hume then asks us to "reverse the foregoing suppositions." If we imagine extreme scarcity rather than extreme abundance or extreme selfishness rather than extreme generosity, here too, Hume argues, justice would have no place because mere rules would be insufficient to constrain people's actions. "Thus," Hume concludes, "the rules of equity or justice depend entirely on the particular state and condition in which men are placed."[81] Because our material conditions are (usually) somewhere between extreme abundance and extreme scarcity, and human nature is (again, under most circumstances) possessed of only moderate benevolence, justice is both possible and necessary. Since we live in neither a golden age nor a Hobbesian state of nature, we both need justice and are able to regulate our actions in accordance with its rules. Later Hume asks us to consider one other counterfactual, namely, that each human being is entirely self-sufficient, and again concludes that under this circumstance, justice would have no place. Interdependence, he concludes, is another feature of the circumstances of justice.[82]

It is in this context that the purportedly troubling passage appears. The passage is another counterfactual thought experiment, the point of which is to emphasize another precondition of justice, namely, the equality of human beings. Hume is making the Hobbesian point that the rough equality of human beings is one of the circumstances of justice. He is, then, implicitly affirming what he explicitly asserts in the essay "Of Polygamy and Divorces," namely, "the natural equality of mankind."[83] In another essay, "Of the Original Contract," Hume asks us to "consider how nearly equal all men are in their bodily force, and even in their mental powers and faculties, till cultivated by education."[84] In the *Enquiry* passage, then, Hume is talking about, and affirming, the actual equality of human beings, by asking us to imagine the counterfactual state of human beings intermingled with inferior creatures.

Furthermore, it is important to emphasize that this is a discussion of the first origins of justice; it is emphatically not an account of the final form of justice. While there has been some disagreement among scholars as to whether the passage is an account of the origins of, or of our approval of, justice,[85] I think it is clear that the former is the right interpretation. While for Hobbes self-interest is both the origin of justice and the source of our obligation to it, Hume's account is more complicated. While self-interest plays a large role in justice's origins in Hume's account, as it evolves we come to endorse it and see it as generating obligations on us and others for reasons beyond self-interest. Hume concludes the section I have been discussing by briefly describing how, from its humble origins, our sense of justice expands: "History, experience, reason sufficiently instruct us in this natural progress of human sentiments, and in the gradual enlargement of our regards to justice, in proportion as we become acquainted with the extensive utility of virtue." "Utility" as Hume uses it here does not mean self-interest but general social benefit. Hume is unambiguous that this "progress of human sentiments" consists in the ever-greater expansion of those to whom we extend its protection—from "families" to "society" and then from relations within a society to the circumstances where "several distinct societies maintain a kind of intercourse for mutual convenience and advantage."[86] Regulating interactions between societies by justice is a mark of progress, and this notion of progress through reflection on and extension of our moral ideas is a fundamental feature of Hume's philosophy.[87] It is a mistake to take the passage as Hume's final word on justice, because it clearly is not. It is only the beginning of his story about where justice comes from.

With this in mind, let us return to the passage itself. If we look at the language that Hume uses, it is clear that he is engaged in a counterfactual, hypothetical thought experiment. He uses the subjunctive: "Were there a species . . ." The creatures he asks us to imagine are "rational [but] inferior . . . both of body and mind." Hume never suggests that such creatures actually exist; if they exist, non-human animals are the only actual case he can think of. The passage is intended to show that "society . . . supposes a degree of equality" which he thereby implicitly affirms. When Hume mentions the "barbarous Indians," we may be able to convict him of ethnocentrism owing to his use of the term "barbarous," but we cannot convict him of racism (or racialism) or conclude that he believes them to be the sort of rational but inferior creatures he asked us to imagine before. Rather, he says that "[t]he great superiority of civilized Europeans above barbarous Indians, tempted us to imagine ourselves on the same footing with regard to them [as we are with regard to nonhuman animals], and made us throw off all restraints of justice, and even of humanity, in our treatment of them." The implication of this sentence, and particularly of the phrase "tempted us to imagine," is that this was a mistake.[88]

The "superiority" to which Hume refers is not the sort of superiority that he asked us to imagine, which is clearly counterfactual, but some other kind. This superiority may be cultural or technological, but we have no reason to think that for Hume it was racial. Hume is not saying that Native Americans were actually inferior in body and mind, and Hume is not justifying their ill treatment. In fact, he notes that Europeans threw off "all restraints of justice, and even of humanity." Not only did Europeans violate their own norms of justice (which is evidence of the limits of their "progress of human sentiments"), but they also threw off "all restraints . . . even of humanity." Hence, for Hume the treatment of Native Americans by Europeans is condemnable on two grounds: they failed to treat Native Americans with justice, and as if that were not bad enough, they even failed to treat them with humanity, the lower standard of treatment to which nonequals like animals are entitled.

Overall, then, though the passage seems troubling at first, it has no racist or racialist implications when seen in context and when we examine what Hume actually says. The point of the section in which it appears is to demonstrate the circumstances of justice, which include moderate scarcity, moderate benevolence, interdependence, and, yes, human equality. The reference to rational but inferior creatures is counterfactual, like the other hypothetical circumstances Hume asks us to imagine, and his reference to American Indians is critical of, not a justification of, their mistreatment at the hands of Europeans.

| | |

CONCLUSION

In the infamous footnote to "Of National Characters" Hume expresses a strong racialist view. Furthermore, he does so in the face of countervailing evidence— evidence on which his contemporary critics could draw in contesting his assertion. This provides some reason to believe that Hume harbored not only racialist beliefs but also racist sentiments. Hume's determination to maintain his basic position, reflected in his careful revision of the footnote, which narrowed its scope but not its essential thesis, is further evidence of this.

However, it is a mistake, I have argued, to believe that Hume's racialism is deeply rooted in his philosophy. On the contrary, Hume's philosophy is overwhelmingly committed to the assumption of the uniformity of human nature. The trouble with the footnote, then, is not that it shows something troubling about Hume's philosophy itself, but rather that Hume was driven to reject his own philosophical doctrines to assert the inferiority of nonwhites, and, later, blacks specifically. To do this, Hume had to go out of his way to ignore much of what he himself had written. But as I noted above, and as other philosophers have pointed out, Hume's philosophy contains the resources to help explain Hume's own racialism, which is a case of "unphilosophical probability," unsupported by the evidence.

If this is correct, some of the charges and labels that have been applied to Hume seem unfair. For example, Morton has characterized Hume's view as "philosophical racism."[89] Hume's racism is, to the contrary, unphilosophical, both in the strict sense in which he uses that term in his analysis of "unphilosophical probability" and in the sense that his racialism is not connected to, and indeed requires a departure from, his philosophy. Similarly, it seems unfair to call the view that Hume expresses in the footnote "Hume's racial law," as Popkin does and Morton does repeatedly.[90] Though the footnote is not a mere casual remark, it is also hardly a thesis that Hume spent much time defending, or even articulating. As such, it is unfair to imply that Hume intended to advance anything as grandiose as a law.

Nevertheless, it is entirely fair to think poorly of Hume for the view that he does express. Though "le bon David" no doubt had many virtues, ability to rise above the racial prejudices of his day was not one of them. But in condemning him in this regard, as I think we should, we ought not make the mistake of believing that Hume's philosophy itself is somehow racially coded. There is no reason to believe, with Eze, that when Hume spoke of human nature, he "meant only a white 'we.' "[91] Indeed, Hume's philosophy—especially his emphasis on the universality of human nature—is incompatible with the racialism he expresses in the footnote. Hume, it is true, was a racialist, and perhaps a racist, but Humeanism is neither.

NOTES

1. "Enquiry concerning the Principles of Morals," in *Enquiries concerning Human Understanding and concerning the Principles of Morals*, ed. L. A. Selby-Bigge and P. H. Nidditch, 3rd ed. (Oxford: Clarendon Press, 1978), 190–91.

2. David Hume, *A Treatise of Human Nature*, ed. L. A. Selby-Bigge and P. H. Nidditch, 2nd ed. (Oxford: Clarendon Press, 1978).

3. "Of Polygamy and Divorces," in David Hume, *Essays Moral, Political, and Literary*, ed. Eugene Miller (Indianapolis: Liberty Classics, 1985), 185; and "Of the Original Contract," in ibid., 467–68.

4. Hume, *Essays*, 197–215.

5. Ibid., 208 n. 10.

6. Aaron Garrett, "Hume's 'Original Difference': Race, National Character, and the Human Sciences," *Eighteenth-Century Thought* 2 (2004): 127–52.

7. Richard J. Herrnstein and Charles Murray, *The Bell Curve: Intelligence and Class Structure in American Life* (New York: Free Press, 1994), 279.

8. Paul Farber has suggested to me that this analysis is anachronistic, as Hume could not have

thought of his own view in this way. While I grant this, I think it is nevertheless an accurate depiction of his view, and the comparison with more recent views does illuminate just how strong Hume's racialism was.

9. Jorge L. A. Garcia, "The Heart of Racism," in *Racism*, ed. Leonard Harris (Amherst, NY: Humanity Books, 1999), 399.

10. Richard Popkin, "Hume's Racism," in his *The High Road to Pyrrhonism*, ed. Richard A. Watson and James E. Force (San Diego: Austin Hill, 1980), 265; Popkin, "Hume's Racism Reconsidered," in *The Third Force in Seventeenth Century Thought* (Leiden: E. J. Brill, 1992), 64, 74. For a critique of Popkin's account of racism, see William Uzgalis's chapter on Berkeley in this volume.

11. Popkin, "Hume's Racism Reconsidered," 64, 66, 72.

12. Annette Baier, "Moralism and Cruelty: Reflections on Hume and Kant," in *Moral Prejudices: Essays on Ethics* (Cambridge: Harvard University Press, 1994), 292.

13. Robert Palter, "Hume and Prejudice," *Hume Studies* 21 (1995): 6.

14. Ibid., 7.

15. Frederick Whelan has suggested to me another motivation for Hume's dismissal of the case of the Jamaican man, one that is consistent with his methodological commitments. In his essay "Of Miracles," Hume argues that we are justified in discounting testimonial evidence when it is incompatible with all of our other knowledge of the world, and especially when we have reason to be suspicious of the motivations of those offering the testimony. A similar argument is made by Charles Taliaferro and Anders Hendrickson in "Hume's Racism and His Case against the Miraculous," *Philosophia Christi* 4 (2002): 427–42. In this respect it is possible to see the last sentence of the note as being consistent with others of Hume's views, but, as I argue below, it remains the case that the racialism of the note as a whole is a significant departure from Hume's usual assumption of the universality of human nature and the equality of humans.

16. James Ramsey, *Essay on the Treatment and Conversion of African Slaves in the British Sugar Colonies* (Dublin, 1784).

17. James Beattie, *Essay on the Nature and Immutability of Truth in Opposition to Sophistry and Scepticism* (Edinburgh: Kincaid and Bell, 1770); for excerpt, see *Early Responses to Hume: Hume's Essays Moral, Political, and Literary*, ed. James Fieser (Bristol: Thoemmes, 1999), 2:255–59.

18. Lord Kames, *Sketches of the History of Man* (Edinburgh, 1774); for discussion, see Robert Wokler, "Apes and Races in the Scottish Enlightenment: Monboddo and Kames on the Nature of Man," in *Philosophy and Science in the Scottish Enlightenment*, ed. Peter Jones (Edinburgh: John Donald, 1988), 155.

19. François Xavier Swediaur, *Philosophical Dictionary; or, the opinions of modern philosophers on metaphysical, moral, and political subjects* (London: G. G. J. and J. Robinson, 1786); for excerpt, see Fieser, *Early Responses*, 342–46.

20. Lord Monboddo, *Antient Metaphysics: Volume Third Containing the History and Philosophy of Men* (London, 1784).

21. Emmanuel Chukwudi Eze, "Hume, Race, and Human Nature," *Journal of the History of Ideas* 61 (2000): 696.

22. Emmanuel Chukwudi Eze, *Achieving Our Humanity: The Idea of the Postracial Future* (New York: Routledge, 2001), 69.

23. Eric Morton, "Race and Racism in the Works of David Hume," *Journal on African Philosophy* 1 (2002): 1–27. http://www.icaap.org/iuicode?150.1.1.3: p. 4.

24. Hume, *Essays*, 383–86.

25. Ibid., 384 n. 7.

26. Richard Popkin, "The Philosophical Basis of Modern Racism," in *High Road to Pyrrhonism*, 92–94; Popkin, "Hume's Racism," 254, 257, 265; Popkin, "Hume's Racism Reconsidered," 65, 66.

27. John Immerwahr, "Hume's Revised Racism," *Journal of the History of Ideas* 53 (1992): 482; Morton, "Race and Racism," 4; Charles Mills, "The Racial Polity," in *Racism and Philosophy*, ed. Susan E. Babbitt and Sue Campbell (Ithaca: Cornell University Press, 1999), 23.

28. Aaron Garrett, "Hume's Revised Racism Revisited," *Hume Studies* 26 (2000): 175.

29. Wokler, "Apes and Races," 155–56, 166 n. 40.

30. Popkin also provides several other pieces of evidence to support his claim, each of which is rather weak. They are that Hume's *Natural History of Religion* does not trace the development of man from ancient Jews to the modern world; that his *History of England* does not derive British history from biblical history; and that the essay "Of Miracles" argues that the account of man's development through Jewish history is implausible ("Philosophical Basis of Modern Racism," 92). Elsewhere, Popkin remarks that "Hume, in contrast to his contemporary William Robertson, does not even bother giving lip-service to the prevailing assumption of the unity of the human species, and its common origin in terms of providential creation" ("Hume's Racism," 257). But Hume's rejection of the biblical account of human origins does not imply an endorsement of polygenism. It has everything to do with the secular character of Hume's thought, and nothing to do, as far as I can tell, with his views on race.

31. Hume, *Essays*, 629 n. i.

32. It should be noted that in "On National Characters" there is one other prejudiced remark about blacks: "You may obtain any thing of the Negroes by offering them strong drink; and may easily prevail with them to sell, not only their children, but their wives and mistresses, for a cask of brandy" (Hume, *Essays*, 214). The context is a discussion, at the end of the essay, of whether physical or moral causes account for the "vulgar" observation "that people in the northern regions have a greater inclination to strong liquors, and those in the southern to love and women" (213). Hume's remark about "Negroes" is one of many stereotypes that he mentions in order to call into question whether the "inclinations" asserted by the "vulgar" are in fact true.

33. *The Philosophical Works of David Hume*, ed. Thomas Hill Green and Thomas Hodge Grose, 4 vols. (London: Longmans, Green, 1874–75).

34. Hume, *Essays*.

35. Beattie, *Essay on the Nature and Immutability of Truth*.

36. Beattie's discussion of Hume's footnote is conveniently reproduced in *Race and the Enlightenment*, ed. Emmanuel Chukwudi Eze (Oxford: Blackwell, 1997), 34–37. However, Eze relies on the original 1770 edition. The revised 1776 edition differs slightly. For both variants, see Fieser, *Early Responses*, 2:255–59.

37. Immerwahr, "Hume's Revised Racism," 484.

38. For the letter, see *The Letters of David Hume*, ed. J.Y.T. Greig (Oxford: Clarendon Press, 1932), 2:299–302.

39. Garrett, "Hume's Revised Racism Revisited."

40. Morton, "Race and Racism," 3.

41. Eze, *Race and the Enlightenment*, 37; Eze, "Hume, Race, and Human Nature," 692; Eze, *Achieving Our Humanity*, 52.

42. Popkin, "Hume's Racism," 266.

43. Immerwahr, "Hume's Revised Racism," 485.

44. Popkin, "Hume's Racism Reconsidered," 75.

45. Immerwahr, "Hume's Revised Racism," 483.

46. Ibid., 485.

47. Morton, "Race and Racism," 3.

48. Ibid., 2.

49. Ibid., 10.

50. Eze, "Hume, Race, and Human Nature"; Eze, *Achieving Our Humanity*, chap. 2.

51. Eze, *Achieving Our Humanity*, 53, 59.

52. Hume, *Treatise*, 73.

53. Eze, *Achieving Our Humanity*, 69.

54. See the following sections of Hume's *Treatise*: "Of the Reason of Animals," "Of the Pride and Humility of Animals," and "Of the Love and Hatred of Animals" (sections 1.3.16, 2.1.12, and 2.2.12), as well as his discussion in the first Enquiry, "Of the Reason of Animals" (section 9).

It should be noted that Eze miscites two of the quotes that he uses (see *Achieving Our Humanity*, chap. 2). The quote on page 68 referenced with note 51 appears not on page 327 of Hume's *Treatise* (as indicated in the note) but on page 73. The quote on pages 68–69 referenced with note 52 appears neither in the *Treatise* section "Of the Reason of Animals" (as Eze indicates in the text on page 68) nor on page 327 of the *Treatise* (as he indicates in note 52), but in the Enquiry section "Of the Reason of Animals," p. 108.

55. Hume, *Treatise*, 176.

56. Ibid., 326, 397.

57. Ibid., 325.

58. I owe this point to Kaveh Kamooneh and Ann Levey.

59. Hume, *Treatise*, 610. Thanks to Ann Levey for pointing out this passage to me.

60. Hume, *Essays*, 467–68.

61. Eze, *Achieving Our Humanity*, 53.

62. Eze, "Hume, Race, and Human Nature," 692.

63. Thanks to James Fieser for assistance on this point.

64. Richard Popkin, "The Philosophical Basis of Eighteenth-Century Racism," *Studies in Eighteenth-Century Culture* 3 (1973): 246; Popkin, "Philosophical Basis of Modern Racism," 93; Popkin, "Hume's Racism," 265.

65. Popkin, "Hume's Racism," 266.

66. Popkin, "Hume's Racism Reconsidered," 64, 66.

67. Popkin, "Philosophical Basis of Modern Racism," 94; Popkin, "Hume's Racism," 259; Richard Louden, "Comments on Emmanuel Chukwudi Eze's *Achieving Our Humanity*," paper presented at the meeting of the American Philosophical Association, Central Division, Chicago, Illinois, April 27, 2002; Timothy Costelloe, "Hume's Prejudice and the Idea of Moral Progress," unpublished manuscript, 2002.

68. Note Hume's use of the word *species* here. As I suggested above, his use of it in the footnote does not imply a polygenetic view but rather is a synonym for "kind."

69. Hume, *Treatise*, 146–47.

70. Ibid., 148.

71. Popkin, "Hume's Racism," 261.

72. Hume, *Treatise*, xvii.

73. Ibid., 13.

74. John M. Werner, "David Hume and America," in *Hume as Philosopher of Society, Politics, and History*, ed. Donald Livingston and Marie Martin (Rochester: University of Rochester Press, 1991), 151–68.

75. David Brion Davis, *The Problem of Slavery in Western Culture* (New York: Oxford University Press, 1988), 457.

76. Hume, *Enquiries*, 190–91.

77. Anne Jaap Jacobson, "Introduction: A Double Re-reading," in *Feminist Interpretations of David Hume*, ed. Anne Jaap Jacobson (University Park: Pennsylvania State University Press, 2000), 9.

78. Hume, *Enquiries*, 183–204.

79. See John Rawls, *A Theory of Justice* (Cambridge: Harvard University Press, 1971), 126–30.

80. Hume, *Enquiries*, 183, 184, 184–85.

81. Ibid., 186, 188.

82. Ibid., 189–92.

83. Hume, *Essays*, 185.

84. Ibid., 467–68.

85. See Joyce L. Jenkins and Robert Shaver, " 'Mr. Hobbes Could Have Said No More,' " in *Feminist Interpretations*, ed. Jacobson, 139.

86. Hume, *Enquiries*, 192.

87. See Annette C. Baier, *A Progress of Sentiments: Reflections on Hume's Treatise* (Cambridge: Harvard University Press, 1991).

88. Arthur Kuflik, "Hume on Justice to Animals, Indians, and Women," in *Hume Studies* 24 (1998): 53–70, 57.

89. Morton, "Race and Racism," 2.

90. Popkin, "Hume's Racism," 258; Morton, "Race and Racism," 1, 4, 6.

91. Eze, *Achieving Our Humanity*, 72.

Rousseau, Natural Man, and Race

BERNARD R. BOXILL

Rousseau is that rarity in philosophy, a great writer, and he is especially impressive when demonstrating and denouncing the corrupting effects of inequality. But he may not have been altogether what he appeared to be. Although he censured imperialism unequivocally, and ridiculed the idea that a European king was entitled to take possession of territories in the New World without regard for the people already living there, his view that these people were stupid and primitive should ring alarm bells:[1] the racist theories developed in the nineteenth century classified these very same people as inferior. Further, despite his egalitarian pretensions, Rousseau recommended the subordination of women, and philosophers who recommend subordinating one part of the human race cannot be trusted not to recommend subordinating another part.[2] Accordingly, since we have lately become alerted to hidden racial biases in certain ostensibly righteous European philosophies, it seems wise to inquire into whether Rousseau too laid traps for non-Europeans in his eloquent tributes to equality.

Rousseau's best work, *The Discourse on Inequality*, is most likely to be helpful on this issue. I will therefore begin by trying to get clear on what he was doing in it. Then I will inquire into whether the theory of human nature that he proposes in it might have contributed even if only inadvertently to the racist theories that were developed in the nineteenth century and continue to dog us today.

| | |

THE DISCOURSE ON INEQUALITY

The Discourse on Inequality is really an extended report of a series of mental experiments in which Rousseau places human beings first in a presocial condition and then in gradually more complicated social environments. His hope was that these experiments would help us to see what we get from the hand of nature, what we get from society per se, and what we get from society as it is complicated in various ways; with this information he believed that we would be able to pinpoint the causes of our corruption and design institutions to reduce it.

The report begins with Rousseau's account of the presocial human being. According to Rousseau, such a being is any ordinary person, one's next-door neighbor, for example, after we have stripped him of "all the artificial faculties he could only have acquired by prolonged progress" (2D, 141). But how do we know what these faculties are? Clearly they must be the faculties people do not need to have from the first in order to avoid extinction. If they acquired such necessary faculties only as a result of a prolonged progress, they would at one time not have had the faculties necessary to avoid extinction, and consequently would not have avoided extinction, contrary to the evident facts. If the faculties we need to have from the first in order to avoid extinction cannot be acquired from a prolonged progress, they must come from the hand of nature, or as we may say, they must be innate.

But the faculties we need to have from the first in order to avoid extinction depend on whether from the first we live in groups, that is are social, or are solitary. By starting with the solitary, presocial being and asking what faculties that being must have from the first to avoid extinction, it may therefore seem that Rousseau begs the question. Why does he not start with human beings living in groups and ask what faculties such beings need to avoid extinction? This is a common complaint, but it fails to appreciate what Rousseau was about. The crucial point here was that Rousseau was following Locke in supposing that we should assume as few innate faculties as we can.[3] Rousseau may have learned from his close reading of Plato's *Republic* that the most obvious consequence of group life is that it makes a division of labor possible and thus increases the stock of goods that we need.[4] Consequently by assuming relative abundance, he could also assume that we do not need to increase the stock of goods that we need, and consequently that we would not need to live in groups to survive. He is not thinking of a fantasy world of milk and honey. He is thinking of places where there are enough fruits, nuts, grubs, roots, and water for a human being to survive. But that not unreasonable assumption enables him to reduce the number of innate faculties he needs to assume. That is, he can start with the assumption that people are not naturally sociable, but naturally solitary. He will then explain why they live in groups by supposing that as scarcity develops and people must live in groups to survive, they acquire sociability and language. The fact that we always (or almost always) find people living in groups can also be explained. Some accident of nature forced some people into scarcity, which then forced them to discover the advantages of group life. Being better able to survive, they displaced the others.

Rousseau lists three faculties necessary to avoid extinction if we live in circumstances of relative abundance. These are self-love or *amour-de-soi*, which he describes as a principle that "interests us intensely in our well-being and our self-preservation"; pity, which he describes as a "natural repugnance at seeing any sentient Being, and especially any being like ourselves, perish or suffer" (2D, 132); and the power to "combine its ideas," which he calls "understanding" (2D, 148). Rousseau believed that these faculties are innate because we need them to avoid extinction even in circumstances of relative abundance. Sociability and the faculty for language are not innate since in such circumstances we can survive without them.

Rousseau supposes then that the swarming multitude of human qualities and faculties beyond these three, including sociability and language, must be acquired by a prolonged progress. This supposition does not follow logically from the claim that self-love, pity, and understanding are together sufficient to account for human survival in circumstances of relative abundance; conceivably human beings have innate properties that are not necessary for their survival. But again relying on Locke's thesis that we should assume as few innate faculties as we can, Rousseau supposes that our only innate faculties are those that are necessary for our survival. All other faculties, any faculty we can imagine human beings surviving without, must be acquired by a prolonged progress. Logically, the prolonged progress could start with solitary human beings. But Rousseau wisely rejected this possibility on the ground that progress among solitary human beings would not be cumulative. Reports of feral children who were always without a language and many of the qualities that we associate with ordinary human beings confirmed the inference (2D, 218). Consequently he maintained that the "prolonged progress" that eventually produces all acquired human qualities is started by interaction with others. Solitary human beings would never acquire new qualities and faculties unless the relative abundance they lived in changed to relative scarcity and they had to start interacting with each other to survive.

To explain how we acquire these new qualities and faculties, scarcity is not enough. Rousseau had to postulate that human beings have another faculty that responds to scarcity by producing new faculties necessary to survive in scarcity but is not itself acquired by a prolonged process. It could not be acquired by a prolonged progress because if it were, human beings would have become extinct with the advent of scarcity. He calls this faculty the "faculty of perfectibility." But this threatens to involve him in contradiction. On the one hand, he seems to argue that the only faculties human beings have innately are those necessary to account for their survival in circumstances of relative abundance. On the other hand, he postulates that human beings have innately a faculty of perfectibility, though this faculty is not necessary to explain human survival in circumstances of relative abundance. Rousseau could avoid the contradiction by dropping the claim that human beings have innately only those faculties they must have in order to survive in circumstances of relative abundance. But then he would still have to explain how we come to have the faculties we need not have to survive in such circumstances, and he could not simply infer that we have these faculties from the fact that we have survived. Kant with his teleological assumptions argued that nature or providence implants these faculties in us, foreseeing that we will need them in some future condition. But Rousseau denies himself this luxury. How then does he solve the problem?

Rousseau is not as clear here as he could be, but what he seems to have in mind is that the faculty of perfectibility is simply the three faculties of self-love, pity, and understanding *when they interact in a certain way*. The qualification *when they interact in a certain way* is essential, for otherwise the faculty of perfectibility would be selected for its survival value, since its parts are, and Rousseau resists that possibility. But if self-love, reason, and pity are the faculty of perfectibility only when they interact in a certain way, and if they need not interact in that way, and we can survive when they do not, then we can say that the faculty of perfectibility is not selected for its survival value, and also that self-love, pity, and understanding are.

Rousseau must have included understanding in the faculty of perfectibility because he claims that the inhabitants of the banks of the Orinoco bind their children's temples with slats, thereby blocking both the development of their reason and the operation of the faculty of perfectibility. The implication is clearly that understanding is part of the faculty of perfectibility. Rousseau must also have supposed that self-love and pity were parts of the faculty of perfectibility for he claims that their interaction gives us morality, which is a property that we do not have innately. As he puts it, "It is from the association and combination which our mind is capable of making between these two Principles, without it being necessary to introduce into it that of sociability, that all the rules of natural right seem to me to flow" (2D, 132, 133). More generally Rousseau's idea seems to be that the passions cause our reason to "perfect itself"; for "it is not possible to conceive of why someone without desires or fears would take the trouble of reasoning." And on the other hand, reason causes the multiplication of the passions because it gives us new ideas as it develops and consequently new things to "desire or fear" (2D, 149, 150).

One might have expected Rousseau to deny that animals have understanding, on the ground that it is the "specific characteristic of the human species," but he claims that animals have understanding and that human beings differ from the animals in this respect "only as more does from less." Indeed, he says, "there is a greater difference between one given man and another than there is between a given man and a given beast" (2D, 148). Since Rousseau claims that animals possess self-love, pity, and understanding, and that the faculty of perfectibility is self-love, pity, and understanding, it seems he must say that animals have the faculty of perfectibility. But he says that the faculty of perfectibility is the specific characteristic of human beings. That is, animals lack the faculty. That is, they do not acquire new faculties the way human beings do. An "animal," Rousseau claims, "is at the end of several months what it will be for the rest of its life and its species is after a thousand years what it was in the first year of these thousand." Human beings, on the other hand, develop a multitude of new qualities. This is perhaps the point he makes most insistently, ridiculing "that fine adage of ethics so much harped on by the ruck of Philosophasters, that men are everywhere the same" (2D, 218, 219).

The objection that animals must have the faculty of perfectibility just because they have self-love, understanding, and pity overlooks the qualification that self-love, pity, and understanding are the faculty of perfectibility only when they interact in a certain way. If the three faculties interact in the requisite way in humans, but not in animals, then human beings would have the faculty of perfectibility but animals would not, though both animals and human beings have self-love, pity, and understanding. To sustain this response Rousseau must explain why the three faculties interact in the requisite way in human beings but not in animals.

Although Rousseau says that self-love, pity, and understanding are sufficient to account for human survival, he does not say they explain animal survival. This may seem odd, for he says that animals have self-love, pity, and understanding. But it is not self-contradictory. The possession of one leg may be sufficient to account for one man's peregrinations, though in fact most men use two legs to move around. Somewhat similarly, Rousseau believed that animals have innately a faculty that human beings lack, namely, instinct, and that while human beings have survived by using only self-love, pity, and understanding, animals have survived using instinct, in addition to self-love, pity, and understanding. Human beings either lack instinct or can choose to restrain it and consequently have free agency (2D, 142, 149). Animals do not have free agency and therefore cannot choose to restrain instinct. As he puts it, "Nature alone does everything in the operations of the Beast, whereas man contributes to his operations in his capacity as a free agent. The one chooses or rejects by instinct, the other by an act of freedom" (2D, 148). Now choosing by an act of freedom requires an exercise of reason, and choosing by instinct does not. That is, because human beings lack instincts and consequently must choose by an act of freedom, they exercise their understanding more often and to a greater degree than animals do. If reason must be exercised at a certain minimal frequency and degree to start interacting with self-love and pity in a way that gives rise to new properties, this would explain why man has, but animals lack, the faculty of perfectibility. If this is correct, we must therefore add free agency to the faculties that make up the faculty of perfectibility. This leaves intact Rousseau's view that the faculty of perfectibility is made up of faculties that are innate and necessary for survival. Since human beings must make choices to survive and do not choose by instinct, they must choose by free agency. Consequently, free agency is necessary for survival and must be innate, just like self-love, reason, and pity.

Rousseau says that human beings lack instincts, choose by an act of freedom, and consequently must exercise their reason.[5] Further, by being exercised in this way, reason begins to interact with self-love and pity to become the faculty of perfectibility. But does this not imply that human beings always have the faculty of perfectibility? Rousseau has to resist this possibility for it implies that the faculty of perfectibility is innate and necessary for our survival. He does so by claiming that the faculty of perfectibility is received in potentiality. He means simply that reason, self-love, and pity existed in us for thousands of years without interacting in the way that makes them the faculty of perfectibility. Rousseau supposes that in the presocial stage of the state of nature, when our needs are simplest and nature most abundant, the human being barely exercises his reason to satisfy his desires. He is hungry and he chooses to eat an apple instead of a pear. He chooses by an act of freedom, but the alternatives are so readily available that he does not have to exercise his reason to make the choice, and as a result it remains undeveloped. As Rousseau puts it, "nothing is so limited" as the mind of natural man in the early stages of the state of nature (2D, 221). During those years human beings are to all outward appearances no different from animals. Indeed like animals they lack the faculty of perfectibility. But they are human beings for the simple reason that they have the faculty of perfectibility in potentiality. That is, they may find themselves in circumstances that force their self-love, reason, and pity to start interacting in the way that produces new faculties and properties. Presumably there are no such circumstances for animals. Consequently animals do not have the faculty of perfectibility even in potentiality.

I insist that Rousseau's natural man is a human being because some people seem determined to deny this. According to one author, for example, Rousseau's natural man is the "missing link," a "midpoint between animals and human beings."[6] This view is based on the fact that some of Rousseau's contemporaries accepted the idea of a "chain of being" and were searching for "missing links" between human beings and other animals. But I see no evidence that Rousseau was interested in this question. His "natural man" is a human being, and he devised the idea of a "natural man" to prove that the human being is a very peculiar kind of creature, namely, one that comes into the world with very few definite qualities but an immense capacity to acquire new qualities. He would have undermined this project if his "natural" man was not a human being but a missing link being human beings and animals.

Robert Wokler also seems to want to make Rousseau's "natural man" into an animal. Thus he claims that it was "truly an orangutan," and that a "fierce and protracted dispute about the factual standing of Rousseau's portrait of the state of nature in the *Discourse* could have been avoided if this simple truth had been perceived."[7] The most charitable reading of this claim that I can think of is that Rousseau based his description of "natural" man on the travelers' accounts of orangutans. But it is highly implausible since Rousseau was very skeptical of those accounts and would not have based any serious theory on them. Neither does Rousseau's speculation that the orangutan was possibly an example of his "natural" man make Wokler's claim any less misleading. First, Rousseau never actually claimed that natural man was an orangutan. On the contrary he suggested experiments that he thought could settle the issue, for example, sexual intercourse between human beings and orangutans to see whether this would produce fertile offspring, though he allowed that this test could not be "tried in innocence" (2D, 218). In any case, Rousseau's natural man has the faculty of perfectibility at least in potentiality. The orangutan does not have the faculty of perfectibility even in potentiality. Consequently, Rousseau's natural man is not an orangutan, even if Rousseau, not knowing that the orangutan did not have the faculty of perfectibility even in potentiality, might have thought that it was. Rousseau's account of how "natural" man lives may be remarkably similar to recent discoveries of how orangutans live, as Wokler claims, but this does not show that natural man is an orangutan. If two things are of the same kind, they should look the same in the same circumstances. But while natural man and orangutan may look the same when each is solitary, they do not look the same when each starts interacting with others of its kind. When natural man begins interacting with other natural men, they invent language and acquire the faculties and properties typical of the human beings we see around us. This is because interaction triggers the faculty of perfectibility that natural man has innately. But even if orangutans started interacting with other orangutans, they would never develop language because they do not have the faculty of perfectibility.

Rousseau is also careful to indicate that no innate faculty draws human beings into interacting with one another; sociability is not innate. He argues that "several foreign causes," that is, environmental factors "which might never have arisen," scarcity especially, drive us out of our solitary conditions and into the extended interaction with others necessary to take advantage of the division of labor and to survive in conditions of scarcity. The interaction prompts self-love, reason, and pity to act on one another so as to become the faculty of perfectibility.[8] By stressing that the causes of the faculty of perfectibility "might never have arisen," Rousseau is indicating that he is rejecting all teleological theories of human history. As I have argued, scarcity is the most important of the foreign causes that actualize the faculty of perfectibility and might never have come about. Rousseau insists that this scarcity is caused by accidental changes in the environment, not by spontaneous increases in man's needs or a spontaneous development of his reason. Following Locke, Rousseau is simply trying to use the weakest assumptions he can about the faculties we have innately, and the assumption that environmental changes cause scarcities that compel us to exercise and develop our reason is weaker in this sense than the assumption that our reason is programmed to develop spontaneously. The exercise of reason leads to an increase in knowledge, and thus to new ideas; these new ideas arouse new desires and fears, and consequently new passions. Reason, self-love, and pity are now interacting in the manner that makes them the faculty of perfectibility. The most important of the new properties it produces is amour propre, namely, self-awareness, the desire to be esteemed by others, and the desire for self-esteem secured through the esteem of others.

The acquisition of new needs and passions could have come to a halt at what Rousseau calls the stage of the "first revolution" and "the best for man." But again some "fatal accident" (2D, 177) pushed us out of it. Rousseau conjectures that this accident was the invention of metallurgy and agriculture and that these inventions led to a division of labor into metal workers and agricultural workers, the introduction of private property in land, and finally dependence and inequality. The mental experiment Rousseau is reporting on here consists of introducing serious economic inequalities into a simple society of equals and then imagining how the people are likely to change, given what we suppose to be innate in human nature. Naturally he has to give some plausible account of how such inequalities might arise, and he speculates that they arise because of the invention of agriculture and metallurgy. But he is not wedded to that account. The crucial experiment could be conducted with the inequalities arising in some other way. Equality might have persisted, Rousseau notes, "if the use of iron and the consumption of foods had always been exactly balanced" (2D, 171). But since "nothing maintained" this balance, random variations in the fortunes of metal and agricultural workers made the emergence of inequality practically inevitable, and this led to vanity, pride, envy, "deceitful cunning," "consuming ambition," and the "ardent desire to raise one's relative fortune, less out of genuine need than in order to place oneself above others" (2D, 180, 181). At this point and no earlier, people developed ambition and what Kant would call "unsocial sociability" and descended into the state of war.

| | |

ROUSSEAU'S THEORY AND RACIAL BIAS

Rousseau was intrigued by travelers' reports of orangutans and pongos, human-looking creatures found in the "Kingdom of the Congo," in the "East Indies," and in the "Kingdom of Loango," far from Europe. He hoped that if these creatures proved to be human beings, perhaps they would turn out to be examples of his "natural" men and would furnish hard empirical evidence in favor of his hypothetical reasoning about human nature. Unfortunately the travelers who described these creatures usually maintained that although they looked somewhat like human beings, they were nevertheless not human. Since they did not say exactly why they took this position, Rousseau conjectured that it was because of the creatures' "stupidity" and "also because they did not speak" (2D, 216). Rousseau thought these were "weak reasons," because of his theory that human language and intelligence develop only in society. He also noted that the reports of the stupidity of orangutans and pongos were unwarranted inferences from facts that were easily consistent with their not being stupid at all (2D, 217). More generally he noted that these travelers were usually "Sailors, Merchants, Soldiers and Missionaries," none of whom could be expected to provide reliable accounts of what they had seen (2D, 218). Rousseau was not being unreasonable when he insisted that we should wait on experiment and more careful observation before we could be confident that orangutans were not human (2D, 217). It was simply good science given that he had a plausible theory that predicted that solitary human beings could be somewhat like orangutans.

But in his fascinating and important book *Enlightenment against Empire*, Sankar Muthu raises interesting questions about Rousseau's determination to hold onto the possibility that orangutans could possibly be natural men. Rousseau, he observes, "managed to humanize certain animals."[9] Since Muthu cites Wokler's essay approvingly in this context, this view may be based on Wokler's misleading claim that Rousseau's natural man is truly an orangutan. But there is a point to Muthu's observation. He wants to suggest, I think, that Rousseau's insistence that there might be strains of very stupid human beings living outside Europe who did not even have a language might have inadvertently provided fodder for the nineteenth-century racist theories that maintained that even if the human-looking creatures living outside Europe were genuinely human, they were very stupid and inferior human beings. Muthu is also concerned about the consequences of Rousseau's habit of using the "savages" of the New World to illustrate his claim that human beings in a state of nature would be stupid, and that intelligence is the product of certain societal conditions that human beings invent and implement. Muthu is careful to point out that Rousseau knew that these "savages" were not examples of his "natural" men. Nevertheless Rousseau uses them to illustrate his views about natural man on the ground that they "of all existing Peoples have so far departed least from the state of Nature" (2D, 165). Presumably his background assumption was that if the Caribs are closest to natural man of all peoples, and things closely related tend to have similar qualities, then the stupidity of Caribs should prove the stupidity of natural man.

Although Muthu's concerns alert us to the possibility that even well-meaning theories can have dire results, I am not convinced that they are altogether well grounded. There are not really many clear cases of Rousseau's use of the stupidity of the Caribs to illustrate his claims about the stupidity of natural man, though his habit of using "Savage man" to refer both to natural man and to people like Caribs may create the impression that there are many such cases. The only clear case that I can find is the one Muthu cites, namely, that the Carib "sells his Cotton bed in the morning and comes weeping to buy it back in the evening, having failed to foresee that he would need it for the coming night" (2D, 151). But even this case is somewhat ambiguous since it illustrates the Carib's lack of foresight rather than his lack of intelligence.

Muthu seems on firmer ground when he notes that Rousseau's frequent comments on the physical prowess of Negroes and New World peoples show how convinced he was of their mental inferiority. Given Rousseau's assumption that Negroes and New World peoples are least removed from the natural state of all peoples, he evidently thought that his comments on their physical prowess implied that natural man was physically even more able and consequently could survive in a solitary condition. Muthu suggests that Rousseau believed that natural man's physical prowess followed from his mental deficiencies, and consequently that he must have believed that Negroes and New World people suffer from mental deficiencies too. Thus he speaks of "Rousseau's contentions that Amerindians' impressive physical characteristics flourish precisely because their mental capacity cannot go beyond the simple association of basic ideas at their stage of historical development."[10] But this reasoning seems flawed. Rousseau did not believe that natural man was physically very able because he was mentally deficient; he believed that natural man did not exercise his mental powers to survive because he was physically very able. By extension, Rousseau did not believe that Amerindians were physically able because they were mentally deficient; he believed that Amerindians did not exercise their mental abilities because they were physically very able. The difference between these two positions is of the last importance for a correct understanding of Rousseau. The first, which I have claimed is mistaken, could easily support racist theories because it suggests that the mental abilities of Amerindians are innately limited and cannot develop to meet the demands of scarcity, so that their physical abilities have to develop if they are to survive. The second, which provides no foothold for racist theories, is that the mental abilities of Amerindians are innately as good as those of other people, but they do not have to exercise these abilities because their physical capabilities are so outstanding. And it is certainly Rousseau's view. The sturdiness of "Savages" he says, "prevents" them "from using their reason" (2D, 160). He does not say that their lack of reason compels them to become sturdy.

Muthu is clear that Rousseau did not intend his views to support racist theories even if they did so in fact. I would like to make a slightly different point: it is impossible or at least highly unlikely that anyone could derive racist theories from Rousseau's views without violating his fundamental principle of making the weakest assumptions possible about our innate faculties. This principle makes it very difficult to justify the characteristic claim of racist theories that some peoples are innately inferior to others. At least it demands that the theorist exhaust all possible environmental explanations for human differences before postulating innate differences.

But what about Rousseau's claims that "Savages," or "Savage Peoples," have remained at the "stage" of the first revolution, while Europeans have long been moved to another stage (2D, 176, 177). His use of the word "stage," and the fact that by "Savages" or "Savage Peoples" he was obviously referring to many of the nonwhite or "colored" people of the world, like Native Americans, Africans, and Tahitians, suggest that he too thought of such people as inferior or backward compared with Europeans. The crucial point to emphasize in responding to this objection is that, following Locke, Rousseau wanted to make the minimal assumptions he possibly could about our innate faculties, and was thus committed to arguing that differences between people are a result of their differing environments, both natural and those they have created, often inadvertently. In particular, Rousseau maintains that intelligence is an acquired faculty and is stimulated to develop at different rates in different kinds of society. Just as one can allow that there are differences in IQ between the races without supporting racist theory, Rousseau can affirm that Europeans are more intelligent than non-Europeans without supporting racist theory either. In both cases, whether or not you support racist theory depends on how you explain the differences. If you maintain that they can be explained only by innate biological differences, then you may provide support for racism. If you maintain that they are explained by environmental factors, especially differences in social institutions, then you do not provide support for racism. But the whole point of Rousseau's *Discourse on Inequality* is to defend the second alternative. One can use his theory to justify the idea that there are innate differences in intelligence between the races only by violating its supreme principle.

One might agree that in general Rousseau wanted to find environmental explanations of all human differences, including intelligence, but object that inborn differences in intelligence must be assumed in order to explain why certain societies create environments that compel intelligence to develop and others do not. So although Rousseau says that the "fatal accident" that took Europeans out of the stage of the first revolution was their "invention" of the "two arts" of metallurgy and agriculture, inventions are not accidents, and if "Savage peoples" failed to make them, it must be because they are innately less intelligent than Europeans. But Rousseau thought that Europeans developed metallurgy and agriculture more effectively than other peoples because Europe was "most abundant in iron and the most fertile in wheat" compared with "other parts of the world" (2D, 177). Evidently, Rousseau assumed that agricultural tools made from iron are more effective than tools made from softer metals like copper and that wheat is more nutritious than other cereals. Because Europe was richer in iron than the other continents, Europeans made better agricultural tools than the equally inventive and intelligent people of American and Africa and had better food. As a result, Europe had an agricultural revolution with all that this entails, while the people of America and Africa remained at the stage of the first revolution.

It may be objected that the fact that Rousseau based his views on Locke's proposal to make minimal assumptions about our innate faculties does not make it impossible for his views to support racism because Locke himself developed a theory of property that justified the European expropriation of the Americas.[11] But this theory of Locke's does not depend on his proposal to make minimal innate assumptions about human faculties. It follows from his view that human happiness and well-being depend on an ever increasing abundance of material goods produced by an ever increasing division of labor and an ever increasing exploitation of natural resources, and Rousseau utterly rejected this view.[12] On the contrary he believed that human happiness depended on human contentment, that is, on a nice balance between our desires and our abilities.

A similar reply can be made to the objection that if Europeans are more intelligent than New World peoples, and their social institutions account for this, it is the duty of Europeans to introduce these social institutions in the New World to make the people there intelligent too. This argument goes considerably beyond the theory Rousseau defends in the *Discourse on Inequality*, and it depends on a suppressed premise that Rousseau would reject, namely, that we ought to take steps to increase general intelligence whatever the costs of doing so. On his account, increases in intelligence are driven by corrupting passions, so that the cost of increasing intelligence is corruption or the danger of corruption. The social institutions that generated the passions that drove increases in intelligence were an extensive division of labor and serious economic inequality. These institutions could be introduced into New World societies and would make the peoples there as intelligent as Europeans, but only at the cost of corrupting them, and this cost is too high.

It may be objected that on Rousseau's account, people must be corrupted before they can establish legitimate societies, because corruption is a necessary condition for the Hobbesian war of all against all that drives people to make the social contract that is the foundation of Rousseau's own legitimate state. Consequently, Rousseau must have believed that for all their defects Europeans were a stage closer to creating legitimate societies than other peoples and consequently that they should conquer the New World societies to prepare them to establish such societies. But this objection confuses the social contract described in the *Second Discourse* with the social contract described in *The Social Contract*. The social contract described in the *Second Discourse* is the result of a Hobbesian war of all against all, to get out of which people establish states. But Rousseau argues that this social contract is a fraud and the states it creates are corrupt. The social contract in *The Social Contract* is an account of the foundation of a legitimate society, and it does not posit a war of all against all. It requires only that people have "reached the point where obstacles to their self-preservation in the state of nature prevail by their resistance over the forces each individual can use to maintain himself in that state."[13] And this implies only that they are no longer self-sufficient. Consequently, the less competitive societies of the New World were, by Rousseau's lights, closer to establishing legitimate societies than the Europeans.

On this account, the European conquest of the New World was one of the greatest catastrophes in human history. Besides the needless death of millions, the conquest and destruction of these societies and the introduction of European social institutions drove the possibility of ever establishing legitimate societies further and further out of reach. When the whole world joined Europe in its greed, pride, hypocrisy, deceitfulness, and cunning, humanity would probably descend into a maelstrom of corruption, war, and death. Rousseau does not mean that nature is steering or leading us onto these disasters, or even that it is useful or illuminating to speak in this way. As I have indicated, he warns repeatedly that a number of accidents that might never have happened thrust Europe onto its present destructive path.

Rousseau's theory of human corruption is clearly nonteleological. Unfortunately, however, Allen Wood creates a potential for confusion by associating it with Kant's, which is teleological. Indeed, Wood says, the "two doctrines are not only compatible, but they are actually *one and the same doctrine.*"[14] My concern is that this contention will lead to unfounded suspicions about Rousseau's theory because the teleological nature of Kant's doctrine gives it the potential to support racist or imperialist theories.

In *Perpetual Peace* Kant declares that "[p]erpetual peace is insured (guaranteed) by nothing less than that great artist nature, whose mechanical process makes her purposiveness visibly manifest, permitting harmony to emerge among men through their discord, even against their wills."[15] Although Kant's use of the word *guaranteed* suggests that he believed that natural processes make peace inevitable, and he expresses similar beliefs not only in *Perpetual Peace* but also in *Idea for a Universal History*, he cannot really have meant to be taken literally.[16] The idea that human competition and corruption, propelled by unsocial sociability, are leading us, without any help from morally motivated actions, to design and set up the just institutions that guarantee peace, that devils could set up a just republican constitution if only they were intelligent enough, is too silly to attribute to Kant. The design and maintenance of just institutions cannot rest on intelligence alone, however enlightened it is. Everyone who has reflected on the matter agrees on this. James Madison revealed the crucial mechanical device in the republican constitution that Kant thought devils could design by recommending a constitution in which "ambition must be made to counteract ambition," but he was clear that such a constitution required at least some virtuous people to ensure its effective operation.[17] He understood that however sophisticated the intelligence that designed such a constitution, that same sophisticated intelligence, coupled with the pride and competitiveness that helped to develop it, would lead some people to think that they could "beat the system," namely, enjoy the constitution's benefits while circumventing its constraints. As Rousseau observes, "If I am told that society is so constituted that every man gains by serving the rest; I shall reply that this would all be very well if he did not gain even more by harming them" (2D, 208). And despite his misleading language Kant probably agrees. Paul Guyer claims that in the first appendix to *Perpetual Peace* Kant "explicitly argues that the moral goal of peace cannot be expected to come about by merely natural means but only through the affirmation of morality by moral politicians."[18] I cannot agree with Guyer that Kant is as explicit about this as he says, for Kant's language there is typically convoluted and indirect, but I agree that what Kant says can bear the interpretation that Guyer gives it, and that charity demands we suppose that interpretation to be correct, for the alternative view that nature alone can guarantee peace is manifestly untenable.

But the fact that Kant believed that peace and justice could be secured only by moral politicians does not tell us what he was trying to do when he argued or seemed to argue that peace and justice could be secured by natural processes alone. One not unreasonable explanation is that Kant was trying to prove that peace was at least possible. He would want to prove this since he believed that we have a duty to secure peace, and this can be true only if peace is possible. But this explanation is not entirely satisfactory. Kant's arguments do not prove, and cannot possibly prove, that natural processes make peace inevitable. But they were clearly designed to prove much more than that peace was merely possible. At the very least they seem designed to prove that natural processes do not implacably oppose our morally motivated efforts to secure peace, and indeed that if they cannot themselves assure the implementation of just institutions, they can sometimes form a tide that watchful moral politicians can take at the flood and channel into such institutions. Clearly if such arguments are successful they will lead us to hope that our morally motivated actions to secure peace will ultimately be successful, for hope is normally aroused not by the belief that a good is barely possible but by a belief that it is at least not unlikely. Since the motivation to act on a duty to secure an end is normally strengthened by a hope that acting on that duty will be successful, this suggests that Kant's object in producing these arguments was to arouse us to hope that we can establish peace, and in this way to encourage us to strive to establish it. Setting aside the now discredited view that Kant objected to using sentiment to support moral motivation, this seems a reasonable way to interpret Kant's apparent attempts to prove that peace is inevitable. If this hypothesis is correct, it tells us finally that Kant could not have wanted his arguments to create even the impression that peace was inevitable since this would spread complacency, undermine our efforts to secure peace, and ensure that we never secure it.

If my reconstruction of Kant's doctrine is correct, *Perpetual Peace* is not so much an academic treatise as a carefully designed scheme to encourage our morally motivated efforts to establish peace, and the means it employs are to get us to hope that such efforts will be successful by persuading us that likely natural trends do not always oppose but actually sometimes second them.[19] I do not intend to suggest that there was anything underhanded or dishonest about this scheme. I concede, indeed I insist, that Kant believed that natural trends were creating circumstances that alert, clever, and morally motivated politicians could use to secure peace. Since Kant could tell that one of the most likely natural trends was Europe's continued conquest and ultimate transformation of the New World into something like its image, he must have assumed that this transformation was among the naturally produced circumstances that moral politicians in different parts of the world could exploit to create the world of republican states that he thought would help secure peace. Notice however that on Kant's view "ambition" constitutes the radical propensity to evil in human nature, so that when he endorses the republican constitution as the most likely to produce just legislation and to restrain a country from war, he is endorsing a constitution that is expressly designed to deal with ambitious people. Indeed, as the claim that intelligent devils could design a republican constitution suggests, and the maxim from Madison makes explicit, such a constitution proposes to exploit ambition to secure justice. Since, however, Rousseau believed that the ambition that made Kant's republican constitution necessary was the peculiar product of European institutions, on his account the first definitive article for world peace in Kant's *Perpetual Peace*, namely, that all states must be republican, could make sense only if Kant believed that by fair or foul means all societies must come to share those European institutions that made human beings ambitious.

Further, it is quite clear that Kant believed this too. Although he unequivocally condemned European imperialism, he was realist enough to understand that the princes and governments of Europe were not going to pay the slightest attention to his exhortations and would continue in their conquest and transformation of the New World.[20] And if unaccountably they desisted or were stopped by unforeseen events, Kant had a backup plan to show how the New World would still be made into the image of Europe. This is the point of his "cosmopolitan right," the third definitive article for a peaceful world in *Perpetual Peace*, entitling individuals of any state to visit other states and to attempt to enter into commerce with the natives of those states.[21] Muthu argues that Kant's cosmopolitan right was not meant to encourage exchanges of goods only.[22] But if it was meant to encourage the exchange of ideas as well, then all the more is it certain that implementing the cosmopolitan right would result in the peaceful change of non-European societies into European societies, for of course in Kant's day Europeans were far more willing and able to visit other countries than non-Europeans were to visit Europe.[23]

It may be objected that Kant did not believe that human nature was as variable as Rousseau maintained, that he believed rather that human beings were everywhere marked by an unsocial sociability that made them aggressive and competitive. If this is correct, the world would not have to become an image of Europe for all states to eventually become republican. But this objection is surely overstated.

Even if Kant believed that human beings everywhere are characterized by unsocial sociability, he also believed that some human beings, the Tahitians especially, were not sufficiently competitive to properly develop their talents.[24] Such people had to become energized by the "spirit of trade" to compel them to start competing and developing their talents, and Kant was confident that "sooner or later" that spirit "dominates every people" and draws them into beneficial worldwide competition.[25] But even if I concede the objection, this only emphasizes yet again how misleading it is to identify Rousseau's doctrine of human corruption with Kant's. Although Rousseau allowed that people start to develop amour propre as soon as they enter society, he argued that it led to serious corruption only when the peculiarly corrupting institutions of European society were introduced. Consequently even if Kant would have argued that the universal quality of unsocial sociability made republican constitutions in all states necessary for peace and justice, Rousseau did not have to draw this conclusion. If Europeans did not spread their ideas and institutions everywhere, if the Caribs and Tahitians and Indians were allowed to go their own ways, a just and peaceful world could include republics in Europe and radically different kinds of constitutions in countries in the New World, the Pacific, and Africa.

This may seem small comfort if Europeans have destroyed these societies or drawn them into the worldwide net of trade, competition, and war, and now for better or worse we all share those Europeans traits that make republican constitutions the best for Europeans. But there may still be cultures that do not breed the competitive ambitious types that can be restrained only by republican constitutions, and Rousseau's doctrine tells us that there is no reason to maintain that these places must adopt republican constitutions. In any case, whatever the facts, the theoretical point I wish to make still stands. Kant's teleological theory envisages the Europeanization of the world and for that reason has the potential for justifying European imperialism or paternalism. Firmly nonteleological, Rousseau's doctrine has no such potential.

Although I have not been able to identify any overt or covert racial biases in Rousseau's philosophy of human nature, it does not follow that it cannot be part of a racist theory. The plasticity Rousseau claims to detect in human nature may have protected the theory he developed from sexual and racial bias, while making that same theory easily exploitable by those bent on mischief. There is no sexual bias in Rousseau's philosophy of human nature as he developed it in The Discourse on Inequality, but he himself used that philosophy of human nature in Emile to justify the subordination of women.[26] I recommend proceeding with extreme caution.

NOTES

1. Jean-Jacques Rousseau, "The Social Contract," in *On the Social Contract with Geneva Manuscript and Political Economy* ed. Roger Masters, trans. Judith Masters (New York: St. Martin's Press, 1978), bk. 1, chap. 9, p. 57. See also "Geneva Manuscript," bk. 1, chap. 5, p. 171. For one of Rousseau's comments on the stupidity of Caribs, see *The Discourse on Inequality*, in Jean-Jacques Rousseau, *The First and Second Discourses and Essay on the Origin of Languages*, ed. and trans. Victor Gourevitch (New York: Harper Torchbooks, 1990), 151 (hereafter 2D).

2. Jean-Jacques Rousseau, *Emile*, trans. Allan Bloom (New York: Basic Books, 1979), chap. 5.

3. John Locke, *An Essay concerning Human Understanding*, ed. Peter Nidditch (Oxford: Oxford University Press, 1975), bk. 1.

4. Plato, *Republic*, trans. G. M. A. Grube, revised by C. D. C. Reeve (Indianapolis: Hackett, 1992), bk. 11, 369bc

5. Or rather, if they do have instincts, they can choose not to follow them. See 2D, 142 and 149.

6. Francis Moran III, "Natural Man in Rousseau's *Second Discourse*," in *Philosophers on Race: Critical Essays*, ed. Julie K. Ward and Tommy L. Lott (Oxford: Blackwell, 2002), 125, 126.

7. Robert Wokler, "Rousseau's Anthropology Revisited," *Daedalus* (Summer 1978): 117.

8. 2D, 168. See also 147 and 177.

9. Sankar Muthu, *Enlightenment against Empire* (Princeton: Princeton University Press, 2003), 43.

10. Ibid., 42.

11. James Tully, "The Two Treatises and Aboriginal Rights," in *An Approach to Political Philosophy: Locke in Contexts* (New York: Cambridge University Press, 1993).

12. I doubt that Locke's theory of the conditions for human happiness was derived from his views about our innate faculties.

13. Rousseau, *Social Contract*, bk. 1, chap. 6, p. 52.

14. Allen Wood, *Kant's Ethical Theory* (Cambridge: Cambridge University Press, 1999), 291.

15. Immanuel Kant, *Perpetual Peace and Other Essays*, trans. Ted Humphrey (Indianapolis: Hackett, 1983), 120.

16. Ibid., 124.

17. James Madison, "The Federalist No. 51," in *The Federalist*, ed. Jacob E. Cooke (Middletown, CT: Wesleyan University Press, 1961), 349.

18. Paul Guyer, *Kant on Freedom, Law, and Happiness* (Cambridge: Cambridge University Press, 2000), 409.

19. See the last sentence of *Perpetual Peace*.

20. Kant, *Perpetual Peace*, 119.

21. Ibid., 118.

22. Muthu, *Enlightenment against Empire*, 195.

23. I do not mean to suggest that Kant thought that we have a duty to compel others to develop their talents. He did not. See Immanuel Kant, *The Metaphysics of Morals* (Cambridge: Cambridge Uni-

versity Press, 1991), 386. But he certainly thought that people everywhere had a duty to develop their talents and that events would compel them to do so.

24. Kant, "Reviews of Herder's Ideas on the Philosophy of the History of Mankind," in *Kant: Political Writings*, ed. H. S. Reiss, 2nd ed. (New York: Cambridge University Press, 1991), 219, 220.

25. Kant, *Perpetual Peace*, 125.

26. See the discussion in Penny A. Weiss, *Gendered Community: Rousseau, Sex, and Politics* (New York: New York University Press, 1993).

| 9 |

Kant's *Untermenschen*

CHARLES W. MILLS

My title is, of course, deliberately chosen to be provocative. In bringing together the moral theorist of the modern period most famous for his putatively uncompromising commitment to the infrangibility of our duty to respect *persons*, and the term *subpersons*, infamously associated with the Nazi movement, I am seeking to challenge how we think about modern Western moral and political philosophy. As such, this chapter is part of a larger ongoing project aimed at ending the marginalization of race within philosophy, and forcing white philosophers to face up to the historic and current implications of nonwhite exclusion.[1] My focus here will be on Kant, as one of the most important philosophers of the modern period, and in the light of the significance of his work for ethics, political philosophy, metaphysics, epistemology, and aesthetics. Kant's pivotal place in the Enlightenment project and the modern canon locates him strategically. If Kant is central as an emblematic figure, and if racist ideas were in turn central to his thought, then this obviously implies a radical rethinking of our conventional narratives of the history and content of Western philosophy. And such a rethinking, as said, is precisely what I am arguing for.

I will divide my discussion into three sections: (1) some general background points about modernity and personhood; (2) Kant's racial views and their implications; and (3) objections and replies.

| | |

BACKGROUND: MODERNITY AND PERSONHOOD

What are *persons*, and why does the concept become particularly important in the modern period? "Persons" is the nonsexist way of referring to humans, instead of

This chapter was originally presented in a longer version at the thirty-sixth annual University of North Carolina at Chapel Hill Colloquium in Philosophy (October 25–27, 2002). I would like to thank the colloquium organizers, especially Bernard Boxill, for the invitation, and my commentator, Pauline Kleingeld, for her detailed comments. I have also benefited from suggestions and comments from Robert Louden and my colleague Samuel Fleischacker.

calling them "men." (With science fiction having opened up our horizons, it would also be appropriately used, as in Kant, to categorize intelligent aliens.) Persons are entities who, because of their characteristics (for example, their threshold level of intelligence, their capacity for autonomy), morally deserve to be protected by certain rights and freedoms, and who are on a normatively level playing field with respect to one another. And the link with the modern period is that whereas in previous ages (the slave states of ancient Greece and Rome, the feudal hierarchies of medieval Europe) moral *inequality* was the norm, modernity is supposed to usher in the epoch when all humans *are* seen as, and treated as, equal rights-bearing persons. In the Athenian polis, slaves were certainly not equal to citizens, nor could the humble serf of the feudal manor dare to put himself on the same level as the lords and ladies who ruled over him. But these distinctions of (class) rank and status are supposed to vanish in the modern period, so that *liberty* and *equality* become the central slogans of the liberalism of both the American and French Revolutions. People may vary tremendously in wealth and social standing, but everybody is supposed to be morally equal, and as such to be entitled to equality before the law and equality of political citizenship.

Now as an *ideal*, this is, of course, a very attractive picture. But the problem with mainstream ethics and political philosophy is that—at least until comparatively recently—this moral egalitarianism has been presented not merely as an ideal but as an accomplished *reality*. In other words, the mainstream narratives of the transition to the modern period represent liberalism as the antifeudal political philosophy for which moral equality is the achieved default mode, the accepted normative standard, from which sexism and racism are then unfortunate but nonrepresentative deviations. And I want to challenge this picture and argue, as feminist philosophers have done over the past three decades with respect to gender, that racial exclusions generally limit this supposed universal equality to Europeans. *Class* distinctions of rank and status are eliminated by the revolutions of the modern period, but preexisting distinctions of gender are not, and distinctions of a new kind—of race—are established by modernity itself. If the supposedly equal "men" are really male, they are also, as philosophers such as Enrique Dussel, David Theo Goldberg, and Lucius Outlaw have argued, generally white.[2]

What I am suggesting, then, is that racism should be seen as a normative system in its own right that makes whiteness a prerequisite for full personhood and generally (the need for this qualification will be explained later) limits nonwhites to "subperson" status. So whereas mainstream narratives tend to assume that adult humanness was usually sufficient, or at least strongly presumptively sufficient, for one's equal moral personhood to be recognized, I am claiming that in reality there were necessary racial preconditions also. In this racist conceptual and normative framework, "person" is really a technical term, a term of art, and non-Europeans are generally seen not as persons but as "savages" and "barbarians." Far from being in contradiction to modernist universalism and egalitarianism, then, racism is simply part of it—since the egalitarian theory's terms were never meant to be extended generally outside the European population. What seem to be racist inconsistencies and anomalies in the writings of the classic political philosophers of the modern period would, if I am right, now turn out to be simple and straightforward implications of racially restricted personhood.

Here is a simple way of thinking about the two rival interpretations under consideration, the mainstream view of modernity (that I am challenging) and my revisionist view. Let T be the (egalitarian) moral/political theory of the modern white Western philosopher in question; p stand for person; and sp for subperson. Then the mainstream view is claiming that for philosopher P:

T asserts egalitarianism for all p, where p is race-neutral. Racist statements are then an exception, and not part of T.

And what I am recommending as an alternative and superior interpretive framework is that, for philosopher P:

T asserts egalitarianism for all p, where whiteness is generally a necessary condition for being p.

T asserts nonegalitarianism for sp, where nonwhiteness is generally a sufficient condition for being sp.[3]

Racist statements are then part of T, not an exception.

Now if this recommendation were accepted, it would, of course, dramatically alter our conception of liberalism and modern Western moral and political theory. Far from being egalitarian and universalist, in supposed sharp contrast to the ideologies of the ancient and medieval world, liberalism too would be revealed to be a multiply-tiered ideology. Persons (those humans meeting the gender and racial prerequisites) would have one standing; subpersons (those humans failing to meet the gender and racial prerequisites) would have a different and inferior standing. So liberalism too would turn out to be a hierarchical political philosophy, though the distinctions are of gender and race rather than of class.

The great virtue of this conceptualization, apart from (I claim, anyway) its correspondence to the actual historical facts, is that it would immediately create a conceptual space for locating the distinctive character of the political struggles of people of color in the modern period in relation to mainstream political philosophy. If liberal universalism already accommodates everybody, if *person* is already race-neutral, then struggles around race, and against racial subordination, are puzzling. (What are they fighting for?) But once we recognize that personhood has been racially normed, they become transparent. Mainstream political philosophy textbooks sanitize and mystify the actual record of the past few hundred years by constructing the West as if white racial domination had not been central to the history of the West. We go from Plato to Rawls without a word being uttered about the racist views of the leading modern Western political theorists and the role of these views in justifying Western political domination over the rest of the world. Acknowledging the racial exclusions in these thinkers' ideologies provides a far more honest and illuminating political framework, since it unites the antifeudal (white) politics of the standard narrative of modernity with the "other" (nonwhite) politics of the alternative narrative of modernity: the anticolonial, antislavery, antiimperialist, and antisegregationist struggles of people of color against racialized liberalism and for the recognition of equal nonwhite personhood. They can then be discussed together rather than in separate Jim-Crowed conceptual spaces.

| | |

KANT'S RACIAL VIEWS AND THEIR IMPLICATIONS

Let us now turn specifically to Kant. Kant is, of course, the famous theorist of personhood, whose deontological (duty-based/rights-respecting) version of liberalism now dominates moral and political discourse, having triumphed over the previously dominant consequentialist (welfare-based/utilitarian) version of liberalism originally associated with Jeremy Bentham and John Stuart Mill. Utilitarian liberalism was the orthodoxy for about a century and a half, but by the midtwentieth century was increasingly perceived to have deep problems of both an operational and, more importantly, a moral kind. The late John Rawls's classic A Theory of Justice was one of the most powerful weapons in the attack on utilitarian theory, and Rawls explicitly drew on Kant for his famous judgment that "[u]tilitarianism does not take seriously the distinction between persons."[4] The weakness of utilitarianism is that it seems, prima facie (utilitarians, of course, have their comeback counterarguments), to permit infringements on the rights of some, say an unpopular minority, if social welfare for the majority could thereby be increased. As a consequentialist theory, it defines the right in terms of good consequences and as such could generate a "right" action or social policy that clearly seems wrong. By contrast, Kantianism defines the right separately from the good, in terms of the categorical imperative to respect other persons. So human rights seem to be set on a far firmer and more trustworthy normative foundation. All persons are morally equal and may not have their basic rights violated.

In this spirit, Allen Wood speaks of what he sees as Kant's "unqualified egalitarianism":

People tend to judge themselves to be better than others on various grounds, such as birth, wealth, honor, power. . . . But [for Kant] these judgments are always mere opinions, without truth, and all social inequalities are therefore founded on falsehood and deception. . . . The reason that Kant's egalitarianism is unqualified is that the worth of every human being is a "dignity"—that is, an absolute and incomparable value.[5]

An inspiring picture—but the problem with it is that, as recent philosophical work by Emmanuel Eze and Robert Bernasconi reminds us (I say "remind" because both writers emphasize that this is old news in other disciplines, if breaking news to contemporary philosophers), Kant is also seen as one of the central figures in the birth of modern "scientific" racism.[6] Whereas previous figures in early racial thought like Carolus Linnaeus and Johann Friedrich Blumenbach had offered only "empirical" (scare quotes necessary!) observation, Kant produced a full-blown *theory* of race. His lectures and writings on anthropology and physical geography are usually ignored by philosophers, but the question is whether this bracketing is theoretically legitimate considering that they map a human hierarchy of racialized superiors and inferiors: white Europeans, yellow Asians, black Africans, red Amerindians.

Consider the following passages (all cited from Eze or Bernasconi).

The racial hierarchy:

In the hot countries the human being matures earlier in all ways but does not reach the perfection of the temperate zones. Humanity exists in its greatest perfection in the white race. The yellow Indians have a smaller amount of Talent. The Negroes are lower and the lowest are a part of the American peoples.[7]

Whites:

The white race possesses *all* motivating forces and talents *in itself.*[8]

[Whites] contain all the impulses of nature in affects and passions, all talents, all dispositions to culture and civilization and can as readily obey as govern. They are the only ones who always advance to perfection.[9]

Asians:

[The Hindus] do have motivating forces but they have a strong degree of passivity and all look like philosophers. Nevertheless they incline greatly towards anger and love. They thus can be educated to the highest degree but only in the arts and not in the sciences. They can never achieve the level of abstract concepts. A great hindustani man is one who has gone far in the art of deception and has much money. The Hindus always stay the way they are, they can never advance, although they began their education much earlier.[10]

Blacks:

The race of the Negroes, one could say, is completely the opposite of the Americans; they are full of affect and passion, very lively, talkative and vain. They can be educated but only as servants (slaves), that is they allow themselves to be trained. They have many motivating forces, are also sensitive, are afraid of blows and do much out of a sense of honor.[11]

Mr [David] Hume challenges anyone to cite a [single] example in which a Negro has shown talents, and asserts that among the hundreds of thousands of blacks who are transported elsewhere from their countries, although many of them have been set free, still not a single one was ever found who presented anything great in art or science or any other praiseworthy quality; even among the whites some continually rise aloft from the lowest rabble, and through superior gifts earn respect in the world. So fundamental is the difference between the two races of man, and it appears to be as great in regard to mental capacities as in color.[12]

The Negro can be disciplined and cultivated, but is never genuinely civilized. He falls of his own accord into savagery.[13]

Native Americans:

The race of the American cannot be educated. It has no motivating force, for it lacks affect and passion. They are not in love, thus they are also not afraid. They hardly speak, do not caress each other, care about nothing and are lazy.[14]

That their [Native Americans'] natural disposition has not yet reached a *complete* fitness for any climate provides a test that can hardly offer another explanation why this race, too weak for hard labor, too phlegmatic for diligence, and unfit for any culture, still stands—despite the proximity of example and ample encouragement—far below the Negro, who undoubtedly holds the lowest of all remaining levels by which we designate the different races.[15]

Americans and Blacks cannot govern themselves. They thus serve only for slaves.[16]

"Miscegenation":

Should one propose that the races be fused or not? They do not fuse and it is also not desirable that they should. The Whites would be degraded. For not every race adopts the morals and customs of the Europeans.[17]

Instead of assimilation, which was intended by the melting together of the various races, Nature has here made a law of just the opposite.[18]

The future of the planet:

All races will be extinguished . . . only not that of the Whites.[19]

Now if the only Kant one knows is the Kant sanitized for public consumption, these views will obviously come as a great shock. Kant believed in a natural racial hierarchy, with whites at the top and blacks and Native Americans ("savages") at the bottom. He saw the last two races as natural slaves incapable of significant cultural achievement, and accordingly (like an old-time southern segregationist) he opposed intermarriage as leading to the degradation of whites. Ultimately, he thought, the planet would become all white.

So what are the philosophical implications of these views? Doing an open-minded investigation into this question requires us, to a certain extent, to bracket what we think we know Kant's philosophy is and not substitute hagiography for theoretical investigation. Accordingly, various authors have been grappling with this question in the English-language secondary literature, and a range of positions has emerged. Pertinent work would include Allen Wood's *Kant's Ethical Thought*; Robert Louden's *Kant's Impure Ethics*; Eze's *Achieving Our Humanity*, building on his Kant article and other related critiques; Tsenay Serequeberhan's "The Critique of Eurocentrism and the Practice of African Philosophy"; Robert Bernasconi's two articles, cited above; and pieces by Mark Larrimore and (jointly) Thomas Hill and Bernard Boxill.[20] Representative positions from the German literature would include work by Rudolf Malter and Reinhard Brandt.[21] These authors variously offer condemnations and defenses of Kant, qualified in different ways, so that a set of characteristic moves is now recognizable.

The position that Kant's defenders have taken is not to deny Kant's racial views but to deny that they have the philosophical implications claimed by Eze, Bernasconi, and others (such as myself). So either Kant's racial views do not affect his philosophy *at all* (the extreme position), or they do not affect it in its *key/central/essential/basic* claims (the more moderate position). The assumption, obviously, is that we have a principled, non-question-begging way to demarcate what is central from what is peripheral to his philosophy, and a similarly principled way of showing how the racial views (and, of course, their implications) fail to penetrate to this inner circle. And the case critics must make is that such a penetration does in fact take place, so that what has been represented as Kant's philosophy in innumerable journal articles, monographs, and textbooks is, insofar as it is racially neutral, quite misleading.

Let us focus on the obvious candidate: the ethics and political philosophy. Kant's claims about the imperative to respect *persons*, his views about the moral state (the *Rechtsstaat*) and its obligations to its citizens, his vision of a future cosmopolitan order where all peoples on the planet will be ruled by universal law are all familiar to us. Now suppose it turns out that not all adult humans are *persons* for him, either (depending on how we want to draw the conceptual geography) because they constitute a separate category of their own, or because within the category of personhood, internal differentiations can be made. In other words, what is supposed to be the starkly polarized moral geography of his theory, with everything being categorizable either as a *person*, with full moral status, or as a *nonperson*, a *thing*, with zero moral status, would have to be redrawn to accommodate the fuzzier category of entities with some *intermediate* status. And what we think we know his various moral, political, and teleological claims to be would all then have to be rethought in the light of this category's existence, so that what holds for the full-blooded, 100 percent, twenty-four-karat persons would not always necessarily hold in the same way for those in this inferior group. If this analysis is correct, it is obviously a radically different picture of the Kant we all thought we knew. The distinction between "Treat all persons with respect," where "person" is assumed to be racially inclusive, and "Treat only whites with respect" (at least here on earth) is obviously not minor and trivial at all. It would mean that his vaunted universalism and egalitarianism are restricted to the white population.

How would the case be made? I think the evidential supports fall into three main possible categories: (1) attempts to demonstrate how Kant's general theoretical claims can be shown to have these implications; (2) citations of specific remarks and passages from Kant seemingly consistent with these implications; and (3) the evidence of textual silence. The last is obviously a tricky category, since silence can speak in more than one way. But if a convincing background theoretical context has been sketched, the failure to address certain topics, or failure to make certain points that would naturally be expected when certain topics are raised, can—in conjunction, of course, with other considerations—at least count as supporting evidence for an interpretation, if not as a definitive proof. Correspondingly, what Kant's defenders have to do is to argue that no such general theoretical ramifications can be proven, that seemingly damning passages can be reinterpreted, quarantined, and/or countered with passages pointing the other way, and that textual silence either has no significance or can be heard differently.

Let us start with (1). Eze takes Kant, inspired by Rousseau's account of how we develop our humanity, to be working with a general theory by which humans transform themselves into moral beings. Hence the significance of Kant's anthropology. Because of his views of natural and immutable racial hierarchy, Eze argues, Kant thought that nonwhites—especially blacks and Native Americans—were not so constituted as to be able to go through this process of self-development and moral maturation. (I focus on blacks and Native Americans as the clear-cut case. As seen above, Asians are just one rung below whites, and though they "can never achieve the level of abstract concepts," Kant does at least describe them as "look[ing] like philosophers." So perhaps, though still inferior, they can parlay this phenomenal appearance into a noumenal payoff.) In other words, there is a certain minimal threshold of intelligence, capacity for autonomy, and so on required to be a full person, and blacks and Native Americans do not reach this threshold. As such, they are all (in my terminology rather than Eze's) subpersons. And Eze argues that for Kant this claim is "transcendentally" grounded, so that as a theorist of scientific racism, Kant has advanced beyond the more empiricist Linnaeus:

> Beyond Buffon and Linnaeus, then, Kant practiced a transcendental philosophy of race. . . . In the *Observations* . . . Kant deployed the transcendentalism of the *Critique of Pure Reason* in order to establish ways in which moral feelings apply to humans *generally*, how the feeling differs between men and women, and among the races. . . . The themes Kant presented in these books . . . give synthesis to the principles and practices he philosophically defined as immanent to humans, but only to white human nature. . . . The inferiority of the Negro, as proposed by Hume, is now in Kant successfully grounded in transcendental philosophy.[22]

If this analysis is correct, the implications for the categorical imperative (CI) could be simply expressed as follows:

> CI: All persons should be treated with respect. GLOSS: "Person" is a technical term, a term of art, signifying beings of a certain level of intelligence and capacity for moral maturity, and on this planet whiteness is a necessary prerequisite for being a person in the full sense. (Whiteness is not sufficient, because of the parallel feminist case with respect to gender.)

Now this, to say the least, would obviously be a radically different way of thinking of the categorical imperative, and insofar as the categorical imperative is central to Kant's moral and political philosophy, Kant's views on race would indeed have major and central philosophical implications. The case could then be buttressed by (2), specific negative passages on blacks and Native Americans such as those cited above, for example that they are savages and natural slaves, that Native Americans are completely incapable of moral education, while blacks need to be educated through flogging (and with a specially constructed split bamboo cane),[23] that race mixing leads to the degradation of whites and is contrary to nature, that only the white race is destined to survive, and so forth. It would be contended that these passages constitute obvious prima facie evidence that Kant did not envisage blacks and Native Americans as fully included in his kingdom of ends, "active citizens" of the polity, beneficiaries of the cosmopolitan order toward which the planet is evolving, and so forth.

Finally, on (3), textual silence, Robert Bernasconi makes the valuable point that, so far as he knows, nowhere in Kant's writings (and remember these comprise numerous volumes) does Kant offer an unequivocal condemnation of African slavery.[24] (Note that one can condemn the *cruelties* of slavery, as some reformers did, while still being anti-abolitionist. Obviously, the ethical desideratum is the principled condemnation of the institution as such.) Yet a more flagrant violation of the prohibition against using one's fellow persons as mere means to an end could hardly be imagined, and it was not as if the Atlantic slave trade was in its infancy at the time he wrote. Whence this puzzling silence, even when the subject of slavery came up in his writings? Obviously, one simple solution to the mystery would be that Kant did not see blacks as fellow persons, even if they were fellow humans.

However, we must now turn to the case for the defense. Above, I distinguished extreme and moderate positions among Kant's defenders. The work of Malter, Wood, and Louden seems to me to fall toward the more extreme end of the spectrum, insofar as they deny that Kant's racial views have any implications for his philosophy at all.

Let us begin with Malter, the most extreme of all, for whom, remarkably, Kant emerges as a committed anti-racist: "The *equality* of all individuals of the human race is for Kant knowable by pure reason. . . . The Kantian theory of race not only does not pave the way for racism, (but) it is the most serious, energetic objection to this—the very worst—madness."[25] Morality for Kant is a priori, not empirical, based on pure reason. So the full personhood of nonwhites is guaranteed as a synthetic a priori truth. But this seems to me to rest on an elision of "human" and "person" of precisely the kind I earlier warned against. What is a priori is that all rational beings are deserving of our respect; it is *not* a priori that all humans are rational beings (in the requisite full sense).

By contrast, Allen Wood concedes Kant's racism but argues that it is overridden by his philosophical commitments. Kant, according to Wood, "conspicuously declines to infer from [his] racialist beliefs . . . that there is any difference in the *human rights* possessed by different peoples," and "[t]he most influential philosophical articulation of these values is Kant's theory of moral autonomy, grounded in the dignity of humanity as an end in itself."[26] Similarly, Robert Louden's *Kant's Impure Ethics* draws a contrast between Kant's *theory* and Kant's *prejudices*, denying that the latter should be taken to modify (what we think of as) the former:

> Kant's writings do exhibit many private prejudices and contradictory tendencies. . . . But Kant's theory is fortunately stronger than his prejudices, and it is the theory on which philosophers should focus. We should not hide or suppress the prejudices, but neither should we overvalue them or try to inflate them into something they are not. . . . The prejudices are not centrally connected to the defining features of his theory of human moral development.[27]

Both writers, then, are offering us a conceptual partitioning of Kant's discourse, on the one hand the philosophical theory (morally egalitarian), and on the other hand views assigned some lower epistemic category, not rising to the level of the theoretical: unthinking prejudice, bigotry, and so on. So though the prejudices are offensive, the theory itself is untouched, quarantined behind a conceptual *cordon sanitaire.*

This is obviously a better argument than Malter's,[28] but I would claim it is still problematic. The question is why we should accept this partitioning. I think there are three possible ways of defending this move: one can claim that Kant's egalitarian theory (henceforth T) is not affected by his racist views because they are in a different conceptual space; one can claim that T represents the essence of Kant's position; and one can claim that T can be reconstructed as a sanitized version of Kant's position. But each of these moves faces problems of its own.

The first is assuming that the racism is subtheoretical and so should be judged to be overridden by T (understood as egalitarian and nonracial). But I began by arguing that racism should be seen as a normative theory in its own right, so this overriding cannot simply be asserted but must be demonstrated. Nor can it casually be inferred from T's apparent race neutrality, as revealed in its vocabulary of "men," "persons," or "humans," for the very question is whether people of color are being conceived of as full persons, fully human.

The second differentiates Kant's essential from his nonessential views and represents the egalitarian T as the essence of his position. But "essential" is ambiguous: does it mean "essential" for our purposes (we later philosophers seeking a usable version of Kant) or "essential" for Kant's view of his own theory? The first shades over into option 3, below; the second needs to prove by non-question-begging criteria that Kant himself did not see the racist claims as crucial to his theory, T.

Finally, the problem with the third is that it is a separate question. While it is, of course, always possible to reconstruct a theory in which personhood has no racial or gender restrictions, the question at issue is what Kant thought. And if Kant himself did not think of nonwhites and women as full persons, then this reconstructed theory cannot really be said to be *Kant's* theory. Most of the theoretical terms will be the same (respect, the kingdom of ends, the categorical imperative), but at least one crucial theoretical term, "person," will not have the same denotation. So while such an enterprise is justifiable from the perspective of developing a moral theory acceptable for our purposes, it cannot be claimed, except in some scare-quotes sense, that this is still "Kant's" theory.

Consider now the moderate position. This position does not deny that Kant's racial views affect his philosophical claims, but it denies that they affect the *central* ones. I take Hill and Boxill's recent joint paper to be a good statement of this line of argument:

> Our position, then, is that, while it is important to notice and block the influence of aspects of Kant's writings that reflect or might encourage racism, the charges of racism do not reach Kant's deep theory. . . . [T]he texts do not in fact support the extreme form of racist beliefs that Eze attributes to Kant, e.g. that some races are not human. . . . Eze succeeds in showing that Kant saw his racial theory as a serious philosophical project, that it was not an offhand, unreflective set of conjectures, and that it deserves philosophical attention. . . . But these concessions do not imply that Kant's central philosophical principles are tainted with racism.[29]

So the presumption is that we have at hand a principled, non-question-begging criterion for distinguishing the deep and central from the shallow and peripheral, and that by this criterion it can be shown that Kant's key theses emerge untouched. A different kind of conceptual partitioning is proposed, which concedes philosophical status to Kant's racial views (they are not just "prejudices") but relegates them to a subordinate status in his thought and maintains the unaffectedness of what are taken to be the key principles.

Now one way of defending this partitioning is to emphasize the differential epistemic status of Kant's moral claims. As just mentioned, Kant famously thought that there were synthetic a priori truths, substantive claims (as against definitional truths like "bachelors are unmarried males") discoverable by pure reason, and that the categorical imperative was one of them. So the reformulation above could be stated as:

CI: All persons should be treated with respect. Status: (supposedly) synthetic a priori truth. → CENTRAL

Auxiliary claim: Whiteness is a prerequisite for personhood. Status: empirical a posteriori claim. → PERIPHERAL

On this basis, then, you could concede that Kant's racial views affect his philosophy, while denying that they affect it *centrally* (deeply, basically, in its key tenets). For you now have a principled demarcation, a conceptual wall, to separate the central from the peripheral.

Opponents of this line of argument have (at least) two moves that could be made in reply. One would be to claim that race also is a transcendental. Whether or not his motivation was to establish centrality by this criterion, this, as we have seen, is Eze's move. But Hill and Boxill argue against this claim and to my mind make some good points: the inferiority of nonwhites seems (to us, obviously, but more to the point, to Kant) more a matter of an empirical a posteriori claim than something that could be determined by pure reason, or as a condition of experience.[30] And Robert Louden, both in his book and in his paper on Eze's book on a 2002 American Philosophical Association Author-meets-Critics panel, is similarly skeptical.[31]

Perhaps Eze has a reply that will vindicate his position. But whether he has or not, I wonder whether he is not setting himself an unnecessarily onerous task in trying to defend his crucial claim, which I take it is the assertion of the centrality of racial views (in Kant and others) to modern Western philosophy. For the alternative move is to *deny* that being a synthetic a priori truth is a prerequisite for being central/basic/deep for Kant, and to make a case by other, arguably non-question-begging and uncontroversial, criteria of "centrality." Certainly for moral and political theory in general the auxiliary claim is absolutely crucial, since it demarcates who/what is included in and who/what is excluded from full membership in the moral/political community.

Consider our moral duties toward nonhuman animals and the environment. As we all know, nonhuman animals, trees, plants, and so on have no moral standing for Kant; his is a classic statement of an anthropocentric moral theory (though *anthropos* here is broader than human, including intelligent aliens). But recently some environmental ethicists have argued for an expansion and modification of the Kantian notion of "respect" to accommodate respect for the earth and other living things. Now would it not seem very peculiar to say that this was *not* a major modification of Kant's theory? This expansion of the scope of beings to which respect is supposed to be extended would have major repercussions for how the theory is applied and how we think of it—if it even counts as the "same" theory any more. Kant's own Kantianism and this nonanthropocentric "Kantianism" are worlds apart in their implications for what is obligatory, prohibited, and permissible for us to do as moral agents.

But it could be replied that even if this is true, this is not a legitimate comparison, since extending "respect" to nonhuman animals obviously requires us to dispense with rationality and the capacity for autonomy as the bearers of moral status, so that Kant's basic principle is altered. In the case of race, however, even if it were true that nonwhites count as subpersons for Kant by virtue of their inferior rationality and diminished capacity for autonomy, deracializing the theory just requires getting rid of a false factual claim, not modifying the basic moral principle.

I would have to concede that there is something to this objection. However, it seems to me that the claim of centrality can still be made. Consider the following example. A well-known twentieth-century figure, whose views (unlike those of the vast majority of philosophers) actually did touch the lives of millions, had a moral philosophy whose terms could be reconstructed (admittedly in a somewhat idealized way) as follows: group G should flourish, are owed respect, should be protected by the state, have their rights respected, and so forth. I am sure everybody will agree that this all sounds very good and commendable. Now suppose I reveal that the thinker I have in mind is Adolf Hitler, and group G are the Aryan race. "Oh, that's quite different!" you will exclaim in horror. But wait, I say, *the central principles, the essential claims,* of his ethical theory are very attractive. It is just—a minor point, this—that because of his empirical beliefs, he wanted to apply them only to a restricted set of the human population. However, surely we can lightly pass over this minor empirical mistake and argue that his basic views remain untouched, since the ideals of flourishing, the respect for rights, and so forth are the really important thing, even if in his own formulation not everybody was included. So could we not say that Hitler's moral theory is, at its core, at the deep level, a nonracial one . . . ?

Now I am not comparing Kant to Hitler. But the point I am trying to bring home is that there is something very strange about dismissing the issue of who gets counted in the moral community as merely a matter of incidental detail. We rightly think that the whole burden of Hitler's moral theory, if it deserves the name, is that it is racially exclusionary, and that once you extend it beyond "Aryans," then obviously it is not the same theory. Even if Hitler had never come to power, even if the Holocaust had never occurred, we would still see this fact of racial restriction as deeply pernicious and as profoundly shaping the theory. How then can it be denied that—whatever their epistemological foundation—these claims about the scope of the populations to which the principles are supposed to extend are indeed philosophically "central" (in theory, and unquestionably in practice)?

So this would be my friendly amendment to Eze's project: even if the "transcendental" claims cannot be sustained, the thesis of philosophical "centrality" can still be defended on other grounds. And the argument is made all the stronger, of course, by the fact that in the case of Kant at least we are not really talking about a mere "empirical" belief but a sophisticated and elaborated theoretical position. Both Eze and Bernasconi see Kant as one of the founders of modern "scientific" racism. So if this is right, then what is involved, while weaker than transcendental necessity, is stronger than empirical fortuitousness: it is a nomological, causal necessity, according to which humanoids of a certain color cannot achieve the basement-level intelligence to be fully moral beings. The color of the skin is a surface indicator of the presence of deeper physico-biological causal mechanisms. If we think of the "ontological" as covering what an entity is, then the physical makeup of a dog will have ontological implications (its capacity for rationality, agency, autonomy, and so on), and so similarly will the makeup of these inferior humans: race does not have to be transcendental to be (in a familiar sense) metaphysical.

The other friendly amendment I would offer—in response to Hill and Boxill's other criticism of Eze, that it is false that Kant regarded nonwhites as nonhuman—is, as discussed earlier, that the case for diminished moral status can be defended (through the "subperson" category) without making such a strong assumption. One does not have to claim that for Kant nonwhites are nonhumans; one just has to assert that for him (and others) humans come in different subcategories and that not all humans make it to the (full) "person" level.

This, then, with variants in (1) (Eze's version is not the only possibility), would be the case for the prosecution: when Kant urged on us the overwhelming importance of respecting *persons*, he was really talking (on this planet) about whites (more precisely, a subset of whites).

|||

OBJECTIONS AND REPLIES

Let us now consider some of the objections that could be made to this case from the defense.

1. *The writings in anthropology and physical geography are separate from, and irrelevant to, the writings in ethics and political philosophy.*

This just begs the question. Since the case for the prosecution rests crucially on the claim that Kant made internal differentiations in the category of human beings, and since it is in these very writings that we find the evidence for the differentiations, they cannot be rejected in advance. This would be to assume that we *know* that when he was speaking of "persons," he fully included nonwhites within the category. But we do not "know" this—we are just assuming it, in keeping with the orthodox view, which is precisely what is being challenged. Eze also makes the useful point that in the course of his academic career Kant gave far more courses on these subjects (seventy-two) than on the moral philosophy (twenty-eight), which would seem to constitute prima facie evidence that he considered them important. Moreover, these subjects were new at the time, and Kant was himself the person who introduced both of them to German universities, drawing on his own research.[32]

2. *Kant's moral community is famously clear-cut in its geography, being starkly divided between persons (with full moral status) and nonpersons or things (with zero moral status). So there is simply no conceptual room for your "subperson" category.*

The "subperson" category is, admittedly, a reconstruction of the normative logic of racial and gender subordination in his thought, a reconstruction that is certainly not openly proclaimed in the articulation of his conceptual apparatus and may seem, prima facie, to be excluded by it. (In a personal communication, Robert Louden points out as an objection to my reading that nowhere does Kant himself use the term *Untermenschen*.) Nonetheless, I would claim that it is the best way of making sense of the *actual* (as against officially represented) logic of his writings, taken as a whole, and accommodates the sexist and racist declarations in a way less strained than the orthodox reading. In other words, there is an ironic sense in which the principle of interpretive charity—that we should try to reconstruct an author's writings so as to maximize their degree of internal consistency—points toward such a concept's being implicit in his thought, since in this way the degree of contradictoriness among his various claims is reduced.

Consider gender. Recent work by feminist theorists such as Pauline Kleingeld and Hannelore Schröder emphasizes the stark disparity between Kant's supposed commitment to unqualified personhood and what he actually says about women. Kleingeld points out that while Kant "asserts both the equality and the autonomy of all human beings," he simultaneously "regards men as naturally superior to women, and women as unfit for the public, political and economic do-

main," implies that women, being guided by "inclination," are incapable of autonomy, asserts that women "have to be legally represented by men," "are under
permanent male guardianship," "have no legal competence, cannot go to court,"
and "lack the right to citizenship," being merely "passive citizens" who do not
have the attributes of lawful freedom, civil equality, and civil independence.[33] So
Kleingeld does not at all want to downplay Kant's sexism. But she thinks the correct approach is to highlight (what she sees as) the tension between his universalism and his gender-differentiated views, and in her comments on my presentation she argued that we should conceptualize his racism in the same way, as being
inconsistent with his stated position elsewhere.[34] By contrast, I would claim that
it is, ironically, more charitable to Kant to see him as tacitly operating with a concept of personhood that is gender- and race-restricted. This reduces the degree of
cognitive dissonance involved in his writings: the *flagrant* contradiction contained in the assertions that women are (full) persons but can be only passive citizens, or that blacks and Native Americans are (full) persons who are simultaneously natural slaves, becomes the less dissonant position that personhood comes
in degrees.

On the other hand, if defenders of the orthodox interpretation reply that
though women and nonwhites are "persons" in a somewhat different way for
Kant, they are nonetheless still *persons* and not "subpersons," then it seems to me
that they face the following simple dilemma. Either (1) they are conceding the
point in all but terminology, so the difference between us becomes merely verbal
and not substantive (though I would claim that my vocabulary, formally divided,
signals the real differentiations in reference, and so is superior to theirs, which
obfuscates these differentiations), or (2) they are so weakening the concept of a
"person," so evacuating it of significant normative content, that it loses most of
the moral force supposedly associated with it.

The German scholar Reinhard Brandt, for example, argues that for Kant
"women and people of color cannot act in accordance with principles of their
own, but can only imitate morality. . . . Therefore from the moral perspective
they constitute intermediate creatures [*Zwischenwesen*] in between the human and
animal kingdoms." This might seem to be an endorsement of something very
like my "subperson" reading. But despite appearances, it is not, for in the very
next paragraph Brandt goes on to conclude: "People of color and women are for
Kant legal persons and enjoy the protection of universal moral and legal principles. . . . Respect for the moral law as such knows no bounds of sex and race."[35]

Brandt does not explain how enjoying "the protection of universal moral and
legal principles" and savoring one's entitlement to gender- and race-neutral respect are compatible with being restricted to passive citizenship or being viewed

as a natural slave who has to be whipped to further one's moral education. If a subcategory exists within "persons" of somewhat-differently-constituted-persons, *Zwischenwesen*, and if this difference in constitution is (as it is) one of *inferiority*, precluding the full array of rights, entitlements, and freedoms of full persons, then what is this but to concede in all but *name* the category of subpersonhood? On the other hand, if it is still possible to be a person in some sense, and yet (as with women) to be denied the basic rights of political participation, or (as with blacks and Native Americans) to be judged to be natural slaves, then what is this "personhood" worth? Would you raise the flag of liberty, man the barricades, prepare to sacrifice your life for it? Obviously not. Such a concept would be a radically etiolated version of the one that is supposed to be the normative soul of the modern epoch. So if personhood in the standard sense is supposed to be a robust notion linked with moral egalitarianism and an associated bundle of moral rights and freedoms that translates into juridical and political equality, then this concept clearly is not it.

3. *Kant was an orthodox Christian and as such a believer in monogenesis, so he could not possibly have accepted such a radical differentiation in the human race.*

See the last five hundred years of global history. Who do you think has been responsible for the origination and implementation of the most important variants of racism over the past half millennium if not orthodox Christians? The opening chapter of George Fredrickson's *Racism: A Short History* is in fact explicitly titled "Religion and the Invention of Racism"—and he is not talking about Buddhism.[36] The two most unqualifiedly racist governments of the twentieth century, Nazi Germany and apartheid South Africa, were both Christian regimes, as was, of course, the American Old South. In general, Christianity's ostensible universalism has never constituted more than a weak, easily overcome barrier against racism. And as recently as the late nineteenth and early twentieth centuries, Social Darwinists had no problem in reconciling monogenesis with the view that some races, though of the same origin as Europeans, and thus human, were "lower," less evolved, and destined for permanent inferiority and/or extinction.

4. *The simple refutation of your thesis is that Kant explicitly condemned European colonialism and urged that Europeans make contracts with Native Americans.*

If, as I claim, people of color, especially blacks and Native Americans, were subpersons for Kant, then how could he have condemned their colonization and demanded that treaties be made with the latter?[37] This is probably the strongest argument in the arsenal of Kant's defenders (it is emphasized by both Wood and Louden).[38] Here is a set of possible moves.

First, one needs to distinguish condemnations in principle of colonialism from condemnations of specific aspects of it. At least some of the passages in his writings seem to be focused on specific colonial atrocities, and insofar as, given my analysis, nonwhites (unlike animals) do have a nonzero moral status, it is not inconsistent with my reading that there should be moral constraints on how people of color are treated. Over the history of European imperialism, there were, after all, many European reformers who deplored its cruelties while still endorsing it in principle and who proselytized for a reformed, enlightened colonialism. So Kant could be one of those people. (And note, as already mentioned, that nowhere does he seem to condemn slavery in principle.)

Second, Robert Bernasconi has argued that even where Kant does seem to condemn colonialism in principle, he is really denying the validity of *one kind* of justification of colonialism, leaving open the possibility that other kinds of justification could be developed.[39]

Finally, there is the fallback position that such passages are simply inconsistent with the theoretical implications (i.e., on the subperson reading) of his work, and that rather than concluding it is the theory which must give way, we should take the opposite tack and conclude that it is these passages that must give way. In other words, rather than claiming that there is complete unity and consistency in all his writings, we could contend that some are inconsistent with others, so the decision has to be made as to which are better supported by the overall logic of his thought. Insofar as we should privilege a theoretically based claim over one that seems lacking in such support, the theory should dominate. This is Eze's own solution in the opening pages of the Kant chapter of his book, where he argues that Kant is *not* entitled, given the assumptions of his own theory, to such condemnation.[40] Obviously, however, there is the danger of circularity here, since defenders of Kant will claim that no such theory has in fact been established, so that where the condemnation is uncontroversial and the putative theory is contested, greater adjudicative weight has to be placed on the specific passages than on question-begging theoretical claims. (Pauline Kleingeld argues that a virtue of her interpretation in contrast to mine is that such passages do not pose a problem for her, since she is claiming that Kant's views do lead to contradictions.)[41]

With respect to Native Americans in particular, though, Maureen Konkle's *Writing Indian Nations* has provided me with some illuminating insights, from real-life history, on the possibilities for reconciling equality and inferiority.[42] Naïve and simpleminded philosophers, bewitched by seemingly obvious syllogisms (treaties are made only with those seen as equals; treaties were made with Native Americans; therefore, Native Americans were seen as equals), would have been lost in dealing with the far subtler minds of colonial jurisprudence, for whom the affirmation of p & $\sim p$ was a routine matter. Konkle begins by pointing out that "[n]o other instance of European colonization produced as many or as significant treaties" as U.S. relations with Native Americans. But this by no means implied unequivocal recognition of their equality. Citing the 1831 and 1832 *Cherokee Nation* cases ("which remain the key cases of Indian law"), Konkle emphasizes that the problem was "to assert colonial authority—tyrannical, imperial authority, of the kind the United States had thrown off in the Revolution—while appearing not to." So while Native peoples were conceded to form sovereign nations, these were also, in Chief Justice John Marshall's formulation, "domestic dependent nations," thus reconciling nationhood with "the necessity of colonial control."

> Indians formed *nations*, he posits, but because they were *Indian* nations and because Indians could be characterized by their essential difference from and inferiority to Europeans, they are in a permanent state of "pupilage" to the United States. . . . [In his concurring opinion, Justice William Johnson] exposes the high political stakes in the concept of Indians' inherent difference: it is the only available means of displacing and denying Native legal claims while retaining the notion of their consent to give up their land, which is still necessary to legitimate EuroAmerican control of territory.[43]

The fact that American justices saw Native Americans as inferior while making treaties with them does not, of course, prove that Kant had a similar view. But I think the actual historical record here demonstrates the mistakenness of the smooth and unproblematic inference from treaty making to the commitment to moral egalitarianism and should alert us that colonial and racial discourse has the ability (as with gender ideology) to take away with one hand what it gives with the other (European givers?).

> 5. *Your attempted critique runs aground on the following simple dilemma: either (1) you are arguing, absurdly, that we must now throw out Kant's moral theory, or (2) you are forced, more reasonably, to wind up conceding (somewhat anticlimactically) that we should keep it, in which case your whole critique has been much ado about nothing.*

If my analysis is correct, then we certainly should throw out Kant's moral theory, since Kant's moral theory makes whiteness and maleness prerequisites for full personhood!

But of course when people make this rejoinder, they do not mean that. What they mean is "Kant's moral theory" in the racially inclusive and gender-inclusive sense, which (if I am right) is not Kant's moral theory at all but a bowdlerized, idealized, and sanitized reconstruction that draws on crucial Kantian concepts but, in its inclusivity, violates Kantian principles. Nonetheless, it will be insisted, that is just a quibble. So this could be thought of as the "So what?" challenge, raised not merely against this analysis of Kant but against parallel analyses of other canonical philosophers. The claim will be made—the claim is made—that from a philosophical point of view, Kant's, or P's, racial views are irrelevant (even if conceded), either because they do not affect his philosophy at all, or because even if they do, even if (it may be grudgingly admitted) my argument goes through, it is in ways that can easily be purged from the theory. So even if P's pronouncements about "men" or "people" were actually only about males and whites, the extension to all humans can readily be made. According to the "So what?" challenge, my kind of project is just sensationalism, "tabloid philosophy,"[44] muckraking, and muckraking without much or any theoretical payoff either.

I think this view is fairly widespread in philosophy, and as I have argued elsewhere, I think it is mistaken. I want to conclude by listing at least three reasons why I think it is wrong.

To begin with, if it is indeed the case that Kant, or more generally P, was just describing whites, or was morally and politically prescribing just for whites in his theory, then surely this is an important fact about his thought that needs to be known and made explicit. Even if P's thought can be easily sanitized, it is still a fundamental misrepresentation to talk as if P were giving race-neutral theories when he is really giving racially differentiated theories. As argued above, there is something deeply troubling and profoundly misleading about racially sanitizing Kant's views and then representing them as if they were the views of the presanitized Kant.[45] Who and what makes the cut in a moral theory is central to what kind of theory it is. Obviously the principle of respect for persons can be extended in a racially indifferent way to include all races. But if this is an extension, it is not a minor technicality that is somehow "already" (essentially, really) implicit in the theory. At the basic level of doing an accurate history of philosophy, then, the official narratives need to be rethought and rewritten. So there are metatheoretical implications for how we think of the development of philosophy. As the discipline standardly presents itself, matters of race are unimportant to its development; Western philosophy is supposed to be universalist and inclusivist. Now it would turn out that matters of race were indeed important to its evolution, at least in the modern period. The colonial dimensions of the thought of, and in some cases actual colonial roles of, Hobbes, Hume, Locke, Kant, Hegel, Mill, and so on would become a legitimate part of the history of modern philosophy.

Second, it could well be that these exclusions do in fact affect the thinker's thought in other ways whose ramifications need to be worked out. In the case of gender, the connection is easier to make, in part because feminists have been laboring on these questions longer than critical race theorists. If you have been generalizing about humanity on the basis of one half of it, then there will obviously be vast areas of history and experience that need to be brought in to correct for these omissions. Political theorists such as Susan Moller Okin have argued against a merely "terminological" gender neutrality, which contents itself with a self-conscious alternation of "he" and "she" without considering how the originally sexist theory's basic conceptual apparatus, assumptions, and pronouncements may have been shaped by these gender exclusions.[46] Do crucial concepts such as "autonomy" need to be given a different emphasis, if a case can be made that a tacitly masculine experience has grounded their formation? Is the disdain for "inclination" linked with its identification with the body and the feminine? It could be argued similarly that genuine race neutrality requires careful rethinking of white philosophy's content in the light of racial domination. If nonwhite "savagery" is the negative antipode against which civilized (white) humanity is going to define itself, then obviously the interlocking conceptual relationships are likely to shape how these concepts of "civilization," and what it is to rise above nature, develop. Both in the descriptive realm, where full humanity is conceptualized in Eurocentric and culturally loaded terms, and in the prescriptive realm, the implications could be far-reaching.

Finally, ignoring the racial exclusions in Kant's (and other modern Western philosophers') moral and political theory obfuscates the distinctive moral topography opened up by recognizing the experience of those persons systematically treated as less than persons. Instead of seeing these exclusions as merely an embarrassment, we should be taking them as a philosophical challenge. Instead of pretending that Kant was arguing for equal respect to be extended to everybody, we should be asking how Kant's theory needs to be rethought in the light not merely of his own racism but of a modern world with a normative architecture based on racist Kant-like principles. How is "respect" to be cashed out, for example, for a population that has historically been seen as less than persons? Should it be reconceptualized with a supplementary group dimension, given that white supremacy has stigmatized entire races as less than worthy of respect, as appropriately to be "dissed"? What corrective measures would be required of the *Rechtsstaat* to redress racial subordination? How is cosmopolitanism to be realized on a globe shaped by hundreds of years of European expansionism? Even if we still want to call the theory "Kantianism," it would be a Kantianism radically transformed by the challenge of addressing the moral demands of the subperson population.

In short, the moral and political agenda of those persons not originally seen as full persons will be significantly different from the agenda of those whose personhood has traditionally been uncontested, and we need concepts, theories, and narratives that register this crucial difference. So that's what.

NOTES

1. For my earlier work on this theme, see Charles W. Mills, *The Racial Contract* (Ithaca: Cornell University Press, 1997), *Blackness Visible: Essays on Philosophy and Race* (Ithaca: Cornell University Press, 1998), and *From Class to Race: Essays in White Marxism and Black Radicalism* (Lanham, MD: Rowman & Littlefield, 2003).

2. My own approach to these matters is within an analytic framework. For approaches from a continental perspective, see, for example, Enrique Dussel, *The Invention of the Americas: Eclipse of "the Other" and the Myth of Modernity*, trans. Michael D. Barber (1992; New York: Continuum, 1995); David Theo Goldberg, *Racist Culture: Philosophy and the Politics of Meaning* (Cambridge, MA: Blackwell, 1993); Lucius Outlaw, *On Race and Philosophy* (New York: Routledge, 1996).

3. The qualification is necessary because of a crucial point of *disanalogy* between race and gender: while there is just one female sex, there are several nonwhite races, and their assigned statuses in racist hierarchies have not historically been the same (as will be seen below for Kant). So while "subperson" is a useful umbrella term, a more detailed treatment would require additional internal divisions.

4. John Rawls, *A Theory of Justice*, rev. ed. (1971; Cambridge: Harvard University Press, 1999), 24.

5. Allen W. Wood, General Introduction, *Immanuel Kant: Practical Philosophy*, trans. and ed. Mary J. Gregor (New York: Cambridge University Press, 1996), xvii.

6. Emmanuel Chukwudi Eze, "The Color of Reason: The Idea of 'Race' in Kant's Anthropology," in *Postcolonial African Philosophy: A Critical Reader*, ed. Eze (Cambridge, MA: Blackwell, 1997), 103–40; Robert Bernasconi, "Who Invented the Concept of Race? Kant's Role in the Enlightenment Construction of Race," in *Race*, ed. Bernasconi (Malden, MA: Blackwell, 2001), 11–36; Robert Bernasconi, "Kant as an Unfamiliar Source of Racism," in *Philosophers on Race: Critical Essays*, ed. Julie K. Ward and Tommy L. Lott (Malden, MA: Blackwell, 2002), 145–66.

7. Quoted in Eze, "Color of Reason," 118.

8. Quoted in ibid., 117.

9. Quoted in Bernasconi, "Kant as an Unfamiliar Source," 147–48.

10. Quoted in Eze, "Color of Reason," 117.

11. Quoted in ibid., 116.

12. Quoted in ibid., 122.

13. Quoted in Bernasconi, "Kant as an Unfamiliar Source," 158.

14. Quoted in Eze, "Color of Reason," 116.

15. Quoted in Bernasconi, "Kant as an Unfamiliar Source," 148.

16. Quoted in ibid., 152.

17. Quoted in ibid., 158.

18. Quoted in Eze, "Color of Reason," 126

19. Quoted in Bernasconi, "Kant as an Unfamiliar Source," 159.

20. Allen W. Wood, *Kant's Ethical Thought* (New York: Cambridge University Press, 1999); Robert B. Louden, *Kant's Impure Ethics: From Rational Beings to Human Beings* (New York: Oxford University Press, 2000); Tsenay Serequeberhan, "The Critique of Eurocentrism and the Practice of African Philosophy," in *Postcolonial African Philosophy*, ed. Eze, 141–61; Bernasconi, "Who Invented?" 11–36, and "Kant as an Unfamiliar Source," 145–66; Mark Larrimore, "Sublime Waste: Kant on the Destiny of the 'Races,'" in *Civilization and Oppression*, ed. Catherine Wilson, *Canadian Journal of Philosophy (University of Calgary)*, supp. vol. 25 (1999): 99–125; Thomas E. Hill Jr. and Bernard Boxill, "Kant and Race," in *Race and Racism*, ed. Bernard Boxill (New York: Oxford, 2001), 448–71.

21. Rudolf Malter, "Der Rassebegriff in Kants Anthropologie," in *Die Natur des Menschen: Probleme der physischen Anthropologie und Rassenkunde (1750–1850)*, ed. Gunter Mann and Franz Dumont (Stuttgart: Gustav Fischer Verlag, 1990); Reinhard Brandt, *D'Artagnan und die Urteilstafel: Über ein Ordnungsprinzip der europäischen Kulturgeschichte* (Stuttgart: Franz Steiner, 1991), 133–36. For these references I am indebted, respectively, to Larrimore and Louden.

22. Emmanuel Chukwudi Eze, *Achieving Our Humanity: The Idea of the Postracial Future* (New York: Routledge, 2001), 104–5.

23. Eze, "Color of Reason," 116.

24. Bernasconi, "Kant as an Unfamiliar Source," 150–52.

25. Malter, "Der Rassebegriff," 121–22, cited and translated by Larrimore, "Sublime Waste," 99–100.

26. Wood, *Kant's Ethical Thought*, 7, 5.

27. Louden, *Kant's Impure Ethics*, 105, 177. In his "Comments on Emmanuel Eze's *Achieving Our Humanity*," APA Central Division Author-meets-Critics panel, 2002, Louden also pointed out that "there do exist ample resources within Kant's philosophy for combating racism. . . . Kant recognizes that the rooting out of harmful prejudices in our thinking is a key part of philosophy's job."

28. In a personal communication, Louden has referred me to a conference paper of his, " 'The Spreading over All Peoples of the Earth': Kant's Moral Gradualism and the Issue of Race," where he explicitly criticizes Malter and distances himself from his position.

29. Hill and Boxill, "Kant and Race," 449–52.

30. Ibid., 453–55.

31. Louden, *Kant's Impure Ethics*; Louden, "Comments."

32. Eze, "Color of Reason," 104.

33. Pauline Kleingeld, "The Problematic Status of Gender-Neutral Language in the History of Philosophy: The Case of Kant," *Philosophical Forum* 25.2 (1993): 134–50; Hannelore Schröder,

"Kant's Patriarchal Order," trans. Rita Gircour, in *Feminist Interpretations of Immanuel Kant*, ed. Robin May Schott (University Park: Pennsylvania State University Press, 1997), 275–96.

34. Kleingeld, comments.

35. Brandt, *D'Artagnan und die Urteilstafel*, 136 (my translation, with help from Ciaran Cronin).

36. George M. Fredrickson, *Racism: A Short History* (Princeton: Princeton University Press, 2002), 17–47.

37. See, for example, Immanuel Kant, *The Metaphysics of Morals*, trans. Mary Gregor (New York: Cambridge University Press, 1991), 86–87, 159; Kant, "Perpetual Peace: A Philosophical Sketch," in *Kant: Political Writings*, ed. H. S. Reiss, 2nd ed. (New York: Cambridge University Press, 1991), 106–7.

38. It is on this basis that Wood argues in *Kant's Ethical Thought* that Kant "declines to infer" differential rights from his racism. But note that Wood does not address the "natural slave" characterization of blacks and Native Americans, which seems a pretty clear statement of inferior rights, especially for a theory founded on autonomy as its central value. Nor (with respect to gender) can he deny that the restriction to "passive citizenship" does indeed follow for Kant from his sexist characterization of women.

39. Bernasconi, "Kant as an Unfamiliar Source," 152–54.

40. Eze, *Achieving our Humanity*, 77–80.

41. Kleingeld, comments.

42. Maureen Konkle, *Writing Indian Nations: Native Intellectuals and the Politics of Historiography, 1827–1863* (Chapel Hill: University of North Carolina Press, 2004).

43. Ibid., 3, 4, 17, 20–21.

44. The phrase, though not the sentiment, is Robert Bernasconi's.

45. Cf. Bernasconi, "Kant as an Unfamiliar Source," 160–62.

46. Susan Moller Okin, *Justice, Gender, and the Family* (New York: Basic Books, 1989), 10–13.

10

Race and Law in Hegel's Philosophy of Religion

MICHAEL H. HOFFHEIMER

> *It is difficult to get the sense of an alien religion from within.*
> *To put oneself in the place of a dog requires the sensibilities of a dog.*
>
> HEGEL, Lectures on Philosophy of Religion (1827)

Georg Wilhelm Friedrich Hegel (1770–1831) was born in Stuttgart and educated at the Protestant seminary at Tübingen. As a young man he worked as a private tutor in Bern and Frankfurt am Main. His early writings herald a lifelong interest in establishing an ethical order (*Sittlichkeit*), a harmonious integration of free individuals in a community based on custom. He welcomed Kant's assault on orthodoxy but felt the need to complete the Kantian revolution and to give it social expression.

He moved to Jena in 1801 to pursue a philosophical career. There he collaborated with Friedrich Wilhelm Schelling in promoting a form of absolute idealism as an alternative to Johann Gottlieb Fichte's subjective idealism. He rose to the position of professor at the University of Jena, and on the eve of the French invasion of the town he published the *Phenomenology of Spirit* (1807), considered by many to be his most original and significant work. Designed as an introduction to his system, the *Phenomenology* traced the history of spirit from the immediate consciousness of sensation to the self-reflective social consciousness that informs the standpoint of the philosophical observer.

During the years of Napoleonic occupation Hegel worked as a newspaper editor in Bamberg and then as rector of a Gymnasium in Nuremberg. He later served as a professor at the University of Heidelberg (1816–18) before moving to Prussia to become a professor at Berlin (1818–31).

From his days in Jena Hegel insisted that philosophy was a science that should be presented in the form of a system. He published the first part of his system, *Science of Logic* (1812–16), but his further efforts to present the system in print appeared in the form of outlines intended for the use of students. He published outlines of his system as a whole, *Encyclopedia of the Philosophical Sciences*, in three editions (1817, 1827, 1831), and he also published an outline of that part of his system that corresponded to his lectures on natural law or political philosophy, *Philosophy of Right* (1821).

He elaborated other parts of the system in cycles of lectures. Material drawn from his manuscripts and from student notes was posthumously published and forms the basis of works such as *Philosophy of History* and *Philosophy of Religion* in which he presented his ideas on race.

|||

HEGEL AND THE TURKS

Except for brief trips late in life to the Netherlands and Paris, Hegel never left the world of Central European towns, remote from ports or commercial centers. He had little opportunity to see, let alone interact with, people from Asia, Africa, or the Americas. His early vision of foreign racial and ethnic groups is revealed in a speech he delivered at his graduation from the Gymnasium entitled "The Deplorable Condition of the Arts and Sciences among the Turks" (1788).[1] During Hegel's last year at the Gymnasium, the ancient role of Turks as the enemy-other had been resuscitated with the renewal of the Russo-Turkish wars. The duchy of Württemberg was aligned with Russia and Austria, and the topic, chosen by the school not Hegel, appealed to the common interest of Protestant and Catholic citizens in the fight against Islam.

Hegel employed a particular criterion of the Enlightenment that derived from Moses Mendelssohn to explain how the supposedly low level of culture in Turkey stemmed from neither religion nor political despotism. He traced perceived defects in that culture to the lack of Turkish state commitment to development (*Bildung*), specifically to the state's failure to support educational institutions. His thesis served a rhetorical purpose, introducing a paean to the duke's patronage of the Gymnasium.[2]

Some scholars, unable to reconcile Hegel's lavish praise for the duke with his youthful republicanism, have concluded that his speech must have been ironic.[3] Yet Hegel's views in it are consistent with other evidence that he wanted to construct a progressive vision of intellectual history that both acknowledged the classical debt to North Africa and Asia and also distanced Mediterranean culture from African and Asian influences. In 1786 he transcribed passages from a book that identified Egyptian influences on Greek thought, and in 1787 he excerpted passages from a source that argued that the Greeks themselves exaggerated the achievements of Persia and Egypt. He also transcribed a statement that such non-Europeans were "still half wild people."[4]

In 1800 Hegel gave more universal form to the negative characteristics he found in the "Oriental spirit." He linked this spirit to a mindset that surrendered willingly to slavery (*Sklaverei*), and he identified this slavish spirit with the emasculating effects he perceived in Asian culture: "Womanly feeling and the *love of women* alone remained a passion the enjoyment of which was not domination."[5]

Many years later, in lectures on the philosophy of history in Berlin, Hegel preserved a special antipathy for Turks and Mongols. He would there assert that the Turks attained no ethical principle (*sittliches Prinzip*), that all science passed to Europe after the Muslim conquest of Istanbul, and that Ottoman rule degenerated into extreme depravity (*grösste Lasterhaftigkeit*) dominated by the most loathsome passions.[6]

Hegel's Gymnasium speech anticipated his later harsh judgments of Turkish civilization. The lack of biographical evidence of significant study of Islamic or Jewish culture in his later years suggests the continuing relevance of his early opinions. As a teenager he grounded defects of Turkish culture in the rawness and crudeness (*Roheit*) of the Turkish people. But he made no use of racial classifications in forming such judgments. Rather than rooting defects of Turkish culture in natural or inherited characteristics, he was led by his commitment to an Enlightenment criterion expressly to deny any inherent lack of talent among the Turks.[7]

| | |

HEGEL AND RACE THEORY

Most Hegel scholars, intent on rebutting the charge that Hegel was racist,[8] have avoided confronting the issue of how his negative judgment of foreign cultures grounded his Eurocentrism. They have likewise turned a blind eye to the prominent role that Hegel gave to race beginning about 1820.

Hegel first discussed race in the 1817 edition of his *Encyclopedia* where he defined race as a condition of "natural mind [*Seele*]" and linked races to geographical origins.[9] He discussed race more fully in 1822 in a manuscript entitled "Diversity of Races" that considered race as a function of both geography and climate.[10]

In these first discussions of race Hegel did not refer to specific races, and he avoided taking positions on the issues of the origin, number, and permanence of races. Since he was probably familiar with the debate between Johann Gottfried Herder and Kant over whether different peoples constituted fixed races,[11] his evasion of those issues probably expressed his own uncertainty. He was even reluctant to employ the term "race," referring at one point to "so-called" races. Yet by including the category of race in his *Encyclopedia*, Hegel signaled that he regarded race as an important issue for philosophy, and by locating it under the category of "natural mind," he indicated that race mattered because of its effect on human consciousness.

Within two years, Hegel was firmly committed to the reality of race. He saw his own contribution to race theory as his insistence that race be explained exclusively as a function of geography and his rejection of historical accounts of racial diversity. He even attempted to prove that it was futile to speculate about the origin of races.[12]

By the mid-1820s Hegel had fully embraced Kant's hierarchy of races. Like Kant, he linked four races to four continents and ranked them in descending order according to their remoteness from Europe:

1. Europeans
2. Orientals (Asians and North Africans)
3. Negroes (sub-Saharan Africans)
4. American Indians

Skin pigmentation was obviously not decisive since Kant and Hegel ranked American Indians below Negroes.[13]

Hegel superimposed on this paradigm nomenclature borrowed from the recent writings of Johann Friedrich Blumenbach.[14] Blumenbach had repeatedly acknowledged his debt to Kant and followed Kant in speculating that all races stemmed from an original white race. Blumenbach coined the term "Caucasian" for this race. But Blumenbach undermined Kant's paradigm by adding a fifth and later a sixth race, and he replaced geographical criteria by anatomical ones.[15] Relying on the configuration of certain features of the skull, Blumenbach concluded that the races most far removed from the stem Caucasian race were "Ethiopians" (Negroes) and "Mongols" (Asians).

Stephen Jay Gould sees Blumenbach's abandonment of the geographical model as the birthplace of modern racial classification.[16] Though Gould believes geographical models were unscientific because they lacked an explicit criterion for ranking, such a criterion was implicitly provided by distance. Races farthest from the stem (white) race traveled farthest and degenerated most completely under the impact of distant environments. Blumenbach's anatomical criteria altered assumptions about the relative affinity of races with consequences for their hierarchical ranking. Moreover, his search for physical signifiers expressed growing doubts about the value of rankings based on intellect and culture.[17] Though Blumenbach had initially assumed that Negroes were inferior to whites in both intellect and capacity for culture, by the late 1780s he maintained Africans were not inherently inferior.[18] Like Herder and Thomas Jefferson, Blumenbach suspected that American Indians stemmed from East Asians and were thus farther removed from Europeans. Yet, on anatomical grounds, he ranked American Indians between whites and Asians, and this subverted the hierarchy that supported Kant's and Hegel's conviction that American Indians were the most inferior humans.

Hegel's lectures in 1825 paid tribute to Blumenbach's preeminence as an authority on race science, and Hegel adopted elements of his theory. But while borrowing Blumenbach's terminology and fivefold classification for the physical features of races,[19] Hegel never applied Blumenbach's scheme to the spiritual traits of races. Moreover, after 1827 Hegel returned to his original Kantian four-race schema.[20]

| | |

APPLICATION TO RACES

Hegel's fullest discussion of specific races occurred in his Berlin lectures on the philosophy of subjective spirit. There he presented Negroes, Mongols, and Caucasians as a sequence that revealed the increasingly objective freedom of spirit. He omitted any extensive discussion of American Indians, but he described them as "a disappearing weak species [*Geschlecht*]."[21]

The progress of spirit was manifested objectively in legal and political institutions. He depicted Negroes as a childish race that institutionalized its contempt for freedom in the practice of slavery, and he characterized Mongols as a higher race that had begun to separate from nature.

Hegel closely associated the incapacity of those races to achieve access to free political institutions to their beliefs. "True freedom is not possible with this identity of spirit with nature [i.e., among Mongols and Negroes]. Here, man can as yet attain to no consciousness of his personality."[22] He believed that only the Caucasian race experienced the subjective capacity for freedom, and he linked this religious consciousness to religious and cultural values that made possible more advanced social organization, especially the consciousness of personal rights.

The linkage of race and religion provided important support for the establishment of religion that Hegel began to advocate after moving to Prussia. In the Heidelberg edition of the *Encyclopedia* he had grounded the state on ethical customs rather than on religion.[23] After moving to Berlin he ascribed to the Christian religion a unique progressive role in history, and he insisted that Christianity was a necessary foundation for the state.[24]

His discussion of other races left no doubt that only Caucasians, specifically those in Christian Europe, were able objectively to establish freedom through the rational institutions of the state.[25] This conviction reprised, probably unintentionally, Linnaeus's ninety-year-old claim that the white race was unique in being governed by laws.[26]

In his lectures on subjective spirit Hegel gave special attention to religious consciousness as the most important subjective criterion that differentiated the four races. For example, he observed that Negroes were higher than American Indians because they were educable, and he supported this by claiming that Negroes were more readily converted to Christianity. He remarked that the Mongol race was higher than Negroes because it embodied a less primitive religious consciousness. He claimed that the religion of the Mongols, unlike that of the Negroes, contained "the presentation of a universal which they venerate as God." But he insisted that the Mongols, unlike Caucasians, were still unable to distinguish gods from men.[27]

Hegel's critique of non-Caucasian religion closely paralleled his conviction that all non-European religions, including Caucasian ones, failed to attain a consciousness of freedom because of their absence of faith in a Trinitarian deity. His commitment to the value of the Trinity had deep roots. He had been fascinated by triangle symbolism since his childhood, and he notoriously conceived of his system in the form of a triad of triads. In theological debates in Berlin Hegel forcefully defended the central importance of the Trinity for Christian doctrine.[28]

He associated both the Trinity and freedom exclusively with Christian Europe: "In Christianity, in the Trinity, lies true liberation."[29] On the one hand, the Christian Trinity, in its commitment to monotheism, differed from trinitarian deities that were venerated in South Asia and North Africa. On the other hand, the Trinity distinguished Christianity from non-Christian monotheistic religions.

The doctrine was especially useful in differentiating Christianity from Islam, whose monotheism Hegel dismissed as expressing a "human lack of freedom." In lectures on subjective spirit, Hegel introduced a dichotomy into the Caucasian race. He divided Caucasians into the "inhabitants of Western Asia" (Muslims) and Europeans (Christians). This was not a racial division but rather one of "national character," but that did not mean he viewed its categories as pliable. Rather he insisted that "national difference is as unchangeable as the racial variety of men."[30]

Hegel's race theory committed him to the judgment that all Caucasian religions were superior to those of non-Caucasians. Thus he defended Islam's single all-powerful God as an advance over the religions of East Asia, which, he claimed, confused deities with finite spirits. He also defended the "universalism" of Islam as an advance over the "limited principle" of Judaism, which, according to Hegel, understood God as a national God of the Jews.[31]

At the same time, he compared Islam unfavorably to all the specific forms of religious consciousness that appeared among Western Caucasians. He insisted that Arabs (the subracial population he most closely identified with Islam) lacked real freedom and history. He complained that the Arabs exhibited no change over time in their national character: "The Arabs are the same as they have always been; completely free, independent, lacking in culture, generous, hospitable, rapacious, cunning. Their religion has wrought no change in their nature and manner of life."[32] He dismissed the Arabs as indifferent to misery, a group that held life and property of little value.[33]

In applying race theory to religion Hegel faced the daunting challenge of finding a common element that characterized all West Caucasian religions from the ancient Greeks to modern Germans and that proved their superiority to all non-European religions including Judaism and Islam. In his first effort he proclaimed generally that religious consciousness in the West rose above abstract, unmediated universalism and thus provided the subjective basis for modern rational thought that grounded a uniquely European "infinite thirst for knowledge, which is alien to other races."[34]

||||

ELIMINATION OF NON-WESTERN RELIGIONS FROM THE *ENCYCLOPEDIA*

After moving to Berlin, in the same years that he was devoting increasing attention to non-Caucasian religions in his lectures, Hegel reduced his coverage of non-Western religions in the formal catalog of his system proper, the *Encyclopedia*.

The earlier presentation of religion in the *Phenomenology of Spirit* (1807) had included three parts, natural religion, religion in the form of art, and revealed religion. Hegel's references in the *Phenomenology* are seldom free from doubt, but most commentators read its discussion of natural religion as referring to ancient religions in Persia, India, and Egypt,[35] and read the section on religion in the form of art as referring to the artistic and religious culture of classical Greece.[36] In other words, the *Phenomenology*'s presentation was chronological, and the pre-Christian religions in it were for the most part dead religions. The sequence within natural religion did not privilege groups geographically closer to Europe, for it placed ancient Persia before India.[37]

The omission of Judaism from the presentation of religion in the *Phenomenology* is troublesome. Perhaps Hegel had already treated Judaism in his earlier discussion of lordship and servitude and meant to avoid repetition; perhaps he considered Judaism to be not quite religion because Jews failed to perceive their God as both universal substance and concrete spirit.[38] In any event, the religions treated in the *Phenomenology* all displayed the progress of consciousness toward the appreciation of a universal spirit, God as He is revealed in the "absolute religion" of Christianity.[39]

The *Phenomenology* was Eurocentric in two ways. First, it treated non-Western religions as pre-Christian, as anticipations of Christianity. Second, it defined Christianity itself through doctrines, symbols, and practices that became consolidated only after it became established in Europe.

In Heidelberg Hegel reduced the place of non-Christian religions in the first edition of his *Encyclopedia*. He confined religion to the first two components of absolute spirit: religion of art and revealed religion.[40] And he restricted non-Christian religion to religion of art, which covered only Greek religion.

In Berlin, in the second and third editions of the *Encyclopedia*, he completely eliminated the vestiges of pre-Christian religion, changing the title "Religion of Art" to simply "Art."[41] This left Christianity as the sole exemplar of religion.

Part of the reason for the elimination of such religions from the *Encyclopedia* lies in the fact that his catalog of the system remained incomplete. Walter Jaeschke rightly emphasizes that Hegel's system included "only a section of the overall conception of the philosophy of religion."[42] Yet Hegel's principles of selection were not arbitrary, and his elimination of non-Christian religions revealed his growing conviction that they did not contain representations of God that were amenable to the scientific presentation attempted in his system.[43] On the contrary, he maintained that some primitive religions did not contain any idea of God, were barely religions, and could not be the subject of scientific study.[44] For these reasons, the history of non-Caucasian religions was not appropriate for the scientific portrayal either in his systematic *Encyclopedia* or in his introductory lectures on the principles of the philosophy of religion.[45]

| | |

EXPANSION OF NON-WESTERN RELIGIONS IN THE
PHILOSOPHY OF RELIGION

While he was working in Berlin to eliminate non-Western religion from the *Encyclopedia*, Hegel was vastly expanding his coverage of them in his philosophy of religion.[46] By defining the central concern of the philosophy of religion as being "with God *as he is [present] in his community*,"[47] Hegel justified the study of actually existing religions, no matter how little rationality they exhibited.

Hegel treated non-Western religions in the middle third of his notes on the philosophy of religion under the rubric "Determinate Religion." Over the years he reworked and augmented his notes on determinate religion until the topic grew to comprise about half of his total text on the philosophy of religion.[48] Race provided an important organizing principle in all four sets of Hegel's notes on the philosophy of religion.

The 1821 Lectures

As early as 1821 Hegel identified Western art, epitomized by Greek classicism, with a distinctive Western vision, which he contrasted to the standpoint of "Orientals." The Orientals, he claimed, were not able to appreciate an independent work of art because they could not achieve a level of free self-consciousness that was able to oppose to itself its own product as object.[49]

Such assumptions about Oriental religion anticipated (and no doubt helped shape) his discussion of the religious consciousness of Mongols in his 1825 lectures on race. The Oriental conflation of religion and art—which Hegel saw simultaneously in idol worship and in taboos against representation of animate objects—prevented a separation that he maintained was essential for both art and religion. This in turn supported his claim that Oriental religion was inherently incompatible with the commitment to the personal rights that established the foundation for civil society and law.[50]

Hegel's deployment of race in 1821 embraced a fertile inconsistency. On the one hand, he associated the religions of Jews and Arabs with the Near East and Africa and characterized them as parts of the "Orient."[51] On the other hand, he included Judaism and Islam with other historical religions of Caucasian Europe, those of the Greeks and Romans, and systematically distinguished the religions of the Jews and Arabs ("religion of sublimity and beauty") from the religion of India ("immediate religion").

The 1824 Lectures

In his 1824 lectures on religion, race played a still more sustained organizing role. The anthropological convictions expressed in his contemporary (1825) lectures on race informed his treatment of specific religions. First, he reorganized the entire first stage of religion so that it was coextensive with "nature religion," the religion of all non-Caucasian races. Second, he subdivided this first stage by race. Moreover, despite earlier disclaimers that the philosophy of religion did not represent a history, Hegel explicitly compared the sequence of specific religions to the stages of life: childhood, youth, maturity.[52]

Hegel subdivided nature religion. Its first form was immediate magic, "the oldest, rawest, crudest form of religion." This was the "first religion"[53] and was practiced by Eskimos, whom Hegel regarded as the most primitive members of the most primitive race, American Indians.[54] He maintained that Eskimos occupied "the lowest rung of spiritual consciousness," but he conceded that their religion was positive insofar as it affirmed that "self-consciousness is something that has power over nature."[55]

Even though he acknowledged that magic was widespread among Africans and present among Mongols and Chinese, he viewed their magic as less raw and primitive than the Eskimos'; and he viewed the magic of the Asians as less primitive than the Negroes'.[56] In his treatment of Africa he was careful to identify magic with the Negroes as a race in order to distinguish it from Islam, which he identified with non-Negroes in northern Africa.

In lectures on the philosophy of history Hegel likewise presented Negroes in Africa as the physical embodiment of the first stages of the phenomenology of consciousness. He characterized their consciousness as still not separated from nature, unaware of the existence of God and law.

> Thus, man as we find him in Africa has not progressed beyond his immediate existence. As soon as a man emerges as a human being, he stands in opposition to nature, and it is this alone which makes him a human being. . . . [H]e is dominated by passion, and is nothing more than a savage. All our observations of African man show him as living in a state of savagery and barbarism, and he remains in this state to the present day.[57]

In his lectures on religion he characterized Negro magic as representing a higher stage, defined by veneration of objects. His examples for this higher stage of magic were drawn from Africa and India, not America.[58] He considered fetishism (which he equated with idol worship) to be higher than magic because it expressed the impulse to objectify, and he located it outside America. He identified higher races with higher forms of fetishism, contrasting the supposed proclivity of Negroes to substitute one fetish for another with the more constant devotion of other peoples to their fetishes (he mentioned the ancient Egyptians).[59] Types of magic corresponded closely to his racial hierarchy. They progressed from the primitive magic of American Indians to the more developed magic of Negroes and (primitive) Asians and culminated in the more developed magic of North Africans and South Asians.[60]

Hegel consistently presented the religions of Asia as on a higher level than those of the American Indians and Negroes. He placed the veneration of living human individuals, which he associated with East Asia, on a higher level than fetishism.[61] And his separate accounts of ancient Chinese religion, Buddhism, and Lamaism provided the transition to religion proper.

Hegel had difficulty classifying Indian religions.[62] In 1824 he ranked Hinduism as a separate second stage of religion, denominating it the religion of fantasy and contrasting it with the more primitive nature religion.[63]

His racial typing informed his organizational treatment of Zoroastrianism. (He identified this religion problematically with the religion of ancient Persia, and he followed both Kant and Blumenbach in regarding Persians as Caucasians.) Accordingly, though plainly less interested in Zoroastrianism than in Hinduism, he was obliged to rank Zoroastrianism as a higher, third stage of religion, the religion of good or light. His short discussion of this religion was designed to prove its doctrinal and ethical superiority over the Hinduism of South Asia.[64] He also considered ancient Egyptians Caucasians rather than Negroes. Accordingly, he identified their religion with a separate, fourth stage, the religion of enigma.[65]

In contrast to the hodgepodge of Asian and Caucasian religions considered as nature religion in the *Phenomenology*, Hegel's organization of religions in 1824 conformed to his racial hierarchy:

1. Nature Religions
   American (American Indian)
   African (Negro)
   East Asian (Mongol)
   Indian
   Persian (East Caucasian)
   Egyptian
2. Religions of the Spiritual for Itself
   Religion of sublimity (Jewish)
   Religions of beauty (Greek, West Caucasian)
   Religion of expediency (Roman)

While this schema successfully separated non-Caucasian religions from the religions of Europe, it resulted in an ambiguous treatment of East Caucasians, for Hegel linked some Caucasians (Persians and Egyptians) to the nature religion of American Indians, Negroes, and Asians. But he linked others (Jews) to spiritual religion. Hegel himself qualified the higher classification of Jews in introductory lectures where he suggested that the God of Judaism was just like the Brahma of Asia, not yet a concrete spirit but rather "a nonsensual being that is only an abstraction of thought that still has no content [*Erfüllung*] that makes it spirit."[66]

The 1827 Lectures

In later lectures, Hegel established still sharper boundaries between religions corresponding to different races.[67] In 1827 he removed the developed religions of Asia (Buddhism and Lamaism) from magic and reorganized the components of nature religion:[68]

1. Religions of Magic
   Less developed (Eskimo, African)
   Confucianism and Taoism
2. Religions of Being-within-Self
   Buddhism
   Lamaism
3. Hinduism

He removed all the religions of East Caucasians from nature religion and pro-vided a separate category for religions that were not yet spirit religions:

4. Religions of Transition
   Persian religion
   Egyptian religion

The 1827 lectures did not, however, segregate the discussions of East and West Caucasians. For the first and only time Hegel reversed the order of the religions of the Greeks and Jews, treating Greek religion before Jewish.[69]

The 1831 Lectures

In 1831 Hegel reorganized the material one last time. Nature religion, which once had embraced all religions up to the Greeks, he now strictly limited to the primi-tive magic of Eskimos, Negroes, and Mongol shamans. He expressed still more strongly his reservation that such nature religion was "properly not religion."[70]

Next he amalgamated those Asian religions that were not primitive under a single heading and separated them from the religions of East and West Cau-casians. Finally he lumped all East Caucasian religions together as "transitional."

1. Nature Religion
2. Religions of Ruptured Consciousness
   Chinese
   Hindu
   Buddhism and Lamaism
3. Religions of Freedom
   Transitional (Persian, Jewish, Phoenician, Egyptian)
   Greek
   Roman

The triumph of race over time was manifested by the move of Jewish religion to the "transitional" category where its privileged status was reduced still further by the fact that it was succeeded by both Phoenician and Egyptian religion.[71]

RACE AND LAW

Hegel maintained that the access of different races to freedom was restricted by their levels of religious consciousness. In his first Berlin lectures on religion (1821), he already generalized that Oriental religion embodied attitudes that were incompatible with the higher social achievements of Europe:

> It is self-evident that a European civil life based on personality, on free and ab-solute rights, is not to be found in such a religion. Genuinely ethical relation-ships—those of family, human benevolence, the obligation to recognize infi-nite personality and human dignity—[become impossible] with savage fancy and abominable deeds.[72]

While praising the spirit of loving renunciation he found in Asian religions, he concluded that this spirit disqualified them from "freedom, right, the rule of law," and he warned that without a foundation in law, the beautiful feeling of love alternates with extreme harshness.[73]

This view informed Hegel's discussion in 1825 of the religion of the non-Caucasian races. According to Hegel, even the Mongols remained unable to rise above an abstract vision of a universal God and unable to recognize the status of humans as persons—unable to achieve attitudes that Hegel saw as prerequisites for achieving and institutionalizing freedom. Because freedom and states were necessary ingredients of history, Robert Bernasconi rightly observes that in "Hegel's account of history . . . only Caucasians can be said to belong to history proper."[74]

The idea that Asian religions prevented the development of spiritual prerequi-sites for law and freedom reappeared throughout Hegel's Berlin lectures on reli-gion. In 1831 he proclaimed that the "dulling of consciousness" that he perceived in Hindu worship was "not far removed from the beast." He insisted that the principle of resignation in Indian religion disqualified Indians from freedom: "Since the specific activity of humans counts for nothing, there is no freedom in India: for freedom entails that particular human goals are regarded as essen-tial."[75]

Hegel never fully worked out his views on the consequences of contact be-tween races. While celebrating the freedom of humans in the abstract, he sug-gested that races were nevertheless subordinate to each other:

> The question of racial variety bears upon the rights one ought to accord to people; when there are various races, one will be nobler and the other has to serve it.[76]

He believed mixed-race offspring shared the characteristics of both parents. Accordingly, he believed intercourse between European colonists and non-Caucasian natives produced a population with greater capacity and aspirations for political freedom than the natives. Yet far from welcoming this development, Hegel feared that mixed-race populations were sources of political instability, and he was ambivalent about the British practice of prohibiting race mixing in India.[77]

While non-Caucasian races could not fully attain freedom, he evidently believed they enjoyed different capacities for benefiting from contact with Europeans. American Indians were the lowest and least educable race for Hegel. He concluded that at least in North America they could neither be educated, colonized, nor reduced to slavery. And his racially informed descriptions of the displacement and elimination of American Indians can be read as ambivalent rationalizations for European colonial genocide.[78]

He described Negroes as prone to cannibalism and slavery, a race that was "industrious" in peace but easily roused to violent passions.[79] But he believed Negroes were more educable than American Indians. Accordingly, he regarded Negroes as suitable slaves. His attitude toward the contemporary institution of black slavery was studiedly ambiguous. Like most contemporaries, he regarded slavery as immoral, calling it an "absolute crime."[80] But he never repudiated race-based arguments for enslavement of particular races, and passages that asserted the natural proclivity of Negroes for slavery could be, and in fact were, read as race-based justifications of slavery.[81] His tendentious descriptions of Africa[82] and his low opinion of the capacity of Negroes for political autonomy suggest strongly that he viewed Africa as an appropriate site for the state-sponsored colonization he advocated in the *Philosophy of Right*.[83]

The only alien group present in Europe was the Jews, and Hegel considered them as a subgroup of the Caucasian race. Though he shared the private anti-Semitism of many of his class, he socialized with converted Jews and supported limited civil legal rights for Jews. Yet he rationalized the extension of such rights by arguing that enfranchising Jews would lead to their complete assimilation into the Christian majority.[84]

|||

CONCLUSIONS

Racial classification played no visible role in Hegel's early intellectual biography, but his treatment of the Turks reveals that he absorbed the prejudices of the day and that a negative view of non-European peoples framed the Eurocentric context in which he formulated the principles of absolute idealism. When he later adopted the idea of race as a category of "natural mind," he applied Kant's four-race racial schema to provide a ranking of the consciousness of American Indians, Negroes, Mongols, and Caucasians.

Hegel devoted special attention to religion in ranking races, and he reworked the philosophy of religion in order to present the sequence of non-Christian religions as an ascending hierarchy of racial types. According to Hegel, the religions of non-Europeans were distinguished by lack of faith in a monotheistic Trinity and an inability to value freedom. He linked such attitudes to the failure of non-Caucasian races to recognize legal rights, to establish political states, and to experience historical progress.

In Berlin Hegel eliminated non-Christian religions from the *Encyclopedia* and excluded America and Africa from history, thus confining the rational contents of his system to the experience of Caucasian Europe. Consequently, the rump race of Western Caucasians survived as the sole vehicle for attributes and aspirations he once identified with humanity. Hegel's philosophy of race thus provided systematic expression to a familiar form of modern Western race consciousness. It defined non-Caucasians as limited by their racial type, but it perceived Caucasians, free from such limits, as the paragon of humanity.

NOTES

1. Hegel's manuscript, now lost, was quoted by Karl Rosenkranz, reprinted in *Gesammelte Werke*, ed. Rheinisch-Westfälischen Akademie der Wissenschaften (Hamburg: Felix Meiner Verlag, 1968–), 1:49–50.

2. Ibid., 1:49.

3. H. S. Harris, *Hegel's Development, 1770–1801: Toward the Sunlight* (Oxford: Clarendon Press, 1972), 43; Jacques D'Hondt, *Hegel biographie* (Paris: Calmann-Lévy, 1998), 34. Rosenkranz, who first published the excerpt and saw the complete manuscript, suspected no irony, but Harris was alert to the possible presence of irony in part because he assumed (wrongly) that Hegel himself selected the topic. Harris, *Hegel's Development*, 44.

4. For the excerpts on Egypt and Persia, see *Gesammelte Werke*, 2:113–14, 175–76. These passages reveal the early roots of the Eurocentric bias Bernasconi argues shaped Hegel's treatment of world history. See Robert Bernasconi, "With What Must the Philosophy of World History Begin? On the Racial Bias of Hegel's Eurocentrism," *Nineteenth-Century Contexts* 22 (2000): 171–201.

5. "Fragments of Historical Studies," trans. Clark Butler, in *Miscellaneous Writings of G. W. F. Hegel*, ed. Jon Stewart (Evanston: Northwestern University Press, 2002), 91, 93.

6. *Vorlesungen über die Philosophie der Geschichte*, in *Sämtliche Werke*, ed. Hermann Glockner, 20 vols. (Stuttgart: Frommanns Verlag, 1949), 11:458–59.

7. We know this part of Hegel's argument only from Rosenkranz's paraphrase. *Gesammelte Werke*, 1:460.

8. Hegel's editors blame his disparaging treatment of non-Western religions on his sources. Hegel, *Lectures on the Philosophy of Religion*, vol. 2: *Determinate Religion*, ed. Peter C. Hodgson, trans. R. F. Brown, P. C. Hodgson, and J. M. Stewart, with the assistance of H. S. Harris (Berkeley: University of California Press, 1987), 2:272 n. 108.; *Vorlesungen über die Philosophie der Religion*, ed. Walter Jaeschke, 4 vols. (Hamburg: Felix Miner Verlag, 1985). But Hegel's racial assumptions influenced his tendentious selection of sources. See Robert Bernasconi, "Hegel at the Court of the Ashanti," *Hegel after Derrida*, ed. Stuart Barnett (London: Routledge, 1998), 171–201. And his insistence that people act in conformity to their race led him to speculate (erroneously and in the absence of any source) that American Indians who supported independence movements must have been of mixed racial ancestry. See Michael H. Hoffheimer, "Hegel, Race, Genocide," *Southern Journal of Philosophy* 39 supp. (2001): 51–52 n. 34. For a list of eminent scholars who downplay the importance of race in Hegel's thought and minimize his racism, see ibid., 48 n. 6.

9. *Enzyklopädie der philosophischen Wissenschaften im Grundrisse* [1817] § 312, *Sämtliche Werke*, 3:234. For later editions, see *Gesammelte Werke*, 19:296, 20:392.

10. "Rassenverschiedenheit," in "Fragment zur Philosophie des subjektiven Geistes," *Gesammelte Werke*, 15:224, translated as "A Fragment on the Philosophy of Spirit (1822/25)," in *Hegel's Philosophy of Subjective Spirit*, trans. and ed. M. J. Petry, corrected ed., 3 vols. (Dordrecht: D. Reidel, 1978), 1:113–15. For the dating, ibid., cxv; *Gesammelte Werke*, 15:301–3.

11. See Robert Bernasconi, "Who Invented the Concept of Race? Kant's Role in the Enlightenment Construction of Race" in *Race*, ed. Bernasconi (Oxford: Blackwell, 2001). These issues had been at the center of public debates between Kant and Herder. See Johann Gottfried von Herder, *Ideas on the Philosophy of the History of Humankind*, trans. Thomas Nenon, in *The Idea of Race*, ed. Robert Bernasconi and Tommy L. Lott (Indianapolis: Hackett, 2000), 26. Herder rejected the limited categories proposed by Kant and viewed humanity as a continuum of different family and national groups. He believed physical features of such groups should be explored in natural history rather than as part of the physical-geographical history of humans. Hegel's treatment of race as part of anthropology expressed a decisive rejection of Herder.

12. He avoided endorsing any competing theories of the origin of races. He insisted, "Whether all human races have proceeded from one couple or from more than one is entirely meaningless to us in Philosophy." *Hegel's Philosophy of Subjective Spirit*, 2:44 (Addition). He argued that the search for historical causes was a function of understanding (as opposed to the superior faculty of reason) and that such a search would be futile because it would overreach available empirical information. "Rassenverschiedenheit," *Gesammelte Werke*, 15:224–27; *Hegel's Philosophy of Subjective Spirit*, 1:113.

13. Petry argues that Hegel believed that races devolved from the original white race. *Hegel's Philosophy of Subjective Spirit*, 1:lviii, 2:451.

14. J. H. I. Lehmann to Kant, January 1, 1799, cited in Antonello Gerbi, *The Dispute of the New*

World: *The History of a Polemic, 1750–1900*, trans. Jeremy Moyle (1955; Pittsburgh: University of Pittsburgh Press, 1973), 332. See Bernasconi, "Who Invented the Concept of Race?"

15. *De Generis humani* (1795 ed.), in *The Anthropological Treatises of Johann Friedrich Blumenbach*, trans. Thomas Bendyshe (London: For the Anthropological Society by Longman, Green, Roberts, & Green, 1865); reprinted as *On the Natural Varieties of Mankind* (New York: Bergman, 1969), 264–76. See Stephen Jay Gould, *The Mismeasure of Man*, rev. ed. (New York: W. W. Norton, 1981), 406–8.

16. Gould, *Mismeasure of Man*, 403.

17. Because American Indians provided a mediating type between Caucasians and Mongolians, he added a fifth, "Malaysian" race to serve as a comparable bridge between whites and Negroes. See Gould, *Mismeasure of Man*, 411–12.

18. See Hans W. Debrunner, "Africa, Europe, and America: The Modern Roots from a European Perspective," in *Crosscurrents: African Americans, Africa, and Germany in the Modern World*, ed. David McBride, Leroy Hopkins, and C. Aisha Blackshire-Belay (Columbia, SC: Camden House, 1998), 7.

19. *Hegel's Philosophy of Subjective Spirit*, 2:46/47, 50/51 (Kehler MS); ibid., 48–59 (Addition). Hegel's reference to the fifth, Malaysian race and his paraphrase of Blumenbach's polemic against Camper leave no doubt that he used the third edition that appeared in 1795. Hegel also briefly adopted Blumenbach's "Ethiopian" but soon resumed *Neger* for Negro. He questioned the distinction between the Malaysian and American races without appreciating its import for Blumenbach. *Hegel's Philosophy of Subjective Spirit*, 2:53 (Addition) (Petry's translation).

20. *Vorlesungen über die Philosophie des Geistes, Vorlesungen*, vol. 13 (Hamburg: Felix Miner, 1994), 39. Bernasconi points out Hegel's inconsistent treatment of the number of races. "With What Must the Philosophy of World History Begin?" 195 n. 40.

21. *Hegel's Philosophy of Subjective Spirit*, 2:60. See Hoffheimer, "Hegel, Race, Genocide," 46–47.

22. *Hegel's Philosophy of Subjective Spirit*, 2:56/57.

23. Cf. *Enzyklopädie der philosophischen Wissenschaften im Grundrisse, Sämtliche Werke*, 7:296–97.

24. This attitude was expressed most clearly in his 1831 lectures. See *Lectures on the Philosophy of Religion*, 1:451–52, 472. But it was anticipated in 1821. "The state must rest essentially on religion; the security of attitudes and duties vis-à-vis the state becomes for the first time absolute in religion." *Lectures on the Philosophy of Religion*, 1:200; *Vorlesungen über die Philosophie der Religion*, ed. Walter Jaeschke, 4 vols. (Hamburg: Felix Meiner Verlag, 1985), 1:109.

25. *Hegel's Philosophy of Subjective Spirit*, 2:56/57 (Addition).

26. According to Linnaeus, American Indians were governed by customs, Asians by opinions, and Negroes by caprice. *Systema naturae* (1735), translated as *The God-Given Order of Nature* (1735), excerpted in Emmanuel Chukwudi Eze, ed., *Race and the Enlightenment: A Reader* (London: Blackwell, 1997), 13.

27. *Hegel's Philosophy of Subjective Spirit*, 2:56/57.

28. See editors' introduction and annotations, G. W. F. Hegel, *Lectures on the Philosophy of Religion*, vol. 1: *Introduction and The Concept of Religion*, ed. Peter C. Hodgson, trans. R. F. Brown, P. C.

Hodgson, and J. M. Stewart, with the assistance of J. P. Fitzer and H. S. Harris (Berkeley: University of California Press, 1984), 64, 127 n. 34, 157 n. 17.

29. *Lectures on the Philosophy of Religion*, 2:156. I have altered the translation, cf. *Vorlesungen über die Philosophie der Religion*, 2:62. For the decisive importance of the Trinity, see also *Lectures on the Philosophy of Religion*, 1:126–28; *Vorlesungen über die Philosophie der Religion*, 2:32–34 (1824). See Walter Jaeschke, *Reason in Religion: The Foundations of Hegel's Philosophy of Religion*, trans. J. Michael Stewart and Peter C. Hodgson (Berkeley: University of California Press, 1990), 232.

30. *Hegel's Philosophy of Subjective Spirit*, 2:66/67.

31. His choice of verb *überwinden* (to prevail or overcome) suggests he viewed Islam as displacing Judaism among the Caucasian inhabitants of West Asia. Ibid., 2: 58/59

32. Ibid., 2:66/67 (Kehler MS).

33. Ibid., 2:58/59. He also referred to the character of West Asians as uniting high sentiments with "excessive vindictiveness and guile."

34. Ibid., 2:61.

35. Hegel himself emphasized that his presentation of the moments of religion was not historical or chronological. Hegel, *Phänomenologie des Geistes, Gesammelte Werke*, 9:365. See *Phenomenology of Spirit*, trans. A. V. Miller (Oxford: Clarendon Press, 1977), 413. But commentators have long identified the Asian and North African referents of Hegel's discussion. Cf. ibid.; *The Phenomenology of Mind*, trans. J. B. Baillie (New York: Harper & Row, 1967), 696–704 (footnotes); H. S. Harris, *Hegel's Ladder*, 2 vols. (Indianapolis: Hackett, 1997), 2:525–73; Jaeschke, *Reason in Religion*, 198. Findlay agrees. J. N. Findlay, *Hegel: A Re-Examination* (New York: Oxford University Press, 1958), 134. Baillie identifies the religion of India as the second component of natural religion. In contrast, Harris speculates that Hegel had in mind primitive vegetarians in Palestine (*Hegel's Ladder*, 2:557). Such diverse readings demonstrate the obscurity of Hegel's discussion.

36. Revealed religion denoted both Roman religion and Christianity. Hegel states explicitly that the religion of art belonged to the ethical spirit that perished in the condition of law, and he identified this condition of law most closely with Rome. *Phenomenology of Spirit*, 454–55.

37. Jaeschke argues against reading the religion of light as a reference to Persian religion and identifies it instead with the God of Israel. *Reason in Religion*, 199–202. Reinhard Leuze discusses the apparent absence of Judaism from Hegel's treatment of religion in the *Phenomenology*. He endorses the traditional reading of the religion of light as a reference to Zoroastrianism. *Die ausserchristlichen Religionen bei Hegel* (Göttingen: Vandenhoeck & Ruprecht, 1975), 166–69, 116–25.

38. Hegel leveled this critique in later years. There are methodological problems with reading his views back into his presentation in 1807, but his understanding of Judaism changed remarkably little, and his later critique neatly explains why he might have considered Judaism under the phenomenology of self-consciousness rather than under either objective spirit (with Greece and Rome) or religion proper.

39. H. S. Harris suggests that the religion of the *Phenomenology* was the religion of Hölderlin, to

which Hegel was drawn in the 1790s and of which Zoroaster was one of the founders. *Hegel's Ladder*, 2:538.

40. His Gymnasium lectures on religion discussed only Christianity, but his pedagogical goal may explain his choice of topics. His lectures for upperclassmen focused on the ethical teachings of Jesus, and his treatment of religion thus associated religion with (Christian) love. Hegel, *Philosophische Propädeutik: Gymnasialreden und Gutachten über den Philosophie-Unterricht*, ed. Karl Rosenkranz, 3rd ed., in *Sämtliche Werke*, 3:225. When he mentioned the gods of "heathens," he did so only to contrast them collectively to the immanence of God in Christ, ibid., 226.

41. Cf. *Gesammelte Werke*, 19:392; *Gesammelte Werke*, 20:543.

42. Jaeschke, *Reason in Religion*, 210.

43. He made this point explicitly as early as his 1821 lectures in Berlin on the philosophy of religion. See *Lectures on the Philosophy of Religion*, 1:197, 197 n. 35; *Vorlesungen über die Philosophie der Religion*, 1:106–7. Hegel repeated this point in different contexts. As one marginal note summarized: "History of religions—difficult." *Lectures on the Philosophy of Religion*, 1:190 n. 16 (1821 lectures); *Vorlesungen über die Philosophie der Religion*, 1:99 n. 98 ("Geschichte der Religionen/Schwer.") He similarly insisted that the "history of religion is not our purpose [*Zweck*]." *Lectures on the Philosophy of Religion*, 1:199 (1821 lectures); *Vorlesungen über die Philosophie der Religion*, 1:108.

44. *Lectures on the Philosophy of Religion*, 1:197, 197 n. 35 (1821); *Vorlesungen über die Philosophie der Religion*, 1:106–7.

45. Jaeschke explores historical assumptions behind Hegel's treatment of determinate religion. Though he goes farther than I toward concluding that Hegel promoted a unitary history of religion, he explores problems with such a reading and identifies passages in Hegel that challenge it. *Reason in Religion*, 279.

46. See Editorial Introduction, *Lectures on the Philosophy of Religion*, 1:13.

47. *Lectures on the Philosophy of Religion*, 1:116 (1824 lectures); *Vorlesungen über die Philosophie der Religion*, 1:33.

48. Editorial Introduction *Lectures on the Philosophy of Religion*, 1:1; Editorial Introduction, *Lectures on the Philosophy of Religion*, 2:1.

49. *Lectures on the Philosophy of Religion*, 1:236, 237n.139, *Vorlesungen über die Philosophie der Religion*, 1:146, 146n. Hegel's lectures (transcribed in the notes cited above) apparently amalgamated Turks with "Orientals" (*Orientale*) and the "Oriental substantiality [*morgenländischen Substantialität*] of consciousness."

50. *Lectures on the Philosophy of Religion*, 2:121; *Vorlesungen über die Philosophie der Religion*, 2:28.

51. *Lectures on the Philosophy of Religion*, 2:129; *Vorlesungen über die Philosophie der Religion*, 2:36.

52. He asserted that the characteristics of the stages were "logically determined by the nature of the concept." *Lectures on the Philosophy of Religion*, 2:237–38; *Vorlesungen über die Philosophie der Religion*, 2:143.

53. *Lectures on the Philosophy of Religion*, 2:272, 273; *Vorlesungen über die Philosophie der Religion*,

2:176–77. Hegel's words do not unambiguously assert that magic is the first religion in point of time; he characterizes magic as the oldest type (*Weise*) and the rawest, simplest, crudest form (*Form*).

54. *Hegel's Philosophy of Subjective Spirit*, 2:62/63.

55. *Lectures on the Philosophy of Religion*, 2:275; *Vorlesungen über die Philosophie der Religion*, 2:179. Hegel repeated his characterization of the Eskimos in his 1827 *Lectures on the Philosophy of Religion*, 2:541, 724; *Vorlesungen über die Philosophie der Religion*, 2:439, 613.

56. Hegel distanced the less primitive magic of the Asians from the first stage of magic that occurs among both the Africans and American Indians. *Lectures on the Philosophy of Religion*, 2:275; *Vorlesungen über die Philosophie der Religion*, 2:179. In 1827 he similarly remarked that the form of magic widespread among Negroes was similar to that among Mongols and Chinese but remarked that it was "developed more fully" (*weiter ausgebildet*) among the latter. *Lectures on the Philosophy of Religion*, 2:542, 725; *Vorlesungen über die Philosophie der Religion*, 2:439, 614. In 1831 his observation that magic was widespread in Africa was the occasion for his introduction of the judgment that Africa constituted "the midpoint for the debasement of consciousness, a debasement that shows itself also in social life in the form of cannibalism and slavery." *Lectures on the Philosophy of Religion*, 2:725; *Vorlesungen über die Philosophie der Religion*, 2:614.

57. *Lectures on the Philosophy of World History*, trans. H. B. Nisbet (Cambridge: Cambridge University Press, 1975), 177.

58. *Lectures on the Philosophy of Religion*, 2:288–89; *Vorlesungen über die Philosophie der Religion*, 2:193.

59. *Lectures on the Philosophy of Religion*, 2:291; *Vorlesungen über die Philosophie der Religion*, 2:195.

60. Hegel's discussion of the veneration of dead bodies led to a digression on the supposed penchant of Africans for cannibalism and slavery. *Lectures on the Philosophy of Religion*, 2:297; *Vorlesungen über die Philosophie der Religion*, 2:201. This paralleled his treatment of Negroes in his lectures on subjective spirit and on the philosophy of history.

61. *Lectures on the Philosophy of Religion*, 2: 293; *Vorlesungen über die Philosophie der Religion*, 2: 197.

62. He also struggled in contemporary writings with whether or not India produced a form of thought that qualified as philosophy. See Robert Bernasconi, "With What Must the History of Philosophy Begin? Hegel's Role in the Debate on the Place of India within the History of Philosophy," in *Hegel's History of Philosophy: New Interpretations*, ed. David A. Duquette (Albany: State University of New York Press, 2002), 42–43.

63. *Lectures on the Philosophy of Religion*, 2:316–52; *Vorlesungen über die Philosophie der Religion*, 2:219–54.

64. *Lectures on the Philosophy of Religion*, 2:352–58; *Vorlesungen über die Philosophie der Religion*, 2:254–59.

65. *Lectures on the Philosophy of Religion*, 2:358–81; *Vorlesungen über die Philosophie der Religion*, 2:195, 259–81.

66. *Lectures on the Philosophy of Religion*, 1:331 (1824 lectures). I have altered the translation; cf. *Vorlesungen über die Philosophie der Religion*, 1:233.

67. Jaeschke notes that the changes in 1827 and 1831 generally adhere to the organizing principles announced in the introductory lectures of 1824. *Reason in Religion*, 243.

68. *Lectures on the Philosophy of Religion*, 2:562; *Vorlesungen über die Philosophie der Religion*, 2:459 (1827 lectures).

69. *Lectures on the Philosophy of Religion*, 2:640; *Vorlesungen über die Philosophie der Religion*, 2:534 (1827 lectures).

70. *Lectures on the Philosophy of Religion*, 2:722. I have altered the translation; cf. *Vorlesungen über die Philosophie der Religion*, 2:612 (1831 lectures). My suggestion that race provided an organizing principle is not incompatible with other influences identified by Jaeschke, *Reason in Religion*, 274–75.

71. The editors are right in noting that this sequence allows Hegel to emphasize the historic connection between Egypt and Greece. *Lectures on the Philosophy of Religion*, 2:66 n. 38. But it is doubtful that this motivated the reorganization because the change introduces more chronological problems than it solves, and Hegel makes little use of the Egypt-Greece connection.

72. *Lectures on the Philosophy of Religion*, 2:121; *Vorlesungen über die Philosophie der Religion*, 2:28 (1821 manuscript).

73. *Lectures on the Philosophy of Religion*, 2:122; *Vorlesungen über die Philosophie der Religion*, 2:28–29 (1821 manuscript).

74. "With What Must the Philosophy of World History Begin?" 184. Bernasconi shows that Hegel's privileging of Caucasians led him to differentiate Persians from Mongols and caused internal inconsistencies in his treatment of Egyptians, whom he wished to amalgamate to Europeans (because of the historical continuity of Greece and Rome) but also—and increasingly in later lectures—to distinguish from Europeans owing to the unfree racial characteristics of Africans. This led Hegel to characterize Egypt as embodying contradiction. Ibid., 185.

75. *Lectures on the Philosophy of Religion*, 2:733 (1831 lectures). I have altered the translation, cf. *Vorlesungen über die Philosophie der Religion*, 2:621.

76. *Hegel's Philosophy of Subjective Spirit*, 2:47 (Kehler's manuscript, Petry's translation). Hegel's discussion of black skin pigmentation and his construction of the excellence or "objective superiority" of white skin immediately follow this quotation. The juxtaposition may support an inference that Hegel meant to provide pseudo-scientific foundation for the particular superiority of whites over Negroes. This is Bernasconi's reading, "With What Must the Philosophy of World History Begin?" 195 n. 39. I suggested an alternative reading in "Hegel, Race, Genocide," 58 n. 72.

77. I discuss the ambivalence and equivocation in Hegel's discussion of race mixing in "Hegel, Race, Genocide," 38.

78. Barck decried Hegel's rationalizing characterization of the genocide of the Indians as a historical "necessity." See Karlheinz Barck, "Amerika in Hegels Geschichtsphilosophie," *Weimarer Beiträge* 38 (1992): 274–78. Ortega wrote with sarcasm of "the peculiar weakness and aptitude of American Indians for evaporating or disappearing" and ridiculed with Hegelian jargon the way that

Indians sought "refuge in not-being." José Ortega y Gasset, "Hegel and America," trans. Luanne Buchanan and Michael H. Hoffheimer, *Clio* 25 (1995): 76.

79. E.g., *Lectures on the Philosophy of World History*, 176, 180, 187. See also *Hegel's Philosophy of Subjective Spirit*, 3: 52/53 (Addition): "Completely good-natured and inoffensive when calm, they commit the most frightful atrocities when suddenly aroused."

80. Hegel's moral condemnation of slavery must be approached in historical context. Before 1830 even American slave owners conceded slavery was immoral. Other German contemporaries denounced slavery unequivocally. Blumenbach protested against drawing political judgments from his race science, "stoutly defended the mental and moral unity of all peoples," and campaigned for the abolition of slavery. Gould, *Mismeasure of Man*, 408. Humboldt argued against any essential distinction among races. Alexander von Humboldt, *Cosmos: A Sketch of a Physical Description of the Universe*, trans. E. C. Otté (London: Henry G. Bohn, 1849), 1:361–62. From this he drew moral and political conclusions: "Whilst we maintain the unity of the human species, we at the same time repel the depressing assumption of superior and inferior races of men." Ibid., 1:368. Humboldt explicitly repudiated the use of racial difference as a justification for slavery. Ibid., 1:369 n.*.

81. Long passages of his descriptions of Negroes in Africa were read during congressional debates in 1860 by a proponent of slavery in the American South. See Michael H. Hoffheimer, "Does Hegel Justify Slavery?" *Owl of Minerva* 25 (1993): 118–19.

82. Mario Casalla, *América en el pensamiento de Hegel: Admiración y rechazo* (Buenos Aires: Catálogos, 1992), 71; Bernasconi, "Hegel at the Court of the Ashanti," 58–63. Eze writes that Hegel's "political philosophy transformed the European historical perspectives into concrete projects of international politics and economics (imperialism, colonialism, and the trans-national corporation)." *Race and the Enlightenment*, 7–8. Carol Aisha Blackshire-Belay claims Hegel "saw Africa as a continent inhabited by a population of people who were yet not ready for their own freedom. It was the responsibility of the Europeans to educate them." "Historical Revelations: The International Scope of African Germans Today and Beyond," in *The African-German Experience: Critical Essays*, ed. Carol Aisha Blackshire-Belay (Westport, CT: Praeger, 1996), 98. Vimbai Gukwe Chivaura cites Hegel's anti-African racism. "European Culture in Africa as Business: Its Implications on the Development of the Human Factor," *Journal of Black Studies* 29 (1998): 189–208. L. Keita identifies Hegel with recent efforts to reduce behavior to race. Review of *Why Race Matters: Race Differences and What They Mean* by Michael Levin, *Western Journal of Black Studies* 23 (1999): 65–70.

83. He treated colonization as the culmination of ethical life. *Elements of the Philosophy of Right*, trans. H. B. Nisbet (Cambridge: Cambridge University Press, 1991), 269 (§ 248). But he also described the geography of Africa as inhibiting European penetration, exploration, and settlement. *Lectures on the Philosophy of World History*, 175. In lectures he presented state-sponsored colonization as a second, higher form of activity, one in which Germany had not yet been active, and he observed that more advanced nations either should or would disregard the rights of "barbarians." *Elements of the Philosophy of Right* 376 (§ 351). For passages on race and colonialism from Hegel's lectures on world history and the philosophy of right, see Eze, *Race and the Enlightenment*, 110–53. Olufemi Taiwo

blames Hegel's false ethnocentric universalism for the absence of Africa as a topic in philosophy. "Exorcising Hegel's Ghost: Africa's Challenge to Philosophy," *African Studies Quarterly: The Online Journal of African Studies*, http://www.africa.ufl.edu/asq/v1/4/2.htm.

84. Hegel argued that granting Jews civil rights would encourage their "self-awareness as legal persons in civil society." And it is "from this root, infinite and free from all other influences, that the desired assimilation in terms of attitude and disposition arises" ("aus dieser unendlichen von allem Andern freien Wurzel die verlangte Ausgleichung der Denkungsart und Gesinnung zu Stande kommt"). *Elements of Hegel's Philosophy of Right*, 296n (§ 270); *Grundlinien der Philosophie des Rechts*, *Sämtliche Werke*, 7: 354n.

11

John Stuart Mill and "The Negro Question"

Race, Colonialism, and the Ladder of Civilization

ANTHONY BOGUES

In the political and intellectual histories of liberalism, J. S. Mill's contribution to the conception of liberty remains one major frame for contemporary liberal political thought.[1] Mill operated in the period of British history generally called "the Victorian liberal era."[2] Some commentators have suggested that the writings of Mill and Jeremy Bentham in England and those of Alexis de Tocqueville in France revised classical liberal principles. They argue that if classical liberalism revolved around the supremacy of the individual and noninterference in economic life (laissez-faire economics), then the emergence of the felicific calculus of utilitarianism and conceptions of broader representative democracy created the intellectual conditions for state and government interventions to design and reengineer the conditions for public welfare and rule. Michel Foucault, however, makes the point that Bentham's panopticon represented a "form of power that rests not on the inquiry but on something completely different, which I call the 'examination.'"[3] What is noticeable about Foucault and others, however, is that they do not review nineteenth-century political thought within a framework of how new forms of government and power are connected to the development of a kind of microphysics of subject formation and individual control, while being shaped by the concerns of empire, colonial power, and race.

Nineteenth-century Europe was not only the "era of Victorian liberalism" but was also a period of empire and colonial domination. It was the period in British history in which colonial empire was the order of the day. And even though the colonies were geographically distant from the "mother country," spatial differences did not negate the fact that the ideas about rule, freedom, civilization, and progress were worked out in direct relationship to colonialism and empire. In this regard Ann Laura Stoler and Frederick Cooper are accurate when they comment that "Europe was made by its imperial projects, as much as colonial encounters were shaped by conflicts with Europe itself."[4]

This means thinking about Mill's political thought can be done on two levels. We can write about and study Mill's political thought narrowly within a framework and in relationship to a set of "internalist arguments" about the genealogy of Western political thought. However, I would suggest that such a procedure silences the ways in which racial slavery, empire, and colonialism were integral to modernity and to modern political thought. Or we can read Mill and his work as partly shaped by the imperial nature of Europe as well as by the political languages and discursive practices of the times. After all, it was Mill himself who noted in his *Principles of Political Economy* that "[t]here needs to be no hesitation in affirming that Colonization, in the present state of the world, is the best affair in which the capital of an old and wealthy country can engage."[5] Following this track, this chapter will attempt to analyze a little-known Mill essay, "The Negro Question," as well as some of the major parliamentary speeches he made while he was chairman of the Jamaica Committee in the British Parliament.[6] Making use of these and some other well-known Mill texts, I will locate some of Mill's central arguments about race, slavery, and colonialism within his paradigm of civilization and progress. The overarching theme of this move is to suggest that meanings of civilization and progress, what Mill generally called "the improvement of mankind," were foundational to his understanding of human nature and consequently central to his political thought. As such they then became important frames for his support of colonial empire.

|||

VICTORIAN POLITICAL THOUGHT

It has been argued by some scholars that as a political figure and political thinker Mill was a radical. I wish to sidestep this dispute for the moment and suggest that Victorian political thought was a mix of many currents that were profoundly shaped by notions of character and civilization.[7] In other words, whether the political thought was Tory, Whig, liberal, or socialist, there was a sharing of common epistemic grounds. Stefan Collini has persuasively shown that a central feature of Victorian political thought was the "idea of character."[8] The "idea of character," Collini maintains, was about "the mental and moral qualities which distinguish an individual or race viewed as a homogeneous whole."[9] Such a definition, he argues, meant both a set of settled dispositions as well as formation. What is critical about the emergence of the "idea of character" in mid-nineteenth-century English political thought is that it was tied to the successful influence of the idea of civilization. By this time as well conceptions about civilization had morphed from their original Latin roots of *civilis* and *civis*, meaning legal and political domains as well as an organized community, into an organizing discursive formation in which a hierarchy of nations and population groups existed.[10]

Within this mix we should add that another preoccupation of nineteenth-century Western thought was the characters of and relationships between biology, race, and evolution. This was the era of Charles Darwin's theories of evolution, which quickly came to profoundly stamp nineteenth-century social thought.[11] Of course we know that Darwin himself was ambiguous about supposed fixed racial inferiority. In his 1871 *Descent of Man*, he argues against then conventionally Western ideas about the centrality of climatic conditions in causing skin color. He notes: "This view has been rejected . . . because the distribution of the variously coloured races, most of whom must have long inhabited their present homes, does not coincide with corresponding differences in climate."[12] But Darwin remains enmeshed within the web of the prevailing conceptions of civilization. He states: "Nor can the differences between the races of man be accounted for by the inherited effects of the increased or decreased use of parts." He then continues, "[W]ith civilized nations, the reduced size of the jaw . . . the increased size of the brain from greater intellectual activity . . . have produced a considerable effect on their general appearance when compared to savages."[13] This conception of civilization not only was present in England but was a central feature of French thought. One of the most important French journalists of the period put the matter well. Gabriel Charmes stated that the duty of French colonialism was to bring "even at the price of spilled blood—peace, commerce, tolerance . . . having taught millions of men civilization and freedom."[14]

The construction of civilization based upon human societal hierarchies and the so-called evolution of the human race with a fixed gaze upon the modernity of European society was a feature of nineteenth-century European thought. What distinguished the different currents was the possibility of character. Could the native/savage become civilized? Did he or she have the potential to be part of the human community? Those who answered in the affirmative while supporting colonial empire advocated a mission of civilization. Those who answered in the negative proclaimed the native a permanent savage beast and claimed that the only real hope for the continued dominance of Europe was the fixed inferiority of the native. Ivan Hannaford has argued that it was this period, which saw the rise of "scientific racism" alongside theories of human evolution, that the essential historical elements of European politics were "eclipsed by a doctrine of force . . . that . . . would express itself in the language of biological necessity, managerial efficiency, and effectiveness in a science of eugenics."[15]

John Stuart Mill was one of those thinkers who offered culture, character, and civilization as explanations for difference and hierarchy.[16] He notes for example that "the problem of character is the determining issue in the question of government" and that the "laws of national character are by far the most important class of sociological laws."[17] Thus for Mill the capacities of civilization to shape human beings were more important than biology. Hence Mill's emphasis on education, training, and the potential for the progress of human nature. Within British society the abolition of the slave trade in 1807 and of racial slavery in the British Caribbean colonies in 1834 occasioned a conflict between those who believed that race was biology and those who felt that race was chance and that the conditions of supposed racial inferiority could be overcome.

|||

THE DEBATE

In 1849, Thomas Carlyle, one of the most important English writers of the day, published in the journal *Fraser's Magazine* the essay "Occasional Discourse on the Negro Question."[18] Both Mill and Carlyle were famous intellectuals at the time, with Mill noting the influence of Carlyle on his thought.[19] The historian Catherine Hall, in an insightful essay on these two figures, makes the point that

> Thomas Carlyle and John Stuart Mill were two of the major middle-class intellectuals and writers of their age. . . . Both had the status to intervene as significant public figures in a political debate. Both were to play a critical part in reformulating ideas about manliness and about English identity.[20]

For Carlyle, the abolition of slavery was a pernicious event in English history. It disturbed the natural human order, making a mockery of the virtue of work as the "gospel of life." Abolition also, he suggested, unsettled the entire meaning of Englishness. This meaning could subsequently be recovered only if forms of servitude were reintroduced into the Caribbean colonies. Carlyle's arguments rested on two ideas. The first was that blacks were naturally inferior to whites and that abolition had not only upset the order but economically ruined the colonies. In this vein, he argued that it was the presence of whites that had been the motor for the development of the Caribbean islands. He observed, for example, that "till the European white man first saw them [they] were as if not yet created, their nobler elements of cinnamon, sugar, coffee, pepper black and gray, lying all asleep, waiting the white enchanter who should say to them, Awake!"[21] This sentiment of course followed the typical discourse about colonization developed in European thought surrounding lands, property, and the rights of conquest.[22]

The second major plank of Carlyle's position was his hostility toward what he contended was black laziness and the refusal of the ex-slave population to work on the former slave master's plantation:

> No Black man who will not work according to what ability the gods have given him for working, has the smallest right to eat pumpkin . . . but has an indis-

putable and perpetual right to be compelled, by the real proprietors of the said land, to do the competent work for his living. This is the everlasting duty of all men, black or white, which are born into this world.[23]

Of course what Carlyle was railing against was the mass movement of the slaves in all the Caribbean colonies away from the old sugar plantations and their establishment of free villages based on small farming and subsistence agricultural production.[24] Carlyle ended his essay with a call for white men to once again "command Black men, and produce West Indian fruitfulness by means of them."[25]

Mill's response to Carlyle's enunciations was swift. In the following edition of the journal, he wrote a polemical essay that challenged the terms of the debate about the meaning of abolitionism, the nature of the imperial polity, and ways in which Carlyle's ideas about human nature were structured. Mill begins by observing that "the history of improvement is the record of a struggle by which inch after inch of ground has been wrung from these maleficent powers, and more and more of human life rescued from the iniquitous dominion of the law of might."[26] For Mill, human society was still in need of great reforms. However, he suggested that the abolition of slavery was one of the greatest achievements of mankind to date. In Mill's thought slavery at that time was "detestable," especially because the laws of England condoned it. From this view Mill saw the abolition of slavery as a triumph "for the cause of justice" (88), freeing the black slaves from "the despotism of their fellow human beings" (88).

Mill also differs from Carlyle not only about slavery but also about so-called black inferiority. Stating that he disagrees with the notion that "one kind of human beings are born servants to another kind" (92) because it is embedded in the idea that every difference among human beings resides in "an original difference of nature" (93), Mill reasons that "human beings are subject to an infinitely greater variety of accidents and external influences than trees" (93). In such a context human difference and hierarchy could be accounted for by character. Since character was something that could be shaped, those who were supposed to be in dire need of improvement were dependent upon the civilized to train them. As a consequence the duty of English society and imperial polity was not to restore slavery but to develop forms of *tutelage*, which could eventually lead the black population into civilization. However, Mill was clear. Until civilization was achieved the freed slaves were not citizens but subjects under British rule. It was from these positions that he would in 1866 again cross swords with Carlyle in the aftermath of the 1865 Morant Bay Rebellion in Jamaica.

The second target of Mill's attack was Carlyle's conception of the centrality of work to human life. For Mill, "the worth of work does not surely consist in its leading to other work, and so on to work upon work without end" (91). While work was necessary for each person's existence, Mill asserted what he called "the gospel of leisure" and noted that "human beings *cannot* rise to the finer attributes of their nature compatibly with a life filled with labour" (91). From this perspective Mill then proposed the continued growth of a Caribbean black peasantry.

Mill's defense of abolitionism and of the British postslavery colonial project of tutelage was an integral part of a sharp debate about the future of British colonial policy. The abolition of slavery and the consolidation of British colonial rule in India, along with the general dissatisfaction among white settlers in Canada, had generated a vigorous debate in British colonial policy circles about the forms of future rule in the colonial empire.[27] At the heart of this debate was whether or not the colonial subject and the ex-slave had the potential for equality or if in the words of Carlyle "[w]e must always master them." If the ex-slaves and the colonial subjects had the potential for political equality, then the issue that faced imperial policy was how to create forms of rule that would construct character and subjects who would over time participate in representative government. In other words the debate agreed on the necessity of despotism in the colonies. Mill makes this clear when he states: "Despotism is a legitimate mode of government in dealing with barbarians, provided the end be their improvement and the means justified by actually effecting that end."[28] Therefore one subtext of the debate was about timing: when could the "mother country" release her children? Of course the hidden assumption and the unanswered question was, who would determine readiness?

So what we have here in the debate between Mill and Carlyle are the following. In one current of English political thought, difference was innate, created by nature, and as a consequence there was no chance of political and social equality for those who were nonwhite subjects of the empire. Another current admitted that the black and colonial subjects were indeed inferior but argued that this inferiority was not ordained by nature and therefore could be overcome by contact with civilization and a process of tutelage. Both currents were united in their belief about black inferiority but disagreed on its root causes and naturalness. For those who thought that this so-called inferiority could be overcome, we should note that the goal was envisioned in terms of white normativity. To become fully human and a citizen, the colonial and black subject had to master the protocols of Western civilization, to become in the words of the nineteenth-century English writer Anthony Trollope a "Creole Negro."

The debate between Carlyle and Mill was an important one in mid-nineteenth-century British political and intellectual history, announcing the high stakes in the argument about Englishness and imperial rule. These elements of the debate would be repeated under sharper political circumstances in the aftermath of the Morant Bay Rebellion.

| | |

COERCION VERSUS TUTELAGE

The 1865 Jamaican Morant Bay Rebellion was a central event not only in nineteenth-century Jamaica but also in the British Empire.[29] The rebellion and its aftermath became known in English political circles as "the Jamaican Affair." The rebellion was centered in one parish of the island colony, St. Thomas. Its leadership was organized around Paul Bogle, a native Baptist preacher and small farmer. Bogle was typical of the ex-slaves that Carlyle had fulminated against years earlier. Living in one of the small districts of the parish, Stony Gut, Bogle and others had developed into a small independent peasantry. As a preacher he developed a close alliance with George William Gordon, a mulatto landowner, who had been born a slave and when freed was given property by his wealthy slave-owning father. The trigger for the rebellion was an incident in the parish courthouse that resulted in a warrant for the arrest of Paul Bogle. When they went to execute the warrant, the police were met by a crowd who promised that they would march into the capital of the parish and "kill all white men and black men that would not join them." The crowd also beseeched the black police officers who attempted to execute the warrant to leave the planters and join them. The crowd urged the police officers with the words "Cleave to the black." On the following day Bogle and members of his community, many of whom he had drilled in quasi-military fashion, marched to the town and the courthouse. In the interim Bogle had written to Edward John Eyre, the colonial governor, asking for the protection of the colonial state. He stated that this protection was needed since he and his community were "her majesty's loyal subjects."[30]

The march gathered momentum, so that by the time it arrived in the capital town, the crowd was an angry one. On the way the marchers attacked a police station and in the town confronted the police and military forces that were posted there. The militia fired upon the crowd. The crowd responded by charging the militia and setting fire to the courthouse. Quickly, the rebels gained control of the town, opened the jails, and released prisoners. The rebellion then spread throughout the parish, and it is the estimation of one writer that at its peak it involved nearly two thousand persons. The colonial governor reacted by establishing a council of war. Arguing that this was but the tip of an island-wide conspiracy to overthrow the colonial government, and with the memory of the Haitian Revolution hovering over the colony, Governor Eyre organized a military force to brutally crush the rebellion. At the end of the day, Eyre unleashed severe repression—439 persons were killed, hundreds were brutally flogged, thousands of houses were burnt, and many of the leaders including Bogle were hanged. Eyre held Gordon responsible for the rebellion and duly executed him.

The scale of the repression caused consternation in the British Parliament, and there were calls for Eyre's removal. However, more important for our purposes was that the rebellion occasioned the creation of two committees. One was the Jamaica Committee, which eventually came to be led by Mill, and the other was a committee to defend Governor Eyre led by Carlyle. The two committees were distinguished as well by their membership. The Jamaica Committee counted among its members Charles Darwin, Thomas Henry Huxley, and Charles Lyell, while Eyre's defense committee drew on persons like Charles Dickens and Alfred Tennyson. The Morant Bay Rebellion then served as a lightning rod in British imperial thought.

For Mill, who had published *On Liberty* in 1859 and *Considerations on Representative Government* in 1861 and had been recently elected to Parliament in 1865, there was nothing more important at that time in English political life than the debate around the consequences of the rebellion and the repressive political and military actions of Governor Eyre. At stake were the issues of liberty and government in an imperial state. He noted in a letter that "not even the Reform Bill [was] more important than the duty of dealing justly with the abominations committed in Jamaica."[31] The events of the "Jamaican Affair" resulted in an investigation by a royal commission. The early efforts of the Jamaica Committee focused on getting an official condemnation of Governor Eyre's actions. Very quickly, however, pushed by Mill, the committee began to advocate both a trial for the governor and compensation for those who were harmed by the colonial state's repression. In one of his opening statements on the issue, Mill argues that the committee's aim, "besides upholding the obligation of justice and humanity towards all races beneath the Queen's sway, is to vindicate, by an appeal to judicial authority, the great legal and constitutional principles which have been violated."[32] In Mill's view the repression conducted in the colony by the Governor Eyre violated the principles of law and civilization. The ex-slaves, though not yet quite civilized, were in Mill's words "her Majesty's subjects." As subjects they were human and entitled to protection under the law. He observes in another speech, "I know not for what more important purpose courts of law exist than for the security of human life."[33] For Mill law and the sanctity of human life were primary values. He observes in a July 1866 speech:

So long as the power of inflicting death is restricted by laws, by rules, by forms devised for the security of the innocent, by settled usage, by a long series of precedents—these laws, these forms, these usages and precedents, are a protection to those who are judged; but they are also eminently a protection to those who judge.[34]

In contrast the Eyre committee believed that the colonial black was subhuman and that the demands of Englishness required that the black colonial subject under imperial rule be treated with drastic coercion when it was thought fit. In their minds since there was no possible potential for development of such subjects, force was a permanent requirement for order. Mill and others thought, however, that while "despotism" was necessary at times, it was only a temporary measure. Once the slaves had been freed, although they were not yet at the stage to be granted political equality, they had to be treated in the courts within the rule of law or tutelage could not succeed. This meant not that the nonwhite colonial subject should be granted political equality but rather that in matters pertaining to the sanctity of human life the treatment in courts should follow forms of limited procedural equality. Therefore, in the British colonies, even though the ex-slaves did not have political liberty and the rights thereof, they were entitled in Mill's view to be treated as human beings. Of course the hidden subtext here was, how could the imperial power claim civility when it behaved in extralegal and barbarous ways? Despotism was necessary for the rule of the colonial empire in the Caribbean, but one had to be careful not to engage in glaring acts of despotism. What Mill ignored was the fact that there was a tight relationship between the practices of colonial despotic rule and the absence of rule of law. As a system of rule, colonialism was about command. It suspended common law and rested upon violence. Its founding violence was conquest. The contradiction that faced Mill was, therefore, how could one justify conquest? He resolved it by turning to civilization as a conceptual frame. Governor Eyre followed the logic of colonial rule. Mill was disturbed by this logic since it seemed to veer off into other directions and also made the colonial power a fixed tyrant. Because he was aware of the relationship between the colonial space and the government in the "mother country," it is clear that Mill wondered about when tyranny would migrate back to the space of the colonial power.

In Mill's view imperial political thought had to rethink its relationship to the colonies—what was the nature of the relationship between the colonial space, imperial ideas, and the construction of the polity? Where did the boundaries of the imperial polity begin and end? In his *Principles of Political Economy*, Mill had noted:

These . . . properties . . . are hardly to be looked upon as countries carrying out an exchange of commodities with other countries, but more properly as outlaying agricultural or manufacturing estates belonging to a larger community. Our West Indian colonies, for example, cannot be regarded as countries with a productive capital of their own . . . the trade with the West Indies is hardly to be considered an external trade, but more resembles the traffic between town and country.[35]

The use of the words *town* and *country* as metaphors to describe the relationship between the West Indian colonies and Britain demonstrates that in Mill's thinking, while the colonies had inferior status, the difference was not unbridgeable. Therefore the colonial subjects deserved at least the sanctity of human life, and the imperial polity in the "British imperial century" was to be organized accordingly. At the same time the imperial polity also had to learn from an earlier phase of British colonialism, one in which Britain had lost the North American colonies. In this new phase, Mill and others argued that the British Empire could successfully maintain its rule only if it was able to exert formal and informal hegemony over the far-flung sites of the empire. Integral to this construction of hegemony was the dissemination of Christianity and Western values. There were of course two agents for accomplishing this task. One was the evangelical movement and the other was education and training. I want to suggest that with this preoccupation in the end the issue of the construction of values became one central aspect of Mill's political thought.

| | |

GOVERNMENT, LIBERTY, AND CIVILIZATION

If for Mill the colonial subjects of the empire were humans, albeit on a lower scale, then how should they be governed and in what ways did the principles of liberty apply to them, if at all? Mill's answer was elaborated in *Considerations on Representative Government*. In chapter 18 of the text, Mill recognizes and agrees with imperial rule:

Free States, like all others, may possess dependencies acquired either by conquest or by colonization; and our own is the greatest instance of the kind in modern history. It is an important question, how such dependencies ought to be governed.[36]

Mill then outlines two classes of colonies. In doing this he suggests that there are people "capable of and ripe for Representative government: such as the British possessions in America and Australia. Others, like India, are still at a great distance from that state" (447). In that context Mill notes that there is a "fixed principle . . . of Great Britain, professed in theory and faithfully adhered to in practice that her colonies of the European race, equally with the parent country, possess the fullest measure of internal self-government" (452–53).

It is interesting here to observe that Mill links the issue of representative government with the so-called superiority of the European. We should also note the distinctions that he makes about colonization and conquest. In the first place the colonial sites are called dependencies, suggesting that they need help and guidance to another stage of human life. Second, by splitting the colonial project from conquest, Mill avoids the hard question of how conquest creates forms of absolute rule since typically the occupier nation has to engage in battles of pacification. Thus by using the political language of dependency Mill avoids one major conflict in his political thought. However, while arguing against natural and inherent racial differences, he continues to uphold the so-called superiority of Europe and its descendants. Turning his attention to what he calls the "backward populations," Mill states that dependencies "must be governed by the dominant country. . . . There are, as we have already seen, conditions of society in which a vigorous despotism is in itself the best mode of government for training the people in what is specifically wanting to render them capable of higher civilization" (453).

In Mill's political thought the ideal form of imperial polity for "backward people" was similar to the rule of a succession of "absolute monarchs guaranteed by irresistible force" (454). For him the problem of imperial rule was central to both the political life and the thought of the period. He writes:

As it is already a common, and is rapidly tending to become the universal, condition of the more backward populations, to be . . . held in direct subjection by the more advanced . . . there are in this age of the world few more important problems, than how to organize this rule, so as to make it a good instead of an evil to subject people; providing them with the best attainable present government, and with the conditions most favorable to future permanent improvement. (454)

It is clear here that Mill knew he was on slippery ground. How could one justify despotic rule and make it a tool for human improvement when by its logic it cannot operate that way? Mill's answer was to proclaim that the task for imperial politics was to find a way to make imperial rule good. This was an entirely unworkable solution. But the root of the problem resided in the ladder of civilization that had captured Mill's political thought.

It was from within this frame that Mill would argue his case in the Jamaica Committee. One intriguing result of the Morant Bay Rebellion was the subsequent political transformation of the colony along with other Caribbean colonies into crown colonies, in which even the right of political equality for whites was rescinded.

It is also important to note that in the early part of the twentieth century Mill's arguments about the nature of imperial rule and its mission of civilization and improvement were again picked up by the British Colonial Office and used against the local native intelligentsia who advocated self-government. Then the colonial power argued that the region was not yet quite ready for political freedom and political equality. One segment of the anticolonial intellectuals vigorously asserted that this was not so. In making their arguments, many of these intellectuals observed that they had mastered Western civilization and were therefore ready.[37]

Since issues of civilization and conceptions about the improvement of mankind lay at the foundations of Mill's thought regarding both race and empire, it is to these issues and conceptions that we again return. Raymond Williams points out that in the nineteenth century civilization came to mean forms of social order and knowledge. He also makes the point that these meanings were also tied to understandings of culture.[38] In nineteenth-century English thought, Matthew Arnold's *Culture and Anarchy* (1869) represented a critical account of the story of culture and its relationship to principles of social and political value. This preoccupation with culture generally informed writings on racial theory. Both Robert Knox in *The Races of Men* (1850) and Joseph-Arthur Gobineau's *Essay on the Inequality of the Races* (1853) deployed theories of culture in which racial hierarchy was the result of cultural developments and achievements. In both these instances, as Robert Young observes:

> Civilization and culture were thus the names for the standard of measurement in the hierarchy of values through which European culture defined itself. . . . The principle of opposition, between civilization and barbarism or savagery, was nothing less than the ordering principle of civilization as such.[39]

For Mill, civilization was both a stage of mankind's improvement and a representation of *certain kinds* of improvement:

> [Civilization] is a word of double meaning. It sometimes stands for human improvement in general, and sometimes for certain kinds of improvement. We are accustomed to call a country more civilized if we think it more improved; more eminent in the best characteristics of Man and Society; farther advanced in the road to perfection; happier, nobler, wiser. But in another sense it stands for that kind of improvement only which distinguishes a wealthy and powerful nation from savages and barbarians.[40]

If we attempt to distill some of the core elements of these improvements advocated by Mill, they would include the advancement of knowledge, the erosion of superstition, and most of all the dominance of a certain kind of character that had to be preserved in order for continuous self-improvement to take place. Implicit in the conception of improvement was the idea of "moving upward." In Mill's thought this process required specific conditions that could be obtained only by the principles of liberty. Mill therefore notes that "the spirit of improvement is not always a spirit of liberty . . . but the only unfailing permanent source of improvement is liberty, since by it there are as many possible independent centers of improvement as there are individuals."[41] Liberty therefore was a precondition for progress and improvement. However it is now clear that there was also in Mill's political thought a precondition for liberty—*civilization*.

Mill differed from many other European thinkers of the period in his views of what distinguished "savages" from civilized nations, that is, in his notion of civilization in its second sense. While joining with those who deployed culture and civilization as markers of racial inferiority, Mill detached civilization from nature, thereby creating the possibility for the black population and the colonial subject to be, one day, fully human—albeit within the frames decided upon by the West. In comparison with, say, Gobineau, Mill was not preoccupied with the decline of civilization. For the former, race was the motor force of history and white supremacy the apex of human achievement. Mill, on the other hand, thought that the driving motor of history was the desire for improvement, although he believed that European civilization was the height of human improvement.

For Mill, empire and colonialism had demonstrated the superiority of Europe. However, that superiority created a bundle of duties. One such duty was to civilize those who were under imperial rule. Mill's political thought therefore was representative of a form of politics in which the conqueror is perceived as the norm and the conquered as children to be taught. If for Mill liberty did not mean only self-determination but also self-development because man was a "progressive being," then the question that faced him was, on what grounds could the colonial subject be made worthy of this human good? His attempts to resolve this question were rooted in the general ideas about the mission of imperial polity. He recognized that there was conquest but justified it on the grounds that the conquered were "savages" and imperial rule was a necessary requirement for civilizing them. His vision was not a fixed racial and colonial order but one in which imperial polity should be geared toward training the colonial child-subject and eventually allowing him or her some degree of political equality.

CONCLUSION

It was this position that might have made Mill a "radical" in his day. However, the limits of this radicalism were revealed in his resignation from the East India Company when he was unable to defeat proposals that gave a modicum of internal self-government to India. His opposition to proposals for Indian internal self-government was based on his thinking that Indians were not yet ready.[42]

Mill's political thought can be treated as emblematic of liberalism in the nineteenth century. In modern political thought liberalism is oftentimes treated as a transcendent political philosophy. It comes into the human world untainted, all sweetness and light. However, I would argue that no proper account of the history of liberalism can be presented without the histories of colonial empire. For liberalism, colonialism was justified on the grounds of a mission of civilization. This mission, called "developmentalism" by Uday Singh Mehta, separates liberalism from its transcendent universalism and makes it a historic political practice and political language.[43] By defining civilization as one condition of liberty, Mill was unable to break the link between race, colonialism, and empire. In the end Mill opposed slavery, rationalized colonialism, and empire and constructed a theory of liberalism that did not recast classical liberalism's foundations of racial exclusions. So while it is accurate to say that Mill's intervention shifted elements of liberal political theory, this shift reinforced the foundational assumptions and the philosophical anthropology of classical liberalism. The assumptions include the rationality of human nature, the privileging of reason as rationality, the relationship between reason and harmony in human life, the position that human nature was both progressive and meliorist, and the existence of a human hierarchy in which conquest was justified. If classical liberalism was preoccupied with the nature of political liberty (what it called natural liberty) and the ways to overcome absolutism, Mill's liberalism accepted the premise that the problem of sovereignty was already solved. The question for him was how to reconcile "man's" desire for self-development with the emergence of representative democratic forms. He writes forcefully:

> The subject of this essay is not the so called "liberty of will," . . . but civil or social liberty: the nature and limits of the power which can be legitimately exercised by society over the individual . . . but in the stage of progress into which the more civilized portions of the species have now entered, it presents itself under new conditions and requires a different and more fundamental treatment.[44]

Thus, the only reason "power can be rightly exercised over any member of a civilized community, against his will, is to prevent harm to others"(emphasis mine).[45]

But Mill's famous harm principle does not fully apply to subjects of colonial conquest or empire. This limitation is reinforced when he further states, "[W]e may leave out of consideration those backward states of society in which the race itself may be considered as in its nonage."[46] Here Mill is using the word race to invoke descent, character, and nation. His emphasis on "nonage," a metaphor for lack of growth, was slightly different from the biological forms of racism in which typologies of the human were fixed and resistant to cultural changes. For Mill race was rooted in cultural and civilizational differences. In this regard he seems to have been in agreement with Charles Darwin's idea that nature had no permanent form. Therefore even if some humans were "savages," with the right training they could be improved. Mill's social-evolutionary framework for the understanding of human nature meant that race as culture and civilization could be used to describe population groups. In this regard therefore he does not escape racialized thinking.

In the end Mill's concern about liberty is rooted in what Charles Mills has felicitously called a "racial contract."[47] This means that Mill's version of liberty is from the angle of those who were conquerors. His concern to grant political equality over time to the colonial subject does not pay attention to the other issues that emerge in the establishment of conquest. By pegging human nature to the concept of civilization, Mill was caught on the ladder of civilization. In the end his liberalism was a practice that could not grant liberty to those who were colonial subjects, nor could it be a condition for their general improvement. For that to happen, the conquered would have to find new grounds for liberty.

NOTES

1. See for example, John Gray's Mill on Liberty: A Defense (London: Routledge, 1996). Of course it is Isaiah Berlin's 1958 lecture "Two Concepts of Liberty" and his arguments about "negative" and "positive" freedom drawing heavily from Mill that continue to frame many discussions about liberty, liberalism, and individualism. Berlin's lecture was published in Isaiah Berlin, Four Essays on Liberty (Oxford: Oxford University Press, 1969).

2. See Richard Bellamy, ed., Victorian Liberalism: Nineteenth-Century Political Thought and Practice (London: Routledge, 1990), for a discussion of the different elements of this stream of political thought.

3. Michel Foucault, Power, ed. James D. Faubion (New York: New Press, 2000), 58.

4. Ann Stoler and Frederick Cooper, "Between Metropole and Colony: Rethinking a Research Agenda," in Tensions of Empire: Colonial Cultures in a Bourgeois World, ed. Frederick Cooper and Ann Stoler (Berkeley: University of California Press, 1997), 1.

5. John Stuart Mill, *Principles of Political Economy, Collected Works of John Stuart Mill*, ed. J. M. Robson (Toronto: University of Toronto Press, 1965), 963 (bk. 5).

6. Some writers have examined the essay but do not pay any attention to his parliamentary speeches. See, in particular, Iva G. Jones, "Trollope, Carlyle, and Mill on The Negro: An Episode in the History of Ideas," *Journal of Negro History* 52.3 (1967): 185–99, and David Theo Goldberg, "Liberalism Limits: Carlyle and Mill on "The Negro Question," *Nineteenth-Century Contexts* 22 (2000): 203–16. For a feminist reading on this debate, see Catherine Hall, "Competing Masculinities: Thomas Carlyle, John Stuart Mill, and the Case of Governor Eyre," *White, Male, and Middle Class: Explorations in Feminism and History* (New York: Routledge, 1992), 255–95.

7. For a useful discussion of the different elements of nineteenth-century English political thought, see Mark Francis and John Marrow, *A History of English Political Thought in the Nineteenth Century* (New York: St. Martin's Press, 1994).

8. Stefan Collini, "The Idea of 'Character' in Victorian Political Thought," *Transactions of the Royal Historical Society*, vol. 35, *fifth series* (1985), 29–50.

9. Ibid., 33.

10. For a useful discussion about civilization and its uses in Western intellectual history and political history, see Thomas C. Patterson, *Inventing Western Civilization* (New York: Monthly Review Press, 1997).

11. Darwin's *The Origin of Species* was first published in 1859. The full title of the text tells us about the centrality of race to ways of thinking about human life. It was titled *On the Origin of the Species by Means of Natural Selection; or, The Preservation of Favoured Races in the Struggle for Life*. For a useful discussion about how issues of selection, struggle, and nature become central metaphors in Victorian thought, see Robert Young, *Darwin's Metaphor: Nature's Place in Victorian Culture* (Cambridge: Cambridge University Press, 1985).

12. Charles Darwin, "On the Formation of the Races of Man," in *Archives of Empire*, vol. II: *The Scramble for Africa*, ed. Barbara Harlow and Mia Carter (Durham: Duke University Press, 2003) p. 161.

13. Ibid., 165.

14. Cited in Alice L. Conklin, *A Mission to Civilize: The Republican Idea of Empire in France and West Africa, 1895–1930* (Stanford: Stanford University Press, 1997), 13. This text contains a fine overview of French colonialism during this period.

15. While Hannaford misses the ways in which earlier forms of racial thinking then come to inform this period and omits the role of the various colonial empires, his insight allows us to begin to understand how questions of education and tutelage then begin to play major roles in the ruling of human beings. See Ivan Hannford, *Race: The History of an Idea in the West* (Baltimore: Johns Hopkins University Press, 1996).

16. One writer who has spotted Mill's preoccupation with civilization is John M. Robson. See his "Civilization and Culture as Moral Concepts," in *The Cambridge Companion to Mill*, ed. John Skorupski (Cambridge: Cambridge University Press, 1998), 338–71. However, Robson does not discuss the imperial context for Mill's preoccupation.

17. John Stuart Mill, *Considerations on Representative Government*, in *Collected Works*, vol. 19 (Toronto: University of Toronto Press, 1984), 421.

18. The essay was later retitled with the word *Nigger* replacing *Negro*.

19. John Stuart Mill, *Autobiography* (London: Penguin, 1989), 132, 185.

20. Hall, *White, Male, and Middle Class*, 264.

21. Thomas Carlyle, "Occasional Discourse on the Negro Question," in *Politics and Empire in Victorian Britain: A Reader*, ed. Antoinette Burton (New York: Palgrave, 2001), 111.

22. A great deal of this is of course rooted in John Locke's theory of property. For a discussion of this see James Tully, *An Approach to Political Philosophy: Locke in Contexts* (Cambridge: Cambridge University Press, 1993).

23. Carlyle, "Occasional Discourse on the Negro Question," 114.

24. For a comparative description of this process in the Caribbean and then in the American South, see Eric Foner, *Nothing but Freedom: Emancipation and Its Legacy* (Baton Rouge: Louisiana State University Press, 1983).

25. Carlyle, "Occasional Discourse on the Negro Question," 115.

26. John Stuart Mill. "The Negro Question," *Collected Works*, vol. 21: *Essays on Equality, Law, and Education* (Toronto: University of Toronto Press, 1984), 87; subsequent references in parentheses in the text.

27. This debate is extensively discussed in Catherine Hall, *Civilizing Subjects* (Chicago: University of Chicago Press, 2002), and Thomas Holt, *The Problem of Freedom* (Kingston, Jamaica: Ian Randle Press, 1992).

28. John Stuart Mill, *On Liberty* (London: Penguin, 1974), 69.

29. For discussion about the rebellion, see Gad Heuman, *"The Killing Time": The Morant Bay Rebellion in Jamaica* (London: Macmillan Press, 1994); Abigail Bakan, *Ideology and Class Conflict in Jamaica: The Politics of Rebellion* (Montreal: McGill-Queen's University Press, 1990); Clinton Hutton, "Color for Color, Skin for Skin: The Ideological Foundations of Post-slavery Society (1838–1865)" (Ph.D. diss., University of the West Indies, Mona, 1992).

30. We should note here that Bogle's political language was reflective of the idea that black Jamaicans who were ex-slaves were subjects of the British crown and therefore entitled to the rights of the rule of law. However, one has to make a sharp distinction between equality that meant that the rule of law operated and equality that granted citizenship and therefore political equality. These two distinctive forms of equality operated within Mill's political thought. The historical research on Bogle and his allies shows that these forms of equality were merged and that they perhaps saw Gordon as a possible political representative for their cause.

31. John Stuart Mill, *Collected Works*, vol. 16 (Toronto: University of Toronto Press, 1988), 1126.

32. Ibid., 21:423.

33. John Stuart Mill, *Public and Parliamentary Speeches*, ed. John M. Robson and Bruce L. Kinzer (Toronto: University of Toronto Press, 1988), 107.

34. Ibid., 112.

35. Mill, *Principles of Political Economy*, 693.

36. John Stuart Mill, "Considerations on Representative Government," *On Liberty and Other Essays*, ed. John Gray (Oxford: Oxford University Press, 1998), 447; subsequent references in parentheses in the text.

37. For the use of these arguments see C. L. R. James, "The Case for West Indian Self-Government," in *The C. L. R. James Reader*, ed. Anna Grimshaw (Oxford: Blackwell, 1995). For the importance of this argument and how it framed Caribbean anticolonial thought, see Anthony Bogues, "Politics, Nation, and PostColony: Caribbean Inflections," *Small Axe: A Caribbean Journal of Criticism* (Indiana University), no. 11 (2002): 1–30.

38. Raymond Williams, *Keywords: A Vocabulary of Culture and Society* (New York: Oxford University Press, 1983), 57–60.

39. Robert J. Young, *Colonial Desire: Hybridity in Theory, Culture, and Race* (London: Routledge, 1995), 94.

40. Cited in ibid., 35.

41. Mill, *On Liberty*, 128.

42. For a discussion about Mill, colonialism, and India, see Uday S. Mehta, "Liberal Strategies of Exclusion," in *Tensions of Empire*, ed. Cooper and Stoler, 59–86.

43. For a wider discussion on nineteenth-century liberalism and empire, see Uday S. Mehta, *Liberalism and Empire: A Study in Nineteenth-Century British Liberal Thought* (Chicago: University of Chicago Press, 1999).

44. Mill, *On Liberty*, 59.

45. Ibid., 68.

46. Ibid., 69.

47. See Charles Mills, *The Racial Contract* (Ithaca: Cornell University Press, 1997).

12

Marx, Race, and the Political Problem of Identity

RICHARD T. PETERSON

While the relation to race and racism is an important question about any modern philosopher, it has special significance for thinking about Marx. For philosophers who were not mainly concerned with social theory or whose work precedes the nineteenth century, issues of race may seem instructive but secondary (at least so far as the stated aims of their own work are concerned). That is not to minimize the importance of these issues for assessing earlier thinkers, since even in the eighteenth century intellectual racialism was sufficiently advanced that assumptions about race could play an important role in understandings of the implications and uses of human reason. Even then thinkers like Hume and Kant were laying the groundwork for accounts of the restricted social application of Enlightenment universalism and were developing a sense of Europeans and intellectuals that connected race to rationality.[1] But however we assess the importance of racism in earlier philosophy, our expectations for Marx can only be correspondingly greater. This is partly because he lives at the time racism becomes an explicit intellectual doctrine, but it is also because of his aim to challenge the failure of the modern world to deliver on the Enlightenment's promise to realize universal principles. If race and racism are characteristic defects of the modern world, then any thinker who claims to challenge that world "at its roots" will have to address these defects. If Marx fails as a critic in this regard, then his critical project comes into question.

Today the occasional depiction of Marx as racist or as Eurocentric figures within a wider skepticism or even dismissal of his work, often by those who otherwise share his desire to challenge systematic inequality and domination.[2] The same holds for treatments of him as an anti-Semite, a charge that has been discussed for decades.[3] Textual evidence can be found for all of these charges, though its meaning is open to debate. The most damning evidence comes from private correspondence, and this raises questions of relevant evidence as well as whether we are properly concerned with the personality of Marx or with his work as a theorist and political figure. This is a difficult line to draw under the best of circumstances, as Foucault points out with his discussion of the nature of an author.[4] But it is especially difficult when dealing with issues of race and racism, which can penetrate so deeply and involuntarily into the personality. Race is in important respects a matter of identity and, especially when not explicitly theorized, can be expressed in a multitude of interrelated ways. Indications from private sources may help evaluate or even locate traces of racial orientations in more public ones. There is the further problem of how to evaluate such traces, since in a racialized society, the question may be less whether an individual shows the effects of racism than how she responds to it. Reliance on letters and other texts never prepared or intended for publication is perhaps unavoidable, but also must be weighed carefully in the light of such considerations.

This chapter will argue that, despite Marx's occasional use of racist language, it is wrong to label him a racist. He was himself both a victim of racist attack and a critic of racism in the politics of his day. The deeper problem about racial themes with Marx is that he failed to take them seriously enough in his theoretical work. The following discussion will examine this failure in the light of historical and political issues that were just coming to the fore in the latter part of Marx's life, in particular, issues about collective identities and loyalties.

| | |

RACE: THE MISSING THEME IN MARX'S SOCIAL THEORY

Perhaps the most significant point about Marx and race is that he does not address race in any systematic theoretical way. That is not to say that he is unaware that racial antagonisms are important, nor is it to say that he is without racial views, as we will see shortly. But race and racism (or, for that matter, the emergence of racialist doctrines) do not become objects of reflection integrated into his theoretical work. They remain "empirical," if by this we mean phenomena that have not been rethought in the terms of a theoretical framework. This point is worth emphasizing for our consideration of the place these themes do occupy in Marx's activity. And it is of interest because in this respect Marx is not so different from virtually all the major philosophers that precede him in the period in which race emerges as a social reality.

Marx's theoretical inattention to the theme of race may not seem surprising given its apparent distance from the themes of political economy that were his main preoccupation and given the relatively undeveloped state of racist theory during his early career. In that regard it is worth recalling that fully developed doctrines of race appear only during his own working life; for example, Gobineau's *Essay on the Inequality of the Races* comes out in 1853.[5] On the other hand, we may also recall that Marx did not lack intellectual resources for responding to the emerging racialist thought. His critiques of political economy and ideology frequently target the modern tendency to cast historical processes and social relations in natural appearances. The biological reductionism and determinism associated with much racism are a suitable focus for the corresponding challenge to reification. Moreover, Marx was concerned from early in his career with grasping the interrelation of naturally given conditions and historical mediations, a point bearing on the uses of physical features like skin color for erecting spurious social divisions. We know from his treatment of gender that biological givens never have unmediated significance in society but are reworked by existing social relations.[6] Similarly, Marx's critical reconstruction of intellectuals' relation to the reproduction of power relations in his account of political economy could have been extended to an account of the role of intellectuals in constructing ideological pseudo-sciences of race.

That none of these materialized may be partly due to the fact that racial conflict as such never became a focus of Marx's attention. As we will see shortly, the problem of racial division among workers was an important problem for him, but this is not the same as seeing this division as bound up with systematic power relations and corresponding social struggles. There is no effort to rethink Hegel's recognition dialectic for race the way Marx does for class.[7] And this in turn may be attributed to the absence of developed struggles around the theme of race. Engels attributed Marx's insights into class conflict to the outbreak of workers' uprisings in the thirties.[8] Perhaps the level of racial conflict had not enabled a corresponding theorization. The difficulties a later thinker like Du Bois encounters with the concept of race despite his focus on racial conflict gives some credence to this suggestion.[9] But if such considerations help us understand the absence of a theorization of race by Marx, they do not illuminate his actual comments about race. And these comments remind us that Marx was not always so consistent in his treatment of the intersection of nature and history, a point sometimes noted by those disturbed by his endorsement of Capital as a work that places the modern economy within the sweep of natural history.[10]

Indeed, some racialist comments couched within the language of evolutionary thought provide a disturbing case in point. Not only does Marx speak as a racialist (by which I mean he talks as though race were an unproblematic idea), but he draws on degeneration theories similar to those found in racist thinking that dates back to Montesquieu and includes Kant. For example, in a letter to Engels (1866) he says that Tremeaux shows "on the existing soil formation of Russia [that] the Slavs become Tartarized and Mongolized, just as he . . . proves that the common Negro type is only a degeneration of a much higher one." Engels, perhaps more versed in the relevant literature, rejects this view out of hand, and Marx seems to drop the theme.[11] Since this is a passing remark outside the area of Marx's main focus, it is difficult to know what to make of it as an indication of his persisting commitments.

The notion of race plays no clear part in his social thought, though he makes free use of the term, if often in contexts not involving the modern division of humanity into biologically defined groups. His indiscriminate usage is perhaps tied to a general but unresolved receptivity to the ideas of biological science (recalling here his use of the notion of the cell form in *Capital*, though there it is a metaphor brought into tight conceptual connection with his general account of commodity relations).[12] Moreover, according to Bertell Ollman, Marx seems to have entertained ideas of reversals of biological change that would result from improved social circumstances.[13]

Surely a decisive consideration is the fact, as we will see below, that Marx explicitly rejects racial division or hierarchy. He makes no use of such notions to justify the denial of rights or the preservation of segregation. Moreover he shows no signs of rejecting the role of blacks as agents in history, a point of some practical consequence when, for example, he calls for the arming of the ex-slaves in the U.S. Civil War.[14]

| | |

RACIST LANGUAGE IN MARX

Before we can draw conclusions from this mixed record, we need to consider what others have taken to be further evidence of Marx's racism.[15] Perhaps the most striking examples come in letters to Engels regarding both their erstwhile comrade Ferdinand Lassalle, a Jew, and Marx's son-in-law Paul Lafargue, a creole from Cuba whose paternal grandmother was a mulatto and whose maternal grandfather was an American Indian.[16]

It is now completely clear to me that he [Lassalle], as proved by his cranial formation and [curly] hair—descends from the Negroes who had joined Moses' exodus from Egypt (assuming his mother or grandmother on the paternal side had not interbred with a *nigger* [in English]). Now the union of Judaism and Germanism with a basic Negro substance must produce a peculiar product. The obtrusiveness of the fellow is also *Nigger*-like [in English]. (Emphasis in the original)[17]

Lafargue has the usual stigma of the Negro tribe: *no sense of shame*, I mean thereby no modesty about making himself ridiculous. (Emphasis added)[18]

What are we to make of such language and stereotyping? That Marx was given to invective is well known. But the use of such racist terms as "Nigger" is in fact rare. And, in the case of Lassalle, it appears only when the political and theoretical differences between the two men emerged and it stays within Marx's private correspondence with Engels. It also disappears with Lassalle's unexpected death. Since it arises after Marx loses confidence in Lassalle's political judgment, there is no reason to think the break itself was racially motivated. Indeed, after Lassalle's death Marx speaks warmly of him and his work. (We will say more about the specifically anti-Semitic language below.)

In the case of Lafargue, one must recall that generally Marx spoke of him too in friendly terms. Moreover, Marx's use of racial language is by no means always to Lafargue's disadvantage: Marx says in another letter that Lafargue's kindness "would go so far to prove that he must belong to a better than the European race."[19] Marx uses racial terminology comfortably and seems disposed to play with ideas of racial origins but appears to have no fixed views that would inform his political judgment. Indeed, in a letter to his daughter Laura and to Lafargue, he discusses Gobineau's theories of racial superiority and says, "[F]or such people it is always a source of satisfaction to have somebody to think themselves entitled to *mepriser* [despise]."[20] Elsewhere, in connection with some of Maine's ideas, he says, "The devil take this 'Aryan' cant!"[21] Marx's use of terms like "nigger" or "jew-boy" is not to be explained away, but neither is it so easy to understand its meaning. This is not the language of a committed racial ideologue, nor is it the language of an unreflective bigot. The fact that he uses a term ("nigger") from another language at least indicates an artificial usage, if not an ironic one. In any case, we cannot simply conclude that Marx is a racist from such language, since the use of racist language is not enough to judge one a racist, if by this we imply a fixed disposition to or advocacy of racist practices. We can conclude that Marx was impressed by racial categories and that they played a role in his social imagination. In this regard it is worth recalling that within his family and inner circle of friends Marx himself was known as "the Moor," in part an allusion to his dark complexion. Some commentators take this as a North African allusion, while Jerrold Siegel insists that it was an ironic reference to Marx's Jewishness.[22] In any case, this self-identification in terms that would otherwise have racially disparaging implications reminds us both of the playful relation to language characteristic of Marx and of the fact that his racialism was by no means a matter of conventional racism. Indeed, race becomes a matter of masks for him, a kind of provisional identification within a world in which the significant lines between humans are drawn in very different terms.

|||

MARX'S CHALLENGE TO RACIAL DIVISION

It is precisely in relation to class solidarity that racial division becomes a serious issue for Marx:

In all the big industrial centers of England a deep antagonism exists between the English and Irish workers. The average English worker hates the Irish as a competitor who lowers his wages and *level of living*. He feels national and religious antagonism towards him. He appears to him in much the same light as the black slaves appeared to the poor whites in the Southern States of North America. Thus antagonism between the proletarians of England is artificially cultivated and maintained by the bourgeoisie. It knows that in this antagonism lies the real secret of maintaining its power. (Emphasis in original)[23]

[Similar antagonisms cultivated in North America] perpetuate *international contradictions*, which are a brake on every serious and honest union between the working class of both countries and a brake on their common liberation. (Emphasis in original)[24]

Racial, ethnic, and national distinctions are barriers to a solidarity whose political success would establish a universal freedom and equality quite at odds with any racist conception of what society can or should be. The point here is that Marx does not overlook the fact that this solidarity must be won in a world in which these divisions exist. On the other hand, it is also noteworthy that Marx's formulation fails to address any specifically racial antagonism. If he rejects the idea of a racial distinction that would qualify class solidarity, he also fails to confront the extent to which specifically racial antagonism blocks the achievement of that solidarity. This is so even when he refers to oppositions that were understood in explicitly racial terms, which was the case not just for the American division between white and black, but also for the British division between English and Irish.[25]

Nonetheless, it may not be an exaggeration to say that in these passages we see a sketch of what was to become a classic socialist approach to racial division. On this view, such division is conceived as the hostility among workers that coincides with apparent or short-term conflicts of interests and is fostered by representatives of the class enemy. Such hostility is a profound problem so far as it blocks class unity among workers, a unity that corresponds to the real long-term interests of the otherwise divided groups. Overcoming racial division is thus a matter of overcoming an illusion. Whatever the immediate cause of conflict, division is not rooted in wider social relations. Acquainting hostile workers with their actual interests and historical conditions becomes the political objective.

Marx does not work out the presuppositions or the strategies of a politics that would combat racial hostility and division. Forswearing race and racism as a theoretical problem means failing to examine what might be distinctive about this division or to ask whether it might itself have some roots in the larger structure of the modern world. In fact, the implicit appeal to the illusory nature of racial antagonism suggests reliance on a liberal Enlightenment strategy for the resolution of conflict through education, through the extension of Enlightenment understood in a rather nonpolitical way. To treat racial antagonism as a matter of ignorance or irrationality is to avoid considering the genesis of these ways of thinking and responding to other workers. More generally, this way of thinking avoids considering the conditions or significance of the emergence of specifically racial and racist identifications and relations.

This is more than a matter of failing to explore the specifics of racial oppression, since it is also a matter of ignoring what might be distinctive about political struggles against racism. As a result, Marx is not in a position to consider issues that later gain considerable importance, for example, about the nature and the value of formation of oppositional or resistance identities in the process of contesting racism. Consequently, he does not consider such questions as the place of such identities within a socialist or democratic movement. In observing these absences in Marx's work, one need not risk the perhaps anachronistic suggestion that he was in a position to deal with such issues. By the same token, these considerations point to the unreadiness of the framework Marx was developing to confront the issues of collective identifications like race and nation that came to haunt the subsequent efforts of the socialist movement.

| | |

THE SPECTER OF ANTI-SEMITISM

The issue of identity becomes more pointed when we turn to another charge frequently made against Marx, that of his alleged anti-Semitism. To what extent we can bring this under the heading of racism is not obvious since anti-Semitism had a long history in Christian Europe before taking on the racialist form that gained currency in Marx's own day.[26] Nonetheless, it may not be an exaggeration to say that Marx was the first major philosopher who was himself a member of a racially stigmatized group. Perhaps his complicated relation to racial language is connected to this fact. He was the object of anti-Semitic attacks, including ones that were cast in explicitly racist terms.[27] At the same time, rival approaches to socialism were often infected by anti-Jewish racism.[28] In this context it is of interest that Marx seems never to have either embraced or rejected a Jewish identity. His letters indicate a resentment over being presented as a Jew, yet he was prepared to work on behalf of a petition in support of the rights of the Jewish community in Cologne.[29] He came from an unreligious family, and his father had officially converted to Lutheranism to protect his legal career. Marx himself married a non-

Jewish woman but lived playfully with the nickname "the Moor," whose connotations, as we have seen, may have been Jewish.

It is particularly in the early writings that commentators find traces of an anti-Semitism that some of them diagnose as Jewish self-hatred. The primary text is "On the Jewish Question," which first appeared in English under the title "World without Jews."[30] In the aftermath of the Holocaust, this was surely a provocative translation of *Zur Judenfrage*, the title given to Marx's reviews of Bruno Bauer's articles on the emancipation of Jews in Germany.[31] Marx's texts are sprinkled with what today is provocative language:

> What is the profane basis of Judaism? *Practical need, self-interest.* What is the worldly cult of the Jew? *Huckstering.* What is his worldly god? *Money.* . . . Money is the jealous god of Israel, beside which no other god may exist. . . . The social emancipation of the Jew is the *emancipation of society from Judaism.* (Emphasis in original)[32]

Hal Draper points out that this kind of stereotyping of Jews was common among radical intellectuals at the time, even in the work of someone like Moses Hess, who later embraced Zionism.[33] Though hardly a justification for such language, this reminds us that Marx is taking up conventional associations of Judaism with commercial activity, though he gives this a distinctive twist when he argues against an exclusively political solution to the oppression of the Jews. Their emancipation will not follow from the strictly political equality that Bauer says will be possible only after they renounce Judaism. Rather, Marx finds political emancipation inadequate, not just for Jews, but for all inhabitants of modern civil society whose alienating relations, rooted in the market, remain in place alongside the liberal secular state and religious freedom (or freedom from religion, as the case may be). Marx thinks Bauer misunderstands both the sources of modern alienation and the place of religion within it. Despite the illusions fostered by any religion, it is not Marx's primary target. He even suggests that to attack religion without addressing its social preconditions is to deprive others of a needed consolation.[34] In Marx's polemic, Jews stand in for the increasingly universal ethos of buying and selling, of reducing all qualities to the quantitative relations of the commodity form. Commerce, including commerce in money itself, was previously marginal, relegated to the Jews. In the modern world, it becomes general. Overcoming Judaism means overcoming not just the general conditions of religion but their specifically capitalist form.

In this light, Marx's use of stereotypes plays on the bad conscience of modern Christianity. The generalization of the commodity form means that in practice everyone has adopted the practices stigmatized as Jewish, everyone has become a

Jew ("The Jews have emancipated themselves in so far as the Christians have become Jews").[35] The irony in this context of the persistence and even deepening of anti-Semitism is not likely to have been lost on Marx. In any case, so far as the issue of anti-Semitism is concerned, it is important that, despite his more radical criticism, Marx does not, like Bauer, reject immediate political emancipation for the Jews any more than he refused to work with the Jewish community in Cologne. If he plays with the prevailing stereotypes, it is for different purposes and without forswearing available relief from anti-Semitic practices.

Still, one may feel uncomfortable about the use of such stereotypes just as one may wonder about the provocative use of anti-Jewish language in the correspondence. Here again Lassalle is a favorite target. For example, Marx writes to Engels in 1859:

> Jew-boy Braun [Lassalle] did not, of course, write me about my manuscript, although four weeks have already elapsed. For one thing, he has been busy with the publication of his own immortal "flaming" work (still, the Jew-boy, even his *Heraclitus*, although miserably written, is better than *anything the democrats can boast of* [in English]). (Emphasis in original)[36]

On another occasion Marx refers to Lassalle as the "Jewish Nigger" and on many occasions speaks of him using what seem to be stereotyping labels (most notably the name "Itzig").[37] If the occasional use of racist language does not make one a racist, the same holds for anti-Semitism (racially conceived or not), particularly if one actively opposes the oppression of Jews and is in fact oneself the victim of attacks by consistent racists. Moreover, the comments we are citing betray a certain complexity of expression and feeling, not only in the respects in which Lassalle is preferred to his "democratic" rivals, but also, it turns out, in the use of terms like "Itzig." Draper cites Heine's account of the use of this term within Jewish communities to deflate the pretensions of one of their members.[38]

Perhaps this observation bears on the inclination of some critics to treat Marx's language as evidence of Jewish self-hatred.[39] Marx's language may well have betrayed a double consciousness: seeing himself emancipated from Judaism, he was loath to countenance an identity that was in any case an occasion for abuse, yet was in no position to transcend this identification as imposed by others. To label the resulting stance as Jewish self-hatred is to impose on Marx an identity that he did not himself embrace, and one can ask on what basis such an imposition can be justified. It may be too much to accuse the accusers themselves of a kind of racialism here, but it is important to remember that describing Marx's language as a symptom of self-hatred presupposes an identity for Marx that he did not himself accept.

At the same time, if we see Marx's own work and its reception as contextualized and informed by an increasingly racialized setting, we have little reason to think Marx himself was clear that this racialization was taking place. He and Engels were disturbed by the anti-Semitism of rival socialists but attributed it to the backward-looking views of the figures in question, advocates of what they labeled "feudal socialism."[40] Once again we see that Marx's practical engagement with racializing phenomena proceeds without any serious theorization of them.

||||

RELIGION, MODERN STRUCTURE, IDENTITY

As we have seen, the bearing of Marx's alleged anti-Semitism on race themes is complicated by the fact that he occupied a world in which anti-Semitism was increasingly cast in biological terms rather than in the religious terms that had prevailed at least since the medieval period. The differences between these kinds of anti-Semitism are important if only because conversion out of a race is not an option, and racists turned to a language and practice that shifted from ghettoization and expulsion to expropriation and extermination. In fact there is a structural background to consider as well, since, in its racist form, anti-Semitism figures in the emergence of new kinds of social identities. Considering these leads us to note that anti-Semitism, like antiblack racism, is not only a matter of hostility and oppression against a particular group. The very racialist identification of these groups is part of a complex recognition process that includes the assertion of dominant racial identities and provides a grid for using modern scientific and moral language to articulate and justify the fate of stigmatized groups.[41]

As an identity, race has features that it shares with some other modern identifications. It is a highly abstract identity, a fact that seems only partly to follow from the biological terms in which it is often couched. It is not only the most general designation of humans below that of the species itself. It is also very abstract in ignoring all of the ways individuals distinguish themselves socially and culturally. As a result, racial identity is also something that all members share indistinguishably (leaving aside issues of mixed race, which are not precisely germane here). There is no ranking when it comes to racial membership. This equivalence of membership within the abstract whole of the group allows for comparisons with nationality. Indeed, Hannah Arendt treats these features of nationalism as conflicting with divisions traced along racial lines within the modern world, though she may pay too little attention to the various ways nationality and race can overlap and reinforce one another.[42]

It is useful to emphasize these features of abstractness and equivalence of racial identities, since they help us think about the connections between such identities and the modern social structure as Marx conceived it. Marx is hardly unique in noting how capitalism undermines the stability and sometimes the existence of preexisting traditions and identities and forces the individual to define her- and himself anew within the world of commodity relations. As Charles Taylor notes, the modern world places a distinctive burden on individuals, since it no longer provides them with fixed positions in a relatively stable world but demands that they adapt themselves to new work, location, institutional settings, and so on.[43] The commodification of relations, like the extension of formal rights and complex legal and bureaucratic structures, requires that individuals adapt themselves to abstractly defined settings and make themselves interchangeable. Old identifications become vulnerable, and new, more abstract group identifications come to the fore. Though Marx describes the destruction of old identifications[44] and theorizes the structural dynamics behind this process, he does not treat the formation of new identities as a theoretical or practical problem of systematic significance. Not only does this failure limit his response to racism and nationalism, it also threatens to short circuit the project of identity formation to which he is committed—that of the working class, a theme to which we will return in a moment.

Marx thus seems to miss the significance of the recasting of anti-Semitism in racial terms. But it is striking that although he usually speaks of issues of anti-Semitism as though they were a matter of the old religious anti-Semitism, his account of religion itself takes into account modern structural change and locates religion within modern institutional relations. Thus he thinks of religion as having become a private matter and as being quite compatible with political emancipation. But, since he treats religion mainly as an expression of alienated consciousness and as an illusory compensation for real alienation, he does not theorize its relation to oppression, racialized or otherwise. Religion expresses the lack of an ethical community rather than being a contributing cause of this lack. Even thinking of anti-Semitism in religious terms might have brought Marx to consider it as a matter of identity imposition and assertion, but as we have seen, Marx never really pursues the issue of identity as deeply as its eventual political importance requires. Religion remains a marker for a failed ethical community, not a medium of political or social assertion.

For us, then, Marx's neglect of the racialization of anti-Semitism is another symptom of his neglect not just of race but of the larger evolution of the nature and importance of social identities. There is a significant part of the story of modernity that Marx is missing, even though it has a great deal to do with his own preoccupations.

EUROCENTRISM

A third issue about Marx that bears on his relation to racism arises with charges of Eurocentrism, particularly in connection with his account of Asian societies or, more specifically, his use of the idea of the Asiatic mode of production. If we take Eurocentrism to mean a distorting privilege given to European models, then it does not obviously count as racism, though implicit assumptions and claims may be racist. But one must accept the racist dimension as a real possibility, given the close associations between European and white racial identity in the writings of philosophers such as Hume and Kant, who posit a link between European identity and rational powers that figures within the articulation of a racialist hierarchy.[45]

In works by these thinkers there is the idea of an inherent inferiority of darker-skinned peoples and a readiness to defend European power over them on grounds of comparative levels of development as measured by Enlightenment reason.[46] This kind of Eurocentrism can be described as racist because of its claims to inherent superiority along racial lines. And it shares with much subsequent racist discourse the interpretation and justification of hierarchy by the use of modern ideas of reason. The inferior are measured by supposedly scientifically determined qualities, including intelligence, and their inferiority is then a justification for the suspension of otherwise prevailing universal norms.

Nothing this extreme appears in Marx. Despite the occasional use of racialist language (of Indians, for example, he speaks of a "certain calm nobility . . . notwithstanding their natural languor"),[47] there is no use of racial ideas in explaining what Marx takes to be a virtual lack of history due to the stagnant logic of "Oriental despotism." Nor is there appeal to racial superiority when he describes the long-term benefits of British rule, whose actual practice he criticizes as barbaric and often incompetent. Nonetheless, there is something like a justification of British colonial domination. After listing what he takes to be the many defects of Indian conditions, Marx offers his historical perspective:

> England, it is true, in causing a social revolution in Hindostan, was actuated only by the vilest interests, and was stupid in her manner of enforcing them. But that is not the question. The question is, can mankind fulfill its destiny without a fundamental revolution in the social state of Asia? If not, whatever may have been the crimes of England she was the unconscious tool of history in bringing about that revolution.[48]

This apparent appeal to a latent teleology (England as "the unconscious tool of history") is open to a number of criticisms, particularly in the light of the subsequent history of colonialism and the imperialist aspects of the postcolonial world. The benefits Marx anticipated for the Indians have as yet to materialize a half century after the end of colonial rule. And the nature of decolonization hardly resembled the process Marx anticipated:

> The Indians will not reap the fruits of the new elements of society scattered among them by the British bourgeoisie, till in Great Britain itself the now ruling classes shall have been supplanted by the industrial proletariat, or till the Hindoos themselves shall have grown strong enough to throw off the English yoke altogether.[49]

Quite apart from the failure of history to match Marx's expectations, there is the problem of the remnants of idealist teleology. In fact, this issue overlaps with other questions about Marx's sense of historical sequence, a sense that was to change as he thought more deeply about actual colonial conditions and as he reflected on the peculiar potentials of Russia.[50] In general, one must be cautious about attributing a consistent teleology to Marx, since this was a main bone of contention in his early coming to terms with Hegel.[51] Nonetheless, there does seem to be a sense of a linear and inevitable line of development in some of Marx's comments, and this does, in the quote above, serve to override objections that might otherwise hold against British policy in India. Still, one can argue that there is nothing inherently racist about such a teleology or, even more persuasively, that there is nothing inherently racist in the claim that a society might benefit from external intervention, even colonial domination. It depends on the circumstances and the stakes. But given Marx's readiness to use problematic ideas to justify the unjustifiable, one may not find these reassurances wholly convincing.

Whatever his intentions, Marx was thinking with ideas that favored European power under the guise of benefiting its victims. Even without explicit racist content, this kind of thought echoes the discursive strategies of Western racism, in which reputedly rational necessity obscures and justifies domination and exploitation of non-European peoples. But such ideological obscurantism is not unique to racism, since a similar mode of thinking can be used within a society to justify existing and previous class or gender exploitation and domination. Moreover, Marx's account is free of the paternalism found in Mill—there is no moral justification for British rule, and in fact the rulers are in no subjective sense presented as enlightened. If there are to be benefits from colonialism, they will have to be wrested from it through conflict. And Marx attributes the potential agency for such change to the Indians. The Indians must and can make something very different of the colonial legacy than what they will inherit from their oppressors. So there is no idea of benevolent tutelage here.

These contrasts with the prevailing racist discourse may be enough to warrant denying that Marx participates in it. But at the same time, he is not well armed to challenge it and does not explicitly try to do so. In fact, we may wonder if he shares too much of this discourse to make a proper challenge to it: we see this not only in the occasional racialist language but also in the occasional appeal to objective historical necessity to justify oppression, and in the failure to see how such intellectual forms serve in the covert articulation of (European) identities that deny to other groups the agency Marx is in principle committed to fostering.

| | |

IDENTITY: TENSIONS BETWEEN CLASS AND RACE

Now we have concluded the survey of what seem to be the most significant issues and debates about Marx's relation to race and racism. From a contemporary perspective, Marx seems implicated in the racialist language of his world. At the same time he challenges racist doctrine and racial division between workers as well as the legal and other social oppression of Jews. Despite considering that there might be benefits to colonialism, he sides with the oppressed and projects their eventual triumph against European domination as their only hope to take advantage of such potential benefits as their oppression may have made possible. From an ethical or political point of view, Marx consistently opposes racist phenomena. But, perhaps because his politics is not informed by reflection on identity, he can at the same time play with racialist language and ignore the concrete politics of racial recognition. Nonetheless, if Marx is by no means free of the influence of a racializing culture, neither does he uncritically embrace it. It seems quite inappropriate to label him a racist.

But, given our wish to measure Marx's work by his own aspirations, we need to take the discussion a step further. Though he was "empirically" against racism, we have seen that Marx does not provide a theoretical account of the issues posed by race and racism. We have noted problems each step along our way: the failure to grasp the specifics of racial oppression or the specifics of resistance to it, the ignoring of the corresponding issues about modern identity formation, and the failure to connect these issues with the evolution of modern social structure. As a consequence, Marx's shortsightedness about race is connected to a general failure regarding modern identity and the politics concerned with it. This has proven to be a fateful gap in Marxist thought, given the subsequent importance of racism, nationalism, and fundamentalism, but also given the tensions between Marxian socialism and the various democratically inclined social movements for which identity has become a central matter.

Yet the question of identity is by no means absent from Marx's thinking. The issue of effective working-class political agency raises a question of identity that he sometimes poses in the language of alienation theory and sometimes in more complex historical terms. By briefly noting problems that arise for Marx in this regard, we can trace some of the implications of his neglect of racial themes in particular and theoretical issues about identity in general.

We can distinguish two respects in which the formation of working-class identity is important for Marx. First, this identity is an ethical as well as a political goal, since the working class is to abolish exploitation and realize the possibility of a society in which the "free development of each is the condition for the free development of all."[52] In Hegelian terms, the revolutionary working class marks the arrival of the concrete universal. But there is something paradoxical about this goal, since, to turn to the second aspect of this identity, the aim is precisely to leave class conditions and relations behind. Indeed, the very framing of the world in economic language now becomes a relic of the long history in which labor predominated over social life, and overcoming capitalism means constructing a world beyond scarcity and a life no longer dominated by questions of production. Individuals would no longer identify themselves in terms of labor, much less in terms of a class, and they would be driven not by interests, if we understand these as implying market orientations, but by new needs proper to freedom and self-development. This implies a transformation of sensibility as suggested by Herbert Marcuse when he speaks of an aesthetic dimension entering everyday life.[53] In this light, working-class consciousness is not an identity that represents a stable goal but is rather inherently transitional.

The point is not that these aspects of the posited working-class identity are at odds with one another, though there may be real tensions between them. But highlighting these aspects may illuminate reasons this identity has proven to be less definite and compelling than many of its political rivals. If the hypothetical postscarcity perspective implies precisely a move away from class identity, the ethical and revolutionary perspective implies a unity and distinctiveness of working-class identification that have rarely been found in practice. As Gyorgy Lukács writes in relation to Lenin, this posited class consciousness always comes "too late": the class is internally divided on the one hand, and opportunities for decisive action may come only through alliances with other classes on the other.[54] There is no need here to go into all the problems of politics, political parties, and class analysis that have resulted from this dilemma.[55]

The more immediately significant point is that the combination of his racialism on the one side and his insensitivity to political issues on the other leads Marx to miss the complexity of the problem of working-class identity. Noting the ambivalence proper to this identity helps us see that it may share some features of the abstractness we have attributed to racial and national identity. Class identity is very general and members have equivalent standing. Of course, to Hegelian-Marxist ears, this charge of abstractness rings false, since the working class is cast as a concrete agency precisely by virtue of its practical positioning and effective knowledge within capitalist society. Organized properly and having acquired the appropriate political understandings, the working class can emancipate society because its socialized activity traverses the constitutive order of the social world. In fact there is no conflict between this kind of concreteness and the aforementioned abstractness of identity. These general features of class position, which undergird claims to effective action as well as to the universal significance or ethical validity of this action, do not of themselves provide specific anchors in historical time and place of the sort associated with a definite identity.

One might say the same of the abstractness of racial or even national identities, which have frequently proven more compelling than class identification. But perhaps it is partly because these lack the concrete anchoring in anything like class conditions that they prove more susceptible to manipulation and adaptation to the contingencies of crisis conditions. They can more easily draw on preexisting traditions and can be made to appear anchored in the specifics of historical time and place. In any case, racial and nationalist identities are articulated and reproduced in the practices of prevailing political and ideological frameworks, while class identity must arise as a repudiation and a critique. Marx tends to treat this difference as a challenge to the ruling class's ideologies and thus as a matter of building from structural conditions to a self-conscious assertion against the class enemy. But without minimizing the question of the ideological representations of class relations, the specific problem of identity for the working class may involve confronting rival modern abstract identities more than accepting the self-understandings of the dominant groups.

This is precisely what Marx's racialism allows him to ignore. More generally, his neglect of identity is paired with his specific neglect of the competing identities that must be challenged for socialist politics to succeed: race, nation, and religion. Because he does not conceptualize the specifically modern problem of identity formation, Marx does not treat rival identities as a problem of structural dimensions. They are seen as holdovers, compensations, or manipulated illusions of secondary importance in the class struggle. In this regard, Marx's uncritical racialism is a serious obstacle, since it undermines any sense that the racial antagonisms Marx does oppose are connected to the formation of racial identity in particular and to modern abstract identities in general. Opposition to racial antagonism remains a matter of confronting ignorance and frustration with a combination of morality and self-interest. To be sure, one should not ignore the honorable political results of this approach, since socialist and communist challenges to racism have been among the most consistent and effective. But the issue of identity goes beyond such strategic questions to the formation of political agency itself.

Apart from attending to the structural conditions and practical importance of identity, a politics of agency must draw from political challenges to imposed identities and the counterassertion of resistance identities. In effect we noted some of the difficulties of this task for working-class identity. Challenges to racist identification have usually been the concern of movements for whom racism is the main target. Marx's idea of the emergence of a universalism that would sweep away racism seems less true to historical experience than the promise of a universalism that might emerge from various specific movements that confront racism. The challenges to prevailing identities within modern society have developed as internal criticisms and reversals of these identities rather than as the assertion of a more expansive perspective like class consciousness. Yet the democratic potential of antiracism, feminism, ecology, and other social movements preserves for them the potential of integration and coordination in the light of shared democratic goals. Today we can imagine a conclusion that the absence of relevant political experience put beyond Marx's reach: perhaps a reconceptualized account of working-class consciousness (or its political equivalent) today would have to be cast as a complex of identities rather than as a unifying single identification.

Such a suggestion can evoke many questions about the meaning of class, the changing organization of production, and so on. These go far beyond the scope of a discussion of Marx and race. We can simply note that a democratic recasting of identities within social movements does raise the issues and concerns of both aspects of working-class consciousness noted above, that of the "concrete universal" and that of the postscarcity utopia. Now something like the former would emerge as a democratic multiculturalism rather than as the assertion of a global perspective, a complex of movements that nonetheless overlaps with questions of the politics of production and distribution. And something like the latter is suggested by movements that have questioned the values of a society driven by imperatives of growth, that challenge consumerism and mount a critique of mass media culture and its promotion of prevailing stereotypes and distortions of social experience.

||||

CONCLUSION

Now we have seen how Marx's racialism affects his critical project. We have argued that Marx cannot be fairly charged with racism, since he opposes racial hostility and oppression on systematic political grounds. But he is a racialist insofar as he accepts the existence of races uncritically and thus fails to rethink their historical emergence and function as modern social identities. Had Marx thought more deeply about race, he might have confronted the issues about identity that come to a head in his work as the question of working-class consciousness. But historically this problem of class identification has turned out to be a weak point of Marxist analysis and politics. The formation of working-class identity has proven more difficult than Marx anticipated, in part because the obstacles of racism and nationalism have turned out to be more intractable than he imagined. The point is not that Marx's racialism prevented him from an intellectual solution that he otherwise could have achieved. Rather, it is that any attempt at a radical democratization of social relations today needs to learn the lesson of Marx's blind spot.

NOTES

1. A useful collection of relevant texts can be found in Emmanuel Chukwudi Eze, ed., *Race and the Enlightenment* (Cambridge MA: Blackwell, 1997).

2. bell hooks provides such a dismissal in her passing characterization of Marx in *Killing Rage* (New York: Henry Holt, 1995), 4.

3. The charge of anti-Semitism can be found in Saul K. Padover, ed., *The Letters of Karl Marx* (Englewood Cliffs, NJ: Prentice-Hall, 1979).

4. Michel Foucault, "What Is an Author?" in *Language, Counter-memory, Practice: Selected Essays and Interviews*, ed. Donald Bouchard (Ithaca: Cornell University Press, 1977).

5. Arthur de Gobineau, *The Inequality of Human Races* (New York: Howard Fertig, 1999).

6. Karl Marx, "Private Property and Communism" (*Economic and Philosophical Manuscripts*), in *Karl Marx: Selected Writings*, ed. David McLellan (New York: Oxford University Press, 1977), 88.

7. I have argued elsewhere that doing so offers a fruitful beginning for a social theory of racial being. Richard Peterson, "Race and Recognition," in *Race, Class, and Community Identity*, ed. Andrew Light and Mechthild Nagel (Amherst, NY: Humanity Books, 2000), 52–67.

8. Frederick Engels, "Socialism Utopian and Scientific," in *The Marx-Engels Reader*, ed. Robert Tucker (New York: Norton, 1978), 699.

9. An article on Du Bois that has become itself the focus of some controversy is Anthony Appiah, "The Uncompleted Argument: Du Bois and the Illusion of Race," in *"Race," Writing, and Difference*, ed. Henry Louis Gates Jr. (Chicago: University of Chicago Press, 1986).

10. Karl Marx, *Capital*, trans. Samuel Moore and Edward Aveling (New York: International Publishers, 1967), 1:18.

11. *Letters of Karl Marx*, 215.

12. Marx, *Capital*, 3–144 (chap. 1).

13. Bertell Ollman, *Alienation* (Cambridge: Cambridge University Press, 1971). While noting

Marx's reference to "inborn racial characteristics" (285 n. 15), citing *Capital* (3:774), Ollman suggests (n. 16) that Marx thought the forces of the environment, if properly marshaled, could remake human qualities transmitted through heredity.

14. Karl Marx and Friedrich Engels, *Selected Correspondence* (Moscow: Progress Publishers, 1955), 133.

15. Leon Poliakov, *The Aryan Myth* (New York: Basic Books, 1971), 244–46.

16. *Letters of Karl Marx*, 250.

17. Ibid., 215.

18. Ibid., 399.

19. Ibid., 250.

20. Ibid., 270.

21. Lawrence Krader, *The Asiatic Mode of Production* (Assey, Neth.: Van Gorem, 1975).

22. Jerrold Seigel, *Marx's Fate: The Shape of a Life* (Princeton: Princeton University Press, 1978), 79.

23. Ralph Fox, ed., *Marx, Engels, and Lenin on Ireland* (New York: International Publishers, 1940), 41.

24. Ibid., 42.

25. Marx and Engels, *Selected Correspondence*, 222.

26. See Poliakov, *Aryan Myth*, for the classic history of the emergence and evolution of religious anti-Semitism.

27. George Lichtheim, "Socialism and the Jews," *Dissent*, July–August 1978, 305.

28. George L. Mosse, *Towards the Final Solution: A History of European Racism* (New York: Howard Fertig, 1978).

29. *Letters of Karl Marx*, 166.

30. Karl Marx, *A World without Jews*, trans. D. Runes (New York: Philosophical Library, 1959).

31. The titles of Bauer's essays are "Die Judenfrage" and "Die Faehigkeit der heutigen Juden und Christen frei zu werden."

32. *Marx-Engels Reader*, 48, 50, 52.

33. Hal Draper, *Karl Marx's Theory of Revolution* (New York: Monthly Review, 1976).

34. A point developed slightly later in the introduction to *The Critique of Hegel's Philosophy of Right*, in *Karl Marx: Selected Writings*, 63–74.

35. *Marx-Engels Reader*, 49.

36. *Letters of Karl Marx*, 435.

37. Ibid., 465 and passim.

38. Draper, *Karl Marx's Theory of Revolution*, 60.

39. For example, Murray Wolfson, *Marx: Economist, Philosopher, Jew: Steps in the Development of a Doctrine* (New York: St. Martin's Press, 1982), 82, 109.

40. Draper, *Karl Marx's Theory of Revolution*, quotes Engels: "Anti-Semitism is the mark of a backward culture" (301). Draper goes on to argue that for Engels anti-Semitism was a kind of detour on which some social elements must journey on their way to a more coherent socialism (413).

41. For a sketch of this kind of conceptualization, see Peterson, "Race and Recognition."

42. Hannah Arendt, *Origins of Totalitarianism* (New York: Harcourt, Brace and World, 1966).

43. Charles Taylor, *Sources of Self* (Cambridge: Harvard University Press, 1989).

44. For example, in the famous passages of the *Communist Manifesto* about the sweeping changes brought about by capitalist development (*Karl Marx: Selected Writings*, 222–31).

45. See Eze, *Race and the Enlightenment*, chaps. 3, 4, and 5.

46. Kant, "From *Physical Geography*," in *Race and the Enlightenment*, ed. Eze, 64.

47. "The Future Results of the British Rule in India," in *The American Journalism of Marx and Engels*, ed. Henry M. Christin (New York: New American Library, 1966).

48. *Marx-Engels Reader*, 658.

49. Ibid., 662.

50. Umberto Melotti, *Marx and the Third World*, trans. P. Ransford (New York: Macmillan, 1977), 114; George Lichtheim, "Marx and the Asiatic Mode of Production," in *Marx's Socialism*, ed. S. Avineri (New York: Atherton, 1973).

51. Marx and Engels challenge Hegelian teleology in *The German Ideology*, e.g., *Karl Marx: Selected Writings*, pp. 171–78.

52. E.g., *Karl Marx: Selected Writings*, 238.

53. Herbert Marcuse, *Eros and Civilization* (New York: Vintage Press, 1962).

54. Gyorgy Lukács, *Lenin*, trans. N. Jacobs (London: New Left Review Books, 1970).

55. Laclau and Mouffe draw conclusions from this history that virtually abandon class analysis altogether: Ernesto Laclau and Chantal Mouffe, *Hegemony and Socialist Struggle*, trans. W. Moore and P. Cammack (London: Verso, 1985).

13

Nietzsche's Racial Profiling

JAMES WINCHESTER

To ask whether or not Nietzsche is a racist is to impose a contemporary question on a thinker who has been dead for more than one hundred years. As long as we remember that it is our question and we do not try to force Nietzsche into a contemporary position, I think we can learn a great deal by posing this question—we will learn both about Nietzsche and about ourselves. Nietzsche was clearly very interested in the concept of race.[1] The word appears more than two hundred times in the Colli-Montinari edition of Nietzsche's work.[2] It also appears frequently in his letters. But frequent discussion does not mean that Nietzsche has an unambiguous theory of race. As is often the case with him, Nietzsche does not form a final definition. Unlike Kant, who strove to find a singular meaning for the term, Nietzsche posits several different definitions of race and expresses widely varying attitudes about whether the term means anything at all.[3] I will not attempt to process Nietzsche's various usages of the term into an overly homogenized and artificial summation. I will concentrate on Nietzsche's later published writings, from *Beyond Good and Evil* to *Ecce Homo*, where Nietzsche discusses the concept most extensively. We will see that his deeply held revulsion toward anti-Semitic racism leads him to reject many of the nineteenth-century prejudices about the supposed racial inferiority of Jews. He does not have much to say about Africans, but he does make mention of them. At one point he suggests that black skin may be a sign of lesser intelligence as well as a sign that one is closer to the apes.[4] Nietzsche clearly shares some of the basic tenets of nineteenth-century race theory. He writes, for example, that race can be determined by hair and skin color as well as the measurement of the skull.[5] Nietzsche is not the racist that some claim that he is, but he does at times adopt some of the thinking on race that was prevalent in his own time but is now widely questioned.

Some of Nietzsche's descriptions of races fly in the face of the prevailing wisdom. He does not glorify the races that were commonly glorified by the racists of his day, and he rejects the prevailing views about the desirability of racial purity. As we will see, he counsels Germans to mix with Jews. He claims that the Germans are not a strong or pure race. Nietzsche praises certain breeding projects of the past and suggests that it is only with the proper breeding that peoples will be able to flourish. Yet at times Nietzsche suggests that his own talk of race and racial breeding is foolish.

Before moving into the heart of the discussion I will briefly explain my use of Nietzsche's notes. In addition to the works that Nietzsche published or prepared for publication, he wrote extensive notes that he himself never published.[6] Six volumes of the *Kritische Studienausgabe* edited by Giorgio Colli and Mazzino Montinari are given over entirely to these notes. There are, in fact, many more pages of notes than there are of works Nietzsche himself published. Some of these notes were edited into a volume entitled *The Will to Power* (first published in 1901 but published in a second, significantly enlarged version in 1906) under the supervision of Nietzsche's sister. *The Will to Power* is by today's editing standards haphazard at best. It combines, for example, passages written at very different times. It also includes only a very small percentage of what the notebooks contain.[7] In what follows, I am interested, first, in Nietzsche's self-understanding. Of course texts often go beyond the author's intentions, and I am also very interested in how Nietzsche's published works may present views that go beyond or contrast with Nietzsche's self-understanding. The notes can be very helpful, but I will write primarily about the works that Nietzsche himself published or prepared for publication. Nietzsche often used his notebooks for thought experiments. Nietzsche published a great deal—he prepared four books for publication during his last productive year. He had plenty of occasions to publish the passages he felt were important. If Nietzsche chose not to publish something, it may very well be because he was unsatisfied with it in some way. Nietzsche may have decided that he did not believe many of the things in the notes. I will often cite the notes, but I will build my interpretation of Nietzsche's conception of race (his self-understanding and that which is contained in the published writings but goes beyond his self-understanding) primarily on the basis of what Nietzsche himself published or prepared for publication.

||||

NIETZSCHE'S EARLY COMMENTS ON RACE

In Nietzsche's early works there are only a few discussions of race. The word is not used in his first published work, *The Birth of Tragedy out of the Spirit of Music*, although it does appear in a draft for a revised introduction to that book.[8] It appears twice in his second book, *The Untimely Meditations*, but in both cases Nietzsche is merely citing someone else, and he does not analyze the concept at all.[9] In one of his five prefaces to unwritten books, Nietzsche uses the word outside of a quotation. These prefaces, written after *The Birth of Tragedy*, were not published during

Nietzsche's lifetime, nor were the works themselves ever written. In the third preface, "The Greek State," he writes that we should recognize the cruel truth that slavery belongs to the essence of culture. He writes that the misery of a few must be increased so that a few Olympians may produce great art. It is this truth that causes the communists and socialists and their "pale descendants, the white race of 'liberals' of every epoch," to be against art and against classical civilization.[10] In 1872 this praise of slavery would have sounded as strange to much of his audience as it sounds to us today. At the same time Nietzsche confounds those who would believe that the white race should rule over the darker races. Whites are clearly not seen as superior in this statement.[11] There are two important points here. First, as we will see, this is hardly the last time that Nietzsche makes the claim that slavery is essential to great culture. Nietzsche is decidedly not a liberal. He believes that great civilizations require slavery. Second, even though Nietzsche in two places speaks of blacks as close to the animals and primitive, it is not the case that he always glorifies whiteness.[12]

In his third book, *Human, All-Too-Human* published in 1878, there are five references to race. For the most part they echo themes that are to be found in Nietzsche's later writings. For example, he writes that sympathy toward others as well as helping others leads to the decline of individuals and to races.[13] In another place, he explains how the progress of a man or a race cannot be reduced merely to the fight for existence.[14] The most prolonged discussion of race in *Human, All-Too-Human* is aphorism 475. It also clearly has ties to Nietzsche's later discussions. Here Nietzsche argues that the European nation-state is weakening as communication and travel are being made easier. The more people travel, the more a mixed race of Europeans is being developed. The nation-state is an artificial construct, and he applauds its dissolution. The Jews have an important role to play, Nietzsche believes, in the cultivation (erzeugen) of a powerful European race. Jews are as useful as any other European race in the production of the new European race, perhaps even more useful. Nietzsche argues that Jews are more intelligent and more energetic than most other European races. Every nation and individual has unpleasant characteristics, and it is gruesome to demand that the Jews be an exception to this rule. Nietzsche writes:

Perhaps the young stock market Jew [*jugendliche Börsen-Jude*] is the most repugnant discovery of the human race. But nonetheless I would like to know how much man must overlook in a complete calculation of a people [*Volk*], a people who thanks to us has had the greatest history of suffering of all people and whom we thank for the most noble man (Christ), the purest way (Spinoza), the most powerful book, and the world's most effective moral laws.[15]

He goes on to say that Jews maintained the banner of enlightenment at the darkest times when Asia threatened Europe. Christianity tried to orientalize Europe, but Judaism helped to occidentalize Europe again—which is to say Europe's task is to continue what the Greeks started. Nietzsche gives no clue here as to why he considers young Jewish stock market boys so repulsive, but I believe it may have something to do with the prevailing stereotypes surrounding Jews and money. Clearly he does not consider Jews, as a race, to be less valuable than other races. Indeed he argues that they are a superior race in many ways. As we will see, this belief that Jews are an important element in the mixture of European races is a refrain that will be repeated right up to the end of Nietzsche's writings. We will also see again the claim that Jews are more rational than other Europeans. The notion that Europeans must set about the task of breeding a superior European race is also repeated in the later work. Nietzsche's estimation of the Jews is all the more remarkable given the prejudice that was prevalent in Germany at the time. Jews were granted full citizenship in the German Reich in 1871, but Jews who had not converted to Christianity were often denied civil service positions, university professorships, and military commissions.[16]

An analysis of breeding is also found in Nietzsche's last discussion of race from *Human, All-Too-Human*. He writes that money is the origin of *Geblütsadel* (noble blood).[17] It is money that allows men to choose the most attractive women and hire the best teachers. It also allows one time for exercise and freedom from hard work. Although we do not see this exact claim in the later works, there are echoes of it. As we will see, the later Nietzsche emphasizes that beauty in humans is not an accident but rather must be cultivated by a rigorous breeding process that spans several generations. He will give two examples—Athens at the time of Cicero and seventeenth-century France—that produced beautiful people as the result of several generations of a sustained breeding effort.[18]

In Nietzsche's next book, *Dawn*, published in 1881, there are only two places where race is explicitly discussed. In an aphorism entitled "The Purifying of the Race," he argues that there are no pure races but only races that have become pure, and this process of purification has happened in only a few cases.[19] Races that are crossbred produce disharmonious bodily forms and disharmonious habits. At first the process of purifying a race might seem like the impoverishment of that race, but once the process of purification has become complete the race will become more powerful. All the power that was previously used in the fight between the disharmonious qualities will now be at the disposal of the race. The Greeks are an example of a race that became pure, and Nietzsche hopes that one day there will be a pure European race and culture.

This claim that the Greeks are a race that has become pure is expanded upon in the *Nachlass*. In a note from spring or summer of 1875 Nietzsche writes that the Greeks are a combination of many different people. He mentions specifically Mongolians, Semites, and Thracians. The Greeks have all of these in their blood, and they also took these peoples' Gods and myths.[20] In another place in the notes, from about the same time, he endorses the project of racial mixing, but this time he wants to mix Asian tranquility with American and European restlessness. Such a mixture will solve the puzzle of the world. The free spirits should take it as their mission to get rid of everything that stands in the way of a "fusion of mankind" (*Verschmelzung der Menschen*), such as the instinct for monarchy, the illusions of wealth and poverty, and health and race prejudices.[21] This breeding project—the mixture of Asians, Americans, and Europeans—is never again mentioned, but Nietzsche never relinquishes the notion that proper breeding is essential to human flourishing.

The first use of the word race in *Dawn* also illustrates Nietzsche's rejection of nationalism and what he refers to as racial prejudice. Nietzsche writes that what allowed Christianity to spread was not its specifically Christian character but the universal pagan nature of its customs.[22] Christian thought is rooted in Jewish and Hellenistic thought and "knew from the very beginning how to raise itself above national and racial isolation and nuances as well as prejudices."[23] Nietzsche rarely has anything positive to say about Christianity, and this section ends with the claim that Christianity was able to incorporate all these different elements only because of its "amazing coarseness and modesty of its intellect in the time of the church building."[24]

Clearly Nietzsche is often less modest than Christianity. He is not afraid, as he writes in other places, to reject entire cultures. Nietzsche consistently rejects what he calls narrow nationalism and racial prejudice, but he is not above criticizing cultures. In his own mind what separates his criticism from the narrow-minded is that he is not merely following the herd. Others have succumbed to the typical national or racial prejudices of the day, but Nietzsche believes himself to be a free thinker. Of course, this is one of the things that interests us most today, namely, to what extent did Nietzsche escape the racial stereotyping of his day. In *On the Genealogy of Morals* (a passage I will discuss in more detail in a moment), Nietzsche writes that Negroes are representatives of prehistoric men who are capable of enduring pain that would drive the best-organized European to despair.[25] Nietzsche seems to intend this as a compliment, but today most would see this claim about Africans as a prejudice. Who today would defend the claim that blacks feel pain less acutely than whites, particularly given that such a characterization could be used to justify the enslavement and maltreatment of blacks? We will also see that even though Nietzsche often scorns anti-Semitism, he sometimes articulates typically anti-Semitic prejudices such as that the Jews of Poland smell or, as we have already seen and will see again, that Jews are particularly good at making money. Perhaps most important, Nietzsche follows the racial thinking of his day by insisting that breeding is essential to human development. In 1881, in a passage from the *Nachlass*, Nietzsche asks, why not create men the way the Chinese create trees that have pears on one side and roses on the other? Nietzsche hopes that with careful breeding one might be able to do away with "the foolishness of races, race wars, national fever, and personal jealousy."[26] This short note illustrates that at the same time Nietzsche questions the validity of the notion of race, he also argues that the breeding of people is possible and could yield good results. Even while Nietzsche scorns much of the racial thinking that predominates in his day, he never gives up the notion that the breeding of humans is not only possible but desirable.

Nietzsche's next work, *The Gay Science*, was first published in 1882, in other words shortly after *Dawn*. Like *Dawn* this first edition of *The Gay Science* contains only two references to the concept of race.[27] In 1887 Nietzsche published a new edition of *The Gay Science*, and in the new sections race is discussed at length. During the 1880s Nietzsche's interest in race increases dramatically. This increased interest is seen not only in his published writings but also in the notebooks.[28] Near the end of the second edition of *The Gay Science* Nietzsche continues to endorse in a section entitled "We Homeless Ones" the notion that Europe needs to overcome nationalism, embrace a wider European culture, and breed a European race.[29] Nietzsche refers to himself as a homeless one, a member of a small group of children of the future. He writes that the children of the future—the homeless ones—are not conservatives who want to preserve the past, nor are they liberals who labor to bring progress. They do not endorse the notions of equal rights and free society. They rejoice in danger, war, and adventure. Echoing his early comment on slavery from the preface to the *Greek State*,[30] Nietzsche argues that a new kind of slavery is needed—for every raising of the human type requires a new type of slavery.[31] Nietzsche emphatically denigrates sympathy for and love of mankind. At the same time, the homeless ones are not German enough to speak of nationalism and racial hatred, which is being expressed by people all over Europe. The homeless ones are too mixed to get caught up in racial self-admiration that characterizes many in Germany. The homeless ones are rather good Europeans. Echoing *Dawn* 70, Nietzsche claims that Christianity played a role in overcoming narrow national chauvinism. Like the early Christians, the homeless ones are willing to sacrifice blood, societal position, and fatherland. This passage is typical of many of the places where race is used in the later Nietzsche's writings. Nietzsche rejects the racial hatred that he sees in the Europe of his day as well as what he sees as misplaced racial self-admiration that is prevalent in his own time, but argues for the breeding of new and better races. Nietzsche believes in racial breeding but thinks that most of the Germans who are talking about racial breeding projects are profoundly mistaken about their own racial makeup and what it would take to improve the race.

| | |

THE PROBLEM OF EUROPEAN RACIAL DEGENERATION

The preface to *The Gay Science*, written in 1886, is a pivotal passage in Nietzsche's writings on race. It emphasizes the link between physiology and thought, a link that is discussed in all of Nietzsche's published writings from 1886 to the end of his productive life in 1888. In this preface, Nietzsche asks if hidden behind one's highest values stand perhaps misunderstandings of the body. Metaphysics is not the result of abstract reason but rather the product of one's physiology. Nietzsche is waiting for a philosophical doctor who would investigate the complete health (*Gesammt-Gesundheit*) of people (*Volk*), times, and races. This philosophical doctor would have the courage to analyze Nietzsche's suspicion that "truths" are really the product of health, growth, power, and life. In other words, our thoughts are really a product of our health—or more precisely our thoughts are the product of the health of our race. Nietzsche becomes that doctor in his last works. In the last five years of his productive life he writes again and again that thought is the product of physiology, but even though he often makes this assertion, the explanations and justifications for the physiological origins of thought are never precisely worked out.

For example, *Beyond Good and Evil* 20 maintains that our thought is controlled by the grammatical structures of our language. The similarity in Indian, Greek, and German philosophies is the result of the similarity of the grammar of these languages. But the grammar of languages is in turn determined, Nietzsche believes, by race and physiology: "the path of specific grammatical functions is in the ultimate ground the path of physiological judgments of worth and racial conditions [*physiologischer Werturtheile und Rasse-Bedingungen*]."[32] Nietzsche goes on to say that this is enough to prove the superficiality of Locke's thesis of the origin of ideas. Our race casts a spell over our thought, or, even stronger, thought is the product of physiology and race. In the Ural-Altaic languages Nietzsche believes the concept of the subject is less developed.[33] This characteristic of their language would be, given Nietzsche's train of thought, a result of their race. Given the racial differences, they will see the world differently than Indo-Germanic people or Muslims. Nietzsche demands that psychology be based on physiology.[34] He also argues that the tempo of a language is based in the race and its metabolism.³⁵ Germans' metabolism is such that they are incapable of *presto*. Having breathed the dry refined air of Florence, Machiavelli can present long, hard, dangerous thoughts at the tempo of a gallop. Germans, with the exception of Lessing, are simply incapable of overcoming their racial metabolism and writing in the tempo of the great Italian masters.³⁶

Race and physiology determine thought, and European thought is in crisis. The solution is to breed a new European race. In *Beyond Good and Evil* 208 we read that Europe is suffering from paralysis of the will. It is ripe with skepticism that comes when races or classes cross after having been separated from each other over long periods of time. It is not race mixing as such that causes skepticism according to Nietzsche. It is rather the sudden mixture of races that have long been separated from each other. The European's will is deeply sick and *entartet* (degenerate). Nietzsche believes that Europe will need to find a way to strengthen its will, for Russia possesses a strong will and will threaten Europe in the next century. Europe must look past the petty politics that have consumed it and see that there is a coming battle for domination of the earth. Europe must strengthen its will to fight against Russia, where strength of the will has been accumulated over a long period of time.

In aphorism 241 of *Beyond Good and Evil* Nietzsche again asserts that one's thought is controlled by one's race. For the most part the good European is beyond "fatherlandishness"—but at times he may still feel patriotic and show other archaic patriotic feelings.³⁷ One's ability to get beyond this fatherlandishness depends upon the speed of digestion. What Nietzsche can overcome in half an hour may take one with a slower digestive process half a year. With those who have an even slower digestive process it could take half a lifetime. Nietzsche can imagine races that have such slow metabolism (shall we call them the sloughs of Europe?) that it would take them half a century to get over their patriotism, their love of land, and return to their reason and become good Europeans. Here again physiology is said to be at the origin of thought, and physiology is rooted in race. This practice of seeking psychological explanations in physiology and linking physiology to race is continued in the next section, where Nietzsche writes that there is a physiological process undergirding the democratic movement in Europe. As Europeans become more and more detached from the physical conditions under which European races originated, they are becoming more supranational and nomadic.³⁸ This process is leading to the creation of a European who is more of a herd animal—Europeans are becoming workers, the democratization of Europe is really preparing Europeans for slavery, that is, it is preparing Europeans to be tyrannized by the strong.

In *On the Genealogy of Morals* race and physiology play a large role in the determination of moral values. Nietzsche writes that philosophy, physiology, and medicine must work together to discover the origins of moral values. We need to ask what is the value of each table of morality. Something can have a value in enabling the survival of a race; this valuation would be different from that of a morality that favors the survival of a few stronger individuals.[39] Nietzsche speaks glowingly here of the "blond beast" or beast of prey. This savage creature has erupted from time to time. As examples Nietzsche cites Roman, Arabian, Germanic, and Japanese nobility, the Homeric heroes, and the Scandinavian Vikings. These are men who have no regard for security but revel in danger and cruelty. In the second essay of On the Genealogy of Morals Nietzsche suggests that Negroes are prehistoric humans (vorgeschlictlichen Menschen) and praises them for their ability to withstand pain. The passage argues that when people were not ashamed of their instinct for cruelty, they were much more cheerful. The bad conscience that has developed in the West is really a sign of the decline of man. Contemporary "hysterical, cultivated little women" (einzigen hysterischen Bildungs-Weibchens) suffer more in one night of suffering than all the animals that have ever been cut open with a knife for the purpose of scientific experiments. William Preston uses this passage to make the claim that Nietzsche is a cruel racist, and there are in fact many places that support this claim.[40] Preston also argues that Nietzsche is equating Negroes to lab animals and that Nietzsche feels that blacks are worth so little that men of distinction will not derive much pleasure in oppressing them. As we have already seen, Nietzsche states unambiguously that cruelty is essential to every "higher" culture. But the ability to endure pain is for Nietzsche a noble trait. Negroes seem to be like blond beasts—noble prehistoric humans who point out the depths to which modern man has fallen. A little later on Nietzsche praises the blond beast as the violent conqueror who knows how to dig its claws into the docile public.[41] Bad conscience develops in the masses whom the blond beast attacks, but not in the blond beast himself. Nietzsche repeatedly praises cruelty, but the ability to suffer and inflict suffering without bad conscience is what makes Negroes and blond beasts more noble than contemporary men.

In the third essay, he suggests that the spread of Christianity is in part a consequence of the problems associated with racial mixing. Christianity has spread because of its ability to sooth "the black melancholy of the physiologically inhibited."[42] Nietzsche writes that on occasion a feeling of physiological inhibition affects large numbers of people. There are many possible causes for this, but one of them is the mixing of races or classes (Stände) that are too different from each other. In a very interesting aside Nietzsche then explains why he equates classes and races here: "Classes always express differences in origin and races: the pain that Europeans feel toward the world, the pessimism of the nineteenth century is in essence the result of a senseless, sudden mixing of classes."[43] In other words, Nietzsche claims that classes have their origin in races. Furthermore the mixing of races that are too different from each other created physiological conditions that led to the rise of Christianity.[44] Christianity is the result of a racial and physiological decline. Not that Nietzsche is against racial mixing. He inveighs here against "senseless mixing" of classes and races. As we will see shortly, he believes that one could do a better job of mixing and produce a new breed of European.

The Anti-Christ also ties together race and religion, in order to link Christianity to racial degeneration.[45] There is nothing accidental about the corruption represented by the Christian Gospels according to Nietzsche. This corruption is not the result of an individual but rather the result of a race. Christianity is the result of several centuries of Judaism. Christianity has, however, far surpassed Judaism—it is three times more effective at lying than its parent. For example, Christianity has convinced the world that it is a religion that does not judge even while it assigns all that stands against it to rot in hell. Christianity learned from Judaism how to convince most of Europe to accept the false concepts of the priest. It succeeded far more than Judaism in instituting lies, according to Nietzsche, but it has succeeded only because Judaism prepared the way. Christians have seduced all of Europe with their underhanded morality. It is a religion of the weak who call themselves good and call the world evil. This calamity could not have happened, according to Nietzsche, without the racial relationship between Jews and early Christians. The early Christians took the Jewish ability to lie and even turned it back on the Jews—that is to say, the early Christians perpetrated the lies that they were good. Whereas the Jews had once claimed that they were the chosen people, Christians were more liberal. One no longer had to be Jewish to be chosen, but nonetheless the dichotomy between chosen and damned continued to be propagated.

For Nietzsche Europe in general and Germany in particular are in a period of racial decline. Nietzsche believes he sees this decline in the patriotism of the Germans and in the democratization of Europe. The rise of Christianity and bad conscience are also attributed to this racial degeneration. The solution to these problems is then appropriately the breeding of a new European race, and Nietzsche has well-developed ideas about how this breeding should be done.

| | |

NIETZSCHE'S BREEDING PROJECTS

In Beyond Good and Evil 200 Nietzsche writes that his time is an epoch of dissolution and this has caused the races to be all mixed up. The people of such a time tend to be weak, and they seek peace from the fight in their souls. On the other hand, there are some people of mixed race who experience this mixture of drives as an incitement to life. If these people inherit in addition a strong drive to self-control and self-trickery, the result is someone like Alcibiades, Caesar (whom Nietzsche calls the first European), Leonardo da Vinci, or Frederic II. In other words, these four people are of mixed race, but they are great individuals who control the many drives that their mixed heritage has bequeathed. It is precisely their mixture and their self-control that make them great. But mixing does not always produce greatness. It produces greatness only when one has the ability to control the mixed soul. In *Beyond Good and Evil* 224 the mixing of races and classes is said to have brought on a chaotic modern soul whose instincts run all over the place. Noble ages and races have delicate palates and are reserved, hesitant, and even nauseated by that which is foreign to them. Nietzsche includes himself among the modern less noble men who are semibarbaric and are more open— who have "taste and tongue for everything." There are advantages to this chaotic soul, for such a soul has secret passages that go in many directions—particularly toward unfinished cultures and toward the half barbaric. Being less noble men, Nietzsche and his contemporaries can appreciate Homer and Shakespeare. More noble times, like the Athens of Aeschylus, would have laughed themselves silly over the bard.

In *Beyond Good and Evil* 244 Nietzsche notes that Germans are often referred to as "deep." This is meant to be a compliment, but this depth is in fact something else and something that, thanks be to God (*Gott sei Dank*), can be eliminated. To debunk the notion that Germans are deep, Nietzsche undertakes a dissection of the German soul. Germans are, Nietzsche writes, a people of the "most enormous mixture and stirred together concoction of races" (*ungeheuerlichsten Mischung und Zusammenrührung von Rassen*). It may even be the case that Germans have a predominance of pre-Aryan elements. Germans are a people (*Volk*) in the middle. They are impossible to get a hold of, more extensive, unknown, unpredictable, surprising, and even more frightening than all other people (again *Volk*). They escape definition. In short, for Nietzsche, the Germans are not a race but a mixture of races.[46]

So the Germans are a *Volk*, a mixture of many races, an "*ungehorere*" mixture. Jews, by contrast, are Europe's purest race. In *Beyond Good and Evil* 251 Nietzsche writes that there are really no Germans who are favorably disposed to the Jews. The Germans are a weak *Volk* who would be easily done away with by a stronger race. The Jews, on the other hand, are the strongest, toughest, purest race living in Europe "today."[47] Jews know how to persevere through the worst conditions. Like Russians, Jews change slowly. They take their time, and they are not stuck in the past but thinking about tomorrow. Those thinking about the future of Europe must take Russians and Jews into consideration. Nietzsche then clearly delineates nations from races—as he has done from his very first discussions of race. Nations are young and in transition. Races such as the Jews are *"aere perennius"*(more enduring than bronze). The Jews could conquer Europe but they are not striving to do so. Instead they are looking for a place to call home. Jews are in search of a place where they would belong and no longer be nomads.

Nietzsche counsels the stronger Germans (for example the noble officer) to mix with the Jews. It would be interesting to see if the Jewish genius for money and patience could be bred into the "art of commanding and obeying" possessed by the Germans. But this aphorism ends with a remarkable passage that calls into question everything Nietzsche has just written.

> But here it seems fitting to interrupt my cheerful Germanic blather (*Deutschthümelei*) and my speech. I am already beginning to touch on what is serious for me, on the "European Problem" as I understand it, on the breeding of a new caste that would rule over Europe.[48]

Kaufmann translates *Deutschthümelei* "Germanomania." My translation of it as "Germanic blather" is perhaps a bit too strong, but *thümelei* is a diminutive, and it is meant to underline that what Nietzsche has been arguing now seems somewhat silly to him.[49] It is as if Nietzsche were saying that the Germans tend to take talk of race, Jews, and Germans too earnestly. Nietzsche is concerned with the "breeding" of a new ruling caste for Europe, but his talk of mixing the "Jewish race" with the German "race" is too Germanic to be taken too seriously.[50]

Nietzsche uses the concept of race extensively, but often in ways that confound the expectations of his readers. Against those who would glorify the Germanic race, he argues that Germans are mixed. To those who warn against the contamination of the German race, Nietzsche counsels race mixing to improve the Germans. Nietzsche wishes to improve the German race by mixing it with Jews. To those who think of whites as the superior race, Nietzsche denigrates the "pale white race," and as we will see he glorifies the race that was bred in India.[51] At the same time in this passage Nietzsche does repeat the often heard stereotype that Jews are good with money. In another place, Nietzsche is decidedly less enthusiastic about mixing with Jews, or at least some Jews. In *The Anti-Christ* he writes: "We wouldn't choose to be near either 'the first Christians' or Polish Jews—both do not smell good."[52] Nietzsche may have escaped some of the racial and ethnic prejudices of his day, but he did not escape them all.

Nietzsche denigrates many of his contemporaries' projects for racial improvement, but he clearly endorses the notion that races can be improved and stresses the importance of doing so. Nietzsche argues that the moral laws formulated by

Christianity to improve mankind have actually led to the creation of a caricature of a man. Christianity has turned man into a sinner. It has hunted down the blond beast and turned this Teuton into a sinner:

> He was stuck between all sorts of terrible concepts . . . there he lay sick, miserable, malevolent toward himself; full of hate against the drive to life, full of suspicion against everything that remained strong and happy. In short, a Christian.[53]

Moral judgments are never to be taken literally. Taken literally, they appear to be merely nonsense. But when viewed as a semiotic, moral judgments are invaluable because they reveal an enormous amount about a culture. Typically those who speak of improving mankind are actually in the business of taking the men who are beasts and making them weaker. In the Middle Ages the church took the "blond beast" (Nietzsche himself puts the term in quotations) and improved him into the noble German. Nietzsche claims that such an improvement is actually a miscarriage. The church turned the blond beast into a sinner. In short, the church turned him into a Christian. Echoing the passage we have already discussed from the third section of *The Genealogy of Morals*, Nietzsche writes that Christianity has made Christians weak; it has made them hate the drives of life and distrust everything that is strong and happy.

As an example of a successful breeding of races Nietzsche cites the Laws of Manu. Actually Nietzsche's understanding of the Laws of Manu comes not from an authoritative edition of that work but from a truncated version found in *Les Législateurs religieux, Manou, Moïse, Mahomet* published by Louis Jacolliot. Nietzsche is impressed that this religion gave itself the task of breeding four races at once: a warrior race, a priestly race, one race of traders and farmers, and a servant race. Nietzsche claims that the type of human that produced these four races is a hundred times milder and more reasonable than the animal trainers who produced the Christians. But the breeding prescribed by Jacolliot's Manu was terrible even by Nietzsche's standards. The Chandalas (the untouchables) are allowed to eat only the impure vegetables—onions and garlic. They may drink water only from the approaches to swamps and the water that collects in the holes made from animal footprints. They cannot wash themselves or their clothes. They may wear only rags taken from corpses, use only broken dishes, have only iron jewelry, and worship only evil spirits. The Chandalas were said to be the result of adultery and incest. Sudra women were also not allowed to help Chandala women in childbirth. The results of these laws were murderous epidemics, awful sexually transmitted diseases, circumcision for boys, and removal of the internal labia for girls. These regulations, Nietzsche tells us, teach us what it is to be Aryan. They teach us what is noble breeding.[54] Moreover, he says that such measures were necessary because they were the only way to render the Chandalas harmless. Nietzsche often writes that "higher men" are in danger of being overwhelmed by "lower" men.[55]

Christianity represents, for Nietzsche, the opposite of the Laws of Manu. Christianity is a countermovement to the morality of breeding represented by these laws. Christianity is the "anti-Aryan religion par excellence" and represents the victory of Chandala values.[56] Gerd Schank writes that in these passages from *Twilight of the Idols* Nietzsche is writing about the biological breeding of a new race but that Nietzsche decisively rejects such a project. Such a breeding of a race is, Schank writes, the false way to raise mankind.[57] Schank argues that for Nietzsche the raising of mankind happens inside the soul of an individual; an individual does not raise mankind by gaining power over others.[58] It is certainly true that Nietzsche often praises those who have wide-ranging souls, but Nietzsche also, at times, clearly states that domination of others is essential to higher individuals. Nietzsche does group the Laws of Manu with other moralities. Like Christianity and Platonic philosophy, these laws are attempts to improve mankind and are based on lies, but the Laws of Manu are said to have produced Aryans, and Christianity is the opposite. Christianity is an "anti-Aryan religion and represents the victory of Chandala values." In *The Anti-Christ* Nietzsche reinforces the notion that Christianity and Manu are opposites and calls the Laws of Manu an "incomparably spiritual and superior work."[59] Nietzsche admires how the Laws of Manu prescribe a way for the noble classes, i.e., philosophers and the nobles, to stand above the masses. These are laws Nietzsche calls life affirming, to which I would add that they are, perhaps, life affirming for some, but certainly not for those who drink the foul water and die in childbirth and epidemics. Whereas Christianity vents its meanness by denigrating women, Nietzsche believes the Laws of Manu treat women with love, respect, and trust.[60] This may be true for the women of the upper class, but allowing the Chandala women to die in childbirth is hardly what I would call love. Next to the Laws of Manu, Nietzsche believes that Christianity looks contemptible.

So against Schank I would argue that Nietzsche is clearly praising what he perceives to be the breeding practices prescribed by the Laws of Manu. But at the same time Nietzsche explicitly equivocates between the terms race breeding and class breeding. It is hard to fathom such praise for a system of laws that would create lower classes and then treat them so ruthlessly that they die in plagues, but such praise is consistent with Nietzsche's praise of slavery. Nietzsche clearly believes in class differentiation. In *Beyond Good and Evil* 258, Nietzsche writes that "the essential thing for a 'good and healthy aristocracy' is that they believe themselves to be the meaning and highest reason of their society." That is why they are prepared, with good conscience, to sacrifice an enormous number of people to slavery.

> The essential characteristic of a good and healthy aristocracy is, however, that it feels itself to be not the means (be it of the kingdom or of the community), but its meaning and highest justification. That it thereby with good conscience accepts the sacrifice of an enormous number of people, who for its sake must be pressed down and reduced to incomplete humans, to slaves, and to tools.[61]

It was a sign of the weakness of the French aristocracy that at the beginning of the Revolution some of its members threw away their privileges and fell victim to the dissolution of their morals. A healthy aristocracy insists upon its privileges. Society's reason to be is not the greatest good for the greatest number. As we have seen, from his earliest writings Nietzsche believed that society should function as support system for noble individuals to exercise their higher duties. Races must be bred, Nietzsche believed, to accomplish this mission.[62]

The later Nietzsche's writings are packed full of advice on how to breed superior races. Even as Nietzsche denigrates traditional theories of improvement, he offers his theories of how to improve a race. As suggested in the praise of the Laws of Manu, Nietzsche writes a few pages later (in a passage I have already cited once) in Twilight of the Idols that the beauty of a race or a family is not an accident, but rather that beauty is the result of the careful work of generations.[63] To create beauty one has to make sacrifices—one must use good taste to rigorously select one's company and one's sexual partners. One must regulate oneself to produce beauty and eschew habit, opinion, and inertia. Nietzsche notes that Cicero was amazed that the men and young boys in Athens were much more beautiful than the women. Their beauty was no accident, according to Nietzsche, but the result of the effort that men had expended, over the centuries, on breeding beauty in themselves. Culture begins, Nietzsche argues, in the body; in other words one must rigorously regulate gestures, diet, and physiology. When one cultivates the body as the Greeks did, one produces an immeasurably greater culture than Christianity, which despises the body.

Nietzsche argues that knowing something about the parents allows one to make inferences about their children.[64] There are three unmistakable characteristics of plebeians: disgusting incontinence, envy, and the insistence that one is always right. Even with the best education one will never get rid of these characteristics. Nietzsche writes that children will inevitably have the qualities and preferences of their parents and their ancestors, and that this is "the problem of race." Today education and culture have become primarily a way of deceiving about the plebeian origins of one's body and soul.[65] Schank argues that Nietzsche uses the word *breeding* in an older sense roughly analogous to "educate."[66] I would agree that this is sometimes the case, but in this section from *Beyond Good and Evil* Nietzsche specifically contrasts education and breeding and argues that there are limits to education. He is arguing that education cannot overcome heredity. The only way then to build a healthy upper class would seem to be to follow the example of the Greeks and the Laws of Manu and rigorously select one's breeding partners. Moreover, in *Ecce Homo* Nietzsche writes that he "did nothing except physiology, medicine, and natural sciences."[67] Kaufmann, in a footnote to his translation, writes that there are two ways the German phrase "*nichts mehr getrieben*" can be read. It could be taken to mean that Nietzsche has studied nothing except these three disciplines, or it could mean, as he translates it, that Nietzsche has not studied anything as intensely as he has studied these disciplines. Kaufmann rejects the first reading because it is biographically false.[68] But much of what Nietzsche writes about himself is biographically false. In fact, Barbara Stiegler has shown that even if the claim is an exaggeration, Nietzsche did spend a great deal of time studying the biology of his day.[69] What makes the statement interesting in either of its renditions is that it reaffirms Nietzsche's claim that physiology is the key to his philosophy, for if physiology is important, then clearly race has an important role to play as well. Even if Nietzsche is never able to convert philosophy into physiology, it is nonetheless certain that he often identified this as his primary goal.

In the *Nachlass*, Nietzsche at times denigrates the notion of race. In a fragment written in the spring or summer of 1888, Nietzsche characterizes race along with freedom, das *Volk*, democracy, tolerance, utilitarianism, *Weiber-Emancipation*, progress, and several other notions as one of the false modern ideals.[70] Yet in his published writings Nietzsche sees many of the problems of Europe as racial problems. He clearly argues that many of the problems that Germans face are racial problems. The proliferation of Christianity, democracy, herd mentality, and bad conscience is a sign of racial degeneration. Nietzsche's solutions to these problems are racial solutions. He clearly endorses the breeding of races—or classes. He has well developed racial profiles. Greeks and Germans are mixed races. Jews are a pure race and therefore stronger than the Germans. He does not endorse racial purity, but he does argue that racial makeup has a great influence on one's spirit. Mixing long-separated races causes skepticism. The mixing of races and classes has led to the chaotic modern soul whose instincts run wild. The breeding of a new European race is discussed over and over again. Although in the middle of a long passage about the breeding of this race, Nietzsche seems to question his own project, suggesting that his talk of racial breeding has descended into Germanic blather, the references to racial breeding are too numerous to ignore. Nietzsche does have a racial project. He wants to "breed a new caste that would rule Europe."[71] But this caste would not be the caste that Hitler envisioned. It would be a mixed race and include Jews. It would be nonetheless a caste or a race that believed itself to be the raison d'être of its society and would therefore, in good conscience, sacrifice, as the Laws of Manu counseled, the lower caste or race to slavery.

Is Nietzsche a racist? At times he clearly is. Occasionally, he clearly uses what we today would recognize as racial stereotypes such as that Africans are more capable of withstanding pain and Jews are good with money. But even as he uses these stereotypes he often seems to be praising Jews and Africans. And occasionally Nietzsche has an inkling of the contemporary questioning of the concept of race. When Nietzsche writes that his own talk of race is beginning to sound like Germanic blather or that race is a false modern ideal, it is a clear indication that Nietzsche shares some of the modern skepticism about the very concept of race.

NOTES

1. Nietzsche uses the word *race* extensively, but he does not discuss some of the most prominent race theorists of his day. For example Arthur de Gobineau, who was famous for his racist philosophy of history, is mentioned only once by Nietzsche—in a letter. His name never appears in either the published works or the *Nachlass*, the notebooks that Nietzsche did not prepare for publication. For a detailed discussion of the relationship or lack of relationship between Nietzsche and Gobineau, see Gerd Schank, *Rasse und Züchtung bei Nietzsche* (Berlin: De Gruyter, 2000), 226–441. For a recent examination of Nietzsche's treatment of Jews, see Jacqueline Scott, "On the Use and Abuse of Race in Philosophy: Nietzsche, Jews, and Race," in *Race and Racism in Continental Philosophy*, ed. Robert Bernasconi and Sybol Cook (Bloomington: Indiana University Press, 2003), 53–73.

2. In most cases I have consulted existing English translations. I greatly admire Walter Kaufmann's translations and Richard Polk's new translation of *Twilight of the Idols* (Indianapolis: Hackett, 1997). The translations, however, are, for the most part, my own based on *Friedrich Nietzsche Sämtliche Werke Kritische Studienausgabe in 15 Bänden*, ed. Giorgio Colli and Mazzino Montinari (Berlin: Deutscher Taschenbuch Verlag, 1980). This edition will be referred to throughout as KSA, with the volume number and page number(s). All citations of the *Nachlass* are from this edition, and all translations of the *Nachlass* are my own. *The Birth of Tragedy, Dawn, Human, All-Too-Human, The Gay Science, Beyond Good and Evil, The Case of Wagner*, and *The Anti-Christ* are composed of consecutively numbered sections. Nietzsche often refers to these sections as aphorisms even if they are longer than aphorisms traditionally are. Therefore, when citing these works, after the title I will give the section or aphorism number. *Twilight of the Idols* and *Ecce Homo* are divided into chapters and then sections. When citing these works I give first an abbreviated title of the chapter and then the section number.

On the Genealogy of Morals is divided into three essays and then section numbers. When citing this work I indicate the essay number and then give the section.

3. For a translation of Kant's most important essay on race, see "Of the Different Human Races," in *The Idea of Race*, ed. Robert Bernasconi and Tommy L. Lott (Hackett: Indianapolis, 2000), 8–22. On Kant's theory of race, see also Bernasconi's "Who Invented the Concept of Race? Kant's Role in the Enlightenment Construction of Race," in *Race*, ed. Robert Bernasconi (Malden, MA: Blackwell, 2001), 11–36.

4. *Dawn* 241.

5. In *On the Genealogy of Morals* Nietzsche writes that all over Europe the suppressed race is gradually getting the upper hand again. One can see this, Nietzsche believes, on the basis of color, the shortness of the skull, and "perhaps in the intellectual and social instincts." Nietzsche, *Genealogy* 1.5.

6. Nietzsche did not publish *Anti-Christ*, *Ecce Homo*, and *Nietzsche Contra Wagner* before he fell into insanity, but since these manuscripts were ready to be published and Nietzsche seemed to have every intention of publishing them, I treat them as on a par with the works that Nietzsche himself published. For a further discussion of my understanding of the *Nachlass* see my *Nietzsche's Aesthetic Turn: Reading Nietzsche after Heidegger, Deleuze, and Derrida* (Albany: State University of New York Press, 1994), 27.

7. On the problems with *The Will to Power*, see Wayne Klein, *Nietzsche and the Promise of Philosophy* (Albany: State University of New York Press, 1997), 181–97. See also Bernd Magnus, "The Uses and Abuses of *The Will to Power*," in *Reading Nietzsche*, ed. Robert C. Solomon and Kathleen M. Higgens (New York: Oxford University Press, 1988), 218–35; and Mazzino Montinari, *Nietzsche Lesen* (Berlin: De Gruyter, 1982).

8. This unpublished draft was written in 1871 and has been published in KSA 7:333. In Kaufmann's translation of *The Birth of Tragedy* 2 the word *race* does appear, but it is the translation of the German word *Gattung*. In section 3 Kaufmann translates *Eintagsgeschlecht* as "ephemeral race." See *The Basic Writings of Nietzsche*, ed. and trans. Walter Kaufmann (New York: Random House, 1992), 18–20.

9. *Untimely Meditations* I, "David Strauss the Confessor and the Writer," section 12. KSA 1:32. Here Nietzsche makes fun of Strauss for saying that it is because of god's will that people are divided into races. Nietzsche says that it is obvious that Strauss has merely stolen this trite pronouncement. In the third Untimely Meditation, entitled "Schopenhauer as Educator," Nietzsche quotes from Walter Bagehot. Bagehot writes that a "Shelley could have never lived in England and a race of Shelley's would have been impossible." KSA 1:352.

10. KSA 1:768.

11. In notes never published by Nietzsche himself, written at the same time Nietzsche also writes of the pale white race in a derogatory way. In these notes there is a piece entitled "Fragment of an expanded version of 'The Birth of Tragedy.'" Here Nietzsche makes the same claim about communists, socialists, and their pale descendants (KSA 7:339–40).

12. *Dawn* 241 and *Genealogy* 2.7.

13. Nietzsche, *Human* 45

14. Ibid., 224.

15. Ibid., 475. There is a section from the notebooks, written in the spring of 1880, that echoes this praise of Judaism. Nietzsche writes "that the Jews, among all nations, have elevated moral sublimity the highest (KSA 9:75).

16. See George M. Fredrickson, *Racism: A Short History* (Princeton: Princeton University Press, 2002), 77.

17. Nietzsche, *Human* 479.

18. Nietzsche, *Twilight of the Idols*, "Raids," 47.

19. Nietzsche, *Dawn* 272.

20. KSA 8:96.

21. KSA 8:306.

22. Nietzsche, *Dawn* 70.

23. Ibid.

24. Ibid.

25. Nietzsche, *Genealogy* 2.7.

26. KSA 9:547.

27. Nietzsche, *Gay Science* 10 and 40.

28. According to the table published by Schank, in the notebooks from 1882 (i.e., the notebooks that have been published posthumously) there are 3 references to the word *race*; in 1883, 1 reference; in 1884, 24 references; in 1885, 33 references; in 1886, 10 references; in 1887, 14 references; and from 1888 to January 1889, 47 references. Schank, *Rasse*, 442–51.

29. Nietzsche, *Gay Science* 377.

30. KSA 1:768.

31. This notion that some must be sacrificed for the improvement of others is also found in the notes from 1881. Here Nietzsche writes "the new problem: whether a part of humanity is to be raised to a higher race at the cost of other humans. Breeding——" (KSA 9:577). The note suggests that Nietzsche believed both in the sacrifice of some for the improvement of others and in the breeding of superior races even while he criticized the racial constructs of many of his contemporaries.

32. Nietzsche, *Beyond* 20.

33. Ural-Altaic refers to the languages and regions of the Ural and the Altai mountains.

34. Nietzsche, *Beyond* 23. In the *Nachlass* Nietzsche seems to contradict this claim. In a note written at about the same time Nietzsche claims that we cannot conclude anything about the relationship of races from the relationship of languages. See KSA 12:14.

35. Nietzsche, *Beyond* 28.

36. Lessing is also distinguished from the Germans in the *Nachlass*. See KSA 11:103.

37. I do not use gender-inclusive language here because I believe for Nietzsche all good Europeans will be men.

38. Nietzsche, *Beyond* 242.

39. Nietzsche, *Genealogy* 1.17.

40. William Preston, "Nietzsche on Blacks," in *Existence in Black: An Anthology of Black Existential Philosophy*, ed. Louis Gordon (New York: Routledge, 1997), 169.

41. Nietzsche, *Genealogy* 2.17.

42. Ibid., 3.17.

43. Ibid.

44. In *Twilight of the Idols* Nietzsche writes that ugliness has a physiological effect on humans: "Physiologically calculated, everything that is ugly weakens and depresses man. It reminds him of decay, danger, and powerlessness. It actually causes him to lose power. One can measure the effect of the ugly with a dynamometer." "Raids," 20.

45. Nietzsche, *Anti-Christ* 44.

46. In the *Nachlass* Nietzsche also argues that the Germans are a mixture. See KSA 11:702–4.

47. In one place in the *Nachlass* Nietzsche calls Jews the oldest and purist of races and therefore the most beautiful. KSA 11:74.

48. Nietzsche, *Beyond* 251.

49. This strategy is common in Nietzsche. See also the last aphorism (296) of *Beyond Good and Evil* where he looks back over the book he has written and laments that what once seemed so young, bad, and full of prickles and hidden roots now seems like boring truths.

50. Dan Conway interprets this passage somewhat differently than I do. He believes that despite what he writes about Germans, Nietzsche wants the ruling caste of the new Europe to be Germanic. Nietzsche sees "the Germans as the rightful heirs and arbiters of European culture." Conway, "The Great Play and Fight of Forces: Nietzsche on Race," in *Philosophers on Race: Critical Essays*, ed. Julie K. Ward and Tommy L. Lott (Oxford: Blackwell, 2002), 190. Against Conway I would argue that Nietzsche constantly denigrates Germans and Germany throughout his later writings. There are a few great Germans, according to Nietzsche. Goethe and Heine are two that he almost always writes of with admiration, but in general Nietzsche believes that Germany is a culturally impoverished nation. For example in *The Case of Wagner* Nietzsche decries the lack of logic in the German audiences. Wagner had no need to have logic in his operas because he was writing for the Germans, not the French. In *Twilight of the Idols* Nietzsche has a section entitled "What the Germans Lack," where he writes that Germans have been making themselves stupid for over a thousand years. There are now no good German books. Goethe is the last German Nietzsche respects. *Twilight*, "Raids," 51. In *Ecce Homo* Nietzsche claims several times that he is not German but Polish and that the Germans are not fit to understand his work. *Ecce*, "Why I Write Such Good Books," 2. He also writes that he does not believe in German culture, only French culture. *Ecce*, "Why I Am So Clever," 3. In the *Nachlass* his criticism of German culture goes even further (KSA 13:644). At times Nietzsche is less critical of Germans and German culture, but Nietzsche seems to be more critical of Germans and German culture than of any other country or culture in Europe.

51. But then again Nietzsche does not always denigrate whiteness. In *On the Genealogy of Morals*,

we find a discussion of the Aryan race, which is, Nietzsche proclaims, white. Against Rudolf Virchow, whom Nietzsche credits with having created a careful ethnographic map of Germany, Nietzsche argues that dark-haired peoples of Germany cannot be Celtic. Germany's dark-haired people are essentially pre-Aryan. Nietzsche further argues that suppressed races are gradually coming to the fore again in Europe, and one can see this on the basis of the emergence of darker coloring and shorter skulls. He says it is even possible that modern democracy, or even more likely modern anarchism and the inclination for the commune, "the most primitive form of society which is now shared by all the socialists in Europe," is a sign of the counterattack of pre-Aryan races. The Aryan race may very well be in a state of physiological decline.

52. Nietzsche, *Anti-Christ* 46.

53. Nietzsche, *Twilight*, "Improvers of Mankind," 2.

54. Of these that Nietzsche cites, the only prescriptions for the Chandalas that are actually found in the Laws of Manu are that their clothes be taken from the burial cloth of the dead, that they eat from broken plates, that their jewelry be made from iron, and that they wander endlessly. See Annemarie Etter, "Nietzsche und das Gesetzbuch des Manu," *Nietzsche-Studien* 16 (1987): 340–52.

55. Barbara Stiegler argues convincingly that Nietzsche does not always recognize the tension in his thought between the politics of health and the politics of greatness. Those whom Nietzsche considers great are often vulnerable to the lower men. Here, for example, the Chandalas constitute a threat to the Sudras. In *On the Genealogy of Morals* the priests through their underhanded methods are able to bring down the Aryans. See Barbara Stiegler, *Nietzsche et la biologie* (Paris: Presses Universitaires de France, 2001), 121.

56. Nietzsche, *Twilight*, "Improvers of Mankind," 4. In another place in *Twilight of the Idols* Nietzsche gives a very different picture of the Chandalas. In section 45 of "Raids of an Untimely Man" Nietzsche writes that almost all of those who are respected today—the scientist, the artist, the genius, the free spirit, the actor, the merchant, and the great discoverer—were once outcasts. All innovators are at one time considered to be Chandalas—they label themselves as such because as geniuses they feel the remarkable separation between themselves and everything that is considered normal.

57. Schank, *Rasse*, 346.

58. Ibid., 330.

59. Nietzsche, *Anti-Christ* 56. In the *Nachlass* Nietzsche also praises the Laws of Manu. See KSA 13:380. Here he calls the Laws of Manua yes-saying Aryan religion.

60. Nietzsche writes in a letter to Köselitz dated May 31, 1888, of having found a copy of the Laws of Manu in French translation. In this letter he refers to the work as the "absolute Aryan product." It is a priestly code of morals that is not pessimistic. KSA 8:325.

61. Nietzsche, *Beyond* 258.

62. In the *Nachlass* Nietzsche argues that decadent (*verfallenden*) races must be annihilated. See KSA 11:69 from the spring of 1884.

63. Nietzsche, *Twilight*, "Raids," 47.

64. Nietzsche, *Beyond* 264.

65. Ibid.

66. Schank, *Rasse*, 335–403.

67. Nietzsche, *Ecce*, "Human, All-Too-Human," 3.

68. Nietzsche, *On the Genealogy of Morals and Ecce Homo*, trans. Walter Kaufmann (New York: Vintage Books, 1969), 286 n. 1.

69. Stiegler, *Nietzsche et la biologie*, 7.

70. KSA 13:514.

71. Nietzsche, *Beyond* 251.

About the Contributors

Robert Bernasconi is the Lillian and Morrie Moss Professor of Philosophy at the University of Memphis. He is the author of *The Question of Language in Heidegger's History of Being* (Humanities, 1985) and *Heidegger in Question* (Humanities, 1993). He is editor of *Race* (Blackwell, 2001), *Race and Racism in Continental Philosophy* (with Sybol Cook, Indiana, 2003), and *The Idea of Race* (with Tommy L. Lott, Hackett, 2000). Bernasconi has published numerous articles on Hegel, recent continental philosophy, race, and social and political philosophy.

Anthony Bogues is the Royce Professor of Africana Studies and Teaching Excellence and Chair of Africana Studies at Brown University. He is associate director of the Center for Caribbean Thought at the University of the West Indies. He is an associate editor of the journal *Small Axe* and an advisory editor for *boundary 2*. Bogues is the author of *Caliban's Freedom: Early Political Thought of C. L. R. James* (Pluto, 1997), *Black Heretics, Black Prophets: Radical Political Intellectuals* (Routledge, 2003), *Empire of Liberty: Desire, Modernity, and Power* (forthcoming), and editor of the critical reader *After Man, The Human: Critical Essays on the Thought of Sylvia Wynter* (Kingston, Jamaica: Ian Randle Press, 2005).

Bernard R. Boxill is the Pardue Distinguished Professor of Philosophy at the University of North Carolina–Chapel Hill. He is the author of *Blacks and Social Justice* (revised edition, Rowman and Littlefield, 1992) and the editor of *Race and Racism* (Oxford, 2001). Boxill is the author of numerous papers on race, justice, and African American philosophy. He is currently at work on a book, *Boundaries and Justice: On International Ethics and Distributive Justice*.

Peter Fenves is the Joan and Sarepta Harrison Professor of Literature at Northwestern University. He is the author of *A Peculiar Fate: Metaphysics and World History in Kant* (Cornell, 1991), "*Chatter*": *Language and History in Kierkegaard* (Stanford, 1993), *Arresting Language: From Leibniz to Benjamin* (Stanford, 2001), and *Late Kant: Towards Another Law of the Earth* (Routledge, 2003). He is also the editor of *Raising the Tone of Philosophy: Late Essays by Kant, Transformative Critique by Derrida* (Johns Hopkins, 1993), co-editor of "*The Spirit of Poesy*": *Essays on Jewish and German Literature and Thought in Honor of Geza Von Molnar* (with Richard Block, Northwestern, 2000), and the translator of Werner Hamacher's *Premises* (Harvard, 1996). Among his current projects is a study entitled *The Messianic Reduction: Walter Benjamin and the Abstention from Philosophy*.

Barbara Hall is Assistant Professor of Philosophy at Georgia State University. She is the author of "On Epistemic Luck" (*Southern Journal of Philosophy*, 1994), "The Origin of Parental Rights" (*Public Affairs Quarterly*, 1999), and "The Libertarian Role Model and the Burden of Uplifting the Race" (*Women of Color and Philosophy*, ed. Naomi Zack, Blackwell, 2000), among other writings.

Michael H. Hoffheimer is Professor of Law at the University of Mississippi. He is the author of *Eduard Gans and the Hegelian Philosophy of Law* (Kluwer, 1995) and *Justice Holmes and the Natural Law* (Garland, 1992). His research interests include the history of law and philosophy, and he has published numerous articles on Hegel, jurisprudence, and legal history.

Anika Maaza Mann is Assistant Professor of Philosophy at Morgan State University. Her current research involves the intersections of race theory and African American philosophy with continental and feminist philosophy.

Charles W. Mills is Distinguished Professor of Philosophy at the University of Illinois–Chicago. He is the author of *The Racial Contract* (Cornell, 1997), *Blackness Visible: Essays on Philosophy and Race* (Cornell, 1998), and *From Class to Race: Essays in White Marxism and Black Radicalism* (Rowman and Littlefield, 2003). His main research interests are in oppositional political theory, particularly around issues of class, gender, and race.

Debra Nails is Professor of Philosophy at Michigan State University. She is the author of *The People of Plato: A Prosopography of Plato and Other Socratics* (Hackett, 2002) and *Agora, Academy, and the Conduct of Philosophy* (Kluwer, 1995). She is editor of *Naturalistic Epistemology: A Symposium of Two Decades* (with Abner Shimony, Reidel, 1987), and *Spinoza and the Sciences* (with Marjorie Grene, Reidel, 1986).

Richard T. Peterson is Professor of Philosophy at Michigan State University. He is the author of *Democratic Philosophy and the Politics of Knowledge* (Pennsylvania State, 1996) and articles on Marx, Foucault, Rawls, and various topics in political and social theory. He is currently working on a book on race and philosophy.

Timothy J. Reiss is Professor of Comparative Literature at New York University. His books include *Against Autonomy: Global Dialectics of Cultural Exchange* (Stanford, 2002), *Knowledge, Discovery, and Imagination in Early Modern Europe* (Cambridge, 1997), and *Mirages of the Selfe: Patterns of Personhood in Ancient and Early Modern Europe* (Stanford, 2003). Reiss is also the editor of seven collections, among them *Sisyphus and Eldorado: Magical and Other Realisms in Caribbean Literature* (second edition, Africa World Press, 2001) and *For the Geography of a Soul: Emerging Perspectives on Kamau Brathwaite* (Africa World Press, 2001). He is a Fellow of the Royal Society of Canada and a Guggenheim Fellow and received the Forkosch Prize in Intellectual History for *The Meaning of Literature* (1992).

William Uzgalis is Associate Professor of Philosophy at Oregon State University. He is the author of several papers on John Locke, including " ' . . . The Same Tyrannical Principle': Locke's Legacy on Slavery" (*Subjugation and Bondage: Critical Essays on Slavery and Social Philosophy*, ed. Tommy L. Lott, Rowman and Littlefield, 1998) and "An Inconsistency Not to Be Excused: On Locke and Racism" (*Philosophers on Race: Critical Essays*, ed. Julie K. Ward and Tommy L. Lott (Blackwell, 2002).

Andrew Valls is Assistant Professor of Political Science at Oregon State University. He is the author of numerous articles and book chapters, including many on issues of racial justice.

He is the editor of *Ethics in International Affairs: Theories and Cases* (Rowman and Littlefield, 2000).

James Winchester is Assistant Professor of Philosophy at Georgia College and State University. He is the author of *Aesthetics across the Color Lines: Why Nietzsche (Sometimes) Can't Sing the Blues* (Rowman and Littlefield, 2002) and *Nietzsche's Aesthetic Turn: Reading Nietzsche after Heidegger, Deleuze, and Derrida* (SUNY, 1994).

Index

Abolition, Britain and, 220–23

Absolute idealism, 194, 207

Abstractness, of identity, 244–45, 249–50

Acosta, José de, 29, 32

Adams, John, 90

Africans, just war theory of slavery and, 35–36, 41n. 64. *See also* Slavery; Slaves; Slave trade

Albornoz, Bartolomé de, 28

Alcohol use, 118, 146n. 32

Althusser, Louis, 69 n. 25

Ambition, 163, 165–66

American Indians. *See* Native Americans

Amsterdam, 19–20, 32, 58

Anachronism, 5–6

Anglican Church, 108–14, 117, 121, 123

Animals, 23–24

    Hume's view, 136–37, 140, 142

    Kant's view, 181–82

    Leibniz's view, 77–78

    Rousseau's view, 153–56, 158–59

Anti-essentialism, 2

Anti-Semitism. *See also* Jews; Judaism

    Marx and, 12–13, 235, 239, 241–44

    Nietzsche and, 255, 259–60

Antislavery tracts, 100

Appiah, Anthony, 6–7

Aquamboe, Kingdom of, 100

Aquinas, Thomas, 18, 19, 23

Arabs, 199–200, 202

Arcos, Miguel de, 41–42 n. 64

Arendt, Hannah, 51, 244

Aristotle, 22–23, 27–28

Arnold, Matthew, 228

Arte de los contratos (Albornoz), 28

Asians

    Hegel's view, 197–99, 202, 206

Kant's view, 174, 177

    Marx's view, 246

Authority, 92

Bacon, Francis, 21

Baier, Annette, 130–31

Balzac, Jean-Louis Guez de, 19

Baptism of slaves, 93, 96, 98, 104n. 23, 116–19

Barbados, 92–93, 109

Barbarians, color as criteria for, 36

Barbarous, as term, 30

Bauer, Bruno, 242–43

Baxter, Richard, 99

Beattie, James, 133–34, 137–38

Bentham, Jeremy, 172, 217

Berkeley, George

    Anglican Church and, 108–14, 117, 121, 124

    ethnocentrism of, 114–17, 119, 124

    Locke contrasted with, 115, 121–23, 125 n. 7, 126 n. 13

    Native Americans, view of, 111–14

    ownership of slaves, 3, 10–11, 117–18, 120

    political philosophy, 121–23, 124

    proposal for college, 109, 110–12, 116–17

    support of slavery, 115–16, 120–24, 126n. 17

    visit to America, 115, 117–20

—Works

    Essay towards Preventing the Ruin of Great Britain, 110

    "Passive Obedience," 122–23

    "Verses on America," 110

Bermuda, St. Paul's College proposal, 110–14, 116–17

Bernasconi, Robert, 10, 173, 178, 183, 187, 206, 214n. 74

Bernier, François, 73–75, 82
Bias, 65
Bible, as justification for domination, 25–27, 35
Black, as term, 41–42 n. 64
Blackburn, Robin, 100–101
Black peoples
    Carlyle's view, 221–23
    Hegel's view, 197, 207
    Kant's view, 174–75, 177, 178
    Mill's view, 221–23
    Nietzsche's view, 259
    religion and, 202–3
    spirit and, 198–99
Blakely, Allison, 19
"Blond beast," 263, 267
Blood purity laws, 58
Blood quanta spectra, 35–36
Blumenbach, Johann Friedrich, 12, 74–75, 197–98, 210 n. 19, 215 n. 80
Board of Trade, 98–99, 101
Bodin, Jean, 24–25, 28
"Body of Liberties" (Massachusetts), 99–100
Bogle, Paul, 223–24, 233 n. 30
Bogues, Anthony, 12
Bosman, William, 100
Bourdin, Pierre, 33
Boxill, Bernard R., 11, 180, 181, 183
Bracken, H. M., 2, 4, 108, 115–16
Brandt, Reinhard, 185–86
Braude, Benjamin, 35
Bray, Thomas, 109, 116
Bredero, Gerbrand Adriaensz, 20
Breeding theories, 255–60, 264–71. See also Racial mixing
Britain
    abolition of slavery, 220–23
    Berkeley's view of, 109–10
    ex-slaves as subjects of, 221, 224–25, 233 n. 30
    Marx's defense of colonialism, 246–47
    Mill's view of government, 226–29
    nineteenth-century colonialism, 217
    slavery and, 20, 42 n. 70, 89–90, 95, 98–99
British Colonial Office, 228

Calvinists, 58, 64
Canada, 222
Capitalism, commodification of identity, 245
Caribbean colonies, 220–23. See also Jamaica
Caribs, 159, 166
Carlyle, Thomas, 12, 220–23, 224
Carolina, 89, 91, 95
Cartesianism, 2. See also Descartes, René
Categorical imperative (CI), 177–78, 181
Caucasians, 197–99, 203–4. See also Whiteness
Cavendish, Lord, 44
Césaire, Aimé, 37
Chandalas, 267–68, 275 n. 54
Character, 12, 218–20, 228–29
    national, 128, 199–200
Charles V, 36
Charlet, Étienne, 20
Charmes, Gabriel, 219
Cherokee Nation cases, 188
Children of slaves, 96–98
China, 79
Chomsky, Noam, 2–3, 4
Christian Directory, A (Baxter), 99
Christianity, 12
    acceptance of slavery, 94, 121
    Europeans as superior, 199, 201
    influence on racism, 186
    missionaries and, 109–14
    Nietzsche's views, 259, 263–64, 266–67
Christian particularism, 76
Christian republic, 82
Civilization, 12, 46, 218–20
    ethnocentric view of, 113–15
    Mill's view, 226–29
Class, race and, 239–41, 248–51, 263–64
Classical liberalism, 217, 230
Classification, 2, 10, 12
Class terms, 81–82, 83
Code noir, 17–18, 35
Codrington College, 109
Colleton, John, 92
Colleton, Peter, 92
Collini, Stefan, 218

Colonialism
  despotic rule required, 225, 227
  Hegel's view, 207, 215 n. 83
  Kant's condemnation of, 186–87
  legitimizing appropriation of land,
    50–51
  Mill's justification of, 227–28
  nineteenth-century, 217
  slavery linked with, 90–91, 94–95
Colonies
  Anglican Church and, 108–14, 117, 121,
    124
  as dependencies, 226–27
  Locke's administration of, 98–99
Columbus, Christopher, 25
Conceptual clarities, 5–6
Conquest, 9
  Hobbes's view, 49–52
  Mill's justification of, 227–28
Consciousness, 196, 199, 207
Consequentialist liberalism, 172
Conway, Dan, 274 n. 50
Cooper, Frederick, 217
Corruption
  Kant's theory of, 163–66
  Rousseau's theory of, 162–63, 166
Council of Trade and Plantations, 89
Cultural racism, 8
Culture, 228. See also Religion
  "Oriental," 195–96
  slavery as essential to, 257, 269
Culture and Anarchy (Arnold), 228

D'Allone, Sieur Abel Tassin, 116
Darwin, Charles, 219, 231
Davis, David Brion, 121, 139
Dayan, Joan, 17–18
Declaration of Independence, 103
De ecclesiastica potestate (Gile of Rome), 25
Degeneration theories, 237, 261–64
De generis humani varietate (Blumenbach),
    74–75
De iustitia et iure (Soto), 25, 27–28
Deontological liberalism, 172
Dependency, political language of, 227

De regimine principum (Giles of Rome),
    23–24, 26
Descartes, René, 16–17. See also Cartesianism
  education, trade, and travel, 18–22
  historical context, 17–18, 38 n. 18
  legal background for thought of, 22–30
  silence on slavery and race, 9, 17, 36–37
  slave/captive equation in, 21–23, 25,
    30–35
  tradition and limits of new thought, 30–37
  —Works
    Discours de la méthode, 17, 19–21, 29
    Epistola ad Voetium, 33–34
    Meditations, 9, 17–18, 30–32
    Passions de l'âme, 31, 32
    Principes de la philosophie, 34
Descent of Man (Darwin), 219
Despotic rule, justification of, 225, 227–28
Developmentalism, 230
Differential treatment, 6–7
Digest (Justinian), 22
Dinet, Peter, 33
Domination, natural, 25–27
Dominicans, 30
Douglass, Frederick, 103
Draper, Hal, 242
Dutch West India Company, 19

East India Company, 229–30
Egalitarian theory, 4, 170–73
Egypt, 76
Egyptians, 205, 214 nn. 71, 74
"Einige patriotischen Gedanken" (Leibniz),
    80–82
Empiricism, 2–3, 6–8, 115–16
Engels, Friedrich, 237, 253 n. 40
English antislavery movements, 120
Enlightenment against Empire (Muthu),
    158–60, 165
Enlightenment thought, 241
  race as central to, 4–5
  as racist, 17–18
Equality, moral, 170
Erasmus, 24
Eskimos, 202

Essay on the Inequality of the Races (Gobineau), 228, 236, 239

Essays Towards a Real Character and Philosophical Language (Wilkins), 80–81, 87 n. 15

Essay towards Preventing the Ruin of Great Britain (Berkley), 110

Essence, 83, 88 n. 19

"Essence, Accident, and Race" (Bracken), 108, 115–16

Essentialism, 2

Ethnocentrism, 113, 119, 124
  racism and, 114–17

Eurocentrism, 12, 48
  of Marx, 246–48

European race, 257–58, 260–61

European racial degeneration, 261–64

Evolutionary theory, 219, 237

Existence, mode of, 9–10, 60, 61–63

Extension, attribute of, 61–63, 64, 70–71 n. 35, 71 n. 41

Extrinsic racist, 6–7

Eyre, Edward John, 223–25

Eyre committee, 224–26

Eze, Emmanuel, 5, 131, 134, 136–37, 144
  Kant, view of, 173, 177, 181, 183–84, 187

Farr, James, 96, 102, 114

Feminist theory, 184–85

Fenves, Peter, 10

Fetishism, 203

Feuerbach, Ludwig, 60

Fichte, Johann Gottlieb, 194

Foucault, Michel, 217, 235

France, 76

Frederickson, George, 4, 186

Freedom, 22, 206
  Spinoza's view, 64–65
  will and, 31–32

Free will, 28–29, 31–32
  rationality and, 32–33

French thought, 219

Friendship, 23

Fundamental Constitutions of Carolina, The, 10, 90–95, 102

Garcia, Jorge, 7–8, 130

Garrett, Aaron, 129, 132, 134

Gausted, Edwin, 109, 117–18

Gender, 184–85, 190

Generational series, 73, 81–83, 87–88 n. 16

Generosity, 31–32, 38 n. 8

Geographical model, 197

German language, 80, 82

Germans, 13
  Nietzsche's view, 255–56, 264–66, 274 nn. 50, 274–75 n. 51

Giles of Rome (Aegidius Romanus), 23–24, 36

Gobineau, Joseph-Arthur, 228, 236, 239

Godwyn, Morton, 94

Goldberg, David Theo, 4

Gold Coast, 100

Gordon, George William, 223

Gould, Stephen Jay, 197

Government, Mill's view, 226–29. *See also* Colonialism

Grace, 33–34, 41 n. 62, 73, 82, 84

Greeks, 170, 258–59

Green, Thomas Hill, 133

Grose, Thomas Lodge, 133

Guyer, Paul, 163–64

Haitian Revolution, 223

Hall, Barbara, 9

Hall, Catherine, 220

Hannaford, Ivan, 219, 232 n. 15

Haraway, Donna, 72 n. 43

Harm principle, 230–31

Hawkins, John, 35

Hegel, Georg Wilhelm Friedrich, 12, 194
  1821 lectures, 202
  1824 lectures, 202–4
  1827 lectures, 204–5
  1831 lectures, 205
  background, 194–95
  Berlin lectures, 198–99, 202–6
  colonialism, view of, 207, 215 n. 83
  elimination of non-Western religions from *Encyclopedia*, 200–201
  Jews, view of, 207, 216 n. 84

Hegel, G. W. F. (continued)
  justification of slavery in, 207, 215nn.
    80, 81
  Marx's response to, 237, 247
  moral condemnation of slavery, 207,
    215n. 80
  origin of races, view of, 197, 209n. 12
  philosophy as science and system,
    194–95, 199–201
  philosophy of religion, 12, 201–5
  race and law, 206–7
  race theory of, 196–98
  rationalizes genocide of Native Ameri-
    cans, 197–98, 207, 214n. 78
  spirit, application to races, 198–200
  Turks, view of, 195–96
—Works
  "Diversity of Races," 196
  Encyclopedia of the Philosophical Sciences,
    194, 196, 198, 200–201, 208
  Phenomenology of Spirit, 194, 200–201
  Philosophy of Right, 194–95, 207
  Science of Logic, 194
Herder, Johann Gottfried, 196, 209n. 11
Hereditary slavery, 95, 96–97
Herrnstein, Richard, 129
Hess, Moses, 242
Hill, Thomas E., Jr., 180, 181, 183
Hinduism/Hindus, 173–74, 203–4, 206
Historia de las Indias (Las Casas), 26, 28
Historia natural y moral de las Indias (Acosta), 29
Historia (Oviedo), 26–27
Hitler, Adolf, 182–83
Hobbes, Thomas, 43–44
  on conquest, 49–52
  early career, 44–45
  on race, 45–49
  racism of, 9, 54
  savages as term, 46–48, 51
  on slavery, 52–54
  state of nature, 45–49, 141, 162
  Virginia Company and, 44–45
—Works
  Elements, 49
  Leviathan, 45–46, 51

Hoffheimer, Michael H., 12
Holland, 9, 19–20, 76
Houstoun, John, 120
Hulme, Peter, 20–21
Human beings
  avoidance of extinction, 151–52
  distinguished from animals, 23–24, 77–78
  innate faculties, 151–57, 160–61
  natural man, 155–56
  presocial, 150–55
  rationality of, 83–84
Human nature, universality of, 127–28, 135,
    137, 139, 144
Humboldt, Alexander von, 215n. 80
Hume, David, 116, 127–28
  belief in superiority of whites, 128–30
  footnote, 128–32
  justice, view of, 139–43
  Kant on, 174
  moral causes, 128, 135
  perception vs. reasoning, 136–37
  philosophy of, 135–39, 143–44
  polygenesis and, 131–32, 134–35, 146n. 30
  racialism/racism of, 2–3, 5, 11, 126n. 13,
    130–31, 134, 143
  revisions of footnote, 132–35
  support of slavery attributed to, 131–32
  universality of human nature, 127–28,
    135, 137, 139, 144
—Works
  Enquiry concerning the Principles of Morals,
    127, 134, 139–40
  "Of Justice," 140–41
  "Of Miracles," 145n. 15, 146n. 30
  "Of National Characters," 11, 128–35
  "Of Polygamy and Divorces," 141
  "Of the Original Contract," 141
  "Of the Populousness of Ancient Na-
    tions," 132
  "Of Unphilosophical Probability," 138,
    144
  Treatise of Animal (Human and Nonhuman)
    Nature, 137
  Treatise of Human Nature, 127, 134, 138
  "Hume's Revised Racism" (Immerwahr), 133

Idealism, 194, 207
Identity, 241–43
  race as, 244–45
  tensions between class and race, 248–51
Immerwahr, John, 133–35
Improvement, concept of, 228–29
Indentured servants, 45
India, 173–74, 222
  Hegel's view, 203–4, 206
  Marx's view, 246–47
Individual, 8, 217
  race as, 63–64
  substance (conatus), 61–64, 71n. 41
Innate faculties, 3, 151–57
  weak assumptions about, 151, 152, 157,
    160–61
Instinct, 154
Institutes (Justinian), 22
Intelligence, Rousseau's view, 160–63
Intrinsic racist, 6–7
Isabel, Queen, 25
Islam, 199–200, 202

Jacolliot, Louis, 267
Jaeschke, Walter, 201, 211n. 37, 212n. 45
Jamaica, 233n. 30
  Morant Bay Rebellion, 221, 223–24, 227
Jamaica Committee, 218, 224, 227
Jamaican Affair, 223–26
James I, 44
Jamestown, 44–45, 50
Jefferson, Thomas, 197
Jesuits, 18–19, 29, 30, 32, 33
Jews, 13, 88n. 21. *See also* anti-Semitism; Judaism
  in Amsterdam, 58–59
  Hegel's view, 207, 216n. 84
  Marx as, 241–42
  Marx's comments on, 238–39, 242–43
  Nietzsche's view, 255–58, 264–66
  role in superior European race, 257–58
  Spinoza on, 64–65
  as strong race, 265–66
Johnson, Samuel, 120
Journal des Sçavants, 74, 75

Judaism, 242, 264. *See also* Anti-Semitism; Jews
  Hegel's view, 199, 200, 202, 204
Justice
  Hume's view, 139–43
  Kant's view, 163–65
  Mill's view, 224–25
  origin of, 141–42
Justification of oppression/slavery
  Bible as, 25–27, 35
  despotic rule, 225, 227–28
  in Hegel, 207, 215nn. 80, 81
  in Kant, 11, 187–88
  in Locke, 95–101
Justinian, 22–24, 29
Just war theory of slavery, 10, 25–27, 29, 91,
    96–97, 99–100, 121–22
  Africans and, 35–36, 41n. 64
  women slaves as contradiction to, 98,
    106n. 46

Kames, Lord, 132
Kant, Immanuel, 11–12, 88n. 23
  anthropocentric moral theory, 181–82
  anthropological/physical geography
    writings, 173–75, 184
  background, 169–72
  categorical imperative, 177–78, 181
  centrality of racial theory to, 175–83
  conceptual partitioning of theory, 179–81
  condemnation of colonialism, 186–87
  debate with Herder, 196
  defenders of, 175–79
  defense of moral theory of, 188–89
  gender, view of, 184–85
  on Hume, 174
  innate faculties, view of, 153
  justification of colonialism in, 11, 187–88
  objections to defense of, 183–91
  personhood, view of, 169, 176, 184–86
  racial hierarchy of, 173–75, 183
  racial mixing, view of, 174–75, 178
  racial sanitizing of, 175–76, 179–80,
    188–89
  racial views and implications, 172–83

Kant, Immanuel (continued)
   scientific racism, influence on, 173, 183
   textual silence of, 176, 178, 187
—Works
   Critique of Pure Reason, 86
   Idea for a Universal History, 163
   Perpetual Peace, 163–65
Kant's Impure Ethics (Louden), 179
Kaufmann, Walter, 270
Kleingeld, Pauline, 184–85, 187
Knox, Robert, 228
Konkle, Maureen, 187–88
Kramer, Matthew, 48–49

Lafargue, Paul, 238–39
La Flèche, 18–19
Land appropriation of, 50–51
Language
   German, 80, 82
   Slavic, 74–76, 79–80
   thought controlled by, 261–62
   used to dominate world, 78
Las Casas, Bartolomé de, 19, 21, 35
   Apologética, 28, 30
   Historia de las Indias, 26, 28
Laslett, Peter, 99
Lassalle, Ferdinand, 238–39, 243
Law
   Mill's view, 224–25
   moral, 266–67
   of nations, 27, 29
   natural, 22–28
   positive, 42 n. 70
   race and, in Hegel, 206–7
Laws of Manu, 267–69, 275 n. 54
Leibniz, Gottfried Wilhelm, 3, 9–10
   Australian inundation analogy, 84–86
   aversion to polemics, 76
   "Einige patriotischen Gedanken," 80–82
   generational series, 73, 81–83, 87–88 n. 16
   geopolitical imaginary, 79–80
   human beings distinguished from ani-
      mals, 77–78
   letter to Sparwenfeld, 74–75, 79–80, 82
   misrepresentation of, 73–75

   political theology, 84–85
   race as term, 80–82, 87 n. 15
   Spinoza and, 59, 68 n. 17
—Works
   Consilium Aegyptiacum, 76–79, 81–82
   "Discourse on Metaphysics," 86
   "A Method to Institute a New, Invincible
      Militia That Can Subjugate the Entire
      Earth, Easily Seize Control over Egypt
      or Establish American Colonies,"
      76–79
   "Monadology," 79
   "A New System of the Nature and Com-
      munication of Substances" (Leibniz),
      75–76
   New Essays in Human Understanding, 74, 83
   Otium hanoveranum, 74, 75
   Sämtliche Schriften, 77
   Theodicy, 84
Lezra, Jacques, 30
Liberalism, 4, 170
   classical, 217, 230
   as nonegalitarian, 170–72
Liberal racism, 114–15
Liberty, Mill's view, 226–29
Limpieza de sangre, 35–36
Linnaeus, Carolus, 177, 198
Locke, John, 2, 83
   administration of colonies, 98–99
   as architect of race–based slavery,
      91–94
   colonialism and slavery linked, 94–95
   contradictions, 89–90, 98
   contrast with Berkeley, 115, 121–23,
      125 n. 7, 126 n. 13
   defense of colonialism, 90–91
   hereditary slavery, view of, 95, 96–97
   innate faculties, view of, 151, 152, 157,
      161
   justification of slavery, 95–101
   just war theory, 91, 96
   power, view of, 92–93
   racism of, 100–103
   slave trade and, 3, 10, 55 n. 9, 89–90, 95,
      98–99, 102

Locke, John (*continued*)
—Works
  Essay on Human Understanding, 84
  The Fundamental Constitutions of Carolina,
    10, 90–95, 102
  *A Paraphrase and Notes on the Epistles of St.
    Paul*, 94, 98
  Second Treatise of Government, 91, 101,
    121–23
  Two Treatises of Government, 90, 92,
    94–95
Lords Proprietors of Carolina, 89, 91, 95,
  102
Lott, Tommy, 47–48, 49
Louden, Robert, 178, 179, 184
Louis XIV, 17–18, 79
Luce, A. A., 122, 123
Lukács, Gyorgy, 249

Madison, James, 163
Magic, 202–3, 205, 212 n. 53, 213 n. 56
Major, John, 23
Malaysian race, 210 n. 19
Malcolm, Noel, 50
Malter, Rudolf, 178–79, 181
Manifest Destiny, 34
Mann, Anika Maaza, 10
Mansfield, Lord Chief Justice, 42 n. 70
Marcuse, Herbert, 249
Maritime image, 21
Marrano Jews, 58
Marshall, John, 188
Marx, Karl
  anti-Semitism and, 12–13, 235, 239,
    241–44
  Capital, 237, 238
  challenge to racial division, 239–41
  Eurocentrism and, 246–48
  identity and, 241–43
  modern structure and, 244–45
  "On the Jewish Question," 242
  private correspondence, 235–36, 238–39
  race missing from theory of, 236–38
  racialism of, 251–52
  racist language in, 237–39, 243

  teleology of, 246–47
  tensions between class and race in,
    248–51
Massachusetts, 99–100
Mehta, Uday Singh, 230
Mendelssohn, Moses, 195
Meno (Plato), 33–34
Mercado, Tomás de, 28, 37
Mersenne, Marin, 19
Mesland, Denis, 20
Mill, John Stuart, 172, 217
  debate with Carlyle, 220–23
  East India Company and, 230
  government, liberty, and civilization,
    view of, 226–29
  harm principle, 231
  Jamaica Committee and, 218, 224, 227
  law and justice, view of, 224–25
  liberalism of, 230
—Works
  Considerations on Representative Government,
    12, 224, 226–27
  On Liberty, 12, 224
  "The Negro Question," 218
  Principles of Political Economy, 218, 225–
    26
Miller, Eugene, 132, 133
Mills, Charles, 5, 11–12, 47, 231
Milton, J. R., 91–92
Mind/body dualism, 17–18, 30–31
Missionaries, 109–14, 116, 118
Modernity, 169–72
Modern philosophy, 1–4
Modern racism, 114
Monads, 73, 81–82
  higher and lower species, 82, 83, 85–86
  race and, 79–83
Monarchs, obedience and, 121–23
Mongols, 197–99. *See also* Asians
Monogenesis, 75, 186
Montag, Warren, 69 n. 24
Montaigne, Michel de, 19, 21, 29, 31, 38 n.
  12
Montesquieu, 128
Moortje (Bredero), 20

Moral causes, 128, 135
Moral equality, 170
Moral law, Nietzsche's view, 266–67
Moral motivation, 163–65
Moral state, 176
Moral system of Descartes, 34–35
Morant Bay Rebellion, 221, 223–24, 227
Moravians, 109
Morton, Eric, 131, 134, 135, 144
Murray, Charles, 129
Muthu, Sankar, 158–60, 165

Nails, Debra, 9–10
Narragansett Indians, 117
National character, 11, 128, 199–200
Nationalism, 244, 259
National predicates, 82
Nation-state, 257
Native Americans
    appropriation of land, 50–51
    culture, destruction of, 113–14, 123,
        125 n. 6
    free will of, 28–29
    Hegel's view, 197–98, 207, 214 n. 78
    hierarchical ranking of, 197–98
    Hobbes's view, 47–48
    Hume's view, 140, 143
    Kant's view, 174–75, 177, 178, 187–88
    Locke's instructions for, 102–3
    missionaries and, 109, 110–12
    Narragansett Indians, 117
    policy of interracial marriage with, 119,
        124, 126 n. 23
    as rational, 28–29
    referred to as savages, 46–48
    treaties with, 187–88
    treatment by Europeans, 118–20, 124,
        140, 143
    used to illustrate state of nature, 158–60
    viewed as sinful, 25–27
Natural, as term, 129
Natural law argument for slavery, 22–28,
    32
Natural man, 11, 155–56, 158–59
Natural mind, 196, 207

Nature religions, 202, 204
Negri, Antonio, 60, 69 n. 25
Negroes. See Black peoples
*New and Accurate Description of the Coast of
    Guinea, A* (Bosman), 100
"New Division of the Earth, by the Different
    Species or Races of Man, A" (Bernier),
    73–75, 82
New Guinea, 100
Nicholson, Francis, 93
Nietzsche, Friedrich
    anti-Semitism and, 255, 259–60
    beauty, view of, 258, 269, 274 n. 44
    breeding theories, 255–60, 264–71
    Christianity, view of, 259, 263–64,
        266–67
    cruelty, view of, 257, 260, 263
    early comments on race, 256–61
    European race concept, 257–58, 260–
        61
    European racial degeneration theory,
        261–64
    link between physiology and thought,
        261–63
    racial thinking of, 13, 255–56, 270–71
    slavery, view of, 257, 260, 268–69
—Works
    The Anti-Christ, 264, 266, 268
    Beyond Good and Evil, 261–62, 264–65,
        268–70
    The Birth of Tragedy out of the Spirit of Music,
        256
    Dawn, 258, 259, 260
    Ecce Homo, 270
    The Gay Science, 260, 261
    On the Genealogy of Morals, 259, 262–63,
        267
    "The Greek State," 257, 260
    Human, All-Too-Human, 257–58
    Kritische Studienausgabe, 256
    Nachlass, 258–59, 260, 270
    Twilight of the Idols, 268
    The Untimely Meditations, 256
    The Will to Power, 256
Noah's curse, 25, 35, 41 n. 63

Non-Christians, as nonhumans, 76
Nonwhites, as subpersons, 170–72
Normative beliefs, 6–8, 170–72, 179

Obedience, passive, 122–23
"Occasional Discourse on the Negro Question" (Carlyle), 220
"Of National Characters" (Hume), 11, 128–35
Okin, Susan Moller, 190
Old Church Slavonic, 75, 76
Oliveira, Fernao de, 28–29
Orangutans, 156, 158
Orientals/Mongols. *See* Asians
"Oriental spirit," 195–96
Original, as term, 129
Origin of races, 197, 209n. 12
Ortega y Gasset, José, 214n. 78
Oviedo, Gonzalo Fernández de, 17, 26–27, 30

Palter, Robert, 130–31
Panopticon, 217
Papal donation, 26–27
Particularism, 76–77
Passive obedience, 122–23
"Passive Obedience" (Berkley), 122
Patriarcha non Monarcha (Tyrell), 92
Paul III, 36
Peace, 163–65
Perfectibility, faculty of, 152–57
Persians, 203–4
Personhood, 97–98, 169–72, 176
  as a priori truth, 178–79, 181
  subpersons, 169, 184–86
  whiteness as prerequisite for, 170–72, 178
Peterson, Richard, 12–13
"Philosophical Basis of Modern Racism, The" (Popkin), 108, 114–16
Philosophy, discipline of, 189–90
Physiology, 197
  thought and, 261–63
Pity, 152–55, 157
Plato, 33–34
Polygenesis, 131–32, 134–35, 146n. 30

Popkin, Richard, 2, 108, 114–16, 125n. 6
  Hume, view of, 130–32, 134, 137–38, 146n. 30
Positive law, 42n. 70
Power, 92–93
  potentia, 60, 63, 69n. 27
Presocial human being, 150–55
Preston, William, 263
Prisoners of war, 91, 96–97
Property rights, 50
Purification of races, 258
Puritans, 108–9
Pythagoras, 79

Quakers, 91, 109

Race
  class and, 239–41, 248–57
  early modern definitions of, 17
  Enlightenment thought and, 4–5
  Hobbes on, 45–49
  as identity, 244–45
  as individual, 63–64
  law and, 198, 206–7
  as modern idea, 1–2
  monads and, 79–83
  Nietzsche on, 256–61
  ontological level, 65–66
  origin of, 197, 209n. 12
  relationship to slavery, 35
  as term, 74, 80–82, 87n. 15, 255
  as web of relations, 63–64
Race and the Enlightenment (Eze), 5
Races of Men, The (Knox), 228
Race theory
  applied to religion, 198–200
  Hegel's contribution to, 196–98
  of Kant, 173–75
Racial contract, 231
Racialism, 6–7
  of Hume, 2–3, 5, 11, 126n. 13, 130–31, 134, 143
  of Marx, 251–52
Racial mixing
  Hegel's view, 206–7

Racial mixing (continued)
  limpieza de sangre, 35
  in New World, 35–36
  Nietzsche's view, 255–59, 263–64
Racism, 6–7
  bias and, 65
  definitions, 43–44, 130
  failure or inaction as, 50
  as form of disregard/ill will, 7–8
  as modern idea, 1–2
  as normative system, 6–8, 170–72, 179
  racialism distinguished from, 6–7
  strong vs. weak, 102, 114
Racism: A Short History (Frederickson), 186
Racist Culture (Goldberg), 4
Rationalism, 2–4
Rationality, 83–84, 230
  free will and, 32–33
  of Indians, 28–29
Rawls, John, 172
Reason, 84–85, 230
  bias and, 65
  East/West dualism, 21
  faculty of perfectibility and, 155
  Leibniz's proposal, 77
  perception vs., 136–37
Rebellions
  Morant Bay Rebellion, 221, 223–24, 227
  obedience and, 121–23
Reiss, Timothy, 9
Religion, 211 nn. 36, 37
  baptism of slaves, 93, 96, 98, 104 n. 23,
    116–19
  determinate, 201, 212 n. 45
  Hegel's philosophy of, 12, 201–5
  as justification for domination, 25–27
  race theory applied to, 198–200
  slaves and, 17, 92–94, 116–19
  universalistic, 114, 115–16
Republican constitution, 163, 165–66
Respect, 182, 190
Rhode Island, 117–19
Rieuwertz, Johannes, 59
Right (ius), 60, 63, 69 n. 27
Ritter, Paul, 77

Roman Empire, 121
Roman law, 28
Ronsard, Pierre de, 38 n. 12
Rousseau, Jean-Jacques, 11, 177
  agricultural revolution, view of, 157, 161
  corruption, theory of, 162–63, 166
  innate faculties, view of, 151–57
  intelligence, view of, 160–63
  Native Americans, view of, 158–60
  natural man, concept of, 155–56, 158–59
  racial bias and theory of, 158–66
—Works
  The Discourse on the Origins of Inequality, 11,
    150–66
  Emile, 166
  Second Discourse, 162
  The Social Contract, 162
Royal Adventurers into Africa, 95
Royal African Company, 89, 95
Russia, 262
Russo-Turkish wars, 195
Rutt, John Towill, 89–90

St. Paul's College proposal, 110–11, 116–
  17
Salamanca debates, 30
Savages, as term, 111
  Hobbes's use of, 46–48, 51
Scarcity of resources, innate faculties and,
  151–57
Schank, Gerd, 268, 270
Schelling, Friedrich Wilhelm, 194
Schlaifer, Robert, 23
Schook, Marin, 32
Schröder, Hannelore, 184
Scientific racism, 173, 183, 219
Searle, John, 3
Self-control, 31–32
Self-interest, 142, 151–52
Self-love, 151–55, 157
Seliger, Michael, 95
Senses, bracketing of, 32
Sepúlveda, Juan Ginés de, 19
Servant, slave vs., 52–54
Sewall, Samuel, 100

Shaftesbury, Earl of (Anthony Ashley
    Cooper), 89, 95, 102–3
Shaftesbury's circle, 94–95, 97, 101–2
Siegel, Jerrold, 239
Silence on race, 9, 17, 36–37, 45, 57, 176,
    178, 187
Simmons, A. John, 104n. 20
Sin, as justification for domination, 25–27,
    29
Six livres de la république (Bodin), 24–25, 28
Slave, servant vs., 52–54
Slave/captive analogy, 21–23, 25, 29–31
    civil conditions and, 34–35
    free will and, 32–34
Slavery. See also Just war theory of slavery
    Berkeley's support of, 115–16, 120–24,
        126n. 17
    as central to colonization, 90–91
    chattel, 91, 100
    Christian acceptance of, 94, 121
    colonialism linked with, 90–91, 94–95
    curse of Ham, 25, 35, 41n. 63
    as essential to great culture, 257, 269
    hereditary, 95, 96–97
    Hobbes on, 52–54
    as legal condition, 17, 22, 27, 35–37
    legitimate vs. illegitimate, 121–23
    Locke's justification of, 95–101
    nation law and, 27, 29
    natural law argument, 22–28
    Nietzsche's view, 257, 260, 268–69
    philosophers' involvement in, 3, 10–11,
        44, 89–90, 95, 98–99, 102, 117–18, 120
    tradition of, 30–37
Slaves
    ancient Greece, 170
    baptism of, 93, 96, 98, 104n. 23, 116–19
    children of, 96–98
    in early modern era, 17
    missionaries and, 109–14, 116
    power of life and death over, 92–93,
        95–96, 101
    religion and, 17, 92–94, 116–19
    as subhuman, 35, 42n. 65

treatment by English colonists, 118–20,
    124
Slave trade
    British, 89–90, 95, 98–99, 120
    Dutch, 19–20, 32
    Portuguese, 19, 35
Slavic languages, 74–76, 79–80
Sociability, 151–52, 156
    unsocial, 163, 165–66
Social contract, 5, 162
Social Darwinists, 186
Social movements, 251
Society for the Propagation of the Gospel in
    Foreign Parts (SPG), 108–11, 118
Soto, Domingo de, 18–19, 25, 27–28, 29
Soul, 115
Space-time, 63, 65
Spain, 18–19, 26–27, 35–36
Sparwenfeld, Johan Gabriel, 74, 75, 79–
    80
Species, as term, 132, 134, 148n. 68
Specific difference thesis, 115
Spinoza, Baruch de, 3
    banned by Jewish community, 58–59,
        67n. 12
    existence, mode of, 9–10, 60, 61–63
    extension, attribute of, 61–63, 64,
        70–71n. 35, 71n. 41
    historical context, 58–59
    on Jews, 64–65
    metaphysics of, 60, 61–63
    ontology of, 57
    political theory of, 60–61
    race and, 63–66
    slavery, view of, 59, 68n. 19
    —Works
    Ethics, 61, 65
    Principles of Cartesian Philosophy, 59
    Theological-Political Treatise, 58, 59, 64–65
Squadrito, Kay, 3
State, 176, 198
State of nature, 9, 60, 97, 141, 158–60, 162
    Hobbes's view, 45–49
Stiegler, Barbara, 270, 275

Stoler, Ann Laura, 217
Strong racism, 102, 114
Suárez de Peralta, Juan, 29, 36
Subject formation, 217
Sublimus Deus (Paul III), 36
Subpersons, 35, 42 n. 65, 169, 184–86
Substance (conatus), 61–64, 71 n. 37, 73
Suma de tratos y contratos (Mercado), 28
Summa theologica (Aquinas), 19

Tahitians, 166
Taylor, Charles, 245
Theory of Justice, A (Rawls), 172
Thought, physiological origins of, 261–63
Tocqueville, Alexis de, 217
Trinity, 199
Trollope, Anthony, 222
Turks, Hegel's view, 195–96
Tutelage, 221–22, 229
Twelve Years' Truce, 19
Tyrell, James, 92

Understanding, 152–55, 157
Universality
    applies to whites only, 11–12
    of human nature, 127–28, 135, 137, 139,
        144
    religious, 114–16
Unsocial sociability, 163, 165–66
Utilitarianism, 142, 172, 217
Uzgalis, William, 10–11, 92, 96, 98–99

"Verses on America" (Berkley), 110
Vespucci, Amerigo, 17, 23, 25, 29–30
Victorian political thought, 12, 218–20
Virginia Company, 44–45, 50–51
Vitoria, Francisco de, 18–19, 25, 27, 41 n.
    64
Voetius, Gysbert, 33–34

Walvin, James, 35
Welchman, Jennifer, 96–98
Werner, John, 139
West Indies, 96
Whelan, Frederick, 145 n. 15
Whiteness
    as prerequisite for personhood, 170–72,
        178
    privileging of, 5, 11–12, 128–30, 198
Wilkins, John, 80–81, 87 n. 15
Will, freedom and, 31–32
Winchester, James, 13
Wokler, Robert, 132, 156, 158
Wood, Allen, 163, 173, 178, 179, 193 n.
    38
Work, 221–22
Working-class identity, 248–51
Writing Indian Nations (Konkle), 187–88

Young, Robert, 228

Zoroastrianism, 203–4, 211 n. 37
Zurara, Gomes Eanes de, 25–26, 35